MONASTIC WISDOM SER

CW01431645

Thomas Merton

An Introduction to Christian Mysticism
Initiation into the Monastic Tradition 3

MONASTIC WISDOM SERIES

Patrick Hart, ocso, General Editor

Advisory Board

Michael Casey, ocso   Terrence Kardong, osb
Lawrence S. Cunningham   Kathleen Norris
Bonnie Thurston   Miriam Pollard, ocso

MONASTIC WISDOM SERIES: NUMBER THIRTEEN

An Introduction to Christian Mysticism
Initiation into the Monastic Tradition 3

by
Thomas Merton

Edited with an Introduction by
Patrick F. O'Connell

Preface by
Lawrence S. Cunningham

CISTERCIAN PUBLICATIONS
Kalamazoo, Michigan

Cistercian Publications

Editorial Offices
The Institute of Cistercian Studies
Western Michigan University
Kalamazoo, Michigan 49008-5415
cistpub@wmich.edu

The work of Cistercian Publications is made possible in part by support from Western Michigan University to The Institute of Cistercian Studies.

Library of Congress Cataloging-in-Publication Data

Merton, Thomas, 1915–1968.
　An introduction to Christian mysticism : initiation into the monastic tradition 3 / by Thomas Merton ; edited with an introduction by Patrick F. O'Connell ; preface by Lawrence S. Cunningham.
　　p. cm. — (Monastic wisdom series ; no. 13)
　Includes bibliographical references and index.
　ISBN 978-0-87907-013-7
　1. Mysticism.　I. O'Connell, Patrick F.　II. Title.　III. Series.

BV5082.3.M47 2007
248.2'2—dc22　　　　　　　　　　　　　　　　2007037374

Printed in the United States of America

TABLE OF CONTENTS

PREFACE

In the 1949–1951 correspondence between the newly ordained Thomas Merton and his abbot, James Fox, later published in *The School of Charity*, there is a discussion about the education of young monks that is extraordinarily interesting. Merton felt that the young men entering the monastery were being educated for the priesthood but that there was no coherent program of monastic formation. At a time when it was universally assumed that choir monks would go on for the priesthood, the education of these young monks was, of necessity, a course of studies laid out by canon law as a prerequisite for ordination, with instructions in monasticism of necessity ancillary to that demand. It is clear that Merton saw something fundamentally out of balance with this arrangement but was unsure how to right the balance. He recognized, as he noted in a letter to Dom James, that it was difficult to see how one could superimpose a monastic curriculum on top of the seminary curriculum. His solution, first as master of scholastics and later as novice master, was to develop a course of instructions for novices and the newly professed that went under the generic name of "monastic orientations."

The net result of Merton's convictions was a whole series of courses designed for novices or, in the case of this volume, a kind of "post-graduate" seminar for newly ordained priests. Anyone who has visited the Merton archives in Louisville can inspect the vast pile of bound mimeographed volumes that give witness to how seriously he took this task of monastic education. How grateful we are that Patrick O'Connell has undertaken the arduous task of seeing some of these volumes to publication. O'Connell has set a high standard with his editions of Merton's novitiate notes *Cassian and the Fathers* (2005) and *Pre-Benedictine Monasticism* (2006), and we are now in his debt with *An Introduction to Christian Mysticism*.

We might begin by noting that in the early 1960s a wide survey of Christian mysticism was somewhat of a novelty. In the standard seminary curriculum there was at least a one-semester cruise through Adolphe Tanquerey's scholastic manual on ascetical theology. To complicate matters, both primary and secondary sources were in short supply in English. Merton compiled these notes nearly two decades before the first volume of the Paulist Press "Classics of Western Spirituality" saw the light of day and a generation before Bernard McGinn published the first volume of his massive history of the subject. As O'Connell notes, Merton, thanks to his linguistic skills, had to draw heavily on Francophone sources and what little was available to him in Gethsemani's library. Wisely, Merton drew on primary texts when he had access to them and studiously avoided the swamp of neoscholastic debates that had been common in the earlier twentieth century about the nature of, and distinction between, ascetical and mystical theology.

For serious students of Merton's work this present volume is an estimable resource and that for at least two compelling reasons. First, these notes, as it were, serve as a foundational level for grasping what stands behind such finished works as *No Man Is an Island*, *Thoughts in Solitude*, *New Seeds of Contemplation* as well as many of his essays on the spiritual life. That Merton wore his learning lightly is, in fact, the case. Behind the limpid prose of his classical works on the spiritual life, however, is a vast well of learning in the sources. This volume is clearly an example of *ressourcement* and as such tells us much about Merton's intellectual and spiritual development. That he was in intellectual dialogue when giving this course with von Balthasar, Daniélou, and Leclercq, those masters of *ressourcement*, should come as no surprise.

Second, I think O'Connell makes a crucial point about Merton's appropriation of an old trope in the Christian mystical tradition. In a distinction as old as Origen's prologue to his commentary on the Song of Songs, spiritual writers have noted that between the stage of purification (*ethike*) and the profound encounter with God (*theologia*) there is the human grasp of the presence of God in the created cosmos which was called *theoria* or *theoria physike*. The later tradition would call that the stage of illumination between purification and union but the point is, and O'Connell correctly notes it, that an appreciation of *theoria* is a crucial key to help explain what seems to be in Merton simply a byproduct of his enormous curiosity: Zen calligraphy, Shaker furniture, the abstract art of Ad Reinhardt, and so on. In fact, it was a new way of "seeing" (*theoria*, at root, mean "gazing") and is part of the contemplative process. The value of *theoria* is, of course, that it means that the penitential life is not an end in itself but a preparation for a new way of seeing.

Merton never pursued this idea in any systematic fashion but one can see in it a kind of a theology of culture broadly understood. Not only did Merton see contemplative union open to every baptized Christian but he strongly asserted that one can cultivate the eye to see in a fresh new way. Not to put too fine a point on it: if one hopes to grasp the mind of Thomas Merton and not be satisfied with clichés and stereotypes then one must take into account these profound academic exercises. They are a key to his understanding of the contemplative life as, for example, he describes it in the opening pages of *New Seeds of Contemplation*.

Finally, a sympathetic reader of this volume needs to advert to the word "introduction" in the title. After all, had Merton done an in-depth study of Augustine or Bonaventure or Eckhart or the great Carmelites this would not have been a book but a set of books. One would better think of this work as a set of blaze marks to work one's way through the complex story of Christian mysticism. One makes that journey with a deeply serious and widely educated guide who is able to point out the salient landmarks of the mystical tradition. "Guide" I think is the right word. Saint John of the Cross never spoke of a spiritual director but frequently spoke of the spiritual guide (*guia*) and the spiritual teacher (*maestro espiritual*) and in Merton one finds both.

In reading these pages I was struck how Merton attempted to mend the long historical rift between systematic theology and the contemplative theology normative in the Church before the rise of scholasticism. He was not spinning out some variety of spiritual gnosis but, rather, recalled to his students, and now, gratefully, to us, the truth of one of Saint Thomas Aquinas's most profound observations, namely, that faith has as its final end not what is articulated but the reality behind that articulation (*non ad enuntiabile sed ad rem*).

Lawrence S. Cunningham
The University of Notre Dame

INTRODUCTION

The series of conferences that comprise *An Introduction to Christian Mysticism* is unique among the courses taught by Thomas Merton during his term as novice master at the Abbey of Gethsemani (1955–1965) in that it was not intended for or presented to the novices. On January 14, 1961, Merton had written to Herbert Mason, "In March and April I have to teach eighteen lectures in mystical theology in the new pastoral course for our young priests, and this is keeping me busy."[1] By the time the lectures actually started the number had expanded to twenty-two (15), to be given twice a week, evidently, during March, April and May.[2] The course duly began on March 1[3] and continued

1. Thomas Merton, *Witness to Freedom: Letters in Times of Crisis*, ed. William H. Shannon (New York: Farrar, Straus, Giroux, 1994), 270.
2. See Merton's letter of March 9, 1961 to Robert Lax: "What makes me most busy at the moment is twenty two lectures on mystical theology. This is some of the vanity which God hath given men to be exercised therein" (Thomas Merton and Robert Lax, *When Prophecy Still Had a Voice: The Letters of Thomas Merton & Robert Lax*, ed. Arthur W. Biddle [Lexington: University Press of Kentucky, 2001], 219). Two lists of preliminary outlines of the course each include twenty-two classes: the earlier, in pencil, indicates the first eight classes as assigned to March, the next six to April, and the last eight to May; for transcriptions of the two outlines, see Appendix A, pages 349–50 (the later outline, in pen), and 351 (the earlier, in pencil).
3. See Merton's journal entry for March 3, 1961: "I started the mystical theology class Wednesday (Mar. 1)" (Thomas Merton, *Turning Toward the World: The Pivotal Years. Journals, vol. 4: 1960–1963*, ed. Victor A. Kramer [San Francisco: HarperCollins, 1996], 97).

through May 19,[4] when Merton noted in his journal, "Finished the official mystical theology course today. Some extra classes to be fitted in where I can."[5] In fact, however, these extra classes continued at least throughout the summer. The Foreword to the mimeographed text of the course notes is dated "Vigil of the Assumption, 1961" (i.e., August 14) (4), but the classes continued at least into the following month. On September 9, Merton wrote to Etta Gullick, "I had a mystical theology course which is getting prolonged by a 'popular demand' which I suspect to be ninety percent nonsense and ten percent pure illusion. And it requires a lot of preparation."[6] The day before, he had noted in his journal, "So I teach and teach, not only novices. This mystical theology class drags on and on. The young priests now want some sort of seminar, and I think it is foolish, a waste of time, yet to please them and soothe my guilt feelings—and perhaps to satisfy my vanity—I suppose I will do it. I wish I could call it love."[7] There is no further mention in journal or letters of the mystical theology course, nor are there any subsequent references to a seminar for

---

4. Omitting two classes during Holy Week (March 26–April 1), this would have been the twenty-second class if the course met twice per week.

5. *Turning Toward the World*, 120; Merton writes of "still slugging {slogging?} along with mystical theology" in a letter of May 10 to Sr. Thérèse Lentfoehr (Thomas Merton, *The Road to Joy: Letters to New and Old Friends*, ed. Robert E. Daggy [New York: Farrar, Straus, Giroux, 1989], 238), but three days later he writes to Abdul Aziz, "I have been taken up with more numerous classes for the last three months, but this is now ending. I will send you the notes of these classes in mystical theology when they are ready" (Thomas Merton, *The Hidden Ground of Love: Letters on Religious Experience and Social Concerns*, ed. William H. Shannon [New York: Farrar, Straus, Giroux, 1985], 48), and on the same day he writes to Mark Van Doren, "For three months I have been pounding away at a mad course in mystical theology and have enjoyed the sweating, but it is finally ending and I enjoy that more. It is always racking to talk about what should not be said" (*Road to Joy*, 41). On the last day of the official course, he tells John Wu, "I have been busy finishing up my course in mystical theology and various other tasks" (*Hidden Ground of Love*, 616).

6. *Hidden Ground of Love*, 353.

7. *Turning Toward the World*, 160.

the young priests, but circumstantial evidence suggests that Merton did continue to meet with the group for some considerable time subsequent to this entry.

While he sounded rather tired of the conferences by this point, he had earlier expressed satisfaction that they were speaking to an authentic desire among the monks attending the course for a deepened awareness of the contemplative dimension of their lives. On March 24, he reflected in his journal on a session held in the new cinderblock cottage that would become his hermitage:

> Wednesday afternoon (rain). The Pastoral Theology group and others came to St. Mary of Carmel—conference on the Spiritual Senses and general discussion. A very happy atmosphere and I think everything was profitable—a kind of opening up. Have never had so much of a sense of the need and the *hunger* of the priests in the monastery for mysticism and contemplation—in a very simple way. It is true that a large part of our difficulties comes from frustration of this deep need and a kind of inarticulate temptation to despair that takes refuge in activities without too much sense.[8]

As he points out in his Foreword, while the "approach has been mainly historical and positive in an attempt to recover some of the rich thought of the patristic and medieval periods" (3), his purpose was less strictly academic than formational,

> an effort to broaden the horizons and deepen the perspectives of mystical theology in a monastic setting. . . . The lectures were intended primarily for monastic priests in a course of "pastoral" theology—that is to say for monks who sought background and contact with sources that would enable them to be of benefit to their brethren in spiritual direction or in that *sapientiae doctrina* which St. Benedict looks for in superiors (3).

8. *Turning Toward the World*, 102.

They reflect Merton's core belief, the foundation as well of his numerous published books on contemplation, that "the Christian mystical tradition is something that has been handed down not only to be talked about but to be *lived*" (4).

Merton's original outlines for the course present an ambitious overview of the mystical tradition that in the event he was not able to carry out fully. The subtitle of the course, "(From the Apostolic Fathers to the Council of Trent)," represents a considerable scaling back of the chronological breadth initially proposed: in the earliest outline, the twelfth class, the beginning of the second half of the course, is labeled "Post Trent—Jesuits—St Theresa." (351)! It is followed by: "St John of the Cross" [13]; "Dark Night" [14]; "Later Carmelites—mod. Debates" [15]; "Semi Quietists etc" [16]; "Modern Writers—Saudreau Poulain" [17]; "Non-Xtian mysticism?" [18]; "Hallaj—Sufis"[9] [19] (n. 20 is left blank, presumably for a second class on this topic); "Byzantine Mysticism" [21]; "St Gregory Palamas" [22]. The semi-Quietists and modern writers were already cancelled on this first outline to make room for two additional classes on "Franciscans—Rhenish Mystics" and "Complete Separation of Myst + Theol" (the latter itself subsequently cancelled) to precede the "Post Trent" class. By the time Merton put together his second outline (349–50) the Jesuits and St. Teresa had moved all the way to class 19 (which was then switched to 20), followed only by "St John Cross Dark Night" (originally 18-19, then 20-21, and finally just 21); "Later Carmelites" (subsequently added to the Jesuits and Teresa class); and "Byz. Myst. Conclusion" (originally two classes reduced to one). In the actual text, however, the Byzantines have disappeared along with the non-Christians. In fact in his Foreword Merton writes, "It has not been possible to carry out our original intention to discuss St. John of the Cross and the Byzantine mystical tradition" (3), though in the final text John of the Cross does

---

9. In his January 14 letter to Herbert Mason, Merton had written, "I want to bring in Hallaj and maybe other Oriental mystics if I have elbowroom" (*Witness to Freedom*, 270).

receive extensive discussion, in a context that reflects a considerable reorientation found in what were evidently the "extra classes" added after the formal conclusion of the course, and more specifically those which were subsequent to the writing of these prefatory remarks in mid-August.[10]

Merton's plans for what was initially to be the first half of the course remain quite consistent in topics, if not in number of classes, in the two outlines, and are followed closely in the actual text of the conferences. After a pair of introductory classes, the topics include: St. John's Gospel, Martyrs, Gnostics, Divinization, Christological Controversies, the meaning of the term "mysticism," Gregory of Nyssa, the spiritual senses, Evagrius, Pseudo-Dionysius, "Western Mysticism," the Dionysian tradition in the West, the Franciscans, the Rhenish mystics, Quietism, and the separation of mysticism and theology. Except for the last two, which are treated only in passing, this list accurately represents the actual development of the course as found in the written notes. The only significant differences between the two versions of the outline for these sections of the course are the omission of mention of Pseudo-Macarius in the second version,[11] and the addition of "Theoria Phys[ike]," which becomes an extremely important section of the course as finally written.

The only topic that receives major attention in this part of the course that is not specifically mentioned in the outlines is Béguine spirituality, which is discussed in some detail under the general heading of "Fourteenth-Century Mysticism" ("The 14th–15th Cents." in a secondary, marginal list on the second outline).

10. Merton notes in his journal that he is "writing up mystical theology notes" on August 11 (*Turning Toward the World*, 150).

11. Merton included a section on Pseudo-Macarius in the "Prologue to Cassian" section of his novitiate course on Cassian and his predecessors (Thomas Merton, *Cassian and the Fathers: Initiation into the Monastic Tradition*, ed. Patrick F. O'Connell, Monastic Wisdom [MW], vol. 1 [Kalamazoo, MI: Cistercian Publications, 2005], 81–88), which may have prompted him to omit discussion of this author here, as was the case with Origen (see below, xxi)—though not of Gregory of Nyssa or of Evagrius.

However, following the section on St. Teresa, the entire rest of the text of the course consists in material not included at all in the projected outlines of the course, namely a lengthy section on "The Spiritual Direction of Contemplatives" followed by a second section on the same topic, subtitled "Direction in the Crises of the Mystical Life" (along with two appendices to be considered later). These sections, which comprise 44 pages of a total of 170 in the mimeographed version of the text proper, evidently owe their existence to the continuation of the course beyond its intended limit of twenty-two classes, and to another project on which Merton was engaged during the period of the "extra classes" of the summer and early fall of 1961.

From indications in Merton's journal and letters, it is possible to get some sense of the progression of classes: during March he appears to be keeping to his schedule, or perhaps even slightly ahead, as he is discussing the topic of the spiritual senses (class 8 on the outlines) at the hermitage during what appears to be his seventh class.[12] But the pace apparently slows subsequently, since in his May 13 letter to Mark Van Doren, less than a week before the formal end of the class, he writes, "I ended up last time Beguines, beguines and beguines. They were wonderful, like the quails around my house. Everybody has forgotten them, but they were very wise and Eckhart learned all the best things he knew from them."[13] In the two remaining "regular" classes he could hardly have progressed beyond the Rhineland mystics, Eckhart and Tauler, and in fact his frequent mentions of Eckhart in letters

---

12. If the classes were held on the same days each week, as seems likely, they were given on Wednesdays (the day on which the first class was held—March 1) and Fridays (the day of the final class—May 19); the entry for March 24 is unclear, since it begins "Wednesday afternoon" but that day was a Friday; presumably he was referring to a class that met two days previous, which would have been the seventh class; if he was mistaken about the day and was actually referring to a class that met on that day, it would have been the eighth class.

13. *Road to Joy*, 41; see also his journal entry from the beginning of that week, Sunday, May 7, in which he writes about reading Dom Porion's book on Hadewijch, his major source for the Béguines (*Turning Toward the World*, 117).

and journal entries of June and July suggest that he may well have continued to discuss these fourteenth-century Germans after the completion of the course proper.[14] Certainly the material on St. Teresa must have been discussed during these extra summer classes, followed by the additional, new topic of spiritual direction (unless this was the subject of the "seminar" that the priests had requested and was thus presented through the fall).

The reason for this unexpected change in focus is explained in letters and journal entries from the summer. In a June 21 letter to Mark Van Doren, he remarks, "I am not writing much at the moment and not intending to write much except for doing chores like an Encyclopedia article (*New Catholic Encyclopedia*, which will probably be stuffy)."[15] He elaborates on the "chore" in a journal entry for June 29: "*New Cath. Encycl.* has repeated its request for one article. I am convinced they do it very unwillingly, merely to get my name on their list. I refused before a ludicrous request to do 300 words on Dom Edmond Obrecht (!!) and now they have asked for 5,000 on spiritual direction and I feel utterly foul for having accepted."[16] There is no further mention of the article until a September 19 letter to Sr. Thérèse Lentfoehr,[17] and then in his journal five days later he writes, "Have to finish article for *Catholic Encyclopedia*,"[18] which he calls a "tiresome task" in a letter of the same day to Dona Luisa Coomaraswamy.[19] Finally

14. See his letters to Etta Gullick of June 10 and July 1 (*Hidden Ground of Love*, 342, 343) and the journal entry of July 4 (*Turning Toward the World*, 137).

15. *Road to Joy*, 42.

16. *Turning Toward the World*, 135.

17. "I have had to write a few articles for a new *Catholic Youth Encyclopedia* which, between you and me and the gatepost, sounds rather useless. But maybe they had a method in their madness, and decided to do something that would have more life in it than the *New Catholic Encyclopedia*. I have a long article to do for them, too, on 'Spiritual Direction'" (*Road to Joy*, 239); his articles on "Contemplation" and "Perfection, Christian," appeared in *The Catholic Encyclopedia for School and Home*, 12 vols. (New York: McGraw-Hill, 1965), 3.228-30, 8.328-32.

18. *Turning Toward the World*, 164.

19. *Hidden Ground of Love*, 133.

on October 10 he writes in his journal, "The other day I finally finished the article 'Direction, Spiritual' for the *New Catholic Encyclopedia.* I should have finished it in August (Deadline Nov. 1, but I wanted to get it done in August)."[20] Work on this article (which ironically ended up not being accepted for publication in the *New Catholic Encyclopedia*[21]) coincided with the concluding phase of the mystical theology course, and prompted Merton either to include a section on spiritual direction at the end of the course itself, or perhaps to make it the subject of the "seminar" requested by his students, if such a continuation of these conferences did indeed take place. The latter supposition is perhaps more likely, as there is no hint of inclusion of this material in the Foreword to the notes, written in mid-August, and in fact it is clear that at that time Merton had no idea that he would include a substantial section on John of the Cross in the second, "spiritual crises" section of the direction material. Given the fact that not quite four weeks separates the writing of the Foreword from the journal entry mentioning the request for the "seminar," the rather abrupt shift in focus, and the quite detailed elaboration of the spiritual direction material, it is at least plausible that this topic became the focus of a somewhat distinct set of conferences, which also allowed Merton to incorporate material from John of the Cross (some of which is related only tangentially to spiritual direction), and which were still related closely enough to the mystical theology material proper to allow them to be included as the two final sections of the written notes.

As for the material in the appendices, Merton's only reference to the first comes in a journal entry for December 14, 1961, where he notes that he is reading the *Scala Claustralium* "for the novices,"[22] an indication that he was intending to use it in regular novitiate conferences and that it was incorporated into the mysti-

20. *Turning Toward the World*, 169.

21. The article has now been published in *The Merton Seasonal*, 32.1 (Spring 2007), 3–17.

22. *Turning Toward the World*, 184.

cal theology notes because of the relevance of the material rather than because he had or was intending to discuss it with the group of young priests to whom the course had been given. The second appendix, on Robert Jay Lifton's book on brainwashing, is related somewhat tenuously to the spiritual direction material and in fact was initially headed "Appendix—to Spiritual Direction" in Merton's original notes,[23] and presumably was added to the notes even later than the *Scala* material, perhaps even in early 1962;[24] it seems unlikely that it was ever discussed with the "seminar," which presumably had stopped meeting by that time, since it is probable that some further mention of the group would appear in the journal if it continued to meet on a long-term basis. In any case, by March 1962, the mimeographed notes on mystical theology had been printed up and not only distributed to those who had been in the course but sent to various interested parties beyond the confines of the monastery, since in a March letter to Sr. M. Madeleva, president of St. Mary's College at Notre Dame, Merton mentions having already sent them to her.[25]

23. Merton subsequently crossed out "to Spiritual Direction" and interlined "II" after "Appendix".

24. A discussion of "brainwashing" in a January 25, 1962 letter to Victor Hammer is clearly dependent on the Lifton book, and suggests that Merton had read it recently and it was fresh in his mind: "As for brainwashing, the term is used very loosely about almost anything. Strict technical brainwashing is an artificially induced 'conversion,' brought about by completely isolating a person emotionally and spiritually, undermining his whole sense of identity, and then 'rescuing' him from this state of near-collapse by drawing him over into a new sense of community with his persecutors, now his rescuers, who 'restore' his identity by admitting [him] into their midst as an approved and docile instrument. Henceforth he does what they want him to do and likes it, indeed finds a certain satisfaction in this, and even regards his old life as shameful and inferior" (*Witness to Freedom*, 6).

25. *Witness to Freedom*, 43; she was writing to inquire why the English mystics, specifically Julian of Norwich, had not been included in the notes (see below, pages xxi, xlix–l); Merton had evidently sent the notes in connection with his role as advisor to St. Mary's faculty who were in the process of setting up a

* * * * * * *

Because Merton's various courses with the novices were open-ended and he had complete control of the schedule, he was able to develop those sets of conferences according to his own designs. The situation with *An Introduction to Christian Mysticism* was quite different: the limited number of classes (at least as originally projected), as well as the broad chronological sweep of the material, imposed certain limitations both on the content and on Merton's ways of dealing with his material. He realized from the start that his survey could not be completely comprehensive, given the time constraints. An initial principle of selection was to focus on the mystical dimension of Christian spirituality, while recognizing the continuum between ascetical and mystical aspects:

> If this "course" is restricted to twenty-two lectures in the Pastoral year, it is obviously taken for granted that much else has been said and taught and assimilated, especially in ascetic theology, before we come to this short series of lectures. Ascetic theology is prescribed in the novitiate. {It presents the} fundamentals of monastic life. The Master of Students should continue the ascetic formation of the young professed monk, deepening his monastic life and, especially, orienting his life of studies and his spiritual growth toward the monastic priesthood. There are retreats, constant sermons and conferences, reading. There is individual direction {and} constant "exercise" in the ascetic life. Hence for all the years of the monastic life through which the student has now passed, he has been subjected *intensively* to ascetic formation and has at least gathered some smattering of knowledge about mystical theology.
>
> Hence the purpose of these lectures is not to cover every detail and aspect of the subject, but to look over the whole field, to *coordinate* and *deepen* the ascetic knowledge that it

---

program in Christian Culture there: see his December 13, 1961 letter to Bruno Schlesinger, a faculty member at the college (*Hidden Ground of Love*, 541–43).

is presumed everybody has, and to orient that asceticism to the mystical life. (15)

Though the heading "ASCETICAL AND MYSTICAL THEOL-OGY" is found in the typescript on the first page of the text proper and is sometimes used to refer to these conferences,[26] the title used on the preceding handwritten page that includes the Foreword is the more accurate "An Introduction to Christian Mysticism," which is therefore used as the title for this volume.

A second principle was to omit certain topics that had been discussed by Merton in novitiate courses and were available in mimeographed form:[27] thus he mentions that despite their importance to the subject he will not be looking in detail at St. Paul's mystical teaching (40), or at Origen (52), or at the Cistercians (18), because they had been discussed in other courses, though references to all of them, particularly the Cistercians, are brought in at appropriate places. Certain other figures that would certainly merit inclusion, such as Jan Ruysbroeck and the English mystics of the fourteenth century, do not appear; they were perhaps originally intended to be included under the heading of "The 14th-15th cents." but were omitted because of time constraints. Merton writes to Sr. Madeleva, who inquired about the absence of the latter group, "The chief reason why Julian of Norwich and the other English mystics are not in the notes I sent is that I did not have time to treat them adequately, and in proportion to my love for them,"[28] though it should be noted that this love actually was

26. See for example Victor A. Kramer, "Patterns in Thomas Merton's Introduction to Ascetical and Mystical Theology," *Cistercian Studies*, 24 (1989), 338–54; this is the title given in the Table of Contents in the "Collected Essays" and it has been pasted in on the title page of some copies of the bound mimeograph.

27. This is not always the case, however: both Gregory of Nyssa and Evagrius had been discussed in detail in Merton's conferences on Cassian and his predecessors but reappear here: see *Cassian and the Fathers*, 52–60, 88–96.

28. *Witness to Freedom*, 43 [March, 1962].

developing during the period when Merton was teaching the Mystical Theology course, as will be seen below.

The other major difference between this set of notes and those of Merton's novitiate courses is the relative absence of extended discussions of primary texts. Aside from the Appendix on the *Scala Claustralium*, not originally prepared for these conferences, only discussions of the *De Oratione* (and to a lesser extent the *Kephalaia Gnostica*) of Evagrius, the poems of Hadewijch, and the writings of Teresa of Avila and of John of the Cross are based mainly on primary source materials. Merton's survey relies heavily, as he himself points out, on secondary sources, especially those currently available only in French, such as the *Dictionnaire de Spiritualité*, the first two volumes of the *Histoire de Spiritualité Chrétienne*, and books such as Jean Daniélou's *Platonisme et Théologie Mystique* (on Gregory of Nyssa) and Hans Urs von Balthasar's *Liturgie Cosmique* (on Maximus the Confessor), easily accessible for the bilingual Merton. But it should be noted that generally Merton does not simply follow a single source in his own discussion of a particular topic or figure. For example in the section on divinization he uses ten different sources, and in his treatment of Meister Eckhart he incorporates material from nine different sources. As a rule, whether he is drawing on multiple sources or relying on one major source, for example the introduction to a French translation of John Tauler's sermons in his section on the fourteenth-century German preacher and mystic, he mainly uses secondary material as a quarry for quotations from the mystics themselves, so that his notes are filled with passages from the figures he is discussing even if few particular texts are discussed *in extenso*. Given the nature of the course, this strategy is both appropriate and effective.

* * * * * * *

This reliance on secondary sources should not be taken as an indication that Merton does not highlight key themes of his own in these conferences. One such theme emphasized from the very outset is the intrinsic relationship between mysticism and doctrine. He notes in his introductory remarks that

> the great mystical tradition . . . is not separated from the dogmatic and moral tradition but *forms one whole* with it. Without mysticism there is no real theology, and without theology there is no real mysticism. Hence the emphasis will be on mysticism as theology, to bring out clearly the mystical dimensions of our theology, hence to help us to do what we must really do: live our theology. Some think it is sufficient to come to the monastery to live the *Rule*. More is required—we must live our *theology*, fully, deeply, in its totality. Without this, there is no sanctity. The separation of theology from "spirituality" is a disaster. (15–16)

While he is critical of a sterile intellectual approach to the Christian life, theology as "a mere product of erudition" in the words of the Orthodox theologian Georges Florovsky (37), he warns against a perspective that would treat theology as "a penance and effort without value, except as a chore to be offered up, whereas spirituality is to be studied, developed, experienced." Merton contends that this devaluation of the doctrinal content of the Christian mystery leads to "experience of experience and not experience of revelation and of God revealing," which is "the death of contemplation" (36). He endorses von Balthasar's evaluation of the Patristic era as an age when "personal experience and dogmatic faith were a living unity" and agrees that "[m]ysticism and experience" must be recognized as "a *servant* of revelation, of the Word, of the Church—not an evasion from service" (36). He finds in the Gospel of John the model of this integration of the doctrinal and the experiential dimensions: "It is a theology; it is mysticism—{there is} no separation between the two; both are one in *our life in Christ*" (38).

Thus union with God is recognized to be profoundly Trinitarian, a process in which the gift of the Spirit unites the believer to the Son, in whom one is united to the Father, as St. Irenaeus declares: "those who have in themselves the Spirit of God are brought to the Logos, the Son, Who takes them and offers them to the Father. From the Father they receive incorruptibility" (51). Merton finds the same idea in Clement of Alexandria: "Through the Scriptures we are drawn by the Spirit to the Father, through the Son" (54). Likewise Merton points to the "*Incarnation* [as] the center of Christian mysticism" (38). The consistent Patristic teaching is that the union of the Word with humanity in the person of Jesus makes possible participation in divine life, both in this life and in eternity:

> The mysticism and the dogmatic theology of the Church are inseparably united in Athanasius, to such a point that they stand and fall together by the single argument of man's divinization by the Incarnation of Christ. . . . Divinization is the result of the Incarnation; more, it is the very *purpose* of the Incarnation. . . . St. Athanasius sums up his whole doctrine: HE BECAME MAN IN ORDER THAT WE MIGHT BECOME GOD. HE MADE HIMSELF VISIBLE IN HIS BODY IN ORDER THAT WE MIGHT HAVE AN IDEA OF THE INVISIBLE FATHER. HE UNDERWENT OUTRAGES FROM MEN IN ORDER THAT WE MIGHT HAVE PART IN IMMORTALITY (*De Incarn.* 54). This gives the complete picture. St. Athanasius is not explicitly concerned with what we would call mystical experience, but his doctrine is the theological foundation for all such experience. (60, 62)

Soteriology is presented as equally central to any authentically Christian experience and interpretation of mystical union. It is only through dying to the alienated, sinful self and rising to new life with and in the resurrected Christ that one shares in the divine life of Trinitarian love. Asceticism is initially identified, based on Mark 8:34, with taking up one's cross (19) through self-denial and following Christ, and is linked to martyrdom as a participation in Christ's death and resurrection that in Ignatius of Antioch becomes an early articulation of mystical union (43). But the paschal journey is not restricted to the literal surrender of life in physical martyrdom: this pattern must be reproduced in any authentic Christian spiritual life. As Merton summarizes, what the martyr undergoes physically every Christian must undergo spiritually:

> The tradition of the martyrs makes it clear that to attain to perfect union with God, a "death" of the self is necessary. . . . How does one die to self? The martyr's case is unambiguous. His exterior, bodily self is destroyed in a real death, and his inner self lives in Christ, raised up with Christ. . . . The ascetic and mystical death to self must in some sense reproduce what is most essential in the martyr's death. Actual dissolution of the union of body and soul is not of the "essence" of this death of the self, but complete liberation from bodily desires seems to be so. . . . We must bear in mind the question of the "death of the self" as we proceed in this course. It will be interpreted variously down the ages (v.g. the mystic death in the Dark Night of St. John {of the} Cross, the stigmatization of St. Francis, etc.) (48)

Merton finds this same focus to be central as well in his own Cistercian tradition:

> We see in Bernard the full mystical explicitation of what is contained and already quite explicit in the Fathers. Observe how the idea of death to ourselves in order to live in Christ is expressed here. It is a mystical transposition of the literal death we saw in the great martyr-theologians. {Note the} classical expressions—the drop of water in the barrel of wine, etc. Note the nature of this "death": it is *"death by absorption into a higher life"*—death brought about by a life—the end of one life by being lifted into a higher life of a more exalted nature. (64)

Thus in Merton's view the mystical and the doctrinal are inseparable. Christian life must be the actualization of the saving mysteries that are professed in faith and celebrated in the liturgy and sacraments. He cites with approval Vladimir Lossky's assertion that defense of dogma is at the same time a defense of the authentic possibilities for sharing the divine life. He summarizes:

> By "mysticism" we can mean the personal experience of
> what is revealed to all and realized in all in the mystery of
> Christ. And by "theology" we mean the common revela-
> tion of the mystery which is to be lived by all. The two be-
> long together. There is no theology without mysticism (for
> it would have no relation to the real life of God in us) and
> there is no mysticism without theology (because it would
> be at the mercy of individual and subjective fantasy). . . .
> Mysticism and theology have one and the same end—they
> culminate in *theosis* or the fullness of the divine life in the
> souls of the faithful. (65–66)

The loss of this interpenetration of doctrine and experience in
the West during the late Middle Ages is for Merton one of the
main reasons for the eclipse of the contemplative life in the centuries since the Reformation, and its recovery is one of the im-
peratives of the renewal of contemporary Christian life, a recovery
that Merton sees as being assisted immeasurably by a revived
awareness of the Eastern Christian tradition, both in the Patristic
era and later, for the East largely was able to avoid the split between doctrine and life that developed in the West with the rise
of the more objective, "scientific" theology of the schools and the
concomitant separation of knowledge and love among the "affective Dionysians" following the lead of Thomas Gallus, along
with the general tendency toward anti-intellectualism that pre-
dominated among spiritual writers from the late Middle Ages
down to modern times; Merton much preferred the idea maintained in his own Cistercian tradition, that love was itself a way
of knowing ("*Amor ipse notitia est*" [84]) to any sharp dichotomiz-
ing of knowledge and love. Though he made no pretensions to
being a systematic theologian himself, Merton makes clear in
these lectures that he considers solid systematic theology neither
a threat nor a distraction to contemplation, but its vitally necessary foundation.

   At the same time, however, Merton is just as clear that neither theology nor mysticism can be reduced to a neat, tidy collection of precise, logically articulated concepts. Hence the central

importance of the *via negativa*, the apophatic dimension, in these notes as in Merton's work as a whole. The Christian life culminates in an encounter with the divine mystery that infinitely transcends words, images and ideas. Hence the importance of the teaching of Gregory of Nyssa, Pseudo-Dionysius, Meister Eckhart, John of the Cross and other teachers of the negative way in these pages, and hence also the critique of Dom Cuthbert Butler's thesis of a tradition of "Western Mysticism" that is basically cataphatic and untouched by the Dionysian emphasis on the luminous darkness in which God must be encountered (168–70), as well as the hint of impatience evident in his discussions of the plethora of labels for degrees of spiritual attainment among later commentators on Teresa of Avila (241). Early in his introductory remarks, Merton states that "the apophatic (dark) tradition . . . is equally important in the East and in the West" (17), and shortly afterwards he expands on this observation in relation to the position of Butler:

> He stresses the special character of *Western mysticism as a mysticism of light*, as opposed to *Eastern mysticism as a mysticism of "night,"* and he concludes that the genuine Western mystical tradition is represented by pre-Dionysian authors: Augustine, Gregory, and Bernard. The later Western mystics, influenced by the introduction of the writings of Pseudo-Dionysius into the West, are, he says, not true to the Western tradition. (This is aimed especially at St. John of the Cross, but also people like Tauler, Ruysbroeck, etc.)

He observes, "This distinction is important and we shall see that it comes close to the heart of the matter in these conferences of ours" (30–31). While he perhaps overstresses the polemical nature of Butler's approach (the abbot draws liberally on John of the Cross and even cites Pseudo-Dionysius in his opening descriptions of mysticism as well as in the "afterthoughts" that are included in the second edition of his book), Merton does raise valid questions, both historical and theological, about any approach to mysticism that would exclude or subordinate the way of

xxviii An Introduction to Christian Mysticism

"unknowing" in contemplative experience. In writing of Gregory of Nyssa, he points out that the emphasis on the divine darkness in his writings is both doctrinal and experiential: it is a refutation of the radical Arian (Anomoean) contention of Eunomius and Aetius that the being of God is intellectually comprehensible (and so incompatible with orthodox Trinitarian dogma) (76–77), and is a description of "an existential contact and communion with the very being of God, which remains unknowable in all its fullness," a darkness that is not mere agnosticism but a recognition, an experience, of the infinite reality of God that is therefore "a *positive* reality and a *light*" and thus "*more true* than any determinate conceptual knowledge of God" (79). Likewise the teaching of the *Mystical Theology* of Pseudo-Dionysius is not the opposite of the cataphatic approach found in the author's other works but its completion. "The originality of his theology is also contingent upon its *unity*. The *Mystical Theology* must not be separated from all the rest of his works. . . . It presupposes all the other Dionysian writings. It presupposes the theology of light and darkness in the *Hierarchies* and the *Divine Names*. It presupposes a strong emphasis on *symbolic and sacramental* theology" (137). Merton attributes the fissure between scholastic and spiritual theology not to the "invasion" of Dionysian thought into the West but to an artificial separation of the *Mystical Theology* from the rest of the Dionysian corpus: "It is quite likely that the writers of the late Middle Ages who, following Denys, broke away from scholastic theology to become professional 'mystical theologians' made this mistake to a great extent" (137). The *Mystical Theology* teaches not just a denial of the adequacy of all conceptual articulations of the divine attributes, but the need to transcend even the very categories of positive and negative theology, which are themselves conceptual expressions that circumscribe the infinite reality of God. Mystical theology is not talk about God, it is encountering a God who cannot be conceptualized; it is, Merton writes,

> beyond both forms of discursive theology, cataphatic and apophatic. It is the FULFILLMENT OF BOTH AND THEIR JUS-

TIFICATION FOR EXISTING. It is a transcendent and experienced theology beyond symbols and discourse. It is not relative (apophatic theology is in relation to the cataphatic which it completes and corrects). Mystical theology stands in relation to no other theology. {It} is a pure immaterial vision beyond intelligence, beyond reflection and self-correction. It is beyond the division of intelligence and will: hence it is not to be called primarily a matter of intelligence or primarily a matter of love: the followers of Dionysius in the West emphasize it as an act of will and thus tend to diminish it. {It is} passive, beyond activity, {at} the summit of the spirit, invaded and possessed by ecstatic love directly given by God, a pure grace, pure love, {which} contacts God in ecstasy. *Ecstasy* {is} a complete break with sense, with intelligence and WITH THE SELF. Here Dionysius goes beyond Gregory and Evagrius: {it is} outside the intelligence, the will, all created beings and the self. This is the important contribution of Dionysius—the full meaning of ecstasy, not just a going out from all things other than the self, but out of the self also. (142–43)

But Merton is also convinced that the tendency on the part of some spiritual theologians to deemphasize or to skip over completely the intermediate levels of symbolic theology has been just as harmful to a full and adequate theology of mystical experience as the unwillingness to move beyond the level of images and ideas into the darkness of unknowing. This accounts for the emphasis in these conferences on *theoria physike*—natural contemplation[29]—the intermediate stage in the model of spiritual

---

29. On September 24, 1961 Merton writes to Abdul Aziz that "the intermediate realm of what the Greek Fathers called *theoria physike* (natural contemplation) . . . deals with the symbols and images of things and their character as words or manifestations of God the Creator, whose wisdom is in them" (*Hidden Ground of Love*, 50). Merton initially provides a brief discussion of *theoria physike* (or *physica*, as he calls it there) in *The Ascent to Truth* (New York: Harcourt, Brace, 1951), 27–28, and again in *The Inner Experience: Notes on Contemplation*, ed. William H. Shannon (San Francisco: HarperCollins, 2003), 67–68.

development first formulated by Evagrius, between the ascetical effort of *praktike* and the contemplative heights of *theologia*—imageless contemplation of the Trinity. As he points out in connection with Dionysius, "both in the West and in the East there developed a tendency to go directly from the ascetic life to contemplation without forms, without passing through *theoria physike*, in the Middle Ages. This is certainly as meaningful a fact as the separation between spirituality and scientific theology, probably much more meaningful. It is here really that the separation has its most disastrous effect" (137).

With their affirmation of the goodness of creation, their appeal to a "sophianic" consciousness, their attentiveness to the "epiphanies" of the hidden *logos*, the principle of order, in Shaker handicrafts and in the primitivist art of the Douanier Rousseau, Merton's reflections on *theoria physike*, drawn particularly from the writings of Maximus the Confessor (as interpreted by Hans Urs von Balthasar), are unquestionably among the most evocative and fully realized sections of this entire set of conferences, and not surprisingly the section that has attracted the most attention from scholars.[30] Merton defines *theoria physike* as "a contemplation according to nature (*physis*) . . . . a contemplation of God

30. See Donald P. St. John, "The Flowering of Natural Contemplation: Some Notes on *Theoria Physike* in Thomas Merton's Unpublished *An Introduction to Christian Mysticism*," *The Merton Seasonal*, 23.2 (Summer 1998), 13–16; and A. M. Allchin, "The Prayer of the Heart and Natural Contemplation: A Foreword to Thomas Merton's Lecture Notes on St. Maximus," in Bernadette Dieker and Jonathan Montaldo, eds., *Merton and Hesychasm: The Prayer of the Heart* (Louisville: Fons Vitae, 2003), 419–29. Kramer's article, though more a survey of the set of conferences as a whole, also devotes particular attention to this section (347–51), as do Allchin in his earlier article, "The Worship of the Whole Creation: Merton & the Eastern Fathers," *The Merton Annual*, 5 (1992), 189–204 (see 195–98), reprinted in *Merton & Hesychasm*, 103–20 (see 109–12); and Basil Pennington in "Thomas Merton and Byzantine Spirituality," *Toward an Integrated Humanity: Thomas Merton's Journey*, ed. M. Basil Pennington, ocso, Cistercian Studies [CS], vol. 103 (Kalamazoo, MI: Cistercian Publications, 1988), 132–48 (see 135–38), reprinted in *Merton & Hesychasm*, 153–68 (see 155–58). This is also the only section of these notes that has been previously published: *Merton &*

in and through nature, in and through things He has created, in history. . . . the *gnosis* that apprehends the wisdom and glory of God, especially His wisdom as *Creator* and *Redeemer*" (122). It is a recognition of the inner coherence, the *logos*, of creatures and of the creation as a whole, a recognition and appreciation of the loving presence of the Creator in the creature; it is the transition point between active and contemplative lives, arising from a synergy between human effort and divine gift, providing "penetrating intuitions" (122) into the intelligibility of all that God has made. While in Evagrius and Maximus *theoria physike* culminates in awareness of pure intelligences, the angelic realm, Merton's focus is above all on the natural world as an epiphany of the divine, on the "sophianic" vision of God's active presence in the world that results not simply in insight but in personal transformation:

> Man by *theoria* is able to unite the hidden wisdom of God in things with the hidden light of wisdom in himself. The meeting and marriage of these two brings about a *resplendent clarity* within man himself, and this clarity is the presence of Divine Wisdom fully recognized and active in him. Thus man becomes a mirror of the divine glory, and is resplendent with divine truth not only in his *mind* but in his *life*. He is filled with the light of wisdom which shines forth in him, and thus God is glorified in him. (125–26)

This indwelling wisdom is not only the source of reformation of the being of the person as reflecting and participating in the divine likeness, but of human activity as sharing in the divine creativity.[31] The human person does not merely observe the

---

Hesychasm, 431–45 (along with the table of contents of the entire text up to but not including the material on spiritual direction: 409–18).

31. The perspective here is very similar to that found in Merton's essay "Theology of Creativity" (Thomas Merton, *Literary Essays*, ed. Brother Patrick Hart [New York: New Directions, 1981], 355–70), first published as part of a three-part symposium in *The American Benedictine Review*, 11 (Sept.–Dec., 1960), 197–213.

sacramentality of God's works but "exercises a spiritualizing influence in the world by the work of his hands which is in accord with *the creative wisdom of God* in things and in history" (126). *Theoria physike* is at the heart of a genuine theology of creativity, which is thus an intrinsic element of the mystical journey to union with God. "God Himself hands over to man, when he is thus purified and enlightened, and united with the divine will, a certain creative initiative of his own, in political life, in art, in spiritual life, in worship: man is then endowed with a *causality* of his own" (126). Conversely, the absence of this sapiential perception of the material world, a purely instrumental relationship to nature, leads to a degradation of creation through an "impersonal, pragmatic, quantitative *exploitation and manipulation* of things" which "is deliberately indifferent to their *logoi* . . . . a demonic cult of change, and 'exchange'—consumption, production, destruction, for their own sakes" (130). Hence authentic contemplation, the cultivation of a consciousness oriented to wisdom, is of tremendous practical importance in a world increasingly tempted by a "demonic pseudo-contemplation, {a} mystique of technics and production" (130).

Merton's emphasis on the importance of *theoria physike* and his characterization of it as *"partly mystical and partly natural,"* marked by "a manifest synergy of God and man in its action" (123) is in accord with his support of the position that the separation of asceticism and mysticism, the *bios praktikos* and the *bios theoretikos*, is "an unfortunate modern development" (21) that treats contemplation as a rarified experience that is limited to the lives of a select few. He rejects the notion that there are "two kinds of Christian perfection, *one ordinary, for all: ascetic perfection; the other extraordinary, abnormal, unique, for very few special souls: the mystical way"* and affirms that "Mysticism and asceticism form an organic whole. . . . Asceticism leads normally to mystical life; at least it disposes for it, though of course the mystical life, its normal fulfillment, remains a pure gift of God" (22). He is thus in sympathy with the position taken by Canon Saudreau and the Dominican school in the early twentieth-century controversy with Poulain about the relationship between asceticism and mysticism that "contemplation is the normal flowering of the Baptismal vocation" (27) (though he would not endorse the conclusion of the former group that the reason that most people do not reach the heights of contemplative union in this life is due to their own culpable failure to respond to grace). The central truth for Merton is that participation in the divine life (*theosis*, divinization) has already been made possible for all through Christ's life, death and resurrection, and the manner in which, or even the degree to which, one experiences this participation in the present life is less significant than the fact that one has responded to the invitation to life in Christ and has committed oneself to the process of journeying with Christ into the infinite abyss of divine love, a journey that according to Gregory of Nyssa's idea of *epektasis*, or unending progress (82), begins in this world but will continue for all eternity. Calculating stages of spiritual development is of limited value when the goal infinitely transcends all limits. Hence Merton's impatience with the myriad and ultimately unsatisfying classifications devised by commentators on St. Teresa of Avila (241), or even with the sharp distinction drawn between acquired and infused contemplation,[32] a distinction unknown to patristic and medieval theologians that "really obscures the essential issue" (121), and can be applied only awkwardly and artificially to such crucial phases of the spiritual life as *theoria physike*. Grace is operative along the entire spectrum of authentic religious experience, and trying to determine at exactly what point that experience can officially be termed "mystical" can be both

---

32. For a thorough recent survey of this issue, strongly critical of the traditional notion of acquired contemplation, see James Arraj, *From St. John of the Cross to Us: The Story of a 400 Year Long Misunderstanding and What it Means for the Future of Christian Mysticism* (Chiloquin, OR: Inner Growth Books, 1999), which includes a brief discussion of Merton's *Ascent to Truth* (202–204); a moderate, non-polemical presentation of the Carmelite position in favor of acquired contemplation is provided by Gabriel of Saint Mary Magdalene, ocd, in "Acquired Contemplation," available in English as the second part of his *St. John of the Cross: Doctor of Divine Love and Contemplation* (Westminster, MD: Newman, 1946).

misleading and harmful. As he remarks concerning the spiritual senses, "It would be fatal for directors to systematically seek out manifestations of each spiritual sense in order to determine whether or not they were dealing with 'a mystic' (!!)" (89).

While Merton affirms the universal call to contemplation in these conferences, he is also particularly concerned to explore how that call is heard and followed in the monastic context in which he and his audience are living. Even though only two of the figures to whom he gives extended attention are monks, and both of these—Evagrius and Maximus—are from the Eastern Church, and although he is quite critical of Dom Butler's efforts to identify a distinctive "Western" mystical tradition based on what he admits "is most familiar in our own Benedictine family" (31), from the outset Merton identifies the purpose of the conferences as "an effort to broaden the horizons and deepen the perspectives of mystical theology in a monastic setting" (3). He is intent on countering any sort of "monastic parochialism" that would restrict the focus of a monk's knowledge and reading to works emanating from the cloister. Having been thoroughly formed in their own Benedictine and Cistercian tradition in the novitiate and juniorate, these students of pastoral theology are ready to have their horizons broadened to encompass the entire mystical tradition of the Church as an integral part of their religious inheritance and a crucial part of their spiritual formation. It is worth noting that Merton's approach to the material leading up to the period of the high Middle Ages, the era of the founding of the Cistercians in 1098, tends to be largely, though not exclusively, thematic, covering as it does the patristic period and the "monastic centuries" that his students would be already familiar with from previous courses, while the material on the later Middle Ages (thirteenth through fifteenth centuries) is more a chronological survey that acquaints the audience with key figures and movements with more breadth and rather less depth. This approach is perhaps due to some extent to the pressures of time, but also makes sure the students have at least some basic familiarity with how the spiritual tradition develops after the "golden age" of Cistercian writers in the twelfth century. The approach changes yet again when Merton reaches the sixteenth century, with a detailed study of Teresa of Avila's teaching on contemplation, which has been so influential on the modern theory and practice of the spiritual life. If Merton thought that this was as far as he would get in the course, as apparently he did, he decided to give his students a thorough exposure to this classic teaching rather than racing to reach the present in what could only have been a superficial and unsatisfying overview. When the classes were unexpectedly extended, rather than resume the chronological survey he elected to turn his attention to the issue of spiritual direction that he had already been researching for the *New Catholic Encyclopedia*, which had the advantage of having practical relevance to a class of monastic priests whose "pastoral" responsibilities would be largely if not exclusively focused on providing direction, to other members of the community and perhaps to non-monastic retreatants and correspondents. Hence the "monastic" focus of these final sections becomes more explicit and prominent, as Merton highlights the value, indeed the superior value, of the "moderate . . . traditional and monastic" approach to spiritual direction, with its emphasis on "both the *spiritual* authority (as opposed to *juridical* authority) of the director and the spontaneity of the relationship between the one directed and the director" (260), as compared with the highly institutionalized and overly casual approaches to direction he labels "type A" and "type B." After this thematic and historical overview of spiritual direction, Merton was able to integrate this material with his earlier discussion of St. Teresa by examining the role of direction in "the crises of the mystical life" (294) as exemplified by Teresa's own experiences, positive and negative, with her directors and to move from there to the teaching of John of the Cross on direction, and more broadly to his teaching on the nights of sense and spirit that have at best an indirect connection with the ostensible topic of spiritual direction, but which enable him to bring the set of conferences to an appropriate conclusion by giving the young monks at least some exposure to a figure of such formative significance to his own spiritual development, and so prominent and influential a "modern" representative of the ancient apophatic tradition of mysticism that Merton had highlighted in earlier sections of the course.

Apparently prompted by factors extrinsic to the course as initially planned, the abrupt shift of subject matter in the two final sections, while ultimately woven, somewhat tenuously, into the overall design, is a reminder that *An Introduction to Christian Mysticism* should not be approached or evaluated as a finished product but as the record of a process, an opportunity to discover what Fr. Louis considered to be essential materials on the Christian mystical tradition with which fully formed members of his monastic community should have at least a basic familiarity. In the absence of recordings of the actual classes,[33] it provides the only access to this unique occasion when Gethsemani's novice master instructed a group composed of professed and ordained monks. As such it occupies a singular place in the series of Merton's monastic conferences. Because of the subject matter it has attracted, and perhaps will continue to attract, somewhat more attention than the novitiate conferences on various aspects of the specifically monastic tradition. But it is important to keep in mind the character of the material as lecture notes and so to avoid higher expectations of consistency, completeness or stylistic polish than such a "genre" is intended to provide. In the section on the spiritual senses, for example, Merton initially states, "When we talk of the spiritual senses we are talking of a very special apprehension of God which is *in no way dependent on* the bodily or interior senses" (83). This is to guard against any inclination simply to identify mystical experience with visions, auditions and other "paranormal" experiences. Yet he later cites with evident agreement the position of Dom Anselm Stolz that "the exercise of the spiritual senses is not a matter of an extraordinary

---

33. Merton's novitiate classes began to be taped only in late April 1962 (for details see *Cassian and the Fathers*, xlvii).

psychological act, nor is it a matter of special spiritual senses in the soul which are *opposed to the bodily senses*, but rather an exercise of the *spiritualized senses* on a mystical level" (91), and sees this approach as in accord with the teachers of the Oriental Church, who "do not try to *account for mystical apprehensions* by pointing to the senses; rather they try to account for the *share of the senses* in mystical experience. Mystical experience is spiritual, and it *reaches the senses in a spiritual way* through and in the spirit. The 'spiritual senses' are thus the senses themselves, but spiritualized and under the sway of the spirit, rather than new spiritual faculties" (91). There is an inconsistency, in fact a flat contradiction, between Merton's initial statement and these later comments, part of a handwritten insert that was not part of the original discussion of the spiritual senses. Had these notes been prepared for publication, Merton would surely have rewritten this section to remove the incompatibility between these statements; as it was, his discovery of new sources providing new perspectives and insights prompted him to incorporate them into the notes without attempting to reconcile them with what had been said earlier. It is interesting to note that it is the class on the spiritual senses that Merton mentions as prompting a lively discussion at the hermitage—perhaps it was consideration of the inconsistency between these positions that accounted for part of the liveliness. In any case, this example makes clear that the notes are a work in progress and need to be regarded as such. This does not diminish the value of these lectures if they are approached as a record of Thomas Merton's ongoing engagement with the Christian contemplative tradition and of his role in communicating the riches of this tradition to other members of his monastic community, rather than as any sort of definitive treatment of Christian mysticism or as a definitive statement of Merton's own knowledge and evaluation of the mystics.

* * * * * * *

In fact it is clear that preparing and teaching this course was as much a stimulus to as a product of Merton's engagement with

the mystical tradition. As so often, his enthusiasm for a particular
figure or topic drew him into deeper exploration. One such figure
is the fourteenth-century Flemish Béguine mystic Hadewijch of
Brabant; Merton's friend, the Carthusian Jean-Baptiste Porion,[34]
had evidently sent Merton his translation of Hadewijch soon
after it was published in 1955, but until now Merton had not paid
it much attention. On May 7, shortly before the "official" course
ends, he comments in the journal, "Have finally after five—no,
seven, years got down to work on the remarkable little book of
Dom . . . Porion on Hadewijch. The introduction is full of information and of sagacious remarks. A really new and clear perspective." He adds, "I am more and more fascinated by the mysticism
of the late Middle Ages, with its defects and its qualities. The
whole scope of the vast movement going back to the Cistercians,
Joachim [de {Fiore}], St. Francis, the Béguines, the Cathari, the
Spirituals, *assimilated* fully by the Church in the great Rhenish
mystics . . . We have not even begun to understand all this, or
appreciate its purport."[35] Merton relied heavily on Porion's introduction for his discussion not only of Hadewijch but of the
entire period, and ended up inserting two handwritten pages of

34. Porion was a Carthusian monk of La Grande Chartreuse who later
became the Procurator General of the Order—two letters from Merton's correspondence with him are included in Thomas Merton, *The School of Charity:
Letters on Religious Renewal and Spiritual Direction*, ed. Patrick Hart (New York:
Farrar, Straus, Giroux, 1990): the first, from February 9, 1952, in which he comments, "You are Carthusian precisely because you are yourself: you are a man
who loves God, in sympathy with Ruysbroeck and Hadjewich [*sic*], etc., in a
Charterhouse" (33); the second (*School of Charity*, 210–11), written March 22,
1964, concerns Merton's dedication to him of his translation of a letter of Guigo the Carthusian (*The Solitary Life* [Worcester: Stanbrook Abbey Press, 1963]).
Dom Porion later collaborated with Merton and Dom André Louf on the statement entitled "Contemplatives and the Crisis of Faith," addressed to the Synod
of Bishops meeting in Rome in October 1967 (published in Thomas Merton,
The Monastic Journey, ed. Brother Patrick Hart [Kansas City: Sheed, Andrews &
McMeel, 1977], 174–78).

35. *Turning Toward the World*, 117 (text reads "Fione").

translated excerpts from the poems of Hadewijch into his conference notes.

Other new or renewed engagement with primary sources had less impact on the actual text of the conferences. On April 2, Easter Sunday, he writes in his journal of beginning to read Gregory of Nyssa's *Homilies on the Canticle of Canticles*[36]—this was apparently after he had discussed Gregory with the class, since the material on Gregory precedes (and overlaps with) the topic of the spiritual senses that was the focus of the March 24 class at the hermitage. On August 19 he records that he has begun to read the *Theologia Germanica*, which the library had just purchased,[37] and eight days later, on the fourth Sunday of August, he mentions the book's teaching "on the heaven and hell we carry about within us, and how it is good to experience within one or the other of these, for there one is in God's hands."[38] While it is unclear exactly where Merton would have been in the now extended mystical theology course, it seems probable that his interest in the work was prompted by his reading of secondary sources in preparing for his classes, rather than his having obtained the text for the purpose of teaching about it, since it is discussed in fairly summary fashion, amounting only to a paragraph, in the notes, and the three brief quotations from the work are not drawn from the translation he read.

36. *Turning Toward the World*, 105; Merton will return to Gregory of Nyssa at the end of the year when a new anthology (*From Glory to Glory: Texts from Gregory of Nyssa's Mystical Writings*) arrives; he writes to Etta Gullick on December 22, "The new book on Gregory of Nyssa by Danielou and Musurillo has been sent me for review by Scribner's. I wonder if it is published in England. It is excellent as far as I have gone with it. A good clear introduction by Danielou and plenty of the best texts, though unfortunately they are all from the old Migne edition and not from the new critical edition of Werner Jaeger" (*Hidden Ground of Love*, 348). Apparently he never wrote a review of the book.

37. *Turning Toward the World*, 153.

38. *Turning Toward the World*, 157; see also the revised version of this passage in Thomas Merton, *Conjectures of a Guilty Bystander* (Garden City, NY: Doubleday, 1966), 165.

A more extensive example of his work on the course leading to deeper knowledge of a writer is Clement of Alexandria. All the citations from Clement in the notes depend on secondary sources, but on the same day he finishes the "official" course (May 19), he records in his journal, "Enjoy Clement of Alexandria. He is underrated and ignored. A great mind and a great Christian, noble and broad and belonging to antiquity, yet new."[39] On August 19 he writes that he has finished reading Clement's *Protreptikos* and has begun his second work, the *Pedagogue*, and adds, "He is certainly one of the Fathers I like best, and with whom I feel the closest affinity."[40] Three days later he writes to Edward Deming Andrews, "I am currently very interested in Clement of Alexandria, one of the earliest Christian 'Gnostics,' and his spirit has much in common with that of Shaker simplicity and joy."[41] By mid-November he has reached the *Stromateis*, the third book of Clement's "trilogy," and on November 14 he contrasts Adolf Eichmann's "sanity" with "the true sanity of Clement of Alexandria. His beautiful, clear, clean doctrines full of peace and light. That we are planted in Christ as in Paradise. His realization of hope in Christ, Life in the Spirit. There is no other true sanity. *Epistemonike Theosebeia* [Understanding fear of God]."[42] Five days later he notes that he is reading the *Stromateis* "with comfort and consolation" and adds, "I see no problem at all in his 'esotericism.' Obviously one cannot tell everybody everything, and there are certain truths for which the vast majority are not and never will be prepared. I cannot talk to the novices about the things which are central in my own spiritual life—or not about many of them, and about none of them directly."[43] He is still reading

---

39. *Turning Toward the World*, 120.

40. *Turning Toward the World*, 154.

41. *Hidden Ground of Love*, 35.

42. *Turning Toward the World*, 179.

43. *Turning Toward the World*, 181; see also the entry for November 21: "Once again I am in favor of the esoteric principles of Clement of Alexandria" (*Turning Toward the World*, 182).

Clement on December 4,[44] and on December 13 writes to Bruno
Schlesinger of St. Mary's College at Notre Dame concerning the
proposed Christian Culture program at the college:

> Here I might mention someone who I think ought to be
> known and consulted as a choragos for our music, and
> that is Clement of Alexandria. In fact I think one might
> profitably concentrate a great deal of attention on the
> Alexandrian school, not only the Christians, but all that
> extraordinary complex of trends, the Jewish and gnostic
> and neo-Platonist, Philo above all, and then the Desert
> Fathers too, just outside. And Origen. And the Palestin-
> ians who reacted against Alexandria, and the Antiochians.
> Here we have a crucially important seedbed of future de-
> velopments. . . . Here again we rejoin the Alexandrians
> and Greeks. The purpose of a Christian humanism should
> be to liberate man from the mere status of *animalis homo*
> (sarkikos) to at least the level of *rationalis* (psuchicos) and
> better still spiritual, gnostic or pneumatic.[45]

His interest in Clement led not just to an extended program of
reading. On August 7 he had remarked on "the marvelous opening of the *Protreptikos* . . . the 'new song'—the splendid image of
the cricket flying to replace by his song the broken string in the
Lyre of Eunomos at Delphi. Though he repudiates the myth he
uses it splendidly. Humanity a musical instrument for God."[46]
Four days later he writes, "The other morning I translated a bit
from Clement of Alex. about Zeus being dead as swan, dead as

44. *Turning Toward the World*, 184; it is not clear whether Merton ever finished the lengthy *Stromateis*: on December 31, 1961 he writes in his journal, "I
haven't read enough of the things I should be reading and want to read: Clement, Gregory of Nyssa" (*Turning Toward the World*, 190).

45. *Hidden Ground of Love*, 543.

46. *Turning Toward the World*, 149; see also the revised version of this passage: *Conjectures*, 170.

eagle, dead as δρακων,"[47] and at some point he translated the passage about the new song as well. He initially thought he might send these excerpts to Robert Lax for his little poetry broadside *Pax*,[48] but eventually it developed into a small book of selections, the original prose transformed into verse, with an introduction.[49] On October 20 Merton noted in his journal, "Worked a little this morning on Clement of Alexandria—the selections and preface. This is satisfying work, because of my love for him."[50] Four days later, he writes to his friend and publisher James Laughlin of New Directions, "Man is now typing a little book I got for you[:] *Clement of Alexandria*, introduction and translations about twenty five pages, selections from his *Protreptikos*, most interesting both to philosophers, religion people, Zens, and Classical scholars. I think you will like this. I think of it as a small format, discreet little book. . . . It could be very attractive. The ms. will be along in a few days."[51] On January 19, 1962 he notes that Laughlin had been to Gethsemani on a visit and agreed to "do the little book on

47. *Turning Toward the World*, 150; see also the revised version of this passage: *Conjectures*, 172.

48. "Maybe for Paxo translate some Clements of Alexandria" (*When Prophecy Still Had a Voice*, 226 [8/16/61 letter]); another letter a week later reports: "Working on Clement of Alexandria" (*When Prophecy Still Had a Voice*, 227).

49. Thomas Merton, *Clement of Alexandria: Selections from the* Protreptikos (New York: New Directions, 1962); the selections, without the introduction, are also found in the translations section of Thomas Merton, *Collected Poems* (New York: New Directions, 1977), 934–42.

50. *Turning Toward the World*, 171.

51. Thomas Merton and James Laughlin, *Selected Letters*, ed. David D. Cooper (New York: Norton, 1997), 181; on November 10 Merton sends the material to Lax, commenting, "Here Clammish of Alexandrig. Too long for Pax after all. Think I do another for Pax, Clammish short introduction with funny sayings about two pages. This too long. This make book for New Directions. Maybe Pax take little bit, like last page. Maybe Jubiless take a little bit. . . . This is just a quick to tell about Clammish" (*When Prophecy Still Had a Voice*, 229–30). There is no indication he ever produced additional material for *Pax*.

Clement and the *Protreptikos*, which is a project I like."[52] Proofs for the book arrived in mid-March,[53] and by the beginning of November it had appeared and was pronounced by Merton to be a "most handsome" volume that made him "very pleased."[54]

While it did not result in any publication, or even find extensive expression in the mystical theology notes themselves, it is clear that Merton's acquaintance with and appreciation of Meister Eckhart developed significantly as a consequence of his involvement with the conferences. In a letter to Dona Luisa Coomaraswamy shortly before the course began, Merton had made a rather general comment on Eckhart, apparently in response to a question from her: "Eckhart I know. We have here a popular edition of him, and I have something in French of his. I like him, and Tauler and Ruysbroeck."[55] It is apparent from subsequent correspondence, however, that even after the "official" conferences have concluded he is still somewhat ambivalent about Eckhart, about whom he writes to his Anglican friend Etta Gullick on June 10, "I like him, but now and again he leaves one with a sense of being let down, when he goes beyond all bounds. He is more brilliant than all the other Rhenish mystics and really more interesting. Yet I like Tauler for a more steady diet."[56] But

52. *Turning Toward the World*, 195; six days later, however, he comments in his journal, "I can perhaps withdraw from publication and write only what I deeply need to write. What is that? The little Clement of Alex. book is not it, I think. Not the way it stands. But it is to be published" (*Turning Toward the World*, 197).

53. Merton writes to Laughlin on March 16, "The *Clement [of Alexandria]* just got in this morning, I don't know how it got held up so long, maybe Fr. Abbot wanted to read it or something. But anyway I will look over the suggestions and shoot it back to you" (*Selected Letters*, 197).

54. Merton to Laughlin, November 2, 1962 (*Selected Letters*, 211); see also his November 17 letter to Ernesto Cardenal (Thomas Merton, *The Courage for Truth: Letters to Writers*, ed. Christine M. Bochen [New York: Farrar, Straus, Giroux, 1993], 136).

55. *Hidden Ground of Love*, 129 [2/12/61].

56. *Hidden Ground of Love*, 342; see also his May 13 letter to his Pakistani correspondent Abdul Aziz, in which he compares the Islamic doctrine of Tawhid (unity) to the idea of "the 'Godhead' beyond 'God'" in Eckhart and the

Mrs. Gullick is an advocate for Eckhart, and sends along an article on him by a former Benedictine, C. F. Kelley, and eventually a book by Vladimir Lossky, already a favorite author of Merton.[57] On July 1 Merton writes to Mrs. Gullick, "And you are of course right about Eckhart. He is more and more wonderful, and when properly interpreted, becomes less 'way out' as our beats say. There is more in one sermon of Eckhart than in volumes of other people. There is so much packed in between the lines."[58] Three days later his journal entry reveals that he is fully drawn into Eckhart's work for the first time:

> I am becoming entranced with Eckhart: I have been won by the brevity, the incisiveness of his sermons, his way of piercing straight to the heart of the inner life, the awakened spark, the creative and redeeming word, God born in us. He is a great man who was pulled down by little men who thought they could destroy him. Who thought they could take him to Avignon and have him ruined and indeed he was ruined in 28 propositions which did not altogether resemble his joy and his energy and his freedom, but which could be brought to coincide with words he had uttered.[59]

Rhenish mystics, which he describes as "a distinction which caused trouble to many theologians in the Middle Ages and is not accepted without qualifications" and "a subtle and difficult theology," adding "I don't venture into it without necessity" (*Hidden Ground of Love*, 49).

57. See *Hidden Ground of Love*, 343 [letter of July 1, 1961], 344 [letter of July 25, 1961]; *Turning Toward the World*, 145 [July 26, 1961], 147 [August 3, 1961].

58. *Hidden Ground of Love*, 343; see also his journal entry for August 6: "Today I read the wonderful sermon on the divine truth in which Eckhart says that as a person about to be struck by a thunderbolt turns toward it, and all the leaves of a tree about to be struck turn toward it, so one in whom the divine birth is to take place turns, without realizing, completely toward it" (*Turning Toward the World*, 148; see as well the revised version of this passage: *Conjectures*, 169).

59. *Turning Toward the World*, 137; see also the revised version of this passage: *Conjectures*, 42–43. On September 16 Merton writes to Pablo Antonio Cuadra, "I have been studying Meister Eckhart, who is tremendous" (*Courage for Truth*, 189).

Thus Merton's engagement with a figure who will be of increasing importance for his work in the last years of his life[60] begins during the course of, though not to any significant extent in the actual text of, his mystical theology conferences.

The expansion of Merton's interest in mystical writers during the months of the mystical theology conferences extended even beyond the authors discussed in the text. He becomes increasingly intrigued with the hitherto anonymous fourteenth-century text *The Mirror of Simple Souls*, mentioned only in passing in the conferences (183–84), and particularly with the possibility (now generally accepted) that it was written by the Béguine Marguerite Porete, who was burned as a heretic at Paris in 1310. Etta Gullick, once again, seems to have called his attention to the book, as he writes to her on May 15, "I have heard of *The Mirror of Simple Souls*.

---

60. Merton will return to Eckhart particularly during the spring and summer of 1966, during his time at the hospital for back surgery and its tumultuous aftermath. See Thomas Merton, *Learning to Love: Exploring Solitude and Freedom. Journals, vol. 6: 1966–1967*, ed. Christine M. Bochen (San Francisco: Harper-Collins, 1997), 38: "The best thing of all was lying reading Eckhart, or sitting up, when I finally could, copying sentences from the sermons that I can use if I write on him. It was this that saved me, and when I got back to the hermitage last evening to say the Easter offices everything else drained off and Eckhart remained as real. The rest was like something I had imagined" [April 10, 1966—Easter Sunday]; two days later, he again writes of Eckhart, transposing his thought, interestingly, into a more "paschal" mode: "Christ died for all that we *might no longer live for ourselves but for him who died for us and rose again.* This is the heart of Eckhart, and remains that in spite of all confusions. At least that is the way I understand him, though he does speak of the Godhead, and living '*in*' the Godhead rather than 'for Christ'" (*Learning to Love*, 39); see also the references to "Eckhart's Castle" and the "little spark" in Merton's hospital poem, "With the World in My Bloodstream" (*Collected Poems*, 615–18). On Merton and Eckhart, see: Oliver Davies, "Thomas Merton and Meister Eckhart," *The Merton Journal*, 4.2 (Advent 1997), 15–24; Robert Faricy, SJ, "On Understanding Thomas Merton: Merton, Zen, and Eckhart," *Studies in Spirituality*, 9 (1999), 189–202; Thomas O'Meara, OP, "Meister Eckhart's Destiny: In Memory of Thomas Merton," *Spirituality Today*, 30 (Sept. 1978), 348–59; Erlinda Paguio, "Blazing in the Spark of God: Thomas Merton's References to Meister Eckhart," *The Merton Annual*, 5 (1992), 247–62.

It is attributed to Marguerite Porete, an unfortunate Beguine who was burned for some very innocent statements. I would like to get to know this book."[61] On July 1 he writes to her, "It would be nice if the *Mirror* were by Marguerite Porete, I feel sorry for her, and would be pleased if it turned out she had after all written a very orthodox spiritual 'classic.'"[62] Early the following year he again refers to the *Mirror* and the question of authorship in letters to Mrs. Gullick,[63] and later that year she secures a copy of it and sends it to Merton, who reflects in a journal entry for October 7, "What a charming and wise book! Yet I think it is Marguerite Porete who wrote it, and she was burned. What sad, impossible things have happened in this holy Church!"[64] Writing to Mrs. Gullick later that month to express his gratitude for the gift, Merton remarks: "Thanks so much for *The Mirror of Simple Souls*. I am really enjoying it, though I find that I have a hard time getting anywhere for great lengths in such books. A little goes a long way. It is an admirable book, but one which one does not really 'read.' I hold it in my hand walking about in the woods, as if I were reading. But it is charming and bold and right."[65] Apparently he does eventually finish reading it, as he writes to E. I. Watkin in May, 1963: "Recently I have read *The Mirror of Simple Souls*, which Etta Gullick lent me. It is a marvelous book, and has some magnificent and original things in it. And is so splendidly written. I understand it is by Marguerite Porete, who was burned at the stake. . . . There is no question that the mystics are the ones who have kept Christianity going, if anyone has."[66]

61. *Hidden Ground of Love*, 341; see also his letter to her of June 10 (342).

62. *Hidden Ground of Love*, 343.

63. *Hidden Ground of Love*, 350 [January 29, 1962], 351 [March 30, 1962].

64. *Turning Toward the World*, 254.

65. *Hidden Ground of Love*, 355.

66. *Hidden Ground of Love*, 583; see also his letter to Etta Gullick of March 24, 1963: "how much I love the *Mirror* and how much I thank you for letting me keep it. It is really one of my favorite books. . . . The language is wonderful, the expressions are charming, and of course I like the doctrine. But I can see how it could have got poor Marguerite in trouble (you see, I am convinced that she

At the very outset of the mystical theology course, no doubt reflecting on his reading in preparation for the conferences, Merton had described himself as "still a 14th century man: the century of Eckhart, Ruysbroeck, Tauler, the English recluses, the author of the *Cloud*, Langland and Chaucer—more an independent and a hermit than a community man, by no means an ascetic, interested in psychology, a lover of the dark cloud in which God is found by love."[67] His interest in Marguerite Porete is part of the same fascination with this era.[68] But even more significant is the blossoming of his love for the English mystics during this same period, prompted by his preparation of a review of a new book by David Knowles,[69] but also in part by his immersion in

---

is the author). As you say, one must fear delusion and heresy in such matters as this, but great simplicity, humility and purity of faith, and above all detachment from a self that experiences itself in prayer, or a self that desires anything for itself, is a sure safeguard" (*Hidden Ground of Love*, 358–59).

67. *Turning Toward the World*, 99.

68. See also his lengthy reflection five days later on the great figures from the following century, who are discussed only briefly in the conference notes: "The saints of the 15th century—are among those who most move me. The collapse of medieval society, corruption of the clergy, decadence of conventual life—and there emerge men and women of the laity *supremely obedient to God*. Especially Nicholas of Flue and Joan of Arc. Complete and simple signs of contradiction to worldliness and system and convention and prejudiced interest. *Not* rebels at all, but completely meek and submissive instruments of God. In them you see clearly and movingly revealed what it is *not* to be a mere rebel but to be obedient to God as a sign to men, a sign of mercy, a revelation of truth and of power. I am drawn to these 'signs' of God with all the love of my heart, trusting above all in their love and their intercession, for they live in the glory of God, and I would not love them if God had not made them 'sacraments' to me. St. Catherine of Genoa also, whom Natasha Spender loves (she keeps wanting me to write about C. of G.). Note especially the fabulous supernatural providence with which St. Joan remained obedient to the *church* while resisting her judges who seemed to be and claimed to be speaking entirely for the Church" (*Turning Toward the World*, 100; see also the revised version of this passage: *Conjectures*, 145).

69. Thomas Merton, *Mystics and Zen Masters* (New York: Farrar, Straus and Giroux, 1967), 128–53; this is a revised version of the review article that first appeared in *Jubilee* (Sept. 1961), 36–40. It is a review not only of David Knowles,

the period for his conferences, though they are mentioned only in passing there. Already on Easter (April 2) he speaks of "reading bits of Dame Julian of Norwich"[70] the day before, and his quotation of her most famous phrase in a journal entry at the end of the same month shows he is still reading her: "There is the level of faith, on which nothing is seen, and yet there peace is evident, and it is no self-delusion to say 'all manner of thing shall be well' because experience has repeatedly proved it."[71] A week later, in the same entry in which he mentions that he has completed his review, he tells himself, "Must get to know Hilton. Have been put off by the {*Goad*} *of Love*, which is not really his."[72] The faithful Etta Gullick sends him a new translation of *The Cloud of Unknowing* in June, and Merton comments in a letter to her of reading both it and Hilton: "I like the Penguin edition of the *Cloud*. It is clear and easy for the contemporary reader. Yet it does lose some of the richness of the older more concrete English. I like the fourteenth-century English mystics more and more. I am reading [Walter Hilton's] *The Scale* [*of Perfection*], which has such a great deal in it."[73] In late August he quotes from "three wonderful chapters in the *Cloud of Unknowing* on Martha and Mary,"[74] but it is above all to Julian that he is drawn: "all this year I have been more and more attracted to her,"[75] he writes in late October.

The English Mystical Tradition (New York: Harper, 1961) but of Eric Colledge's anthology *The Medieval Mystics of England* (New York: Scribner's, 1961) and of Thomas Traherne, *Centuries of Meditations* (New York: Harper & Brothers, 1960).

70. *Turning Toward the World*, 105.

71. *Turning Toward the World*, 113 [April 29, 1961].

72. *Turning Toward the World*, 117 [May 7, 1961] (text reads "*Guard*").

73. *Hidden Ground of Love*, 343 [July 1, 1961].

74. *Turning Toward the World*, 156 [August 26, 1961]; on the *Cloud*, see also Merton's Foreword to William Johnston, *The Mysticism of the Cloud of Unknowing: A Modern Interpretation* (New York: Desclée, 1967), ix–xiv; second ed. (St. Meinrad, IN: Abbey Press, 1975), vii–xii.

75. *Turning Toward the World*, 173 [October 23, 1961]. On Merton and Julian, see Thomas Del Prete, "'All Shall Be Well': Merton's Admiration for Julian of Norwich," *Spiritual Life*, 39.4 (Winter 1993), 209–17.

On Christmas day his journal reflection is based on Julian: "the main thought of my heart (it has been a thought of the heart and not of the head) is that while Christ is given to me as my life, I also am given to Him as His joy and His crown (Julian of Norwich) and that he wills to take delight in saving and loving me."[76] Two days later, in a long passage, he declares, "I think the gift of this Christmas has been the real discovery of Julian of Norwich. I have long been around her, and hovered at her door, and known that she was one of my best friends, and just because I was so sure of her wise friendship I did not make haste to seek what I now find." He describes her as "a true theologian, with a greater clarity and organization and depth even than St. Theresa," and praises the way in which she ponders the meaning of her visionary experience: "she really elaborates the content of revelation as deeply experienced. It is first experienced, then thought, and the thought deepens again into life, so that all her life the content of her vision was penetrating her through and through." He is struck above all about the way in which she is able peacefully to live in the midst of the "apparent contradiction" between her confidence in the ultimate eschatological conviction that "all shall be made well" and her submission to the Church's doctrine of the damnation of the reprobate. This steadfastness serves as an inspiration and a model for Merton: "I believe that this 'wise heart' I have prayed for is precisely in this—to stay in this hope and this contradiction, fixed on the certainty of the 'great deed'— which alone gives the Christian and spiritual life its true, full dimension."[77] In a letter to Clare Boothe Luce written this same week he calls Julian "a mighty theologian, in all her simplicity and love,"[78] and in March of 1962, writing to Sr. Madeleva to explain why Julian and the other English mystics were omitted from the mystical theology notes, he calls her "without doubt

---

76. *Turning Toward the World*, 189.

77. *Turning Toward the World*, 189; see also the revised version of this passage: *Conjectures*, 191–92.

78. *Witness to Freedom*, 26.

one of the most wonderful of all Christian voices" and "with
Newman, the greatest English theologian," above all because she
has grounded her thinking and writing in "her experience of the
substantial center of the great Christian mystery of Redemption. . . . the objective mystery of Christ as apprehended by her,
with the mind and formation of a fourteenth-century English
woman."[79] She has become, as Merton writes to Jacques Maritain
at the end of 1962 (comparing her to Maritain's wife Raïssa): "that
mystic that I love above all others."[80] It is somewhat ironic that
in a text entitled *An Introduction to Christian Mysticism* the mystic
he loves above all others is not even mentioned, but it was a love
that developed during and after the time when the conferences
were given, and, one may presume, a love that was prepared for
and nourished by the process of researching, composing and
delivering these conferences, particularly those focused on the
fourteenth century.

As this series of journal and correspondence comments on
Julian suggests, for a full appreciation of the mystical theology
notes it is important that they be situated in the context of the
time frame in which they were composed and delivered. The
course was given during the period when Merton was engaged
in revising his early writings on contemplation, a process that
began in 1958 with his essay "Poetry and Contemplation: A Reappraisal,"[81] a reworking of his 1947 essay "Poetry and the Contemplative Life,"[82] continued with the drafting in 1959 of what
became *The Inner Experience*, developed from the pamphlet *What*

79. *Witness to Freedom*, 43.

80. *Courage for Truth*, 33.

81. Thomas Merton, *Literary Essays*, 338-54; first published in *Commonweal*,
October 24, 1958.

82. Thomas Merton, *Figures for an Apocalypse* (New York: New Directions,
1947), 95–111; first published in *The Commonweal*, July 4, 1947. For a comparison
of the two versions, see Patrick F. O'Connell, "Poetry & Contemplation: The
Evolution of Thomas Merton's Aesthetic," *The Merton Journal*, 8.1 (Easter 2001),
2–11.

Is Contemplation? of 1947,[83] and culminated in the transformation of *Seeds of Contemplation*[84] into *New Seeds of Contemplation,*[85] an undertaking that Merton was working on at the very time that the mystical theology conferences were being developed and given.[86] Like the new versions of these works, *An Introduction to Christian Mysticism* provides evidence of Merton's mature view of the contemplative life, seen no longer *"as a separate department of life"* but as all of life viewed and lived in the context of God's love, *"the very fullness of a fully integrated life,"* as the new "Author's Note" to the poetry essay strikingly puts it.[87] The classes also overlap, if only slightly, what William Shannon has called "the Year of the Cold War Letters," (October 1961–October 1962),[88]

83. Thomas Merton, *What Is Contemplation?* (Holy Cross, IN: St. Mary's College, 1948); a revised version, published in England by Burns & Oates in 1950, is readily available: Thomas Merton, *What Is Contemplation?* (Springfield, IL: Templegate, 1981). For a discussion of this work and its relationship to *The Inner Experience*, see William H. Shannon, *Thomas Merton's Dark Path: The Inner Experience of a Contemplative* (New York: Farrar, Straus, Giroux, 1982), 17–33, 72–113, and his introduction to *The Inner Experience*, vii–xvi.

84. Thomas Merton, *Seeds of Contemplation* (New York: New Directions, 1949).

85. Thomas Merton, *New Seeds of Contemplation* (New York: New Directions, 1961); for a comparison of the various versions of *Seeds/New Seeds*, see Donald Grayston, *Thomas Merton: The Development of a Spiritual Theologian* (Lewiston, NY: Edwin Mellen Press, 1985) and Ruth Fox, OSB, "Merton's Journey from *Seeds* to *New Seeds*," *The Merton Annual*, 1 (1988), 249–70; see also Grayston's parallel-text edition of the versions: *Thomas Merton's Rewritings: The Five Versions of Seeds/New Seeds of Contemplation as a Key to the Development of His Thought* (Lewiston, NY: Edwin Mellen Press, 1989).

86. See the journal entry for September 23, 1961: "This week—finished quickly the galley proofs of *New Seeds of Contemplation*" (*Turning Toward the World*, 164).

87. *Literary Essays*, 339.

88. William H. Shannon, *Silent Lamp: The Thomas Merton Story* (New York: Crossroad, 1992), 215; note also that at the very time that Merton and James Laughlin were discussing the publication of Merton's selections from Clement they were also preparing his collection of articles by various authors on the atomic threat, *Breakthrough to Peace: Twelve Views on the Threat of Thermonuclear*

when Merton's newly reawakened social conscience first began to find expression in articles on war, non-violence, and eventually race, poverty and the environment. In fact, the very first of the 111 letters collected and distributed in mimeographed form[89] is one from late October to Etta Gullick in which Merton thanks her for sending articles on Eckhart and E. I. Watkin's *Poets and Mystics*, with its "chapter on Julian, whom I love dearly";[90] the collection also includes three later letters to Mrs. Gullick, all of which include material related to the mystics,[91] along with two to Bruno Schlesinger, including the one recommending Clement of Alexandria,[92] and the letter to Sr. Madeleva on the mystical theology notes themselves and on Julian,[93] clear evidence that for Merton contemplation and action, an interest in mysticism and a passion for justice, were not alternative but correlative, both essential ways of being faithful to God's will for humanity.

An Introduction to Christian Mysticism is not a definitive or exhaustive treatment of its subject. It is, as the title indicates, an introduction, and is even, as its Foreword states, "imperfect and incomplete." But it does provide, as the Foreword also states, by far the most extensive "historical and positive" treatment in all of Merton's writings of the "rich thought" of the Christian mysti-

---

Extermination (New York: New Directions, 1962); see *Turning Toward the World*, 195: "J. Laughlin was here Tuesday and Wednesday and we worked on the Peace paperback. He will also do the little book on Clement and the *Protreptikos*, which is a project I like" [January 19, 1962].

89. These letters, hitherto available scattered through the five volumes of Merton's collected letters, have now been published together: Thomas Merton, *The Cold War Letters*, ed. William H. Shannon and Christine M. Bochen (Maryknoll, NY: Orbis, 2006).

90. *Hidden Ground of Love*, 346–47.

91. *Hidden Ground of Love*, 348-50 [December 22, 1961], 350-53 [March 30, 1962], 355–56 [October 29, 1962].

92. *Hidden Ground of Love*, 541–43 [December 13, 1961], 543–45 [February 10, 1962].

93. *Witness to Freedom*, 43–44.

cal tradition, and is therefore a valuable witness both to Merton's own knowledge of and interest in that tradition, and to what topics, figures and movements he considered it important for contemporary monks, and by extension contemporary educated Christians, to be aware of. *An Introduction to Christian Mysticism* is thus both a complement to the other writings of its period and a uniquely significant document in its own right.

* * * * * * *

The text of *An Introduction to Christian Mysticism* exists in two versions. Included in Volume 13 of Merton's "Collected Essays," the 24-volume compendium of published and unpublished materials assembled and bound at the Abbey of Gethsemani some time after Merton's death and now available at the abbey and at the Thomas Merton Center at Bellarmine University in Louisville, is a 188-page mimeographed text headed "AN INTRODUCTION TO CHRISTIAN / MYSTICISM / (From the Apostolic Fathers to the Council of Trent.) / Lectures given at the Abbey of Gethsemani." It consists of the unnumbered title page; an unnumbered "Foreword" page; seven unnumbered "Table of Contents" pages, headed "ASCETICAL & MYSTICAL THEOLOGY"; 170 numbered pages of the body of the text; one unnumbered title page reading "APPENDIX TO MYSTICAL THEOLOGY / Appendix I. / The SCALA CLAUSTRALIUM."; four numbered pages of Appendix 1; four numbered pages of Appendix 2. Except for the title and Foreword pages, the fifth page of the table of contents, and the Appendix 1 title page, all the mimeographed pages are two-sided. This version of the text would have been distributed to the students at some point towards the end of the course or shortly after it was finished, and was also sent to other monasteries and various correspondents.

Also at the Bellarmine Merton Center is the original text of *An Introduction to Christian Mysticism*, composed by Merton himself, which he would have had in front of him as he was giving the conferences and which was the basic source for the retyped mimeographed text. It consists of 156 pages, partly typed and partly handwritten, on unlined three-ring paper, heavily modified by handwritten additions included both on the pages of text themselves and on the otherwise blank verso pages, with passages marked for insertion on the recto pages opposite. One hundred ten of the pages are typed, 44 are handwritten, and two are partly handwritten and partly typed. The text begins with three preliminary handwritten pages: an epigraph from Evelyn Underhill; the title and Foreword page (marked to be typed as two separate pages); an outline of the course (later version). Then follow 141 pages of the text proper: the numbering runs from page 1 to page 121 (the number "77" is skipped but number "82" is used twice),[94] with twenty additional pages inserted with numbers followed by letters.[95] The final twelve pages, all handwritten, consist of a title page for Appendix 1, four pages of Appendix 1, five pages of Appendix 2, and two additional pages of notes on Gordon Zahn's book *German Catholics and Hitler's Wars*.[96] In addition, a preliminary handwritten outline of the course is inserted after page 69.

94. Pages 1–7 (the first two unnumbered) are typed; 8–9 (handwritten), 10–23 (typed; # 18 handwritten; # 22 corrected by hand for typed # 20), 24 (typed), 25 (handwritten), 26–60 (typed; # 46 handwritten; ## 59, 60 corrected by hand for typed ## 58, 59), 61 (partly handwritten, partly typed), 62–67 (typed), 68 (partly handwritten, partly typed), 69 (typed), 70–72 (handwritten), 73–74 (typed), 75–76, 78 (handwritten), 79–82 (typed), 82–86 (handwritten), 87–105 (typed; # 90 corrected by hand for typed # 89), 106–10 (handwritten), 111–21 (typed).

95. Pages 7a-b (handwritten), 9a-b (typed), 23a-b (handwritten), 27a (handwritten; unnumbered, but referred to as 27a in a note on the previous page), 66a-c (handwritten), 68a-b (handwritten), 78a-b (typed), 98a-d (typed), 115a-b (typed).

96. See Merton's March 1962 letter to Frank Sheed praising this book, published by Sheed and Ward, as "a most important and very well-done job of work" (*Witness to Freedom*, 45); Merton perhaps associated it with Lifton's book on brainwashing and so inserted his notes on it at the back of the mystical theology notes, but the material is not labeled an appendix and is not included in the mimeograph, so it does not seem to have been considered an actual part of the mystical theology material.

This version of the text, typed and handwritten by Merton himself, serves as copy text for the present edition of *An Introduction to Christian Mysticism*, with the following modifications: the epigraph, which Merton subsequently incorporated into the Foreword, the two versions of the outline of the course, and the two pages of notes on the Zahn book have not been included as part of the text; they have been transcribed and included in the Textual Notes found in Appendix A; Merton's occasional jotted notes for announcements to the class are not considered text material and are included neither in the text nor in the textual notes;[97] the Table of Contents from the mimeograph and the occasional places in the mimeograph where the typist has followed Merton's directions to incorporate quotations from printed material that he did not type or write out himself are included in the text—these latter additions are listed in the Textual Notes in Appendix A.

All substantive additions made to the text, in order to turn elliptical or fragmentary statements into complete sentences, are included in braces, as are the few emendations incorporated directly into the text, so that the reader can always determine exactly what Merton himself wrote. No effort is made to reproduce Merton's rather inconsistent punctuation, paragraphing, abbreviations and typographical features; a standardized format for these features is established that in the judgement of the editor best represents a synthesis of Merton's own practice and contemporary usage: e.g., all Latin passages are italicized unless specific parts of a longer passage are underlined by Merton, in which case the underlined section of the passage is in roman type; all other passages underlined by Merton are italicized; words in upper case in the text are printed in small caps; periods and commas are uniformly included within quotation marks; patterns of abbreviation and capitalization, very inconsistent in the copy text, are regularized. Latin passages in the original text

---

97. These are found on verso pages opposite pages 15, 23, 41, 43, 49, 57, 94, 98a, 100, 118, and the third page of Appendix 1.

are left in Latin but translated by the editor in the notes. All references to primary and secondary sources are cited in the notes. All identified errors in Merton's text are noted and if possible corrected. All instances where subsequent research and expanded knowledge affect Merton's accuracy are discussed in the notes.

The textual apparatus does not attempt to record every variation between the different versions of the text. Errors, whether of omission or of mistranscription, in the mimeograph version of the text where this is not being used as copy text, are not recorded since they have no independent authority vis-à-vis the copy text. Notes on the text record:

a) all cases in which a reading from the mimeograph version is substituted for the copy text—generally limited to the typist following Merton's own instructions for expanding the text; in those cases where Merton's direction to expand the text is not followed, the text is left as it is, the direction is recorded in the textual apparatus, and the addition is included in the explanatory notes;

b) all on-line corrections Merton made in the process of typing (i.e., crossing out one word or phrase and immediately substituting another);

c) all handwritten additions or alterations to the original text.

Thus the textual notes allow the interested reader to distinguish between the preliminary draft of Merton's notes and the additions that he made, presumably before actually delivering the conference lectures. Since these conferences were given only once, the additions were made during the same general period as the original drafting of the text, but they do serve to indicate how Merton continued to rework his material as he prepared the conferences.

A list of suggestions for further reading is included as a second appendix, consisting first of other sources in Merton's published works where figures and topics from this volume are discussed, followed by a list of important recent studies on the major figures and topics of this volume, that will provide helpful updating on material discussed by Merton.

* * * * * * *

In conclusion I would like to express my gratitude to all those who have made this volume possible:

- to the Trustees of the Merton Legacy Trust, Robert Giroux, Anne McCormick and Tommie O'Callaghan, for permission to publish the *Introduction to Christian Mysticism* conferences;
- to the late Robert E. Daggy, former director of the Thomas Merton Center, Bellarmine College (now University), Louisville, KY, for first alerting me to the project of editing Merton's monastic conferences, and for his encouragement in this and other efforts in Merton studies;
- to E. Rozanne Elder, director of Cistercian Publications, for continued support for the project of publishing Merton's conferences;
- to Brother Patrick Hart, ocso, for his friendship, for continued encouragement in the publication of the volumes of the conferences in the Monastic Wisdom series, for which he serves as editor, and for facilitating my research visits to the library at the Abbey of Gethsemani;
- to Professor Lawrence S. Cunningham of the University of Notre Dame, for graciously accepting an invitation to provide the Preface for this volume;
- to Paul M. Pearson, director and archivist of the Merton Center, and Mark C. Meade, assistant archivist, for their gracious hospitality and valued assistance during my visits to the Center;
- to the Gannon University Research Committee, which provided a grant that allowed me to pursue research on this project at the Merton Center and at the Abbey of Gethsemani;
- to Mary Beth Earll of the interlibrary loan department of the Nash Library, Gannon University, for her tireless efforts in locating and acquiring various obscure volumes;

- to library staff of the Hesburgh Library of the University of Notre Dame, the Mullen Library of The Catholic University of America, the St. Anselm's Abbey Library, Washington, DC, and the Friedsam Memorial Library of St. Bonaventure University, for assistance in locating important materials in their collections;
- again and always to my wife Suzanne and our children for their continual love, support and encouragement in this and other projects.

AN INTRODUCTION TO CHRISTIAN MYSTICISM

(From the Apostolic Fathers to the Council of Trent)

Lectures given at the Abbey of Gethsemani

FOREWORD

These notes are imperfect and incomplete and probably contain many errors. It has not been possible to carry out our original intention to discuss St. John of the Cross and the Byzantine mystical tradition. Hence the series is unfinished. These lectures represent an effort to broaden the horizons and deepen the perspectives of mystical theology in a monastic setting. The approach has been mainly historical and positive in an attempt to recover some of the rich thought of the patristic and medieval periods, and especially material that has not hitherto been available in English. The lectures were intended primarily for monastic priests in a course of "pastoral" theology – that is to say for monks who sought background and contact with sources that would enable them to be of benefit to their brethren in spiritual direction or in that *sapientiae doctrina* which St. Benedict looks for in superiors.[1] The guiding principle underlying all that is said here may be expressed in words borrowed from a non-Catholic writer who has not otherwise been quoted or consulted by us – namely, Evelyn Underhill: "The essence of mysticism being not a doctrine but a way of life, its interests require {the existence of} groups of persons who put its principles into effect."[2] The idea

---

1. *The Rule of St. Benedict in Latin and English*, ed. and trans. Justin McCann, OSB (London: Burns, Oates, 1952), c. 64: "*Vitae autem merito et sapientiae doctrina eligatur*" (144); ("Let him [the abbot] be chosen for the worthiness of his life and for the instruction of his wisdom") (McCann translates: "the merit of his life and his enlightened wisdom" [145]).
2. Evelyn Underhill, "Medieval Mysticism," *The Cambridge Medieval History*, ed. J. R. Tanner, C. W. Previté-Orton, Z. N. Brooke, vol. 7, ch. 26 (Cambridge:

that mysticism has "principles" which one can, of set purpose, "put into effect" may be a little misleading: but in any case, the Christian mystical tradition is something that has been handed down not only to be talked about but to be *lived*.

Vigil of the Assumption, 1961

Cambridge University Press, 1932), 781; the bracketed words are missing in the Foreword but were included in the quotation of the same sentence that had originally been placed as the epigraph for the entire volume, apparently before the Foreword was written.

Table of Contents[3]

3. The numbering and lettering of the Table of Contents, particularly of the subsections, frequently do not correspond precisely to the divisions of the text itself; pagination is provided only where it is present in the mimeograph.

ASCETICAL AND MYSTICAL THEOLOGY

I. Introduction

1. *Aim of the Course*

If this "course" is restricted to twenty-two lectures in the Pastoral year, it is obviously taken for granted that much else has been said and taught and assimilated, especially in ascetic theology, before we come to this short series of lectures. Ascetic theology is prescribed in the novitiate. {It presents the} fundamentals of monastic life. The Master of Students should continue the ascetic formation of the young professed monk, deepening his monastic life and, especially, orienting his life of studies and his spiritual growth toward the monastic priesthood. There are retreats, constant sermons and conferences, reading. There is individual direction {and} constant "exercise" in the ascetic life. Hence for all the years of the monastic life through which the student has now passed, he has been subjected *intensively* to ascetic formation and has at least gathered some smattering of knowledge about mystical theology.

Hence the purpose of these lectures is not to cover every detail and aspect of the subject, but to look over the whole field, to *coordinate* and *deepen* the ascetic knowledge that it is presumed everybody has, and to orient that asceticism to the mystical life. The main task will be to *situate* the subject properly in our life. It belongs right in the center, of course, {in order} to give the monastic priest, the future spiritual director and superior, *a proper perspective* first of all, then to deepen his knowledge of the Church's tradition and teaching, to make him fully acquainted with the great mystical tradition, which is not separated from the dogmatic and moral tradition but *forms one whole* with it. Without mysticism there is no real theology, and without theology there is no real mysticism. Hence the emphasis will be on mysticism as theology, to bring out clearly the mystical dimensions of our theology, hence to help us to do what we must really do: live our theology. Some think it is sufficient to come to the monastery to live the *Rule*. More is required—we must live our *theology*, fully, deeply, in its totality. Without this, there is no sanctity. The separation of theology from "spirituality" is a disaster.

This course will also strive to treat of *some of the great problems* that have arisen

a) in the ascetic life, and in its relation to mysticism;

b) in the mystical life itself: conflicts, exaggerations, heresies, aberrations, and the frustration of true development.

We must realize that we are emerging from a long period of combined *anti-mysticism* and *false mysticism*, one aiding and abetting the other. {The} strongly rationalist character of our culture has affected even theologians, and they have become shy of mysticism as "unscientific." On the other hand, {there has been a} flowering of irresponsibility and illuminism, {a} multiplication of visionaries, etc.

Finally, however, the course will concentrate on the great witnesses of the Christian mystical tradition, with *emphasis on a return to patristic sources.* What we propose to try to do, if possible (and probably we will not do it), {is} to cover the following ground (after a preliminary survey of the fundamentals of mysticism in *St. John's Gospel*):

1. The great tradition of the Fathers—the beginnings of Christian mysticism in and with theology—{they are} inseparable; St. Athanasius and Irenaeus; the Cappadocians, following Origen and Clement—especially *Gregory of Nyssa*, {the} Father of Christian mysticism; then *Evagrius* and the Desert tradition; Pseudo-Macarius, who had tremendous influence in the Oriental tradition (hesychasm); above all, *Pseudo-Dionysius*, who wrote the first tract *De Mystica Theologia* and is the fountainhead (with

Gregory of Nyssa) of the apophatic (dark) tradition which is equally important in the East and in the West.

2. Tracing the apophatic tradition down into the West, we will see the growth of mystical theology in the modern sense, the splitting off of a specialized group of thinkers *in reaction against* scholastic "scientific" thought, and their creation of a separate theology of the interior life; then the Rhenish mystics, on down through the Carmelites; the Jesuit anti-mystical reaction; the great St. Teresa and St. John of the Cross; the Quietist heresy.

3. We will pursue this line of thought through modern developments, when mystical theology becomes more and more of a backwater and a specialty; controversy in the seventeenth and eighteenth centuries about semi-Quietism, about acquired and infused contemplation; this is really a low ebb of mysticism, but it has been exhaustively treated in the twentieth century.

4. After the complete, or almost complete, extinction of mystical theology in the nineteenth century, a revival of interest starts; {the} impulse was given, first of all, it would seem, by non-Catholic and non-religious thinkers—"scientists," pragmatic thinkers like William James, with his objective and phenomenological study of *The Varieties of Religious Experience.*[4] Then Catholics react: Poulain[5] is a Catholic William James. But first Saudreau[6] restores

---

4. William James, *The Varieties of Religious Experience: A Study in Human Nature, Being the Gifford Lectures on Natural Religion Delivered at Edinburgh in 1901–1902* (New York: Longmans, Green, 1902).

5. Augustin-François Poulain, sj, *Des Grâces d'Oraison* (1901; 10th ed., Paris: Beauchesne, 1922); ET: *The Graces of Interior Prayer: A Treatise on Mystical Theology,* trans. Leonora L. Yorke Smith (St. Louis: B. Herder, 1950); this work was first published in 1901, thus predating James.

6. Auguste Saudreau, *Les Degrés de la Vie Spirituelle* (1896; 6th ed., Paris: P. Téqui, 1935); ET: *The Degrees of the Spiritual Life: A Method of Directing Souls according to Their Progress in Virtue,* 2 vols., trans. Dom Bede Camm, osb (London: Burns, Oates & Washbourne, 1907); Auguste Saudreau, *La Vie d'Union à Dieu et les Moyens d'y Arriver* (Paris: C. Amat, 1901; 3rd ed., 1921); ET: *The Life of Union with God, and the Means of Attaining It: According to the Great Masters of Spirituality,* trans. E. J. Strickland (New York: Benziger, 1927); Auguste Saudreau, *L'État Mystique: Sa Nature, ses Phases* (Paris: Vic & Amat, 1903); ET: *The Mystical State:*

{a} traditional idea of contemplation as the normal end of the Christian life; controversies in modern times, voluminous literature on mysticism as a specialty in the early twentieth century, debates and problems, perhaps not as deep as it seems.

5. If it is still possible we might investigate non-Christian "mysticism" and see what it is, and evaluate its claims. Finally we ought to consider the mystical tradition of the Oriental Church since the lamentable separation.

It will be seen that much has had to be left out—much that is very important. What is omitted is presumed to be easily attainable in other courses or in readings:

a) foundations of Christian mysticism in Scripture. We will only give a brief consideration to some of the most fundamental ideas in St. John's Gospel. The rest has either been exposed in other conferences or courses, or can be easily found in the proper sources.

b) the Cistercian school of mystics has been treated elsewhere by us.[7] Rather than take up our limited time with them here, we will simply remark on them when it is relevant to point out some similarity or some contrast. However it must be remembered that the Cistercian school is to be credited with a very important development in mystical theology. St. Bernard and William of St. Thierry are of *primary importance* in the history of Christian mysticism.

Its Nature and Phases (New York: Benziger, 1924); *Les Faits Extraordinaires de la Vie Spirituelle: État Angélique—Extase—Révélations—Possessions* (Paris: Vic & Amat, 1908); Auguste Saudreau, *Manuel de Spiritualité*, 3d ed. (Paris: P. Téqui, 1933).

7. See "Introduction to Cistercian Theology," a set of conference notes for a course given by Merton as master of students and found in volume 15 of "Collected Essays," the 24-volume bound set of published and unpublished materials assembled at the Abbey of Gethsemani and available both there and at the Thomas Merton Center, Bellarmine University, Louisville, KY; see also "Cistercian Fathers and Monastic Theology," a set of conference notes for a course given by Merton to novices in 1963, which may be a revision of earlier novitiate conferences, in volume 20 of "Collected Essays."

c) the tradition that Butler[8] has called "Western Mysticism" will seem to be here neglected—again, for the same reasons. It is treated elsewhere. One lecture will be sufficient. ({See} reading lists.)

2. *Various Approaches to the Subject*

A. *Asceticism.* Here we are on relatively simple and familiar ground. {The} dictionary definition (*Oxford Dictionary*) {is}: "Ascetical—pertaining to or treating of the spiritual exercises by which perfection and virtue may be attained, as in *Ascetical Theology*"; "an ascetic—One of those who in the early church retired into solitude, to exercise themselves in meditation and prayer, and in the practice of rigorous self-discipline."[9] It comes from the Greek *askein*: to adorn, to prepare by labor, to make someone adept by exercises. (Homer uses it for "making a work of art."[10]) {It was} applied to physical culture, moral culture and finally *religious training*. It means, in short, training—spiritual training. The ascetes not only trained themselves in the spiritual warfare, but bound themselves to do so by public profession of perfect chastity. Hence ascetic theology is in practice, for us, simply the study of the training, the methods and principles by which we are to live out our public consecration to Christ and to Christian perfection. The whole of Christian aceticism is summed up in Mark 8:34: "*If any man would come after me, let him deny himself, take up his cross and follow me!*" A negative side {involves} renunciation, abnegation of self; a positive side {consists in the} following of Christ; {the} development of the Christ-life in us; development of the *life of grace* in us; cooperation with the Holy Spirit more than conformity with a moral or ascetic system.

---

8. Dom Cuthbert Butler, *Western Mysticism: The Teaching of SS. Augustine, Gregory and Bernard on Contemplation and the Contemplative Life*, 2nd ed. ([1922]; London: Constable, 1926).

9. *The Oxford English Dictionary*, ed. James Murray, corrected edition, 13 vols. (Oxford: Clarendon Press, 1933), 1:679.

10. Homer, *Iliad*, 23:743: "a highly wrought [ἤσκησαν] Sidonian bowl."

Extremes to avoid {include}:

a) *laxity*—asceticism must be *real*. {We} must not cherish illusions. {There is} no spiritual life when we are merely attached to ease, comfort, human consolations.

b) *Pelagianism*—undue trust in quantitative asceticism—in severity as such, as if severity were equal to perfection. It is *not true* {that} "the more you punish yourself physically, the more perfect you are."

c) *Gnosticism*—the idea that by heroic feats of asceticism we can *force our way* stubbornly into the realm of mysticism.

d) *oversimplification*—making the entire ascetic life consist in one virtue such as "obedience" or "patience," or one practice such as "fasting" or "manual labor," letting everything else go! The *wholeness* of the ascetic life must be maintained.

Read: two important sections from de Guibert—{the} article *"Abnegation"* in *DS* I, col. 105 bottom, and 108 bottom to 109 end.[11]

---

11. Joseph de Guibert, "Abnégation: III. Notion Précise et Doctrine de l'Abnégation," *Dictionnaire de Spiritualité Ascétique et Mystique* [*DS*], ed. F. Cavallera *et al.*, 17 vols. (Paris: Beauchesne, 1932–95), vol. 1, cols. 101–109: "On this central role of abnegation, the texts could be multiplied indefinitely: the main ones have been indicated above (II, Tradition). There are two reasons for its importance. First of all, in the spiritual life, it is in practice the decisive point, the dominant strategic position whose loss or gain determines the battle for sanctity. This is proven by experience: in studying the lives of 'failed saints,' that is, of priests, religious, or simple faithful—excellent, fervent and zealous, pious and devout, but nevertheless, not 'saints' in the full sense—one will discover that what they lacked was not a deep interior life, nor a sincere and vital love for God and souls, but rather a certain fullness of renunciation, a certain depth of abnegation and completeness in self-forgetfulness, which would have given them over completely to the work of God in them, an attitude which in contrast strikes us in true saints" (cols. 105–106); "As far as practice is concerned in the matter of abnegation, what is important is to follow the working of grace rather than seeking to anticipate it: to let the supernatural light reveal to the soul, or at least allow it to understand, gradually, the fields extending further and further, the more and more intimate dimensions where renunciation should be practiced. To show with discretion how to make progress, one should point out that God will give a growing understanding of abnegation; it would be imprudent in this matter to

The *separation* between asceticism and mysticism is an unfortunate modern development:

a) {In the} classical distinction of the Fathers, one led naturally to the other: {one begins with the} *bios praktikos*, active or

---

want to impose by authority what God has not yet made clear. It is faithfulness to insights already received, to the small abnegations of daily life, which prepares the soul for greater sacrifices and deeper insights. It would be imprudent to put before souls artificially, or for them to put before themselves in their imagination, heroic sacrifices to which God has not yet led them along the paths of wisdom. Moreover, in such a case there would be danger not only of discouragement but of illusion if, carried away by fantasies of sacrifices that God has perhaps never required, we end up without courage to face those more down-to-earth sacrifices that are asked of us in our ordinary life. This discretion to follow grace rather than wanting to outrun it will be the better way to bring about the second aspect of a fruitful practice of abnegation, peace and interior calm. This should be properly understood: it is not a question of asking that abnegation cost nothing; it is by definition a cross, a hard and demanding path. But it is quite different from a painful sacrifice that tears us apart in the depths of ourselves, or from inquietude, an anxious preoccupation and focus on oneself that unsettles and paralyzes: such an approach deprives one of peace and should be avoided in the practice of abnegation. There should be no self-vilification over an omitted sacrifice, or discouragement about a missed opportunity for self-renunciation; humble peace in the face even of our cowardice is the indispensable condition for true generosity. Such an attitude assumes that trust in God, separated from all trust in ourselves, will be sufficient to allow us to follow the way of abnegation. The critical moment comes when the soul, having responded faithfully to the initial promptings of grace along this path, feels these promptings becoming more pressing and more demanding, and asks itself with the terror of someone throwing himself into a void, 'Where am I going to end up?' It is at this point that the soul must have the humility not to focus on itself and its inadequate powers, but surrender itself completely in an act of blind trust in God and of generosity with no second thought. How many fervent souls have remained half-way to sanctity because they get stuck at this point, because they have not committed themselves to or have not persevered in these attitudes. Finally, the soul should be more oriented to the positive dimension of abnegation, to its loving aspect, seeing it as the liberation of charity in oneself, as a more complete conformation to Christ, rather than as destruction and negation. This will be immersing oneself in the full truth of reality, and will also be the way of practicing abnegation in peace and interior joy" (cols. 108–109).

ascetic life, practice and training in virtue until perfection is achieved in the relative sense of freedom from inordinate passion. Then one is prepared for *bios theoretikos*, contemplative life. But these two are simply parts of the same whole.

b) In modern times there has arisen a supposed division between two kinds of Christian perfection, *one ordinary, for all: ascetic perfection*; the *other extraordinary, abnormal, unique, for very few special souls: the mystical way.*

We shall always presuppose the classic meaning is understood. Mysticism and asceticism form an organic whole. {There is} no mysticism without asceticism. Asceticism leads normally to mystical life; at least it disposes for it, though of course the mystical life, its normal fulfillment, remains a pure gift of God.

Tanquerey[12] is supposed to divide ascetic and mystical theology as follows: *ascetic*—all the theory and practice of the spiritual life up to but exclusive of infused contemplation; mystical theology: "all that pertains to infused contemplation from the beginning of the prayer of quiet to the union completed in the spiritual marriage."[13] We do not intend here to ascend the ladder of perfection according to Fr. Tanquerey, nor to maintain this clear separation—not eleven classes of ascetic theology followed by eleven classes on infused contemplation!

De Guibert prefers to lump them together under one term, "spiritual theology": "This term explains that the science of the spiritual life is a part of theology, and that ascetical and mystical cannot be separated, and that both have a common purpose, the spiritual perfection of man."[14] I do not like too much the term "sci-

---

12. Adolphe Tanquerey, *The Spiritual Life: A Treatise on Ascetical and Mystical Theology*, 2nd ed., trans. Herman Branderis (Tournai: Desclée, 1932).

13. Joseph de Guibert, sj, *The Theology of the Spiritual Life*, trans. Paul Barrett, ofm cap. (New York: Sheed and Ward, 1953), 9; de Guibert is summarizing the position of Tanquerey, whose definition of ascetical theology he quotes directly earlier in the same sentence.

14. De Guibert, *Theology of the Spiritual Life*, 10–11 (which reads "theology, that" and "separated, and finally").

ence of the spiritual life," but in general I agree with de Guibert's approach here. However, I do not intend to follow the lines laid down in his text either.

B. *Mysticism.* Here we are on more difficult ground. Nowhere is it more important to define your terms and show where you really stand. The word mystic (which will be fully defined below) originally meant "one who was initiated into the mysteries." It has a general, vague sense of someone who experiences mysterious, esoteric, supra-rational or irrational states, feelings, intuitions.

a. *Wrong use of the word* (sometimes as a term of contempt) identifies mysticism with occultism, spiritualism, theosophy, or mere aestheticism, {an} escape into feeling. {There is a} danger of identifying mysticism with narcissism, in some form or other. Hence, {we must recognize} the importance of self-forgetfulness in relation to true contemplation and *not* encouraging souls in self-consciousness, self-awareness, the taste for self-awareness, etc., yet {one must} develop true personalism and spontaneity, as we shall see. Sometimes mysticism is wrongly used to *praise* those who are merely in subjective reaction against dogma or liturgy or set forms of religious life. Mysticism tends easily to be equated with individualism. *Bergson*[15] is responsible for a distinction between "two sources" of morality and religion: (a) static: institutional, authoritarian, dogmatic; (b) dynamic: personal, independent and spontaneous (inspired). There may be a grain of truth behind this, but it must not be exaggerated. The two tendencies really exist but do they lead to two essentially different kinds of religion?

b. *The non-Christian, scientific approach*: William James, {in his} *Varieties of Religious Experience,* studies hundreds of cases of experience, sometimes mystical, sometimes not, {making} very

---

15. Henri Bergson, *Les Deux Sources de la Morale et de la Religion* (Paris: Librairie Félix Alcan, 1932); ET: *The Two Sources of Morality and Religion*, trans. R. Ashley Audra and Cloudesley Brereton (New York: Henry Holt, 1932).

little qualitative distinction between them. {He} studies them clinically as "case histories" but ends up with a sober admission that these experiences exist and must be taken into account as being at least of great subjective validity in those who experienced them. James says: "Mystical experiences are, and have the right to be, authoritative for those that have had them, and those who have had them not are not in a position to criticize or deny the validity of the experience; the mystic is invulnerable and must be left in undisturbed possession of his creed."[16] In a way he is more open to the acceptance of all mystical experience than the theologian who sharply distinguishes. We are less tolerant. We believe that there are standards of judgement that can and must be objectively applied—those of revelation. However James ends by concluding: "It must always remain an open question whether mystical states may not possibly be superior points of view, windows through which the mind looks out upon a more extensive and inclusive world."[17]

This is the standard position of the educated non-Catholic in America today—cf. {the} new book *Mysticism and Philosophy* by W. T. Stace.[18] We need not be unhappy about it. In actual fact, the witness of religious experience is something that has a profound effect on the non-religious man today, unless he is a complete rationalist and sceptic, or a professional atheist. It is through this witness, rather than through apologetic arguments, that such men can more easily be reached.

c. *The Catholic approach*—in the nineteenth century, {there was} very little mystical theology {except for the} formal textbook approach of men like Scaramelli.[19] {But note the} unique case of

16. While Butler (*Western Mysticism*, 137) presents this as a direct quotation, it is actually a summary of James, 422–24.

17. James, 428, quoted in Butler, *Western Mysticism*, 137.

18. W. T. Stace, *Mysticism and Philosophy* (Philadelphia: Lippincott, 1960).

19. Giovanni Battista Scaramelli, sj (d. 1752), *The Directorium Asceticum, or, Guide to the Spiritual Life*, 8th ed., 4 vols. (London: Burns, Oates & Washbourne, 1924).

Baron Von Hügel.[20] Görres' *Mystik*[21] {is} criticized by Butler[22] for having "two volumes" for divine mysticism and two on diabolical mysticism.

{The} twentieth century: first of all the resurgence of interest in Catholic mysticism in the twentieth century was in large part a reaction stimulated by non-Catholic studies, an attempt at once to correct errors of the rationalistic approach, to "defend" Catholic mysticism, {and to} separate it from other forms of spirituality and pseudo-spirituality. To some extent a book like Poulain's *Graces of {Interior} Prayer*[23] is an imitation, along Catholic lines, of the secular phenomenological approach, scientific studies of documents and cases, but in a theological setting. Butler's *Western Mysticism* is perhaps also to some extent affected. Inductive study of the texts {characterized these works}.

Before World War II the tendency is a multiplication of more or less *controversial* studies, with varying approaches, all affected by the general atmosphere of debate over certain central questions, such as the nature of mystical prayer, the vocation to mystical prayer, {the} problem of {the} distinction between acquired and infused contemplation, etc. We will discuss later[24] some of the main currents of controversy, especially Poulain, Saudreau.

After World War II the approach is more *unified.* The controversial aspect is in the background. {There is an} atmosphere of

20. Friedrich von Hügel, *The Mystical Element of Religion as Studied in Saint Catherine of Genoa and Her Friends*, 2 vols. (New York: E. P. Dutton, 1908).
21. Johann Joseph von Görres (d. 1848), *Die Christliche Mystik*, 5 vols. (Regensburg: G. J. Manz, 1836–42); *La Mystique Divine, Naturelle et Diobolique*, trans. M. Charles Sainte-Foi (Paris: Mme. Vve Poussielgue-Rusand, 1854–55).
22. Cuthbert Butler, osb, *Benedictine Monachism*, 2nd ed. (New York: Longmans, Green, 1924), 65, quoted in *Western Mysticism*, 128.
23. Text reads "*Mystical.*"
24. Merton does not in fact return to this modern controversy, as according to his original outlines he had intended to do; an overview of the different positions is provided by Butler in his "Afterthoughts" to the revised edition of *Western Mysticism* (xiii–lxii), and by J. V. Bainvel in his Introduction to the 10th edition of Poulain (xxxii–cxii).

collaboration and general teamwork: the outstanding works of this period are often the products of *special teams* (v.g. {the} collaboration of Bouyer, Leclercq, Vandenbroucke and Cognet in the new *Histoire de Spiritualité*[25]), or else the works of individual authors are still done by men who otherwise appear on these "teams." The great monument of the post-war period is the *Dictionnaire de Spiritualité*,[26] started by men who were engaged in the controversies of the previous period, but including all the best minds writing in French at the present time. Note: the "teams" began to appear in the '20s, though still engaged in controversy, for instance: the Jesuits of the *Revue d'Ascétique et de Mystique* (hereafter *RAM*) {and} the Dominicans of *La Vie Spirituelle* (hereafter *VS*). (Discuss these two publications.) Also {note the} importance of *Études Carmélitaines*; {as well as the} sessions

25. *Histoire de Spiritualité*, 4 vols.: Louis Bouyer, *La Spiritualité du Nouveau Testament et des Pères* (Paris: Aubier, 1960); Jean Leclercq, François Vandenbroucke, Louis Bouyer, *La Spiritualité du Moyen Age* (Paris: Aubier, 1961); Louis Bouyer, *La Spiritualité Orthodoxe et la Spiritualité Protestante et Anglicane* (Paris: Aubier, 1965); Louis Cognet, *La Spiritualité Moderne*, Part 1: *L'Essor: 1500–1650* (Paris: Aubier, 1966) (the last two volumes were issued after this series of conferences and were therefore unavailable to Merton). The first three volumes were later translated as *The Spirituality of the New Testament and the Fathers*, trans. Mary Perkins Ryan (New York: Seabury, 1963); *The Spirituality of the Middle Ages*, trans. Benedictines of Holme Eden Abbey (New York: Seabury, 1968); *Orthodox Spirituality and Protestant and Anglican Spirituality*, trans. Barbara Wall (New York: Seabury, 1969) (Bouyer writes [213] that this volume was originally intended as an appendix to the final volume on modern Catholic spirituality, but was issued separately when that projected volume swelled to two parts; that volume, the second part of which never appeared, was not translated into English). References will be given both to the original French (which Merton used), and to the English translations.

26. Publication of the *Dictionnaire* had actually begun in 1932 with the appearance of the first fascicle; the complete volume 1 appeared in 1935; publication was severely slowed (though not completely interrupted) by World War II (a fascicle of volume 2 appeared in 1944); at the time of writing, four volumes had appeared, taking the *Dictionnaire* up through the letter "E"; three more volumes (through "I") would appear during Merton's lifetime.

in psychology and spirituality at Avon-Fontainebleau.[27] Note {that} after the war new reviews have brought in a Biblical emphasis ignored before World War II, {and the} influence also of {the} liturgical revival. There is no lack of magazines; the quality however is not always high.

Some characteristic attitudes to mystical theology. {In the} *early period* (before World War II): note the inadequacy of a few early writers like Dom Savinien Louismet[28] who made "contemplation" something so broad and vague that it embraced almost any type of affective piety. *Canon Saudreau*, in 1896, {made an} effort to recover {the} traditional notion of Christian mysticism through {the} study of {the} Fathers and "mystical writers," centered mainly on {the} thesis that "contemplation is the normal flowering of the Baptismal vocation"[29] and all Christians should or at

27. International Conference of Religious Psychology, sponsored by the French Carmelites; see for example *Mystique et Continence: Travaux Scientifiques des VIIe Congrès International d'Avon*, held Sept. 27–30, 1950 and published in *Études Carmélitaines*, 32 (1952).

28. Savinien Louismet, OSB (d. 1926), *The Mystical Knowledge of God: An Essay in the Art of Knowing and Loving the Divine Majesty* (New York: P. J. Kenedy & Sons, 1917); *The Mystical Life* (London: Burns, Oates & Washbourne, 1917); *Mysticism, True and False* (New York: P. J. Kenedy & Sons, 1918); *Divine Contemplation for All, or The Simple Art of Communing with God* (London: Burns, Oates & Washbourne, 1921); *The Mystery of Jesus* (New York: P. J. Kenedy & Sons, 1922); *Mystical Initiation* (New York: P. J. Kenedy & Sons, 1923); *The Burning Bush: Being a Treatise on the Ecstatic Contemplation of the Blessed Trinity* (Nw York: P. J. Kenedy & Sons, 1926).

29. This quotation is not found in *The Degrees of the Spiritual Life*, which does not refer to baptism at all; chapter VI of Book V, entitled "How Contemplation is Less Rare than is Commonly Supposed" (2.71-94) does maintain that "the contemplative way is the one to which souls who give themselves up without reserve to the service of God are ordinarily called" (2.76). Nor is it found in Saudreau's *Life of Union with God*, *The Mystical State*, *Les Faits Extraordinaires de la Vie Spirituelle* or *Manuel de Spiritualité*; it is also not used in Saudreau's contribution to the article "Contemplation" in the *Dictionnaire de Spiritualité* (vol. 2, cols. 2159-71). The idea, though not the exact wording, is found in a letter of Juan Arintero quoted by Butler in *Western Mysticism*: "Perfection lies in the full development of baptismal grace" (xlii) (taken from Bainvel's Introduction to Poulain, lxxi).

least can aspire to it. *R. Garrigou-Lagrange* {is known for} taking up the arguments of Saudreau and supporting them by a theological synthesis of St. Thomas and St. John of the Cross.[30] This was the standard "Dominican" thesis in the '20s and '30s, strongly propounded by *Fr. Arintero*.[31] *A. Poulain, sj* divides mystical and ascetical ways of perfection, {and} supports the doctrine that acquired and infused contemplation are distinct. {He takes} a phenomenological approach (see above). {This is at the} center of the controversy of early twentieth-century mystical theologians. {He} tends to encourage those who identify mysticism with visions, extraordinary experiences. (READ Butler, *Western Mysticism*, p. 131[32]—{a}

30. Reginald Garrigou-Lagrange, *Perfection Chrétienne et Contemplation selon S. Thomas d'Aquin et S. Jean de la Croix*, 2 vols. (Paris: Éditions du Cerf, 1923); ET: *Christian Perfection and Contemplation according to the Teaching of St. Thomas Aquinas and St. John of the Cross*, trans. Sr. M. Timothea Doyle (St. Louis: Herder, 1937); see also Reginald Garrigou-Lagrange, *Les Trois Ages de la Vie Intérieure, Prélude de Celle du Ciel* (Paris: Éditions du Cerf, 1938); ET: *The Three Ages of the Interior Life, Prelude of Eternal Life*, trans. Sr. M. Timothea Doyle (St. Louis: Herder, 1947–48).

31. Juan González Arintero, *The Mystical Evolution in the Development and Vitality of the Church*, trans. Jordan Aumann (St. Louis: Herder, 1949); Juan González Arintero, *Stages in Prayer*, trans. Kathleen Pond (St. Louis: Herder, 1957).

32. "It is a fact to be deplored that devout souls are apt to be frightened of mysticism by the presentations commonly made of it nowadays, whereby it is almost identified with a quasi-miraculous state of visions, revelations, and extraordinary favours frequently affecting the body; so that it is placed on a sort of pedestal, as a thing to be wondered at and admired respectfully from beneath, out of reach of all but the small number of select ones called by God to a privilege so exceptional, the very thought of which as a thing to be practically desired would be presumption." Butler does not explicitly mention Poulain here, and it is at least questionable if the reference is to him; while Poulain limits mysticism proper to a quasi-experimental perception of God, i.e. to the highest levels of the contemplative life, he does not in fact emphasize these phenomena, and in his "Afterthoughts" Butler notes the "general agreement" that exists between the conflicting positions (of Poulain and Saudreau) on "the sharp distinction between contemplation and even mystic union in itself, and the accidental accessories that often accompany it—visions, locutions, raptures,

critique of Poulain's position.) *A. Stolz*,[33] a Benedictine, writing in the '30s, returns to the Fathers and endeavors to correct the perspectives of these other writers by a reappraisal of what the Fathers really taught, independent of any modern thesis to be defended. His work may not in all things be satisfactory but it is an attempt at recovery of {a} sane perspective. *Dom C. Butler*: as an example of the early approach, study the opening of his prologue. He claims that he is going to study "the ways of the mystics."[34]

What is a "mystic"? {The} *Oxford Dictionary* says: "An exponent of mystical theology; also, one who maintains the importance of this—one who seeks by contemplation and self-surrender to obtain union with or absorption in the deity, or who believes in the spiritual apprehension of truths inaccessible to the understanding."[35] This is a very sound definition, for general purposes: it aims at including non-Christian "mysticisms" (absorption in the deity); it includes the vitally important notion of self-surrender; it emphasizes the paradoxical ambition to grasp "spiritually" truths that are not "understood."

---

trances, and so forth. This is important, for in recent times the tendency has been to throw more and more emphasis on this the non-essential and, it may be added, undesirable side of mysticism, and indeed in great measure to identify mysticism with it" (xli).

33. Anselm Stolz, OSB, *Theologie der Mystik* (Ratisbon: Friedrich Pustet, 1936); *Théologie de la Mystique* (Chevtogne: Éditions des Bénédictins d'Amay, 1947); ET: *The Doctrine of Spiritual Perfection*, trans. Aidan Williams, OSB (St. Louis: Herder, 1938).

34. This is not a direct quotation from Butler, but a summary of his statement that his purpose in *Western Mysticism* "is to set forth, in their own words, as a co-ordinated body of doctrine, what three great teachers of mystical theology in the Western Church have left on record concerning their own religious experience, and the theories they based on it" (3).

35. *Oxford English Dictionary*, 10:175, which reads "maintains the validity and supreme importance of 'mystical theology'; one who, whether Christian or non-Christian, seeks . . . absorption into the Deity, . . . believes in the possibility of the spiritual apprehension of truths that are inaccessible . . ."

Approaching the "mystics," Butler says: they may be read for their theology; they may be studied as witnesses to religious experience.[36] His concern is to study the statements of the mystics about their religious experience and to evaluate it, determining *whether or not it is objectively true*.[37] (In this {he was} probably reacting against the attitude typified by William James, Bergson, etc.) In particular, he confines himself to St. Augustine, St. Gregory and St. Bernard. He studies carefully all the important texts in which they explain what they mean by, and what they have experienced in, "contemplation"; and then he takes up such related problems as the relation of contemplation and action, both in the individual and in the Church.[38]

One of the most characteristic theses of Butler merits a special word here. He stresses the special character of *Western mysticism as a mysticism of light*, as opposed to *Eastern mysticism as a mysticism of "night,"* and he concludes that the genuine Western mystical tradition is represented by pre-Dionysian authors: Augustine, Gregory, and Bernard.[39] The later Western mystics, influenced by the introduction of the writings of Pseudo-Dionysius into the West, are, he says, not true to the Western tradition. (This is aimed especially at St. John of the Cross, but also people like Tauler, Ruysbroeck, etc.[40]) This distinction is important and we

---

36. These are the first and third approaches to mysticism he mentions; the second is the psychological (or psycho-physiological), that would examine the bodily concomitants of higher states of prayer (*Western Mysticism*, 3).

37. The "Epilogue" to Part I (in the revised edition) treats of "The Validity of the Mystics' Claim" (133–54).

38. Part I of *Western Mysticism* (17–154) focuses on the meaning and experience of contemplation, Part II (155–223) on the relationship of contemplation and action.

39. For a more recent examination of Butler's thesis, see Rowan Williams, "Butler's *Western Mysticism*: Towards an Assessment," *Downside Review*, 102 (1984), 197–215.

40. Butler's tone is in fact much less polemical than this statement suggests, and clearly recognizes the value of the teachings of John of the Cross, whom he quotes frequently, as well as of Tauler and Ruysbroeck.

shall see that it comes close to the heart of the matter in these conferences of ours. However it must be said that Butler's thesis is an oversimplification, and that the division has implications that cannot be fully accepted by anyone who really wants to understand Christian mysticism. It tends to put undue emphasis on a particular branch of Christian mystical theology, and exalts St. Augustine as the "prince of mystics,"[41] at the expense of the great tradition we propose to study. What Dom Butler has given us is, in fact, what is most familiar in our own Benedictine family. But even then we must realize the importance of Greek influences in William of St. Thierry and even in St. Bernard himself.

After World War II—some important studies, written before or during the war, began to have a great influence in the late '40s. Among these, worthy of special mention are those which threw light on the great Greek mystical theologians—for instance: Daniélou, *Platonisme et Théologie Mystique*[42] (St. Gregory of Nyssa); von Balthasar, *Liturgie Cosmique*[43] (St. Maximus) {and} *Présence et Pensée chez S. Grégoire de Nysse*;[44] not to mention the studies of Hausherr[45]

---

41. Butler, *Western Mysticism*, 20.

42. Jean Daniélou, SJ, *Platonisme et Théologie Mystique: Doctrine Spirituelle de Saint Grégoire de Nysse*, rev. ed. (Paris: Éditions Montaigne, 1953).

43. Hans Urs von Balthasar, *Liturgie Cosmique: Maxime le Confesseur* (Paris: Aubier, 1947); this is a translation of the original German version: *Kosmische Liturgie: Höhe und Krise des griechischen Weltbildes bei Maximus Confessor* (Freiburg: Herder, 1941). A revised edition entitled *Kosmische Liturgie: Das Weltbild Maximus' des Bekenners* (Einsiedeln: Johannes Verlag, 1961) has recently been translated by Brian E. Daley, SJ as *Cosmic Liturgy: The Universe According to Maximus the Confessor* (San Francisco: Ignatius Press, 2003).

44. Hans Urs von Balthasar, *Présence et Pensée: Essai sur la Philosophie Religieuse de Grégoire de Nysse* (Paris: Beauchesne, 1942); now available in English as *Presence and Thought: Essay on the Religious Philosophy of Gregory of Nyssa*, trans. Mark Sebanc (San Francisco: Ignatius Press, 1995).

45. Irénée Hausherr, "Le *Traité de l'Oraison* d'Evagre le Pontique (Pseudo-Nil)," *Revue d'Ascétique et de Mystique*, 15 (1934), 36–93, 113–70; Irénée Hausherr, "Le Traité de l'Oraison d'Evagre le Pontique," *Revue d'Ascétique et de Mystique*, 40 (1959), 3–26, 121–46, 241–65, 361–85; 41 (1960), 3–35, 137–87.

and Viller[46] on Evagrius Ponticus, and his influence on St. Maximus (in *Revue d'Ascetique et de Mystique—RAM*). Note also the tremendous importance of the textual studies of St. Gregory of Nyssa by Werner Jaeger[47] and the restitution to Gregory of the authorship of the *De Instituto Christiano* in its full text,[48] hitherto ascribed to St. Macarius; also the clarification of the problem of Pseudo-Macarius.[49] These are technical matters, but their effect is beginning to make itself felt through the work of great popularizers like Bouyer.[50] Note also the resurgence of Cistercian studies, with Dom Leclercq,[51] Dom Déchanet (on William of St. Thierry),[52]

46. M. Viller, "Aux Sources de la Spiritualité de S. Maxime: Les Oeuvres d'Evagre le Pontique," *Revue d'Ascétique et de Mystique*, 11 (1930), 156–84, 239–68.

47. Gregory of Nyssa, *Opera*, ed. Werner Jaeger *et al.*, 10 vols. (Leiden: E. J. Brill, 1952–1990).

48. Werner Jaeger, *Two Rediscovered Works of Ancient Christian Literature: Gregory of Nyssa and Macarius* (Leiden, Brill, 1954).

49. I.e., that both homilies and letters traditionally ascribed to the fourth-century Egyptian hermit Macarius the Great were actually written by a Syrian in the late fourth century with possible Messalian tendencies; for the most recent discussion, see Columba Stewart, osb, *'Working the Earth of the Heart': The Messalian Controversy in History, Texts, and Language to AD 431* (Oxford: Clarendon Press, 1991); for Merton's discussion of this material see Thomas Merton, *Cassian and the Fathers: Initiation into the Monastic Tradition*, ed. Patrick F. O'Connell, Monastic Wisdom [MW], vol. 1 (Kalamazoo, MI: Cistercian Publications, 2005), 81–88.

50. Merton is presumably referring here primarily to the first volume of the *Histoire de la Spiritualité*, but Bouyer was a prolific author on topics of spirituality and monasticism.

51. Leclercq was a prolific author and editor on monastic topics; Merton will refer particularly to his seminal work *The Love of Learning and the Desire for God: A Study of Monastic Culture*, trans. Catherine Misrahi (New York: Fordham University Press, 1961); for the correspondence of Merton and Leclercq, see *Survival or Prophecy?: The Letters of Thomas Merton and Jean Leclercq*, ed. Patrick Hart (New York: Farrar, Straus and Giroux, 2002).

52. Jean Déchanet, osb, *Aux Sources de la Spiritualité de Guillaume de Saint-Thierry* (Bruges: Beyaert, 1940); *Guillaume de Saint-Thierry: L'Homme et son Oeuvre* (Bruges: Beyaert, 1942); the latter has been translated as *William of St. Thierry:*

and the translations of works of Ailred, William, etc. {A} new edition of St. Bernard[53] {is being prepared}. Studies for {the} eighth centenary of St. Bernard {have been published}.[54] Gilson's *Mystical Theology of St. Bernard*[55] (written long before, during World War I) remains a landmark in the new development of mystical theology. Since the war, mystical and ascetical theology has followed the line suggested by Fr. de Guibert at the Gregorianum, and has tended more and more to call itself "spirituality." (He coined the term "spiritual theology.") *In the secular field* since the Second World War, there has been an ever increasing and widening interest in Oriental mysticism, due to more and more numerous popularizations. In the West there has been, particularly in America, a great fad for Zen Buddhism, due to the influence of the great work of Daisetz Suzuki,[56] who is one of the most important influences of the mid-twentieth century, at least in America and England.

The Man and his Work, trans. Richard Strachan, Cistercian Studies [CS], vol. 10 (Spencer, MA: Cistercian Publications, 1972).

53. *Sancti Bernardi Opera, ad Fidem Codicum Recensuerunt*, ed. Jean Leclercq, C. H. Talbot and H. M. Rochais, 8 vols. in 9 (Rome: Editiones Cisterciences, 1957–1977).

54. *Bernhard von Clairvaux: Mönch und Mystiker*—Internationaler Bernhardcongress, Mainz, 1953 (Wiesbaden: F. Steiner, 1955); *Mélanges Saint Bernard*—XXIVe Congrès de l'Association Bourguignonne des Sociétés Savantes (8e Centenaire de la Morte de Saint Bernard) (Dijon: Association des Amis de Saint Bernard, 1954); *Festschrift zum 800 Jahrgedächtnis des Todes Bernhards von Clairvaux* (Wien: Herold, 1953); *Bernard de Clairvaux* (Paris: Éditions d'Alsatia, 1953); *Sint Bernardus: Voordrachten Gehouden aan de R. K. Universiteit te Nijmegen bij Gelegenheit von het Achtste Eeuwfeest van zijn Dood* (Utrecht, Antwerp: Het Spectrum, 1953).

55. Étienne Gilson, *The Mystical Theology of St. Bernard*, trans. A. H. C. Downes (New York: Sheed & Ward, 1940).

56. Merton possessed copies of *Essays in Zen Buddhism*, series one, two and three (London: Rider, 1958) and *Manual of Zen Buddhism* (London: Rider, 1956); for Merton's correspondence with Suzuki, see Thomas Merton, *The Hidden Ground of Love of Love: Letters on Religious Experience and Social Concerns*, ed. William H. Shannon (New York: Farrar, Straus, Giroux, 1985), 560–71.

Orthodox Mysticism—after the Second World War an important manual by Vladimir Lossky, *Théologie Mystique de l'Église d'Orient*,[57] has opened up the forgotten world of Byzantine mysticism, solidly based in the Greek Fathers. Studies of St. Gregory Palamas, by Meyendorff,[58] appearing at the end of the '50s, and the new works of Fr. Paul Evdokimov,[59] promise that there will be a very rich flowering in this field. It is here that we must look for future developments, along with the area where attempts are being made to understand non-Christian mysticism in the light of our own contemplation. Here Louis Massignon, with his studies on Al Hallaj in the '20s,[60] was a pioneer.

57. Vladimir Lossky, *Théologie Mystique de l'Église d'Orient* (Paris: Aubier Montaigne, 1944); ET: *The Mystical Theology of the Eastern Church* (London: James Clarke, 1957).

58. Jean Meyendorff, *St. Grégoire Palamas et la Mystique Orthodoxe* (Paris: Éditions du Seuil, 1959); ET: John Meyendorff, *St. Gregory Palamas and Orthodox Spirituality*, trans. Adele Fiske (Crestwood, NY: St. Vladimir's Seminary Press, 1974); Jean Meyendorff, *Introduction à l'Étude de Grégoire Palamas* (Paris: Éditions du Seuil, 1959); ET: John Meyendorff, *A Study of Gregory Palamas*, trans. George Lawrence (London: Faith Press, 1964).

59. Merton was particularly interested in *La Femme et le Salut du Monde* (Paris: Casterman, 1958) and *L'Orthodoxie* (Paris: Delachaux et Miestlé, 1959) (see his appreciative statements on the latter in his journal entries for August 10, 1960 and January 26, 1961 in Thomas Merton, *Turning Toward the World: The Pivotal Years. Journals, vol. 4: 1960–1963*, ed. Victor A. Kramer [San Francisco: HarperCollins, 1996], 90, 91), but also in Evdokimov's articles on monasticism and other topics; for Merton's mistake in thinking that Evdokimov was a priest, and Merton's interest in Evdokimov in general, see Rowan Williams, "Bread in the Wilderness: The Monastic Ideal in Thomas Merton and Paul Evdokimov," in Basil Pennington, ocso, ed., *One Yet Two: Monastic Tradition East and West*, CS 29 (Kalamazoo, MI: Cistercian, 1976), 452–73; reprinted in Bernadette Dieker and Jonathan Montaldo, eds., *Merton and Hesychasm: The Prayer of the Heart* (Louisville: Fons Vitae, 2003), 175–96.

60. Louis Massignon, *La Passion de Husayn Ibn Mansur Hallaj: Martyr Mystique d'Islam*, 4 vols. (1922; Paris: Gallimard, 1975); ET: *The Passion of Al-Hallaj: Mystic and Martyr of Islam*, trans. Herbert Mason, 4 vols. (Princeton: Princeton University Press, 1982); for Merton's correspondence with Massignon, see

A Few Remarks. What has been said so far is a rambling introduction, necessarily imperfect and incomplete, to the very rich and varied literature in mystical and spiritual theology. Make no mistake, there is very much in this field. It is a very active study at the moment; much is being done. Behind this intellectual effort is a very real *spiritual rebirth*, not the spurious and superficial supposed "religious revival" that has driven people to church since the atomic bomb, but the deeper revival, the awakening of the basic need of man for God, which has made itself felt in at least a small number of Christians forming elites in countries where the last war had its deepest effects—France, Germany, Italy. This "spiritual hunger" is a matter of intimate concern to us because we are doubtless in the monastery for this reason alone. Hence this study we are about to undertake is absolutely *vital to our vocation*. In a sense we will be trying to face "THE" questions which are at the very heart of our spiritual life. We are here looking at a spiritual movement of which we form a part, and not a negligible part. However, it is not merely a matter of study and reading. We must become *fully impregnated in our mystical tradition. Audite et intelligite traditiones quas Deus dedit vobis.*[61] The mystical tradition of the Church {is} a collective memory and experience of Christ living and present within her. This tradition *forms and affects the whole man*: intellect, memory, will, emotions,

---

Thomas Merton, *Witness to Freedom: Letters in Times of Crisis*, ed. William H. Shannon (New York: Farrar, Straus, Giroux, 1994), 275–81.

61. "Hear and understand the traditions that God has given us" (*"Antiphon: Feria Quarta Hebdomada Tertia in Quadragesima,"* in J. P. Migne, ed., *Patrologiae Cursus Completus, Series Latina* [*PL*], 221 vols. [Paris: Garnier, 1844–1865], vol. 78, col. 756C). In a journal entry for March 8, 1961 Merton quotes this passage and comments, "Moved by this Benedictus antiphon [Lauds]. At a time when all the healthy traditions are vanishing or being corrupted or destroyed. We have no memory (as Coomaraswamy says—and as Plato said); instead of traditions we have neuroses. The loss of tradition is an important factor in the loss of contemplation—in the fact that contemplation is blocked and sidetracked by neurosis. Neurosis as false religion and false contemplation" (*Turning Toward the World*, 99).

body, skills (arts)—all must be under the sway of the Holy Spirit. {Note the} important human dimension given by tradition—its *incarnate* character. Note especially the *memory*. If we do not cultivate healthy and conscious traditions we will enter into unhealthy and unconscious traditions—a kind of collective disposition to neurosis (N.B. delinquency). Read and *commit to memory* the words of God. (N.B. the value of reading *Dante*, in whom poetry, theology, mysticism and life are *all one*—his guide to {the} vision of God is St. Bernard.[62])

Theology and Spirituality—the divorce between them. For some, theology {is} a penance and effort without value, except as a chore to be offered up, whereas spirituality is to be studied, developed, experienced. Hence {there is an} experience of *spirituality* {but} not {an} experience of *theology*—this {is} the death of contemplation. {It promotes} experience of experience and not experience of revelation and of God revealing. {Note the} danger of reading "mystical symptoms." Perhaps in our modern world we are witnessing a kind of death agony of spirituality—a real crisis has been reached.

Von Balthasar, in *Dieu Vivant* (12),[63] contrasted the Fathers, in whom personal experience and dogmatic faith were a living unity. Mysticism and experience is a *servant* of revelation, of the Word, of the Church—not an evasion from service. (However, his accusation of the Spanish mystics is exaggerated and false. They were truly biblical and certainly served the Church very objectively.[64]) The "saints" today do not exist for theology. What

62. Bernard takes over from Beatrice as Dante's guide in Canto XXXI of the *Paradiso* and continues through the next two cantos to the close of the poem: see Dante Alighieri, *The Divine Comedy: Paradiso, I: Italian Text and Translation*, trans. Charles S. Singleton (Princeton: Princeton University Press, 1975), 346–81.

63. Hans von Balthasar, "Théologie et Sainteté," *Dieu Vivant*, 12 (1948), 15–31.

64. Von Balthasar, "Théologie et Sainteté," 24: "Les descriptions de sainte Thérèse et de saint Jean de la Croix ont pour objet les états mystiques, et c'est dans ces états que, à parler grossièrement, on atteint ce qui peut s'y reveler d'objectif. La mystique espagnole se tient ici au role diamétralement opposé

dogma text would quote St. Thérèse? {This is} a great impoverishment for the theologians, the saints and the Church herself. Remember that theology is a *sanctuary*.

Fr. Georges Florovsky has said, {in} *Dieu Vivant* (13), "In this time of temptation and judgement *theology becomes again a public matter, a universal and catholic mission.* It is incumbent upon all to take up spiritual arms. Already we have reached a point where theological silence, embarrassment, incertitude, lack of articulation in our witness are equal to temptation, to flight before the enemy. Silence can create disturbance as much as a hasty or indecisive answer"[65] (especially silence on a vital question of *theology to be lived* in the monastery—or giving a stone instead of bread). *"It is precisely because we are thrown into the apocalyptic battle that we are called upon to do the job of theologians. . . .* Theology is called not only to judge [scientific unbelief] *but to heal.* We must penetrate into this world of doubt, of illusion and lies to reply to doubts as well as reproaches"[66] (but not reply with complacent and ambiguous platitudes!—{it} must be {the} word of God *lived* in us). "A theological system must not be a mere product of erudition. . . . It needs the experience of prayer, spiritual concentration, and *pastoral concern. . . .* We must answer with a complete system of thought, by a *theological confession. We must experience in ourselves by intimate suffering all the problems of the soul without faith who does not seek. . . .* The time has come when the refusal of theological knowledge has become a deadly sin, the mark of complacency and of lack of love, of pusillanimity and of malignity."[67] (Clearly

---

à la mystique dogmatique de la Bible." ("The descriptions of Saint Teresa and of Saint John of the Cross have for their object mystical states, and it is in these states that, to speak rudely, one reaches what can be revealed objectively. Spanish mysticism is shown here in a role diametrically opposed to the dogmatic mysticism of the Bible.")

65. Georges Florovsky, "Les Voies de la Théologie Russe," *Dieu Vivant,* 13 (1949), 58.

66. Florovsky, 59–60.

67. Florovsky, 60.

for us monks the problem lies not in reading Poulain etc. but in becoming *first of all real theologians*.)

Now let us turn to St. John "*the* theologian."

{II.} Mystical Theology in St. John's Gospel

This is only the briefest outline. There is sufficient material for a whole course of lectures, for St. John is *the* theologian—the greatest mystical doctor of the Church. His Gospel is the true source of all Christian mysticism, together with the Epistles of St. Paul. What are the bare outlines, the "bones" of his mysticism? It is a theology; it is mysticism—{there is} no separation between the two; both are one in *our life in Christ.*

Chapter 1: The Word, the true light, in Whom all things are made, comes into the world to enlighten it (John 1:1-5). He enlightens those who, *receiving Him by faith*, are *reborn as sons of God* (John 1:11-13) in a spiritual transformation ({the} *basis of the doctrine of "divinization" in the Greek Fathers*). The *Incarnation* (John 1:14) is the center of Christian mysticism. Those who do not know Christ are in darkness. Those who receive Him *see His Glory—receive of His fullness* (John 1:14, 16). God indeed *is invisible* (John 1:18; 1 Tim. 6:16; 1 John 4:12) but *His light comes to us in Christ* (John 1:18, 14:6-14, 12:35-37, 3:19) and we *know Him in Christ* (i.e. the *Father* manifests Himself in the Son) (12:44-50, 14:7-9).

Chapter 3: The theme of *rebirth in Christ* is developed. Sacramental mysticism {is} introduced:

a) a sacramental rebirth (by baptism) (3:5);
b) which gives us the Holy Spirit to be our Life;
c) a rebirth to *everlasting* life by faith in Christ (3:14-16).

Chapter 6: Sacramental mysticism {is} developed—the *Eucharist*:

a) We receive the Incarnate Word and live by Him not only in faith but *in the mystery of Eucharistic communion*, which is the fullness of faith and love (6:32-35);
b) This food gives us everlasting life, {the} *resurrection of {the} body* (6:39-40, 48-56);

c) Trinitarian mysticism: the Father draws us to the Son (6:44-46; cf. Matt. 11:27);

d) Christ lives in us when we eat His Body and we live in Him (6:57);

e) This is the same kind of union, of "circumincession," as the life of the Father in the Son (6:58).

Chapter 13: Sacramental mysticism continued—the "sacrament" of the washing of the feet {is a} sign of union in Christ by charity and mutual service—the "mystique" of the worship of God in humble service of one's brother (13:6-10, 13-17, 34-35)—cf. chapter 15: *love of one another as Christ has loved us—even to death* (15:12-13, 17). *Some Remarks*: {it is} interesting to take chapters 6 and 13 together as expressions of the same Eucharistic theology—the washing of the feet in chapter 13 as a "sacramental" sign of union in Christ. Service of one another {involves the} *consent* to being served, then serving (Peter's struggle), in token of the fact that Christ has "emptied Himself" for us even to death. Liturgy should be seen in the light of this sign of *agape*. Liturgy {is thus} not just signs of *worship* or of *sanctification* but of God present in Christ, in us, in our love for one another (external sign—interior life—Reality). When the *sign* is properly placed, its meaning is effected. The eucharistic sign {is both} the "yes" of God, giving Himself {and} the "yes" of our own hearts, giving ourselves to one another in Christ. We can say paradoxically: a full *Amen* can lead to sanctity and contemplation (!!) leading up to the full expression of Trinitarian life in the Church (17:21-23). From the *sign* to the *realization*: this is living theology. Realization fulfills and goes beyond {the} sign; contemplation fulfills and goes beyond liturgy.

Chapter 14: We are to follow Christ into a new realm (13:36, 14:2-4, 16:22-23, 28). He is the way to the Father (14:6). The Father will give all we ask in Christ's Name (14:13)—*He will send the Holy Spirit*, {the} Spirit of Truth Whom the world cannot receive (14:17, 15:26-27). *We shall know Him*—He will be in us (14:17); we shall know Christ in us and in the Father (14:20-21, 23, 15:10). {The} only condition {is} that we keep His commandments (14:21-23)—

{a} mysticism of the commandments or *words* of Christ (14:23, 15:3, 15:7; cf 17:5 f.). {The} Holy Spirit brings to mind Christ's words (14:26, 16:13-14). Christ must go for {the} Spirit to come (16:7).

Chapters 15-16: Abiding in Christ—{the} Vine and {the} Branches: {there must be a} *purification* of the branches for fruitfulness (15:2). Life {means} abiding in Christ (15:4-7), obeying Christ as He obeys {the} Father (15:10, 9). {This entails} persecution by the world (15:18-27, 16:1-6, 20-22, 17:13-14). In this persecution the Spirit will give testimony of Christ (15:26-27) and will judge the world (16:9-11).

Chapter 17: Christ has power over all flesh, to give life to all, for {the} glory of the Father (17:1-3). Eternal life {is} knowledge of {the} Father in {the} Son (17:3). The Son gives the word of the Father to those who are given Him by the Father (17:5-8, 14). The word of God in us causes opposition and persecution (17:14); *the word of the Father sanctifies us in truth* (17:17); *the word {is} transmitted to others by {the} Apostles, and all who receive it are in Christ and protected by His love* (17:20). *"That all may be one"* {is a prayer that the} fullness of Trinitarian life {may be} expressed in {the} Church (17:21-22-23). *Conclusion*:

a) on earth—to be "made perfect in one" glory (love) *manifested* (17:23; cf. 16:27-28);

b) out of this world—to the Father in Christ—*in His glory* (17:24).

Further important New Testament texts: it is not our intention to go into the mystical doctrine of St. Paul, as this has been done in another course (see notes {on} "Sanctity in Epistles of St. Paul"[68]). However it is necessary to mention at least two points:

1) The heart of the doctrine of St. Paul is the mystery of Christ, that is to say not only the Incarnation of the Son of God

---

68. This is a course Merton gave to scholastics in 1954, found in "Collected Essays," vol. 23, and published as "Sanctity in the Epistles of St. Paul," ed. Chrysogonus Waddell, ocso, *Liturgy OCSO*, 30.1 (1996), 3–27; 30.2 (1996), 3–23; 30.3 (1996), 15–33; 31.1 (1997), 7–26; 31.2-3 (1997), 3–20.

Who emptied Himself etc. (Phil. 2:5-11), but the unity of all in Him, the recapitulation of all in Christ (Ephesians 1:10), otherwise the Mystical Body of Christ.

2) The doctrine of the Mystical Body is inseparable from Paul's teaching of our *divinization* in Christ. This is a complete transformation beginning at Baptism when we become new men, dying and rising with Christ, and ending when Christ is all in all, when the one mystical Christ reaches His full mystical stature (Ephesians 4:1-16). This is the work of the Holy Spirit (*id.*), {the} Spirit of Love.

3) The doctrine of divinization is a doctrine of the renewal in the same image or likeness to Christ in the Spirit (see Col. 1:15-19; 2 Cor. 3:17 ff.).

4) The mysticism of St. Paul implies a *growing consciousness* of this mystery in us until we reach a full mystical understanding of the mystery of Christ in ourselves. Comment briefly on Ephesians 3:14 ff.: the Father, source of sanctification, strengthens by the Spirit "in the inner man" "that Christ may dwell in your hearts . . . . that you, rooted and grounded in love may *comprehend* with all the saints [{n.b. the} Church {as the} center of contemplation] the love of Christ which *surpasses all knowledge*." These are themes that are later exploited by Christian mystics thoroughly and completely.

Another *important Pauline text* must not be neglected here, 2 Cor. 12:1-10: the great visions of Paul (caught up into the third heaven—note his vision of Christ at his conversion: {the} same?). At the same time {note} his continued weakness and his complete dependence on grace—{cf.} the *value* of his weakness, and the fact that the great works of Paul and his mysticism came *first*, the weakness after. {This is} important for the realities of the Christian life (pastoral note).

Two crucial texts from the *Acts*: Acts 2:1: Pentecost {is} crucial for Christian mysticism, a basic source. {It is} the descent of the Holy Ghost upon the Church. {Note also the} importance of Peter's explanation, {the} fulfillment of {the} promise in Joel. Mystical life {comes} from the Spirit, {and is lived} in the Church, as {a} *witness of the Living and Risen Christ.* (Note {the} typological use of Ps. 109 {and its} implications for Christian mysticism—its scriptural roots. {The} Holy Spirit illuminates {the} mind to see {the} meaning of Scripture in the mystery of Christ and His Church.) {It reveals the} action of Christ in His Church (v. 33); {the} common life {is the} expression and witness of the presence of Christ in His Church. Note—a very ancient formula, going back to St. Hippolytus, {states,} "I believe in the Holy Spirit, in the Church, for the resurrection of the flesh."[69] Another text ({the} Anaphora of the *Traditio Apostolica*) {reads}: "calling together into unity all the saints who communicate [sacramentally] in order to fill them with the Holy Ghost."[70] The work of the Church is to fill generation after generation with the Holy Ghost and all His gifts. (Pastoral note: see spiritual direction in this light.) {In} Acts 7:44 f., Stephen, in his long speech explaining {the} Scriptures (he is *full of {the} Holy Ghost* [6:3]), finally reaches the erection of the temple and explodes against the Jews. {He denounces} the earthly standards which have supplanted the heavenly in Judaism: hence they "resist the Holy Spirit." Conflict {is} precipitated: they rush at him. He is *full of the Holy Spirit,* and as they rage at him he looks up and sees *Christ in the glory of God.* They take him out to stone him and as he dies he forgives them. This brings us to the topic of *mysticism and martyrdom* in the early Church.

III. Martyrs and Gnostics

A. *Martyrdom*—martyrdom was early regarded as the summit of the Christian and therefore of the mystical life:

---

69. Hippolytus, *Traditio Apostolica*, c. 21 (see Hippolyte de Rome, *La Tradition Apostolique*, ed. and trans. Dom B. Botte, osb, Sources Chrétiennes [SC], vol. 11 [Paris: Éditions du Cerf, 1946], 51; in the second edition [1984], Botte considers the last phrase an interpolation [87]; see also Pierre Nautin, *"Je Crois à l'Esprit Saint dans la Sainte Église pour la Résurrection de la Chair":* Étude sur l'Histoire et la Théologie du Symbole, Unam Sanctam 17 [Paris: Éditions du Cerf, 1947]).

70. Hippolytus, *Traditio Apostolica*, c. 4 (*La Tradition Apostolique*, 33).

1. Martyrdom is a perfect *union with Christ*, a perfect *following of Christ*. It is the perfect fulfillment of Christ's command to leave this world for Him. It follows Him perfectly and in all truth "out of this world to the Father."[71] It is a perfect sacrifice of love, a total giving of oneself as Christ gave Himself for us.

> I would have you think of pleasing God—as indeed you do—rather than men. For at no later time shall I have an opportunity like this of reaching God; nor can you ever have any better deed ascribed to you—if only you remain silent. If only you will say nothing in my behalf, I shall be a word of God. But, if your love is for my body, I shall be once more a mere voice. You can do me no greater kindness than to suffer me to be sacrificed to God while the place of sacrifice is still prepared. Thus forming yourselves into a chorus of love, you may sing to the Father in Jesus Christ that God gave the bishop of Syria the grace of being transferred from the rising to the setting sun. It is good to set, leaving the world for God, and so to rise in Him (taken from St. Ignatius to the *Romans*, n. 2; Fathers of the Church, *Apostolic Fathers*, p. 108-9[72]).

By martyrdom he becomes in the fullest sense a Christian, a real Christian, a "word of God" and not merely a "voice." "It is good to set, leaving the world for God, and so to rise in Him" (death and resurrection in Christ, in cosmic symbolism). In n. 3 he says with the help of their prayers, his martyrdom will make him a "Christian not only in name but in fact."[73] Why? because by martyrdom the power (of the Holy Spirit) is enabled to work in him, *substituting itself for his own power.* "Christianity is not the work of persuasion, but, wherever it is hated by the world it is a work of power" (p. 109).[74]

---

71. John 13:1.

72. *The Apostolic Fathers*, trans. Francis X. Glimm, Joseph M.-F. Marique, SJ, Gerald G. Walsh, SJ, The Fathers of the Church [FC], vol. 1 (New York: Christian Heritage, 1947).

73. *Apostolic Fathers*, 109 (which reads ". . . not merely in name . . .").

74. N. 3 (which reads ". . . whenever . . .").

I am writing to all the Churches to tell them all that I am, with all my heart, to die for God—if only you do not prevent it. I beseech you not to indulge your benevolence at the wrong time. Please let me be thrown to the wild beasts; through them I can reach God. I am God's wheat; I am ground by the teeth of the wild beasts that I may end as the pure bread of Christ. If anything, coax the beasts on to become my sepulcher and to leave nothing of my body undevoured so that, when I am dead, I may be no bother to anyone. I shall be really a disciple of Jesus Christ if and when the world can no longer see so much as my body. Make petition, then, to the Lord for me, so that by these means I may be made a sacrifice to God. I do not command you, as Peter and Paul did. They were Apostles; I am a condemned man. They were free men; I am still a slave. Still, if I suffer, I shall be emancipated by Jesus Christ and, in my resurrection, shall be free. But now in chains I am learning to have no wishes of my own (*idem*, n. 4).[75]

Note the eucharistic imagery.

I am already battling with beasts on my journey from Syria to Rome. On land and at sea, by night and by day, I am in chains with ten leopards around me—or at least with a band of guards who grow more brutal the better they are treated. However, the wrongs they do me make me a better disciple. "But that is not where my justification lies." May I find my joy in the beasts that have been made ready for me. My prayer is that they will be prompt in dealing with me. I shall coax them to devour me without delay and not be afraid to touch me, as has happened in some cases. And if, when I am ready, they hold back, I shall provoke them to attack me. Pardon me, but I know what is good for me. I am now beginning to be a disciple; may nothing visible or invisible prevent me from reaching Jesus Christ. Fire and cross and battling with wild beasts [their clawing and tearing], the breaking of bones and mangling of members, the

75. *Apostolic Fathers*, 109–10.

grinding of my whole body, the wicked torments of the devil—let them all assail me, so long as I get to Jesus Christ (*idem*, n. 5).[76]

Seeing that all things have an end, two things are proposed to our choice—life and death; and each of us is to go to his appropriate place. As there are two currencies, the one of God, and the other of the world, each stamped in its own way, so the unbelieving have the stamp of the world; those who, in charity, believe have the stamp of God the Father through Jesus Christ. And, unless it is our choice to die, through Him, unto His passion, His life is not in us (Ignatius to {the} Magnesians; *idem*, n. 5; p. 97).

    la. *The Mystical Theology of St. Ignatius*: {The} basic idea {is} of the hidden, transcendent and *silent* Godhead, in Whom is all reality, indeed Who is Himself the Real and the Father. As silence is to speech, so the Father is to the Son. *To hear and possess the silence of the Father* is the real objective of reception of the Word. "Whoever truly possesses the Word of Jesus can also hear His silence, that he may be perfect, that through his speaking he may act and through his silence be known" (Ephesians, 15).[77] *Christian perfection* (he does not yet say *gnosis*) is penetration into this silence and this reality of the Word in the Father. He who penetrates to the inner silence of God can himself become a word of God— and Ignatius must himself be a "word" in his martyrdom. He who fails to be a "word" remains only a "voice"—incomplete. But the Romans must "be silent" if Ignatius is to be a word. Here we come upon the profound idea of God present as "silence" within the Church—the silence of the bishops. From this silence

---

76. *Apostolic Fathers*, 110.

77. This translation is not that found in *Apostolic Fathers*, 93; it is apparently a modernized version of the translation found in J. B. Lightfoot, ed. and trans., *The Apostolic Fathers*, 2nd ed. (London: Macmillan, 1889), II.2.548: "He that truly possesseth the word of Jesus is able also to hearken unto His silence, that he may be perfect; that through his speech he may act and through his silence he may be known."

God speaks in the testimony of Christians. For Ignatius, martyrdom must be understood in relation to this mysticism of *silence* and *presence*. Note: not only martyrdom is a manifestation of God in us, but even *our simplest everyday acts* are produced by Christ living in us. "Carnal men can no more do the works of the spirit than those who walk in the spirit can do the things of the flesh; nor can faith do the things of infidelity nor infidelity the things of faith. Since you do all things in Jesus Christ, even those things are spiritual which you do according to the flesh" (to {the} Ephesians, n. 8; p. 90).[78]

2. Martyrdom is a gift of God—it must not be sought deliberately by our own will (see *Martyrdom of Polycarp*, c. 4; Fathers of {the} Church, *Apostolic Fathers*, p. 153[79]). But it should be accepted with humility and joy when God offers it as a great gift.

3. Asceticism is a preparation for martyrdom. It is to be seen in explicit reference to the possibility of martyrdom. This includes the acceptance of providential sufferings. Ignatius suffers already from the "beasts" (his guards) on the boat to Italy.

4. Tertullian,[80] with characteristic exaggeration, thought that *only* martyrs could be united immediately to God after death. However, all agree martyrdom brings man direct to God.

5. Martyrdom is a second baptism. It is the perfect fulfillment of our baptismal vocation. In baptism we die to the world and rise in Christ sacramentally. In martyrdom we do so in all truth. St. Cyprian says: martyrdom is a baptism "in which the angels baptize, in which God and His Christ exult, a baptism after which there is no more sin, a baptism which consummates the progress of our faith, which unites us to God as soon as we have left the world. In the baptism of water we receive the remission of sin, in the baptism

---

78. This reads ". . . spirit do the things . . ."

79. This chapter mentions one who "had forced himself and some others to come forward voluntarily" and then apostasized; it concludes, "For this reason, therefore, brethren, we do not approve those who give themselves up, because the Gospel does not teach us this."

80. See *Histoire de Spiritualité*, vol. 1, 258, n. 58; ET: 208, n. 58.

of blood the crown of virtues" (*Ad Fortunatum*).[81] Note: in this text we do not of course yet have the "three ways," but here purification is the beginning, the whole life of virtue is the illuminative life, and we reach "union" in martyrdom, the crown and fulfillment of the ascetic life, the supreme mysticism. {There is here} at least an adumbration of the three ways, culminating in union.

5{a}. Martyrdom is the crown of the eucharistic life. We have already seen the famous reference, the eucharistic implications of Ignatius' "I am the wheat of Christ." *Origen* refers to martyrdom as the "supreme eucharist"[82]—the perfect thanksgiving of the Christian. {Here are} implications that the eucharistic life, together with the ascetic life of virtue, points directly to martyrdom. The eucharist is the *food of martyrs* as it will also be the bread of virgins. N.B. Secret of the Mass of mid-Lent: "The sacrifice from which all martyrdom took its beginning."[83]

6. In all these texts we have seen suggestions of a relationship between the martyr and the monk. With the end of the persecutions, the monk will take over the ascetic life of the martyr. His ascetic life will be the substitute for martyrdom. Mystical Union (expressed first of all as *gnosis*) will bring him to see God at the summit of the ascetic life as the martyr saw Christ on leaving the body. St. Ephrem (fourth century) speaks especially of *monastic vigils* as a martyrdom. "The martyrs gave witness during the day, the ascetics bear witness during their vigils. . . . Crucify your body all night long in prayer. . . . If you do not yield to sleep, count yourself among the martyrs. Be a martyr in vigils and may this martyrdom be a matter between you and God alone" (*Exhortatio ad Monachos*, 5[84]). Afflictions, macerations, fasts, etc.

---

81. *PL* 4, col. 654AB; quoted in *Histoire de Spiritualité*, vol. 1, 258; ET: 208.

82. *Histoire de Spiritualité*, vol. 1, 259; ET: 208.

83. See the Secret of the Mass for Thursday of the third week of Lent: ". . . *sacrificium . . . de quo martyrium sumpsit omne principium*" (*Missale Romanum ex Decreto Sacrosancti Concilii Tridentini Restitutum* [New York: Benziger, 1944], 104).

84. Quoted in Gustave Bardy, "Dépouillement," *DS* 3, col. 461, from *Ephraem Syri Hymni et Sermones*, 4 vols., ed. T. J. Lamy (Malines: H. Dessain,

make the monk equal to the martyrs. (Note the Syrian emphasis on corporal penance.)

Summary on Martyrdom:

a) The tradition of the martyrs makes it clear that to attain to perfect union with God, a "death" of the self is necessary.

b) How does one die to self? The martyr's case is unambiguous. His exterior, bodily self is destroyed in a real death, and his inner self lives in Christ, raised up with Christ.

c) The ascetic and mystical death to self must in some sense reproduce what is most essential in the martyr's death. Actual dissolution of the union of body and soul is not of the "essence" of this death of the self, but complete liberation from bodily desires seems to be so.

d) We must bear in mind the question of the "death of the self" as we proceed in this course. It will be interpreted variously down the ages (v.g. the mystic death in the Dark Night of St. John {of the} Cross, the stigmatization of St. Francis, etc.). Clement of Alexandria speaks of a *"gnostic martyrdom."*[85] The *ecstatic* character of Christian mysticism is already adumbrated in Clement. This ecstatic character is most important and must never be underestimated. However, this does not imply an "alienation of the senses" or a psycho-physical (violent) experience. *Clement* of Alexandria already speaks of the ascetic life as a martyrdom. "Whosoever leaves father and mother etc. . . . that man is blessed because he realizes not the ordinary martyrdom but the *gnostic martyrdom*, living according to the Rule of the Gospel out of love for our Savior. FOR GNOSIS IS THE UNDERSTANDING OF THE NAME AND THE KNOWLEDGE OF THE GOSPEL"[86] (*Stromata*, IV:4). This brings us to the theme of *Christian Gnosis*.

1886–1902), 4.214-16; the first sentence quoted here actually follows the rest of the passage. (This text is actually apocryphal, according to Dom Edmund Beck, OSB, in "Ascetisme et Monachisme chez Saint Ephrem," *L'Orient Syrien*, 3 [1958], 273–98.)

85. *Histoire de Spiritualité*, vol. 1, 261; ET: 210.

86. *Histoire de Spiritualité*, vol. 1, 261; ET: 210.

B. *Gnosis*. There is no explicit doctrine about a properly so-called contemplative life in the Gospels. We have seen above that all is included in our life in Christ, our life in the Church, the sacramental life of charity which culminates in the knowledge of Christ through the Spirit, and the return to the Father. But the Alexandrians, uniting Hellenistic philosophy with the Gospel in a living and highly valuable synthesis, began to look at the Christian knowledge of God in the light of a "contemplative summit" of Christian experience and "philosophy." This was not a perversion of Christian truth—it threw new light on the full meaning of the Christian life in the Spirit.

Revaluation of Christian Gnosis: Bouyer (*Histoire de la Spiritualité Chrétienne*, vol. 1) protests against the accusations of syncretism that have been levelled against Clement and Irenaeus for the last two hundred years.[87] The term *gnostic* has itself been in bad favor since the nineteenth-century critics attached it to the Gnostic heretics. But the term belonged originally to the orthodox gnostics, the Christians. Irenaeus always defends the Christian as the genuine gnostic; the heretics are always pseudo-gnostics. Hence the Gnostic heresy has no real right to the name of gnostic, which ought to be restored to its proper place in the history of theology. *St. Justin*, martyr and philosopher, initiated the Christian *gnosis* (i.e. philosophy), a rational and also contemplative understanding of the Gospel message, with a view to communicating it to the pagan intellectual. *St. Irenaeus* ({a} Syrian who became bishop of Lyons) reacted against the Gnostic heresy as anti-biblical, anti-ecclesiastical {and} anti-humanistic.

Characteristics of the pseudo-gnostics: the Gnostic heresy is predominantly a mixture of Jewish, hellenistic and oriental elements superimposed on Christianity. The Christian elements remain superficial. {The} Gnostic system rejects the Biblical cosmogony and replaces it with the pseudo-scientific concepts of

87. Bouyer says one hundred years, and does not mention Irenaeus (*Histoire de Spiritualité*, vol. 1, 262; ET: 211).

the day. Christ stands at the summit of a mystical ascent through aeons, angelic realms.

Dualism: {the} God of the Old Testament {is presented as the} enemy of Christ. The body is evil—{it} is a tomb of the soul (*soma sema*[88]). Hence the doctrine of the *Incarnation* is rejected. The visible universe comes from an evil principle, etc. Note the important implications of all this for the ascetic life. {It is a} distortion of true Christian asceticism. False mysticism inevitably results, {marked by} hatred of the flesh {and} illuminism. The Gnostics insisted that *only gnostic illumination* really saved. Hence only a minority, an elite, is really saved. This minority is *initiated into special* mysteries inaccessible to the ordinary faithful. The initiates are the true *gnostics*. The effect of their gnosis is *a rescue from matter and an escape into the realm of pure spirit*. This kind of solution to the problems of the spiritual life will remain a *constant temptation* all through Christian history. We find various forms of it constantly recurring.

The reaction of St. Irenaeus—Adversus Haereses:

a) He opposes to the esoteric tradition of the gnostic, *the public tradition of the Church*. True Christian gnosis is enlightenment by the Holy Ghost present in the Christian community, the body of Christ. In the midst of the Church the Spirit is permanently a "pledge of incorruptibility and a confirmation of our faith."[89] Note {the} emphasis on incorruptibility, i.e. resurrection, as opposed to liberation from the flesh. Above all Irenaeus defends the *unity of the Scriptures* against the pseudo-gnostics. True Christian gnosis is arrived at precisely by a grasp of the unity of God's revelation, culminating in the recapitulation of all in Christ. Without this understanding, man remains in illusion, and does not yield himself to the Holy Spirit.

---

88. "the body [is] a tomb" (*Histoire de Spiritualité*, vol. 1, 267; ET: 215).

89. *Adversus Haereses*, III.24.1 (J. P. Migne, ed., *Patrologiae Cursus Completus, Series Graeca* [PG], 161 vols. [Paris: Garnier, 1857–1866], vol. 7, col. 966B), quoted in *Histoire de Spiritualité*, vol. 1, 280; ET: 227 (where it it cited as III.38.1).

b) *Recapitulation of all in Christ*: as opposed to the Gnostic pleroma, {Irenaeus presents} the idea of Christ as Pleroma as already developed by St. Paul. Existence in the image and likeness of God is restored to the Christian in Christ. {Note the} importance of this doctrine of image and likeness in Christian mysticism: we shall meet it again.

c) *Trinitarian mysticism*: those who have in themselves the Spirit of God are brought to the Logos, the Son, Who takes them and offers them to the Father. From the Father they receive incorruptibility.

d) *Incarnation and Redemption in Irenaeus*: in opposing the pseudo-gnostics he places great emphasis on the Incarnation. Human nature being assumed by the Word, man becomes capable of *divinization*. "God became man in order that man might become God."[90] This dictum will be taken up by St. Athanasius,[91] etc. St. Basil will even say, "Man is a creature who has *received orders to become God*."[92] Incarnation and divinization henceforth are closely associated in the Fathers. *Objections*: Harnack has objected[93] that this emphasis on the Incarnation makes it automatically redemptive and therefore the Cross has no more importance. This is false—clearly Christ by His obedience, His redemptive death on the Cross, liberates man from sin and restores in him the divine life, if man himself will take up his own

---

90. See *Contra Haereses*, Book 5, Preface: "*qui propter immensam suam dilectionem factus est quod sumus nos, uti nos perficeret esse quod est ipse*" ("Who, because of his measureless love, became what we are in order to enable us to be what He is") (*PG* 7, col. 1120B); and *Contra Haereses*, III.19.1: "*Propter hoc enim Verbum Dei homo; et qui Filius Dei est, filius hominis factus est, commistus Verbo Dei, ut adoptionem percipiens fiat Filius Dei*" ("For this reason the Word of God became human, and he who was the Son of God became the Son of Man, so that, united with the Word of God man might become by adoption the Son of God") (*PG* 7, col. 939B).

91. *De Incarnatione*, 54 (*PG* 25, col. 192B).

92. St. Gregory Nazianzen, *Oratio 43: In Laudem Basilli Magni*, 48 (*PG* 36, col. 560A), quoted in Lossky, *Mystical Theology*, 124.

93. See *Histoire de Spiritualité*, vol. 1, 284–85; ET: 230–31.

cross and imitate the obedience of his Master—especially in martyrdom.

Conclusions: gnostic is never a term of reproach for Irenaeus. Nor is it a term for {an} esoteric elite. *All {the} faithful can and should be gnostics.* However there are varying degrees of perfection. Gnosis, {the} study of Scripture and contemplation of its mysteries, shows Christ at the center of all history, and {focuses on} recapitulation, {the} summing up of all in {the} power of the divine mercy uniting all to God in Him. This is {the} gnosis-mysticism of Irenaeus.

Clement of Alexandria the gnostic: time does not permit an extended study of the very important Alexandrian School. For Origen, see our notes on *Cassian and the Fathers*.[94] But it is necessary to refer at least in passing to Clement's idea of the "true" (Christian) gnostic, especially as we shall meet this again, where Clement influences Fénelon in the seventeenth century. There are certain very positive elements of great importance in Clement:

1) His characteristic use of *non-Christian philosophy, as contributing to Christian gnosis.* {See} *Stromata* VI:9:[95] just as the Jews received the Law, the pagans received philosophy from God. This equation of the philosophy of Plato with the Law of Moses, of Socrates as an obscure precursor of Christ, gives the gnosis of Clement a strongly philosophical cast. This was dictated to some extent by the mission of the school of Alexandria where pagans came to be instructed along with Christians.

2) However, though gnosis implies a broad living synthesis of philosophy, Judaism, and revelation, it is not mere human

94. *Cassian and the Fathers*, 23-29.

95. While he begins to touch on this topic at the end of chapter 9, the following chapter (*PG* 9, cols. 299/300D-303/304C), entitled *"Gnosticum verum etiam scientiarum humanarum cognitionem sibi comparaturum tanquam fidei adjutricum atque ad res divinas percipiendas animum praeparantium"* ("The true gnostic unites in himself the understanding of human sciences along with the assistance of faith in order to prepare the mind to grasp divine realities") focuses particularly on the contributions of pagan learning to Christian gnosis.

syncretism. Over and above intellectual effort and study, *gnosis is a gift of God*, in fact the gift of God par excellence. He defines gnosis as a "certain divine knowledge . . . born from obedience to the precepts, . . . which teaches man to enter into the possession of God" (*Stromata* III:5).[96] Gnosis is a *seeking* for God: "*To seek the Face of God by all possible means.*"[97] It comes to us "from the Father by the Son."[98]

3) The gnostic is therefore called to know God, to possess God, to *see God*. This is not merely intellectuality: it is a spiritual gift, a mystical vision. (The term mystical is not yet used,[99] but it should be clear that gnosticism equals mystical contemplation for Clement. However, it is still *debatable*.)

4) The gnostic ascent to the gift of divine vision is also an ascent to divinization *through purification*. By constant prayer the gnostic leads an "angelic life."[100] He is liberated from the passions and from the flesh and "purified by light."[101] There is a negative emphasis on the body (cf. Platonism). "The gnostic soul must be freed from its bodily wrapping. . . . Carnal desires must be got rid of; the soul must be purified by light . . . but most men put on their mortal element as snails put on their shells, and roll up in their passions like hedgehogs" (*Stromata* V).[102]

---

96. *PG* 8, col. 1148BC, quoted in Joseph Moingt, "Écriture Sainte et Vie Spirituelle," II.A.7: "Clément d'Alexandrie," *DS* 4, col. 146.

97. *Stromata*, VI.10.81 (*PG* 9, col. 301C), quoted in Moingt, col. 146.

98. *Stromata*, V.11 (*PG* 9, col. 109B), quoted in *Histoire de Spiritualité*, vol. 1, 327; ET: 266.

99. But cf. *Stromata*, VII.10.57 (*PG* 9, col. 480C), quoted in Jules Lebreton, "Clément d'Alexandrie," *DS* 2, col. 961, which refers to "mystical stages" (τὰς προκοπὰς τὰς μυστικὰς).

100. See *Stromata*, IV.25.155, VII.10.57, VII.14.84 (*PG* 8, col. 1365A, *PG* 9, cols. 481B, 517A).

101. *Stromata*, V.11.67 (*PG* 9, col. 104A), quoted in Bardy, "Dépouillement," col. 460.

102. *Stromata*, V.11.67-68 (*PG* 9, col. 104A), quoted in Bardy, "Dépouillement," col. 460.

5) However the ascesis of the gnostic is built, above all, on faith, hope and charity. Gnosis is associated with the perfection of charity. It enters into the mystery of the divine *agape*. {The gnostic} is united with Him in the mystery of His love. Gnosis is primarily a unified view of the whole mystery of salvation as expressed in Scripture but also as experienced in the loving union of the gnostic with the divine light.

6) Reading of the Scriptures is hence the royal road to gnosis. The Scriptures are God's way of educating man for Sonship. Those who have meditated on the Scriptures become "Theodidacts."[103] Through the Scriptures we are drawn by the Spirit to the Father, through the Son. This implies first of all the spiritual understanding of what is *veiled by the letter* of Scripture. "As the sea belongs to all but one swims in it, one sails on it for business, one fishes in it; and as the earth belongs to all but one voyages on it, one ploughs it and one hunts on it, another builds on it or mines it, so Scripture—one draws forth from it simple faith, one bases his conduct upon it, and one finally GAINS FROM IT THE FULLNESS OF RELIGION AND ATTAINS TO GNOSIS."[104]

7) The perfect gnostic must unite in himself *three essential elements*:

(1) fulfillment of all the precepts;

(2) *theoria*, contemplation ({a} unified grasp of {the} agape-mystery);

(3) the instruction of others.

Note this arrangement, which will become traditional. It is not yet the same idea as we find in St. Thomas[105] but it is on the way to it, and obviously from the same Hellenic sources.

---

103. "those taught by God" (*Stromata*, I.20.98-99 [*PG* 8, col. 816B], quoted in Moingt, col. 146; cf. I Thess. 4:9).

104. *Eclogae Propheticae*, 28 (*PG* 9, col. 713A), quoted in *Histoire de Spiritualité*, vol. 1, 329-30; ET: 269.

105. The reference is evidently to the three traditional categories of the spiritual life, popularly associated with Aquinas, as Merton has already done in the Epilogue to *The Seven Storey Mountain*: "Practically anyone who realizes

8) Clement describes the summit of the gnostic life in very
strong terms (*Stromata* VII:57): gnosis, after purification, leads

_____

the existence of the debate can tell you that Saint Thomas taught that there were
three vocations: that to the active life, that to the contemplative, and a third to
the mixture of both, and that this last is superior to the other two. The mixed
life is, of course, the vocation of Saint Thomas's own order, the Friars Preachers" (Thomas Merton, *The Seven Storey Mountain* [New York: Harcourt, Brace,
1948], 414); Merton goes on to point out that Thomas sees the contemplative life
as superior to the active, and "proves it by natural reason in arguments from a
pagan philosopher—Aristotle" (414) and to look at the three lives as successive
phases of spiritual development: "First comes the active life (practice of virtues, mortification, charity) which prepares us for contemplation. Contemplation means rest, suspension of activity, withdrawal into the mysterious interior
solitude in which the soul is absorbed in the immense and fruitful silence of
God and learns something of the secret of His perfections less by seeing than
by fruitive love. Yet to stop there would be to fall short of perfection. According
to Saint Bernard of Clairvaux it is the comparatively weak soul that arrives at
contemplation but does not overflow with a love that must communicate what
it knows of God to other men. . . . With this in mind, Saint Thomas could not
fail to give the highest place to a vocation which, in his eyes, seemed destined
to lead men to such a height of contemplation that the soul must overflow and
communicate its secrets to the world" (415). Saint Thomas discusses the active
and contemplative lives in the *Summa Theologiae,* 2a 2ae, q. 179–82, where he
does support, with various qualifications, the traditional position of the superi-
ority of the contemplative life (*Summa Theologiae,* ed. Thomas Gilby, OP, *et al.,* 61
vols. [New York: McGraw-Hill, 1964–80], vol. 46); but Aquinas does not look at
the categories of the spiritual life as successive phases, and in art. 2 of q. 179 he
explicitly excludes the idea of a third level—the so-called mixed life (6/7-10/11).
It is in a later *quaestio,* on whether a religious order dedicated to the contemplative life is superior to one devoted to the active life (2a 2ae, q. 188, art. 6), that he
maintains that an order that shares the fruits of its contemplation is the best: "*Et
hoc praefertur simplici contemplationi. Sicut enim majus est illuminare quam lucere
solum, ita majus est contemplata aliis tradere quam solum contemplari*" ("And this is
preferred to simple contemplation, for just as it is better to illumine than merely
to shine, so it is better to give to others the things contemplated than simply to
contemplate") (*Summa Theologiae,* 47: 204/205). The phrase "*contemplata tradere*"
thus becomes associated with the "mixed life" even though Thomas himself
had not endorsed this category. (Merton himself used "Contemplata Tradere"
as the title for the second last chapter of *Seeds of Contemplation* [New York: New
Directions, 1949], 182; in *New Seeds of Contemplation* [New York: New Directions,

man INTO THE DIVINE NATURE.[106] "The Son of Man became Man in order that you might learn how man becomes God."[107] The "intimate light" of gnosis leads to a "summit of repose."[108] This light is so positive that Clement even speaks of contemplating God *face to face* (even in this present life)—probably not in the strict sense in which this would be used only of vision in heaven. It is "sure knowledge and apprehension."[109] Here he is stressing the positive side of a mystical experience that will also be put in more negative terms (including by Clement himself). He is not expressing, probably, a *different kind of experience*, differing in essence. He sees a different modality of the one experience. "The perfection of the gnostic soul is to go beyond all purification and all liturgy and be with the Lord there where he is immediately under HIM."[110] This is important: mysticism is an ascent *beyond* the acts of an exterior life, however holy. It is implicitly an *ecstasis*. Note this is something quite different from saying that liturgy, etc. are not to be used as means in the spiritual life, that they are imperfect *means*. They are simply not the *end*. However note that this very positive expression of the vision of God in contemplation will be taken up later by other mystics—for instance Richard of St. Victor: in the *Benjamin Major* (*PL* 196), he speaks of seeing God, *"quasi facie ad faciem intuetur, Deum qui per mentis excessum extra seipsum ductus, summae sapientiae lumen sine ullo involucro,*

1961], 268, the title is replaced by the English translation "Sharing the Fruits of Contemplation"). A helpful discussion of the issue of the active and contemplative lives in Aquinas is provided by Simon Tugwell, OP in the introduction to his translations from Aquinas in *Albert and Thomas: Selected Writings* (New York: Paulist Press, 1988), 279–86, 290, in which the relevant texts are also found: 2a 2ae, q. 179–82 (534–85); q. 188, art. 6 (628–32).

106. *PG* 9, col. 480C.
107. *Protrepticus*, 1.8 (*PG* 8, col. 65A), quoted in *Histoire de Spiritualité*, vol. 1, 334; ET: 273, and Irénée Dalmais, "Divinisation: II. Patristique Grecque," *DS* 3, col. 1378.
108. *Stromata*, VII.10.57 (*PG* 9, col. 480C), quoted in Lebreton, col. 961.
109. *Stromata*, VII.10.57 (*PG* 9, col. 481A), quoted in Lebreton, col. 961.
110. *Stromata*, VII.10.57 (*PG* 9, col. 481A), quoted in Lebreton, col. 961.

figurarumque adumbratione, denique non in speculo et aenigmate, sed simplici, ut ita dicam, veritate contemplatur."[111] This is a very strong statement.

10) Finally Clement, in a distinction that would hardly make him popular with present-day theologians, seems to echo the Gnostic idea of a separation between the ordinary faithful and the perfect. The simple faithful do not have gnosis. The gnostic *does* form part of an elite who have access to a hidden knowledge.

Note: Dom Leclercq shows how monastic theology and especially *Cistercian theology*, nourished by experience, is truly a *gnosis* in the best sense of the word (see {The *Love*} *of Learning and* {the *Desire for*} *God*,[112] pp. 266,[113] 269,[114] 271 ff.,[115] especially p. 275, 280).

111. Col. 147AB, which reads ". . . *intuetur, qui . . . semetipsum . . . sine aliquo . . . figurarumve . . . non per speculum et in aenigmate, sed in simplici, ut sic dicam, . . .*": "He looks upon God face-to-face, as it were, who is led beyond himself in ecstasy and contemplates the light of supreme wisdom without any veil, without any semblance of forms, not in a mirror, darkly, but, as I say, in simple truth."

112. Merton has written *Desire of Learning and Love of God*.

113. "On the whole, the monastic approach to theology, the kind of religious understanding the monks are trying to attain, might better be described by reviving the word *gnosis*—on condition naturally that no heterodox nuance be given it. The Christian *gnosis*, the 'true *gnosis*' in its original, fundamental and orthodox meaning is that kind of higher knowledge which is the complement, the fruition of faith and which reaches completion in prayer and contemplation."

114. "To speak of gnosis and to differentiate between two knowledges or two degrees in the understanding of faith by no means implies echoing the difference which certain gnostics of antiquity or certain heretics of the twelfth century found between the simple believers—*credentes*—and the 'perfect' who receive a different teaching: this meant in those times a secret esoteric doctrine reserved for the initiate. The monastic theologians are speaking of two different ways of knowing the same mysteries."

115. These pages focus on "Theology and Contemplation" (271–77) and "A Spiritual Theology" (277–81); Leclercq wrote on page 275 of self-knowledge and the knowledge of God as the two complementary and correlative aspects of monastic theology and on the influence of Augustine's theory of divine illumination of the Word on monastic writers; he quotes M.-D. Chenu on page 280 on the elevation of wisdom over detached objective learning as a characteristic of monastic theology that makes it of permanent value.

"Monastic theology is a *theology of admiration* and therefore greater than a theology of speculation" (p. 283).

IV. Divinization and Mysticism

We will consider three aspects of this question, especially in the Cappadocian Fathers: A. Divinization; B. Mysticism; C. The Spiritual Senses.

A. *Theosis—Deificatio—Divinization.* First of all it must be quite clear that the idea of divinization is to a great extent expressed in terms resembling those used by ancient Greek philosophy, and also by the neo-Platonists, contemporary with Clement and Origen. It is a term of which modern theologians are afraid, because of pantheistic implications. Paul in Acts 17:28 {says,} "we are God's offspring," quoting Epimenides and Aratus.[116] Read {the} speech at the Areopagus—Paul's appeal to Hellenic wisdom. For Plato, man had to recover his likeness to God by an ascent to contemplation of eternal ideas, purifying himself of the sensible, especially intellectually. For Plotinus, man is by nature rooted in God, or rather the soul is by nature divine, and must recover its lost identity by purification. For Paul, *resurrection* must fulfill the vocation of all as sons of God. The idea of divinization is not baldly expressed in Scripture in that term, but there are many scriptural themes that are used by the Fathers, and it is evident that the center of the Christian mystery as we have seen it in St. John and St. Paul is the transformation of man in Christ, indeed the recapitulation of all in Christ.

Some basic scriptural themes on divinization {include}:[117]

a) Man {is} made in the image and likeness of God (Gen. 1:26-27).

b) Our divine adoption (Gal. 3:26; 4:5); participation in {the} divine nature (2 Pet. 1:4).

---

116. See Dalmais, col. 1376 (which mentions Aratus but not Epimenides).
117. See Dalmais, col. 1376.

c) We are called to be perfect as the Father is perfect, {in} Godlike charity (Matt. 5:44 f.).

d) {The} vision of God makes us like unto God (1 Cor. 13:12; 1 John 3:2).

e) We shall participate in the resurrection and enjoy incorruptibility (1 Cor. 15:52).

Hence Clement can say that *gnosis is divinization*. For Clement, *divinization* (which he treats in the light of Platonism and of the Greek mystery cults) is the summit of a divine *pedagogy*: from philosophy to faith, from faith to *gnosis*, from *gnosis* to {a} *union of love*. Clement already points to *something beyond gnosis*—a union with God as friend to friend.[118] It is the restoration of the divine image in us, in the likeness of Christ. Hence it is more than mere speculation. "Christ by a heavenly doctrine divinizes man" (*Prot.* 11).[119] {According to} Origen: "Mind is divinized by what it contemplates" (*en ois theorei theopoietai*).[120] Origen also brings our divinization into {a} *closer relationship with the Incarnation.* "The human and divine natures were united [in Christ] in order *that by communion with what is divine, human nature might become divine*, not only in Jesus but in all those who, by faith, embrace the life that Jesus has taught and which leads to friendship and community with God" (*Contra Celsum* 3:28, quoted in *DS*, III:1379[121]). A wonderful text of *Hippolytus* is quoted by Bouyer (*Hist. Spir.* 1, p. 498[122]):

> Thou who living on this earth hast known the heavenly King, thou shalt be the familiar friend of that God, and the co-heir of Christ, being no longer submitted to passions or to sicknesses. For thou shalt have become God. All the trials thou hast endured, being man, God has sent them to

---

118. *Stromata*, VII.10 (*PG* 9, col. 481A), quoted in Dalmais, col. 1378.
119. Quoted in Dalmais, col. 1378.
120. *In Joannem*, 32.17 (*PG* 14, col. 817A), quoted in Dalmais, col. 1379.
121. *PG* 11, col. 956D.
122. ET: 417–18.

thee because thou art man. But on the other hand, all the goods that are natural to God, God has promised to give them to thee when thou hast been begotten to immortality and deified. In obeying His holy precepts, in making thyself good by imitation of His goodness, thou shalt be like unto Him and honored by Him. For God is not poor, He who has made thee also a god in view of His glory.[123]

St. Athanasius is at the same time the great doctor of divinization and the defender of the divinity of the Word against the Arians. This fact is very significant. The mysticism and the dogmatic theology of the Church are inseparably united in Athanasius, to such a point that they stand and fall together by the single argument of man's divinization by the Incarnation of Christ. One might also say that the emphasis of St. Athanasius is so strong that it almost constitutes an exaggeration and that one must remember that what he says about the Incarnation must not make us forget the prime importance of the Cross and the Redemption of man. Some important texts (taken from {the} interesting commentary on the treatise of Athanasius, *De Incarnatione Verbi*, Introduction, Sources Chrétiennes, p.92 ff.[124]). Divinization is the result of the Incarnation; more, it is the very *purpose* of the Incarnation. "God gave the Word a body in order that in Him we might be renewed and divinized" (*Ad Adelph.* 4).[125] (Note: already in Ignatius of Antioch, v.g. *Romans* 2, there are implications of divinization.[126]) "It is for us that the Word assumed a body, in order that in Him we might be renewed and divinized. . . . The Son

---

123. *Philosophoumena*, X.34 (the very end of his work *Against Heresies*) (*PG* 16, col. 3454BC—published as a work of Origen).

124. Athanase d'Alexandrie, *Contre les Païens et Sur l'Incarnation du Verbe*, ed. and trans. T. Camelot, OP, SC 18 (Paris: Éditions du Cerf, 1947).

125. *Contra Arianos*, 2.47 (*PG* 26, col. 248B), quoted in Athanase, *Contre les Païens*, 93, n. 1. (Merton has misread the citation, which is somewhat unclear.)

126. See the final sentence of this chapter: "It is good to set, leaving the world for God, and so to rise in Him" (*Apostolic Fathers*, 109); see Dalmais, col. 1376, for other passages relating to divinization in Ignatius.

of God made Himself man in order to divinize us in Himself. . . . We do not participate in the body of an ordinary man but we receive the body of the Word and in Him we are divinized" (*Contra Arianos* 2).[127] "Man could not have been divinized by union with a simple creature, if the Son of God were not true God. . . . We would not have been delivered from sin and from malediction, if the flesh taken on by the Son of God were not by nature human flesh. . . . So too man would never have been divinized if the Word Who made Himself flesh was not by nature from the Father and His own true Word. Such a union was effected in order to unite to Him who by nature belongs to the divinity, him who is by nature man, *in order that his salvation and divinization* might be assured" (*Contra Arianos* 2).[128]

Note: the effectiveness of this argument of St. Athanasius depends on the fact that *divinization and salvation* are regarded as one and the same thing. It is our destiny to be united to God in the One Son of God. We are called to "be sons of God in Christ."[129] Divinization is our last end. This is the vocation of all Christians, not simply of a special elite. There must have been a fundamental agreement between Athanasius and the Arians—in other words both parties, while being divided on the question of the divinity of the Word, must have been agreed on the fact that divinization was the last end of the Christian. Divinization means immortality, the vision of God, the restoration of our lost likeness to God, and all these mean *a sharing in the divine life*. Further, "the Word made Himself visible in His body in order that we might come to know the Invisible Father" (*De Incarn.* 54; see below).[130] Thus the Lord

---

127. The three sentences (translated from Athanase, *Contre les Païens*, 93) are actually from three different sources: *Contra Arianos*, 2.47 (*PG* 26, col. 248B); *Ad Adelphium*, 4 (*PG* 26, col. 1077A); *Ad Maximum*, 2 (*PG* 26, col. 1088B).

128. *Contra Arianos*, 2.70; *PG* 26, col. 296AB (Athanase, *Contre les Païens*, 93–94); the text reads "by the Word . . ." rather than "by the Son of God . . ."

129. *Contra Arianos*, 3.19 (*PG* 26, cols. 361C-364A), quoted in Dalmais, col. 1381 (somewhat condensed).

130. *PG* 25, col. 192B, quoted in Dalmais, cols. 1380–81.

gives us *supernatural* and *gratuitous knowledge* of the Father. The Father is revealed to us in the Son even in this present life, in order *that through the Son we may come to the Father and be divinized.* Furthermore, the doctrine of the *mystical body* is clear in Athanasius. We are divinized as members of Christ. In the *De Incarnatione,* Athanasius tells us to consider the works of Christ and recognize that they are divine, to realize that *by His death* (Athanasius by no means ignores the redemptive death of Christ) He has given us immortality, and that He has become the *choregos*[131] in the great work of divine providence. (Note {the} implicit comparison of the economy of redemption to a dance.) Then St. Athanasius sums up his whole doctrine: "He became man in order that we might become God. He made Himself visible in His body in order that we might have an idea of the invisible Father. He underwent outrages from men in order that we might have part in immortality" (*De Incarn.* 54).[132] This gives the complete picture. St. Athanasius is not explicitly concerned with what we would call mystical experience, but his doctrine is the theological foundation for all such experience.

Note St. Athanasius renews all the same arguments in order to prove the divinity of the Holy Spirit. "If this participation in the Holy Spirit communicates to us the divine nature it would be madness to say that the Spirit is of a created nature and not of the divine nature. That is why *those in whom He is present are divinized*" (*Letters to Serapion*).[133] This makes it quite clear that our divinization is *already a reality,* and yet in some sense it is to be progressively unfolded and deepened until it reaches an ultimate perfection in heaven. *St. Basil* takes this up even more clearly (see *DS* III:1382): "The Paraclete like the sunlight taking possession of a very clear and pure eye will show you in Himself the image of the Invisible; in the blessed contemplation of the image you will

---

131. "chorus leader," "producer"—a term taken from Greek drama.

132. *PG* 25, col. 192BC (Athanase, *Contre les Païens*, 90).

133. *Letters to Serapion*, 1.24 (*PG* 26, col. 585C), quoted in Dalmais, col. 1381.

see the inexpressible beauty of the archetype. . . . It is from this that everything flows: foretelling of the future, understanding of mysteries, comprehension of hidden things, distribution of charisms, participation in the life of heaven, singing and dancing in choir with the angels, unending joy, permanent dwelling in God and likeness to God, and finally, the supreme object of desire, *to become God*" (from *De Spiritu Sancto*).[134] Here we have the mystical life not so much included in divinization as leading up to the full flowering and manifestation of the divine life in us, which has begun with the granting of the Holy Spirit at baptism.

A note: in the Fathers as well as in the Bible and ancient religions generally, the idea of divinization is connected with that of *sacrifice*. The victim accepted by God becomes "His" and therefore divine, and those who partook of it communed with God (n.b. Leclercq, p. 271).[135] The Christian who opens himself totally to God is "divinized"—i.e. is accepted and becomes God's possession, and is filled with glory and the Holy Spirit (cf. John 17:1, 19 etc.; cf. {the} use of the word τελείωσις—especially in Hebrews[136]). The sacrifices of the New Law are truly *consummated*. In the New Law, our sacrifices are consummated in and with the sacrifice of Christ, and we ourselves become τελειοι—consummate—perfect. This consummation is not mere moral perfection but the transformation of the whole man in the glory of the Resurrection.

A note: *divinization in the Cistercian Fathers*. St. Bernard is in the great tradition—this must be mentioned at least in passing.

---

134. *De Spiritu Sancto*, 9.23 (*PG* 32, col. 109BC).

135. Here Leclercq points out the correspondence in the development of monastic theology between the "objective" dimension of the mystery of salvation "as related by Holy Scripture and as it is lived in the liturgy," and the "subjective" dimension of appropriating this salvific action in one's own spiritual life, "which interiorizes the mystery in the soul of each of the faithful."

136. See Heb. 7:11: "If then perfection [τελείωσις] was by the Levitical priesthood (for under it the people received the Law), what further need was there that another priest should rise, according to the order of Melchizedek, and said not to be according to the order of Aaron?" Related forms of the word are found at Heb. 5:14, 12:2.

The classical text is *De Diligendo Deo* X:27-28. Read the translation in Gilson (pp. 130–32): all the qualities of true and pure love which take us out of ourselves and transform us in God. Bernard concludes: SIC AFFICI DEIFICARI EST.[137] Note the timidity of the translations into English: "To be thus affected is to become one with God" (Connolly[138]); "Thus to be affected is to become Godlike" (Gilson, who at the same time gives the Latin [p. 132—note {the} *misprint* in {the} English version[139]] and adds a reference to St. Maximus' *Ambigua*[140]). For Bernard, divinization is the mystical marriage. This implies a considerable development of the doctrine. We see in Bernard the full mystical explicitation of what is contained and already quite explicit in the Fathers. Observe how the idea of death to ourselves in order to live in Christ is expressed here. It is a mystical transposition of the literal death we saw in the great martyr-theologians. {Note the} classical expressions—the drop of water in the barrel of wine, etc. Note the nature of this "death": it is *"death by absorption into a higher life"*—death brought about by a life—the end of one life by being lifted into a higher life of a more exalted nature (see Durrwell, *Resurrection*, p 228[141]). Conclusion: we can say with William of St.

---

137. *PL* 182, col. 991A.

138. *Saint Bernard on the Love of God*, trans. Terence L. Connolly, sj (New York: Spiritual Book Associates, 1937), 38.

139. It reads *"deificare"* rather than *"deificari"*.

140. Gilson, 132, n. 195: the reference, to *Ambigua*, c. 2 (in the translation of John Scotus Erigena) (*PL* 122, col. 1202AB) is given in Gilson, 26–27.

141. "In our Lord, life consummates and consecrates death, and similarly in us death is brought about by a life. It is death by absorption into another's life. This death is not a separation of soul and body; it is the end of one life by being lifted into a higher life whose nature is incompatible with the first" (F. X. Durrwell, cssr, *The Resurrection, A Biblical Study*, trans. Rosemary Sheed [New York: Sheed & Ward, 1960], 228). See Merton's comment in his journal for April 16, 1961: "Durrwells's [sic] book on the *Resurrection*, sent by Frank Sheed, is excellent when you get into it. A remarkable insight into the visible and institutional aspect of the Church as something provisional, belonging along with death and suffering to the time of imperfection. A necessary corrective. Too

Thierry, *FESTINA PARTICEPS ESSE SPIRITUS SANCTI*.[142] William makes our transformation in Christ a matter of perfect mystical union of wills: "*Velle quod Deus vult, hoc est jam Deo similem esse; NON POSSE VELLE NISI QUOD DEUS VULT HOC EST JAM ESSE QUOD DEUS EST*" (*Golden Epistle*, II:5).[143] He qualifies, this is not pantheism (see *DS*, III:1410).[144] *Pastoral note*: {the} Cistercian emphasis {is} on purity of love and self-forgetfulness, {on} forming souls for contemplation {in} simplicity, tranquillity, liberation from "self."

{*Note*} *the implications of this treatment of divinization by the Fathers in the Anti-Arian controversy*:

1) It makes very clear the close relationship between mysticism and theology. In a certain sense it shows them to be one and the same thing. By "mysticism" we can mean the personal experience of what is revealed to all and realized in all in the mystery of Christ. And by "theology" we mean the common revelation of the mystery which is to be lived by all. The two belong together. There is no theology without mysticism (for it would have no relation to the real life of God in us) and there is no mysticism without theology (because it would be at the mercy of individual and subjective fantasy).

---

many evils are excused by a passionate and one-sided attachment to the Church as a juridical institution" (*Turning Toward the World*, 108).

142. "Hasten to be a sharer of the Holy Spirit" (*Speculum Fidei* [*PL* 180, col. 384B, which reads: "*Festina ergo . . .*"], quoted in André Fracheboud, "Divinisation, IV: Moyen Age: A. Auteurs Monastiques du 12e Siècle," *DS* 3, col. 1408).

143. "To will what God wills, this is to be like God; to be able to will nothing except what God wills is to be what God is" (*Golden Epistle*, II.3.15 [*PL* 184, col. 348B, which reads: "*Velle autem . . . similem Deo . . .*"], quoted in Fracheboud, "Divinisation," col. 1410.

144. "*Quibus enim potestas data est filios Dei fieri, data est potestas, non quidem ut sint Deus, sed sint tamen quod Deus est, sint sancti, futuri plene beati, quod Deus est*" (*PL* 184, col. 348B) ("For to these is given the power to become sons of God, a power to be not as God is but rather what God is, to be holy, to be fully blessed in the future, which is what God is") (on this issue see Gilson, 212–14).

2) Mysticism and theology have one and the same end—they culminate in *theosis* or the fullness of the divine life in the souls of the faithful.

3) Lossky (p. 8)[145] points out that *the struggle of the Church to safeguard the purity of dogma in every age* is at the same time a struggle to guarantee to each Christian *free access to mystical union*. St. Irenaeus against the *Gnostics* defended the very concept of deification as man's last end. St. Athanasius, etc. against the *Arians* defend {the} divinity of {the} Word because {the} Word opens to us the way to deification, {and} against the Macedonians, who deny the divinity of the Holy Spirit who deifies us. {Likewise} St. Cyril, etc. against {the} *Nestorians*, because Nestorianism separates {the} humanity and divinity in Christ; {the} Cappadocian Fathers against {the} *Monophysites* and Apollinarians, to show that the fullness of human nature has been united to God in the Word ("what has not been assumed is not saved"[146]); St. Maximus against {the} *monothelites*, to safeguard the action of the human will necessary for salvation and union, {and} against {the} *iconoclasts* to reaffirm the possibility of divine mysteries being expressed in material forms. "In each case the central preoccupation is always one thing that is at stake: the possibility, the mode, or the means of union with God" (*op. cit.*, p. 8). Note: Pseudo-Denis the Areopagite in his theory of the *theandric energy* in Christ contributes to the mystical clarification of dogma: two wills, two liberties in "one single energy"; two natures united in "one theandric conscience";[147] the human conscience of Christ *within* the

---

145. ET: 10.

146. St. Gregory Nazianzen, "Letter 101, to Cledonius" (*PG* 37, col. 181C, 184A).

147. Merton seems to be somewhat imprecise here. In *Letter* 4 Pseudo-Dionysius speaks of "theandric energy" (θεανδρικὴν ἐνέργειαν) (*PG* 3, col. 1072C), but not of a "single" energy (monoenergism), a term that later will be favored by the monophysite Severus of Antioch (though a variant text of the passage does read "a single theandric energy" [μιαν θεανδρικὴν ἐνέργειαν]: see Jaroslav Pelikan's Introduction to Pseudo-Dionysius, *The Complete Works*, trans. Colm Luibheid [New York: Paulist, 1987], 20); also, he does not use the term "na-

divine conscience—this is the pattern for the soul, one with God in Christ.

B. *Theoria Mystike, Theognosis: Mystical Contemplation*

So far we have seen that Christian mysticism begins before the term mysticism is used. The essence of the concept of mystical union is contained in the doctrine of St. Ignatius Martyr. The concept of contemplation is first developed under the term *gnosis*. The Fathers, unanimous in stating that divinization is the end of the Christian life, stress the transformation of the Christian in Christ. In all these treatments there has been present the acknowledgement that our gnosis and divinization involve a *transitus*, a passing over into a hidden realm, so that our "life is hidden with Christ in God."[148] This implies that the experience of union with Christ is a *hidden* experience, something secret and incommunicable, an experience of something that is hidden on the ordinary levels of Christian life. Hence we must discuss the first appearance of the concept of mysticism and mystical experience in Christian tradition.

1. The Greek classical term, *mystikos*, refers to the hidden *rites* of the mystery religions—not to a hidden experience, but to the mystery which is revealed only to the initiates and through which they pass. It does not refer directly to an "experience," certainly not to a spiritual experience in our sense of the word. Bouyer stresses this[149] in order to prove that Christian "mysticism" is not a simple carry-over from the pagan mystery cults. However, it may be remarked that implicitly one who has been initiated and passed through the secret rites has "experienced" what it means to be an initiate. He has not merely learned a few new rubrics, unknown to others. Bouyer also insists that mysticism in the pagan sense is not a "hidden doctrine" based on an

---

ture" (φύσις) with regard to the humanity of Christ. See René Rocques, *L'Univers Dionysien: Structure Hiérarchique du Monde selon le Pseudo-Denys* (Paris: Aubier, 1954), 310–11, especially 311, n. 6, and 309, 312.

148. Col. 3:3.

149. *Histoire de Spiritualité*, vol. 1, 485; ET: 406.

ineffable personal experience. However he admits that poets and philosophers developed "mystical" doctrines based on rites of which they had knowledge and which remained secret. These "mystical" doctrines were difficult and recondite and, we might add, tended to be "spiritual."

2. Christian use of the term mystic (*mystikos*):[150] Clement and Origen take over the pagan term and use it in reference to the spiritual (mystical or typological) *sense of Scripture*. For them the mystical sense is the *real* sense. To discover the mystical sense is to penetrate to the real meaning of revelation and hence to penetrate into the hidden things of God, the mystery of Christ. This mystery, the *mysterion* of the Cross, is the central reality of all cosmic life: the salvation of the world, the recapitulation of all in Christ. Hence, as we have seen, the "gnostic" is the man who has entered into this "mystical" understanding of Scripture. Originally, the mystical sense of Scripture is: (a) that which points to Christ; (b) that which deals with invisible realities of faith; (c) that which is spiritual and not carnal, i.e. not involved in {the} "letter" of the Law and of Scripture. It cannot be too often repeated that this "mystical sense" of Scripture is not a hidden *idea about* God or a mere complex of difficult or secret truths. It is a *reality experienced and lived*. One might say that for the Fathers the letter tended to be doctrine and law, the spirit tended to be *reality and life*. Their theology was therefore not simply constructed with the literal elements of revelation; it was built on an experience of the ineffable reality of revelation, or of God revealed in the mystery of Christ. Hence it is clear that already to enter into the mystical sense or real sense of Scripture, which is interior and spiritual, one must "die to" the letter, to the exterior and apparent meaning; one must "go beyond," one must "stand outside" (*ekstasis*) the apparent meaning. This does not necessarily imply a strict *opposition* between the letter and the spirit, but simply a fulfillment of the letter in the spirit. (*De facto* the opposi-

---

150. See *Histoire de Spiritualité*, vol. 1, 486; ET: 407.

tion gets to be overstressed.) Hence in any case the way is prepared for a "*theoria*" which requires an abandonment of what is "seen" and a going beyond to what is "not seen." This need not yet be mystical in the modern sense of the word. Examples: the "mystical sacrifice" of the Eucharist as opposed to the bloody sacrifice of the Old Law: the "*real*" sacrifice, not the appearance; "mystical bread"—the Body of the Lord; {the} "mystical table" (altar), "mystical action" (Mass), "mystical water" (baptism).[151]

3. *Theognosis*, and *theoria mystike*—mystical contemplation. According to Bouyer, *Origen* in a characteristically "gnostic" passage in his commentary on St. John (13:24), speaks of Christ as our guide in "mystical and ineffable contemplation"[152]—i.e. to the spiritual understanding of Scripture. *This text* is not a commentary on John 13, v. 24 but on chapter 4, the line "*Spiritus est Deus et qui adorant eum in spiritu et veritate oportet adorare.*"[153] This takes up nn. 21-25 of Tome XIII of the *Commentary in Joannem* of Origen.[154] He explains how God is the "incorporeal light"[155] illuminating the mind, the incorporeal fire purifying us, the incorporeal Spirit giving us life and leading us to Himself. "He who is deprived of the divine Spirit is made earthly; he who disposes himself to receive the Divine Spirit and receives Him, is renewed and created afresh."[156]

But how are we to know the Divine Spirit? No one knows the Father but the Son. We come to know God in the following way:

a) The Son reveals to us how God is Spirit.

b) We must adore Him in Spirit and truth, not in the letter which killeth.

---

151. See *Histoire de Spiritualité*, vol. 1, 488–89; ET: 409.

152. *In Joannem*, 13.24 (*PG* 14, col. 440C): see *Histoire de Spiritualité*, vol. 1, 489; ET: 410.

153. "God is Spirit, and whoever worships him must worship in spirit and in truth" (Jn. 4:24).

154. *PG* 14, cols. 432C-444B.

155. *In Joannem*, 13.23 (*PG* 14, col. 437/438B).

156. *In Joannem*, 13.24 (*PG* 14, col. 437/438C).

c) We must worship Him no longer in figures and types but like the angels who worship Him without the "shadows"[157] that intervene, in intelligible and heavenly things (he does not fully explain {this idea} here—evidently {it is} more immediate).

d) (The angels) SUMMUM ILLUM SACERDOTEM SECUNDUM ORDINEM MELCHISEDEC PRO ORANTIUM ATQUE EGENTIUM SALUTE HABENTES DUCEM CULTUS MYSTICI ATQUE INEFFABILIS VISIONIS.[158] We only have the Latin here.[159] It is possible that Bouyer, who considers this the first example of the use of "mystical contemplation" in Christian tradition, is mistaken. He unites *mystici* with *visionis*. It is quite possible that the phrase is to be divided into (Christ the) *"ducem cultus mystici"* (i.e. {the} familiar concept of *choregos* always introduced in connection with angels) {and} *"et ineffabilis visionis."* It is then the "cult" that is mystical rather than the "vision" (this is ineffable). The point is not too important. The meaning of the text is clear enough. To definitively decide, one would have to see the Greek.

Note {the} predilection of {the} Greek Fathers for "mystic" in connection with *angelic adoration of God*. The angels do not "discuss the divine essence" says Chrysostom (*Incomprehensibility*

---

157. *In Joannem*, 13.24 (*PG* 14, col. 439/440C).

158. "having that high priest according to the order of Melchizedek as leader of the ritual of the mystical and ineffable vision [or: of the mystical ritual and ineffable vision], for the salvation of those praying and acting" (*PG* 14, col. 439C, quoted in *Histoire de Spiritualité*, vol. 1, 489–90; ET: 410).

159. Merton does not mean that this text, like so much of Origen's work, survives only in Latin translation, but rather that the text of the *Patrologia Graeca* at Gethsemani consisted only of the Latin translations, not of the Greek originals. In fact, the original Greek does confirm that Bouyer's translation of the passage is correct and that "mystical" belongs with "vision" not with "cult": "τὸν κατὰ τὴν τάξιν τοῦ Μελχισεδὲκ ἀρχιερέα ὁδηγὸν ἔχοντες ὑπὸ τῶν δεομένων σωτηπίας λατρείας καὶ μυστικῆς καὶ ἀπορρήτου θεωρίας" ("having a high priest according to the order of Melchizedek as guide of worship and of mystical and ineffable vision, for the salvation of those in need") (note the additional "καὶ" in the Greek before "μυστικῆς," which has no corresponding "*et*" in the Latin).

of God I, SC p. 100-102),[160] but they "sing triumphal and mystic odes," i.e. the *sanctus*. Dom Leclercq (*Love of Learning and Desire for God*, p. 120) says Origen's *Commentary on the Canticles* was "*less mystical and more psychological*" than that of Gregory of Nyssa, which was more concerned with the *sacraments* and more pastoral. Note {the} objectivity of "mystical" in this ancient sense.

With the Cappadocian Fathers, whatever may be the use of terms, we have clear references to "mystical contemplation." We shall see this especially in Gregory of Nyssa. First, a text from St. Gregory Nazianzen, a "classical" description of mystical contemplation in Platonic language:

> It appears to me that there is nothing preferable to the state of that man who, closing his senses to exterior impressions, escaping from the flesh and from the world, enters into himself and, retaining no further contact with anything human, except in so far as necessity obliges, conversing with himself and with God, lives above visible things and carries in himself divine images, always pure, having truly become, and becoming each day more and more, the spotless mirror of the divinity and of divine things, receiving their light in his light, their resplendent clarity in his own weaker light, already plucking in hope the fruit of future life, living in communion with the angels, still on this earth and yet out of this world, lifted up into supernal regions by the Spirit (from *Oratio* II:7, quoted by Bouyer, *Hist. Spir.* I, 418[161]).

Here we have at any rate the conception that to enter into the contemplation and possession of things hidden, one must "die to" exterior experience and rise from death on a new level. This is the kind of text that sometimes misleads:

---

160. Jean Chrysostome, *Sur l'Incompréhensibilité de Dieu*, trans. Robert Flageliere, intro. Ferdinand Cavallera, sj and Jean Daniélou, sj, SC 28 (Paris: Éditions du Cerf, 1951).

161. ET: 347 (*PG* 35, col. 413C, 416A).

a) Its Christian elements are only implicit; it is more typically pagan.

b) It exploits too emphatically a supposed "separation" and incompatibility between the sensible and the spiritual; {there is an} overstress on "introversion."

c) It does not stress the action of grace.

Such texts should therefore not be studied alone and out of their context and out of the whole orientation of the writer to whom they belong.

The Mysticism of the Cappadocian Fathers

1. *Its special importance*: here we come upon the first great Christian mystics. This applies especially to St. Gregory of Nyssa, in a lesser degree to St. Gregory Nazianzen. St. Basil is more an ascetic and dogmatic than a mystical theologian, though himself a mystic. St. Gregory {of} Nyssa on the other hand is the Father of Christian mysticism much more truly than Clement or Origen. What we have seen so far prepares the way for Gregory of Nyssa and for his truly and strictly mystical theology. The *great originality* of Gregory of Nyssa is to be stressed.

a) True, he uses Platonic elements and language, but this must not blind us to the originality and depth of his *experience*. He clearly goes beyond Origen, his master, in the field of truly mystical experience, rather than intellectual penetration of the spiritual sense of Scripture.

b) This originality is all the more apparent now that the authorship of the *De Instituto Christiano* has been definitively restored to him by Werner Jaeger, while at the same time the full text of this important treatise has been discovered.[162]

---

162. The text of the treatise generally called *De Instituto Christiano* had been published in what Jaeger calls an "abridged and mutilated form" (*Two Rediscovered Works*, 3, n. 1) in PG 46, cols. 287–306; the authentic text appears in Jaeger's edition of *Gregorii Nysseni Opera vol. VIII, I: Gregorii Nysseni Opera Ascetica* (Leiden: Brill, 1952), 1–89; Jaeger's conclusion (*Two Rediscovered Works*, 174–207) that the *De Instituto Christiano* was the source for the *Great Letter* of

In St. Gregory of Nyssa the dogmatic writings, even those which are purely controversial, have a direct orientation to the mystical life. His replies to *Eunomius* and *Apollinaris* are a defense of basic truths of the mystical life, especially of the divine transcendence and of the necessity to know God "by unknowing." The treatise *De Hominis Opificio*[163] is not merely speculative, but considers man as created for contemplation and union with God. He develops the conception of man which reached William of St. Thierry via Scotus Erigena: man as *psyche (anima)—homo animalis; nous (ratio)—homo rationalis; pneuma (spiritus)—homo spiritualis.*[164]

Pseudo-Macarius, rather than vice versa, has subsequently been widely challenged by other scholars, who consider that Gregory, or his disciples, produced a revised text of the *Great Letter*: see Reinhart Staats, *Gregor von Nyssa und die Messalianer*, Patristische Texte und Studien, 8 (Berlin: De Gruyter, 1968), as well as his 1984 edition of the two texts (*Makarios-Symeon: Epistola Magna. Eine Messalianische Mönchsregel und ihre Umschrift in Gregors von Nyssa 'De Instituto Christiano'* [Göttingen: Vandenhoeck & Ruprecht, 1984]); M. Canévet, "Le 'De Instituto Christiano' est-il de Grégoire de Nysse?" *Revue des Études Grecques*, 82 (1969), 404-23; Vincent Despres, Introduction to *Pseudo-Macaire: Oeuvres Spirituelles: Homélies propres à la Collection III*, SC 275 (Paris: Éditions du Cerf, 1980); arguments summarized by George A. Maloney, SJ in the Introduction to his translation of *Pseudo-Macarius: The Fifty Spiritual Homilies and the Great Letter* (New York: Paulist, 1992), 10–11 and 28, n. 5.

163. *PG* 44, cols. 123C–256C.

164. In the *Golden Epistle* (*A Letter to the Brethren at Mont Dieu*), trans. Theodore Berkeley, OCSO, Cistercian Fathers [CF], vol. 12 (Kalamazoo, MI: Cistercian Publications, 1976), William uses the framework of three levels of spiritual development: "there are beginners, those who are making progress and the perfect. The state of beginners may be called 'animal,' the state of those who are making progress 'rational' and the state of the perfect 'spiritual'" (1:12 [25]). See also Déchanet, *William of St. Thierry: The Man and His Work*: "What strikes one about the book on the soul is the fact that three-quarters of it comes from St. Gregory of Nyssa's *De hominis opificio*" (39); and Déchanet, *Aux Sources de la Spiritualité de Guillaume de Saint-Thierry*, 56, which points out that William used the translation made by Scotus rather than that by Dionysius Exiguus; this translation, which survives in only one manuscript, was discovered by Dom Maïeul Cappuyns: see his *Jean Scot Erigène, Sa Vie, Son Oeuvre, Sa Pensée* (Paris: Desclée de Brouwer, 1933), 173–76; he later published the translation in "Le *De Imagine* de Grégoire

However, returning to the question of "mysticism" in Gregory {of} Nyssa, we find it still means *primarily the penetration of the hidden sense of Scripture.* See {the} *Prologue to Canticle of Canticles*— his purpose is "by proper contemplation" (*theoria*) to open up the *"philosophy hidden in the words"* (of the Canticle).[165] In *Homily* 1 he says his exposition itself will be a *mystike theoria*[166] or mystical contemplation of the Canticle of Canticles. Contemplation is the apprehension of the mystical meaning of Scripture, but this mystical meaning is not a *new concept*—it is a *reality*—a *divine* reality apprehended in a *spiritual experience.* This is *gnosis mysterion*[167] (mystical) based on *cathara politeia*[168] (pure life, ascetical) and it is the function of *all* Scripture to open up *both* to us.

The influence of the Cappadocians and especially Gregory {of} Nyssa is of the utmost importance. It extends in many different directions:

a) *Evagrius* and the Desert School, and hence through *Cassian* ({a} disciple of Evagrius) to the West.

b) *Pseudo-Dionysius* and the mysticism of night, hence also to the West once again, and particularly to the Cistercian Fathers, especially *William of St. Thierry.* Note: the Cistercians are heirs of St. Gregory of Nyssa in three ways: first, through the Origenist current, secondly through Cassian, then through the Dionysian movement which however affects fewer of our Fathers ({it} hardly touches Bernard).

c) *Pseudo-Macarius* and through him the Syrian tradition, Isaac of Nineveh, etc.

de Nysse Traduit par Jean Scot Erigène," *Recherches de Théologie Ancienne et Médiévale*, 32 (1965), 205–62.

165. *PG* 44, col. 756A.

166. *PG* 44, col. 765A.

167. *PG* 44, col. 757A (Prologue, which reads γνῶσιν μυστηρίων [*gnosin mysterion*]).

168. *PG* 44, col. 757B (Prologue, which reads καθαρὰν πολιτείαν [*katharan politeian*]).

d) *St. Maximus* and the main line of Oriental (Byzantine) mysticism.

Example of the Cappadocian influence: the doctrine of St. Bernard on "pure love,"[169] by which the image of God is perfected in man and the "lost likeness" is recovered, is a legacy of the Cappadocian tradition. In the Cappadocian Fathers we find the familiar division of spiritual men into three classes: slaves; mercenaries; sons[170]—according to the disinterestedness of their love for the Father. This is the basis of St. Bernard's *De Diligendo Deo*.[171] Note that the division is already adumbrated in Clement of Alexandria, *Stromata* IV[172] (on which Fénelon bases his "pure love"[173]).

The Mysticism of Night: in St. Gregory of Nyssa (particularly the *De Vita Moysis*) we find the first clear Christian formulation

169. See Gilson's discussion of "pure love" (140–49), an analysis particularly of *Sermon* 83 on the Songs of Songs.

170. See St. Basil's Preface to his *Long Rules*, in *Ascetical Works*, trans. M. Monica Wagner, CSC, FC 9 (Washington, DC: Catholic University of America Press, 1950), 277, and St. Gregory of Nyssa, *The Life of Moses*, trans. Everett Ferguson and Abraham J. Malherbe (New York: Paulist, 1978), 136–37.

171. See Bernard of Clairvaux, *On Loving God*, 34–38 (cc. 12–14), trans. Robert Walton, OSB, in *The Works of Bernard of Clairvaux: Treatises II*, CF 13 (Washington, DC: Cistercian Publications, 1974), 125–30; these chapters were originally a letter to the Carthusians that Bernard appended to the *De Diligendo Deo* as a conclusion.

172. See Clement of Alexandria, *Stromata*, IV.6 (*PG* 8, 1241AB), and *Stromata*, VII. 2 (*PG* 9, col. 409A).

173. See François de Fénelon, *Le Gnostique de Saint Clément d'Alexandrie*, opuscule inédit de Fénelon, ed. Paul Dudon (Paris: Beauchesne, 1930) and *L'Explication des Maximes des Saints*, now available in English as *Explanation of the Maxims of the Saints on the Interior Life*, in Chad Helms, ed. and trans., *Fénelon: Selected Writings* (New York: Paulist, 2006), 207–97; see also Gabriel Joppin, *Fénelon et la Mystique du Pur Amour* (Paris: Beauchesne, 1938), especially "Le Gnostique de Saint Clément d'Alexandrie" (126–30), François Varillon, *Fénelon et le Pur Amour* (Paris: Éditions du Seuil, 1957), and Pierre Pourrat, "Charité: V.5.11: Fénelon," *DS* 2, cols. 621–22; Fénelon's teaching on pure love in the *Explication* was condemned by Pope Innocent XII in 1699 after intense pressure from King Louis XIV and Bishop Bossuet.

of *apophatic mysticism*—mysticim of darkness, unknowing, or night. However, it must be remembered that this had already been anticipated by the Platonists and Philo Judaeus, and there is probably a *link with Oriental thought*, however obscure. The apophatic mysticism of the Christian Fathers is a definite resemblance to Oriental mysticism. But it should not be rejected or dismissed precisely for this reason. It is an important fact. There is nothing whatever to be gained by calling Gregory of Nyssa and Pseudo-Dionysius "Buddhists" and then having no more to do with them. This oversimplification would bring with it its own punishment. It would cut us off from what is actually the main line of the Christian mystical tradition, even though it may not appear to be so.

The Reason for Apophatic Mysticism: why did Gregory {of} Nyssa stress the mysticism of "night" and "unknowing"? The dogmatic reasons for this are to be sought in the treatises of St. Basil[174] and then of St. Gregory {of} Nyssa *Against Eunomius*;[175] cf. also the homilies preached by St. John Chrysostom "On the Incomprehensibility of God." The *Eunomians* or *Anomeans* {were} Arians who held that the essence of God could be and was *clearly known*. {This led to} a false and oversimplified intellectualism in contemplation. The divine essence could be apprehended intellectually and exhaustively in the mere fact that one accepted the supposed revelation of God as "not engendered."[176] Once one "saw" the "truth" of this (heretical) postulate that the Father alone, the "not-engendered," was God, one entered into the full light of the divine essence and God Himself had no more light than this. The Son and the Holy Spirit {were} both "creatures" of God. Note that this is a complete evacuation of all mystical content from Christianity. Note that once again Christian mysticism

---

174. *Liber Eunomii Apologeticus* (*PG* 30, cols. 835B–868C).

175. *Contra Eunomium Libri Duodecim* (*PG* 45, cols. 243B–1122B).

176. See J. N. D. Kelly, *Early Christian Doctrines*, revised ed. (San Francisco: Harper & Row, 1978), 249: since only the Father is ingenerate (ἀγέννητος), by definition only the Father is truly God.

is inextricably bound up with the revelation of the Three Divine Persons. Now an added note is imperative: *that the essence of God transcends all knowledge by a creature.* St. Gregory of Nyssa declared that the doctrine of the Eunomians was not theology but "technology"[177] (referring to the fact that the Word is simply an instrument by which God makes other created beings).

　　Note: the *Homilies* of *St. Chrysostom On the Incomprehensibility of God* are to be studied in connection with the apophatism of Gregory {of} Nyssa. These homilies are *not in themselves mystical.* They are preached to the ordinary faithful, and do not presuppose a deep supernatural experience, only the ordinary life of faith nourished by the liturgy and by a deep *living awareness of the reality of God*, especially in the liturgical mysteries. But the living awareness of the majesty of God is precisely in proportion to our realization that He is beyond our knowledge. Not only is His *essence* incomprehensible to us but above all His *judgements*, His *gifts*, His *rewards*, His *mercies*. All these statements {are} based on St. Paul, v.g. Rom. 11:33, 1 Cor. 2:9, 2 Cor. 9:15, Phil. 4:7. Where {the} Anomeans stress the "clear [intellectual] knowledge of God"[178] in a concept, Chrysostom reacts forcefully. Such a concept is purely a *mental figment, an idol.* Besides it is heretical. But even concepts that are not false must not be confused with genuine experience of God. The experience of divine truth is not the comprehension of an intellectual concept, not the light generated by the understanding of an abstract truth. Chrysostom replaces this intellectual light (really "curiosity") with the *experience* of the "fear of God," {a} traditional interpretation of the text that "The fear of the Lord is the beginning of wisdom."[179] Note this is not a denial of intellectual study or of theology. It is the removal of a *false experience* which is shallow and illusory, and the restoration of the true basis of Christian experience, which is the fear of the

　　177. See Chrysostome, *l'Incomprehensibilité*, 13.

　　178. See Chrysostome, *l'Incomprehensibilité*, Introduction I: "Saint Jean Chrysostome et l'Anoméisme" (7–15).

　　179. Prov. 1:7; this passage is actually never quoted in the sermons.

Lord, sacred awe, born of faith and nourished by participation in the liturgical mysteries "with the angels."[180] ({A} pastoral comment: the atmosphere of *curiosities* {is} fatal to true contemplation.) Hence the homilies of Chrysostom, while not dealing directly with the mystical life, are in actual fact supremely important as guaranteeing true conditions that make that life possible: once again {we see} the sense of the Christian mysteries, worship in spirit and in truth. St. Chrysostom prays:

> Let us invoke Him as the inexpressible God, incomprehensible, invisible and unknowable; let us avow that He surpasses all power of human speech, that He eludes the grasp of every mortal intelligence, that the angels cannot penetrate Him nor the seraphim see Him in full clarity, nor the cherubim fully understand Him, for He is invisible to the Principalities and Powers, the Virtues and all creatures without exception; *only the Son and the Holy Spirit know Him* (*Incomprehensibility of God* III; SC p. 166).[181]

The Mystical Ascent: very briefly, the ascent to God in Gregory of Nyssa (*De Vita Moysis*) is a passage from *light* to *obscurity* to *total darkness*. To penetrate into the total darkness is to enter into the holy of holies, the sanctuary of God. There is a two-fold symbolism: Moses' experiences with the burning bush and on the mountain, and finally the tabernacle divided into the "Holy," the inner part which is pure but still accessible to the people, and the "Holy of Holies" which is forbidden to the people. The mystical life has three stages ({the} classical division):

1. Light, the burning bush: purgation—we die to the passions by *apatheia*.

2. Cloud (obscurity): illumination (*gnosis*)—we die to intellectual knowledge on {the} natural level and attain to *theoria* (*physica*).

---

180. See Chrysostome, *l'Incomprehensibilité*, Introduction III: "La Terreur Sacrée" (33–45).

181. *Homily* 3.

3. "Holy of Holies," Deep Darkness: union—not *gnosis* but *ousia*.[182]

It is supremely important to see how clearly Gregory goes beyond *gnosis* to *ousia* by love. Definitely for him *gnosis* is not an end but a *beginning*.

{Gregory provides an} example of the "first darkness," {the} entrance into the revelation of God's hidden designs and judgements. Gregory says of St. Basil, "Often we have seen him enter into the *gnophos* [darkness] where God was found. The inspiration [*mystagogia*] of the Spirit alone made known to him what was unknowable to others, so that he appeared to be enveloped in the darkness where the Word of God is hidden" (quoted in *DS* II:1873).[183] This is a *relative* darkness. Things of God *hidden to man can however be revealed*. The real step is beyond *gnosis*, beyond illumination (even in darkness); it is a union with God in *ecstasis*, a going out of one's own being to become one with the being of God. This divine essence *cannot be known* by a created intellect as it is in itself, says Gregory. This ecstasy is a *mystical death*. This transformation is accomplished by the replacement of *gnosis* by *agape*. The following points are vitally important:

1. It is therefore a death of love, but on the highest mystical and existential level.

2. It is not love considered as {having} a purely ethical or psychological value.

3. It is certainly not love as the love of an isolated subject for a well-defined object.

4. It is an existential contact and communion with the very being of God, which remains unknowable in all its fullness. The darkness, however, is a *positive* reality and a *light*. It is *more true* than any determinate conceptual knowledge of God.

---

182. "knowledge . . . being, substance."
183. *In Laude Fratris Basilii* (*PG* 46, col. 812C), quoted in Jean Daniélou, "Contemplation chez les Orientaux Chrétiens: III. La Contemplation de Dieu: D. Mystique de la Ténèbre chez Grégoire de Nysse."

A pertinent quotation from the *Homilies in Cantica* ("In the night on my bed I sought Him whom my soul loveth"): what is the *mystical night?*

> Night designates the contemplation [*theoria*] of invisible things after the manner of Moses who entered into the darkness where God was, this God who makes of darkness His hiding place (Ps. 17:12). . . . Surrounded by the divine night the soul seeks Him who is hidden in darkness. *She possesses indeed the love of Him* whom she seeks, but the Beloved escapes the grasp of her thoughts. . . . *Therefore abandoning the search* she recognizes Him whom she desires by the very fact that His knowledge is beyond understanding. Thus she says, "Having left behind all created things and abandoned the aid of the understanding, by faith alone I have found my Beloved. And I will not let Him go, holding Him by the grip of faith, until He enters into my bedchamber." The chamber is the *heart, which is capable of the divine indwelling when it is restored to its primitive state* (PG 44:892-893).[184]

This is a description of mystical union. N.B. this is not to be understood as a sales talk. We don't *preach* mysticism. It is not something that can be taught, still less a proper subject for exhortation.

The familiar example of Moses appears here as everywhere. Note the special importance of:

a) Possession by love and not by knowledge.

b) *Abandonment of the search for clear knowledge,* and rest in liberty and unknowing. A simple characteristic of the mystical soul is its awakening (a real awakening, to transformation, conversion of mind) to the fact that it really need not seek Him Whom it already possesses—plus an ability to rest in darkness and unknowing, without care and without concern over conceptual knowledge. Where this ability to rest is not found, there may

---

184. *In Cantica*, 10, quoted in Daniélou, "Contemplation," col. 1875.

be a sentimental or intellectual operation of "unknowing" followed by a blank and by sleep. This is not mysticism!

c) Distinguish the intellectual *via negativa*, or apophatic *speculation*, from real apophatic *contemplation*. The former is dialectical and discursive. It reasons. The latter is intuitive and is produced by love.

d) Note the essential role of purity of heart, spiritual virginity, return to the primitive, paradisiacal state.

e) The experience of the *indwelling of God by faith*.

Ecstasis in Gregory of Nyssa: is this something beyond darkness? It is beyond the darkness of *gnosis*. But {it} is another aspect of the union with God in darkness in the state we have just described. It is *theologia*. It is a "going out" from itself by the soul under the pressure of the divine transcendence. It is connected with awe and *admiration*. It suddenly seizes upon the soul and takes it out of itself. It is also referred to as *sobria ebrietas*—a term borrowed from Philo.[185] "In this drunkenness, David went forth from himself and entered into ecstasy and saw the invisible beauty, after which he pronounced the memorable word, 'Every man is a liar'" (quoted in *DS* II:1878).[186] It is a vigilant sleep: "I sleep and my heart watches."[187] Another good text from the *Homilies in Cantica*: "Then the activity of the heart is exercised in all its purity and the spirit contemplates realities from on high *without any impression coming to trouble it in its repose*. The soul takes joy in nothing but the contemplation of reality, and letting all bodily activity fall asleep by purity and nudity of spirit, she receives the manifestation of God in a divine vigil" (*PG* 44:993).[188]

---

185. "sober intoxication": *In Cantica*, sermons 5, 10, 12 (*PG* 44, cols. 873B, 990B, 1032B); *In Ascensionem Christi* (*PG* 46, col. 692BC) (see Daniélou, "Contemplation," cols. 1878–79, and *Histoire de Spiritualité*, vol. 1, 52, n. 90 [ET: 31, n. 90]; also 435 [ET: 362]).

186. *In Cantica*, 10 (*PG* 44, col. 989D).

187. Song of Songs 5:2, quoted in *In Cantica*, 10 (*PG* 44, col. 992C).

188. Quoted in Daniélou, "Contemplation," col. 1879 (there should be an ellipsis after ". . . repose.").

Elsewhere: "All carnal passion being extinct in us we burn lovingly with the flame of the Spirit alone" (*id.* 773).[189]

Epectasis—a characteristic and personal doctrine of Gregory of Nyssa is that of *epectasis*, the ever-increasing growth of love and desire and penetration into the inexhaustible ocean of divine light. As there is no limit to the infinite, even in heaven we will continue to grow, in a certain manner, in love and knowledge. This is the teaching of St. Gregory of Nyssa. Daniélou describes epectasis as "a desire that is perpetually fulfilled without ever exhausting its object and which therefore goes on in a progress that has no end" (*DS* II:1884).

C. *The Spiritual Senses*: the doctrine of the spiritual senses plays a central part in Gregory of Nyssa. His teaching of *apophatic* mysticism and unknowing is accompanied paradoxically by an insistence on the *existential reality* of the mystical experience. It is a true experience of God, analogous to the direct perception of a sense object by the bodily senses. But the analogy is rather the other way round: the experience of God by the spiritual senses is in fact *more direct* and more *immediate* than the perception of a sensible object by the bodily senses. The mystic has to appeal to ordinary sense experience in order to attempt to express an experience which is ineffable because even *more immediate* than an experience by the exterior senses. We must understand when the mystic says he is "touched" by God it means that he experiences not only something analogous to a bodily touch but far more, in a spiritual order, which cannot be expressed directly. He is really *touched* by God, and this touch is experienced as what it is. J. Daniélou[190] praises Gregory's use of the spiritual senses, following Origen of course. (We bypass Origen here—reference is made to his doctrine of spiritual senses in *The Fathers and Cassian*.[191]) This

---

189. *In Cantica*, 1 (PG 44, col. 773D), quoted in Daniélou, "Contemplation," col. 1881.

190. See Daniélou, *Platonisme et Théologie Mystique*, 225–26, and the discussion below, 92–96.

191. *Cassian and the Fathers*, 29.

Origenist use of spiritual senses is more *Biblical* (*gustate et videte* . . .[192]). It is quite true that when the Bible wishes to express the experience of God it is always in the language of the senses. But at the same time we must realize that there must be a distinction between genuinely spiritual experience which is *eo ipso*[193] not sensible, and an interior spiritual experience in which the senses (of the body or at least the interior senses) have a part.

Clarification:

a) When we talk of the spiritual senses we are talking of a very special apprehension of God which is *in no way dependent on* the bodily or interior senses. Hence we are discussing a special class of mystical experiences which are not "mystical phenomena," not visions, etc.

b) The exercise of the spiritual senses is then *analogical*.

c) In this exercise, *grace*, or the action of the Holy Spirit, *supplies* for the action of the senses, whether exterior or interior, by definition excluded and impossible. Hence it is no longer true to say that in mystical experience there is *nihil in intellectu quod non prius in sensu*.[194] St. Bonaventure defines spiritual senses as *"usus gratiae interioris respectu ipsius Dei"*[195] (for this see {Olphe-Galliard}[196] in *Études Carmélitaines, Nos Sens et Dieu* [1954], p. 180 and ff.).

d) The mystical action of {the} spiritual senses must also not be confused with the literary use of ordinary sensible data in order to convey or express the inexpressible. There are many mystical texts where sense experience is used allegorically, or

---

192. "Taste and see [that the Lord is good]" (Ps. 33 [34]:9).

193. "in and of itself"; "by its very nature."

194. "There is nothing in the intellect that is not first in the senses" (quoted in M. Olphe-Galliard, sj, "Les Sens Spirituels dans l'Histoire de la Spiritualité," *Études Carmélitaines*, 2: *Nos Sens et Dieu* [1954], 180).

195. "the exercise of interior grace with respect to God Himself": *Commentary on the Sentences*, *III*, D. 13, dub. 1, *Sancti Bonaventurae Opera Omnia*, ed. PP. Collegii S. Bonaventurae, 10 vols. (Quaracchi: Collegium Sancti Bonaventurae, 1882–1902), 3:291, quoted in Olphe-Galliard, "Sens Spirituels," 186.

196. Merton consistently misspells this name as "Olphe Gaillard."

metaphorically. This is a literary and poetic, one might say an aesthetic, function of the senses, and must not be explained by the term "spiritual senses": v.g. in the poem "Dark Night" when St. John of the Cross speaks of going down a secret stairway, and in disguise.[197] These are poetic images.

e) *Special Problems created by the Doctrine of the Spiritual Senses in the West*:

1. The doctrine of the spiritual senses which began with Origen is *united* in Gregory of Nyssa with apophatic mysticism in a *perfectly integrated wholeness*. The two approaches to the phenomenology of mysticism balance and correct one another. The doctrine of the spiritual senses develops *both* in Western and Eastern Christendom. In an early, simple and traditional form we find a sane and unassuming doctrine of the spiritual senses not so much *exposed* as *supposed*—in St. Benedict and St. Gregory the Great: in the *Rule*—*apertis oculis ad Deificum lumen*;[198] *aurem cordis*;[199] in St. Gregory—*palatum cordis*;[200] *in aure cordis*.[201] The advantage is that the doctrine remains simple, concrete, biblical, and is not an analysis or systematization of experience but simply a statement of loving knowledge: *Amor ipse notitia est*.[202] There is

---

197. *The Complete Works of Saint John of the Cross*, ed. and trans. E. Allison Peers, 3 vols. (Westminster, MD: Newman Press, 1946), 1.10.

198. "Let us open our eyes to the divine light" (*Rule*, Prologue, 1 [McCann, 6/7]).

199. "[incline] the ear of thy heart" (*Rule*, Prologue, 1 [McCann, 6/7]).

200. "the palate of the heart" (*Epistola* 17 [*PL* 77, col. 921A]).

201. "in the ear of the heart" (used frequently by Gregory: see *PL* 75, col. 706B [*Moralia*, Bk. 5, c. 29]; *PL* 76, cols. 535B, 535C, 902B, 927C, 948A, 1150B [*Moralia*, Bk. 30, c. 5; *Homelia in Ezechiel*, Bk. 1, 6.39, 12.19, Bk. 2, 2.18; *Homelia in Evangelia*, I.18.1]; *PL* 77, col. 1130D).

202. "Love itself is a kind of knowledge" (St. Gregory the Great: *Homily* 27.4 [*PL* 76, col. 1207A]; St Bernard, *De Diversis*, 29.1, quoting Gregory [*PL* 183, col. 620BC]); see also the similar phrase "*Amor ipse intellectus est*" used by William of St. Thierry in his *Disputatio adversus Petrum Abaelardum* (*PL* 180, col. 252C), in the *Epistola ad Fratres de Monte Dei* (*PL* 184, col. 356A) and in his *Commentary on the Song of Songs* (*PL* 180, cols. 491D, 499C).

no theorizing about the spiritual senses. The statements made are often rather vague and offhand, so that one is never quite sure if they involve more than a literary metaphor. The best and most traditional source for the spiritual senses is the *rite of baptism* (q.v.).[203] We regret that we have to pass over the very important relation of the spiritual senses to the sacramental life in which they are principally developed.

2. But the doctrine of the spiritual senses is sometimes over-emphasized, to the detriment of the apophatic element. Where this happens, the impression is created that mysticism is simply sensible experience on a miraculous plane—objective visions of the Sacred Humanity of Christ, etc.

203. In the rite of baptism of adults, the priest made the sign of the cross successively on the ears, eyes, nostrils and mouth of the person to be baptized, saying in turn: "*Signo tibi aures, ut audias divina praecepta, . . . oculos, ut videas claritatem Dei. . . . nares, ut odorem suavitatis Christi sentias. . . . os, ut loquaris verba vitae*" ("I make the sign on your ears, that you might hear the divine commands, . . . on your eyes, that you might see the light of God, . . . on your nostrils, that you might be aware of the odor of the sweetness of Christ, . . . on your mouth, that you might speak the words of life"); soon afterward, he prayed, ". . . *omnem caecitatem cordis ab eo (ea) expelle . . . et ad suavem odorem praeceptorum tuorum laetus (-a) tibi in Ecclesia tua deserviat*" (". . . drive away all blindness from his (her) heart . . . and may he (she) serve you in your Church, made joyful by the sweet odor of your commandments"); after the salt was blessed, the priest said to the catechumen, "*Accipe sal sapientiae*" ("Receive the salt of wisdom") and prayed, ". . . *hoc primum pabulum salis gustantem, non diutius esurire permittas, quo minus cibo expleatur caelesti*" (". . . may You no longer allow the one tasting this food of salt for the first time to hunger or to be satisfied with anything less than heavenly food"); later in the ceremony, the priest placed his hand on the head of the one to be baptized and prayed, ". . . *ut digneris eum (eam) illuminare lumine intelligentiae tuae*" (". . . that you might deign to enlighten him (her) with the light of your understanding"); shortly afterward, touching the ears and nostrils of the baptizand with saliva, he declared, "*Ephpheta, quod est, Adaperire . . . In odorem suavitatis*" ("*Ephpheta, that is, be opened . . . In the odor of sweetness*") (*Rituale Romanum* [New York: Benziger, 1953], 26, 27–28, 29, 40, 42); except for the initial signing of the senses, all these rites were also part of the baptism of infants (11–12, 12–13, 14, 15).

3. In actual fact the doctrine of the spiritual senses tends to be emphasized in Western mysticism especially in the traditions of St. Augustine and St. Bonaventure and precisely where there is most emphasis on the Sacred Humanity of Christ. In this tradition we find "The Presence of Christ the Spouse is the proper object of contemplation and *each of His perfections is the particular object of one of the spiritual senses*" ({Olphe-Galliard,} *art. cit.*).[204] Hence the spiritual senses flourish in "bridal mysticism," and especially in reference to the *kiss of the Spouse*, mystical embraces, *wounds of love*. The full flowering of the spiritual senses comes in participation in the sufferings of Christ and in *stigmatization* which is miraculous, involves the body, and {is} *peculiar to Western mysticism*. This aspect of mysticism tends therefore towards the miraculous and "extraordinary."

4. In the West, there is a tendency for theologians who are not themselves mystics, *in reaction against genuine but apophatic mysticism*, to overemphasize the spiritual senses. Cardinal Peter D'Ailly, reacting against Ruysbroeck and the Rhenish mystics, wrote a whole treatise based on "spiritual senses."[205] This tends towards *complication and rationalization*. The spiritual senses become *materialized*. The "spiritual senses" are objectified as *new entities* "grafted on to the theological virtues and the gifts of the Holy Spirit."[206] They are *systematically categorized* and labelled: spiritual light = a perfection of faith and gift of understanding; taste and touch {are} associated with charity and {the} gift of wisdom; smell and hearing—no doubt there are some fantastic attempts to fit in "spiritual smell" with hope?

5. *Poulain* is one of those who has made the spiritual senses absolutely central in his doctrine on mysticism. After having distinguished ordinary and mystic prayer, the latter beginning with the prayer of quiet, he distinguishes mystical prayer by its

204. Olphe-Galliard, "Sens Spirituels,"187.
205. According to Olphe-Galliard ("Sens Spirituels,"190), thirteen chapters of *Compendium Contemplationis*.
206. Olphe-Galliard, "Sens Spirituels,"185.

"fundamental characteristics" (see especially chapters 5 and 6).[207] These characteristics he divides into *principal* and *subsidiary*. The principal characteristics of mystical prayer according to Poulain are: (1) the "felt presence of God";[208] (2) the interior possession of God by the interior senses. The subsidiary characteristics:[209] {the} mystical union or act is independent of our own will; {it} gives a knowledge of God that is obscure or confused; {it} is partially incommunicable; {it is} not produced by reasoning or by the consideration of sensible images or of creatures; {it} varies in intensity; {it} involves less effort than meditation; {it is} accompanied by sentiments of repose, love, suffering, etc.; {it} efficaciously inclines {the} soul to different virtues; {it} acts upon the body and is acted upon by the body in return; {it} impedes certain interior acts (ligature).[210] Remarks: in general, if we take into account what Poulain says about "ligature" and about the obscurity of mystical prayer, we can see that there are elements in this which tend to preserve the apophatic quality of mystical prayer. However, the fact that he places all the emphasis on the *felt* presence of God and on possession of God by the spiritual senses seems to be regrettable and likely to create a completely wrong idea of the real nature of mystical prayer. In speaking of the felt presence of God Poulain is evidently trying to contrast it with an intellectual and abstract knowledge of God. But the words "felt presence" are inadequate and misleading. Poulain does take into account the fact that there is a mystical prayer in which God is experienced only as "absent"—i.e. in the Two Nights.[211]

The spiritual senses according to Poulain:

207. Poulain, 64–113.
208. Poulain, chapter 5: "First Fundamental Character of the Mystic Union: God's Presence Felt."
209. Poulain, chapters 7-14: Ten Subsidiary Characteristics (114–99).
210. Poulain, chapter 14 (178–99).
211. Poulain, chapter 15 (200–19).

a) He makes clear that they have nothing to do with the ordinary exterior or interior sense; {it is} not a matter of imagination.[212]

b) They are *intellectual and direct perceptions* of "the existence of other beings"[213] (God and angels) on a spiritual and mystical level. They are an "angelic type of intuition";[214] analogously akin to the external senses, they perceive the presence of God (always of course as object).

c) The sense of *touch* belongs to the lower degrees of mystical prayer. The sense of *sight* operates only in the highest level of mystical prayer. The sense of spiritual *touch* gives a "sensation of imbibition or immersion"[215] in God. (The expression is a typical barbarism. It probably would be better to render it in the less offensive but more vague "oceanic feeling," which is used by psychologists and which Freud asserted he "never had"[216]—though the oceanic feeling is not necessarily mystical.) Spiritual touch

212. Poulain, 88.

213. Poulain, 88 (not a direct quotation).

214. Cf. Poulain, 88–89 n.

215. Poulain, 91: "a sensation of imbibition (saturation), of fusion, of immersion."

216. In the opening pages of *Civilization and Its Discontents* (trans. James Strachey [New York: W. W. Norton, 1961]), Sigmund Freud describes the "feeling as of something limitless, unbounded—as it were, 'oceanic'" described in a letter from a friend (identified in a note [12] as Romain Rolland, writing on December 5, 1927), who commented, "One may . . . rightly call oneself religious on the ground of this oceanic feeling alone, even if one rejects every belief and every illusion" (11); Freud goes on to remark, "I cannot discover this 'oceanic' feeling in myself" (12). In a December 26, 1961 letter to Jeanne Burdick, Merton wrote, "Freud did not think much of a mysticism which was described as 'an oceanic feeling' and I think in a way he was rather right in his suspicion of it, though he was a great old puritan that man! Oceanic feeling is not something that has to be rejected just because it might suggest a danger of narcissism. But pure love, disinterested love, is far beyond the reach of narcissism and I think even old Freud would have caught on that this was an equivalent of mature and oblative love in the ordinary psychophysical sphere" (*Hidden Ground of Love*, 110).

"can become an embrace"[217]—i.e. "sudden and affectionate clasp-
ings"[218] take place.

Poulain does well to emphasize the existence and reality of
the spiritual senses, but his treatment tends to objectify and to
materialize them, and therefore it is misleading. It would be fatal
for directors to systematically seek out manifestations of each
spiritual sense in order to determine whether or not they were
dealing with "a mystic" (!!).
    M. {Olphe-Galliard} (*Études Carmélitaines, art. cit.*): while ad-
mitting the pitfall of oversystematization into which theologians
of the present day fall when treating this subject, he does little
to simplify his ontological explanation of the spiritual senses:[219]
they are gratuitous gifts working in the spiritual organism ani-
mated by grace; they are virtually contained in baptismal justification (true, see {the} rite of baptism); they are "grafted on to
the virtues and gifts" (!!) (and I suppose they are suspended from
the fruits and beatitudes). They are not habits or faculties but
special acts of perfected habits, etc., etc. This kind of theology
explains little. It easily degenerates into pure verbalism. However
M. {Olphe-Galliard} is more helpful and illuminating when he
distinguishes between the spiritual senses which are related to
the *intellect* and those which are related to the *will* [220] (though we
will see this psychological approach is also unsatisfactory). Those
senses that perfect an act of the intellect attain to God *mediately*,
that is to say, through an interior effect: *in aliquo effectu interiori*[221]—

217. Poulain, 108.
218. Poulain, 85.
219. Olphe-Galliard, "Sens Spirituels," 185–86: it should be noted that he
is presenting St. Bonaventure's teaching on the spiritual senses here.
220. Olphe-Galliard, "Sens Spirituels," 186, summarizing Karl Rahner,
"La Doctrine des Sens Spirituels au Moyen Âge, surtout chez S. Bonaventure,"
Revue d'Ascetique et de Mystique, 14 (1933), 263–99.
221. "*in aliquo effectu interiori cognoscitur* [*Deus*]" ("God is known in some
interior effect") (Olphe-Galliard, "Sens Spirituels,"188, quoting Bonaventure, *II
Sent*, D. 23, a. 2, q. 3 [*Opera Omnia*, 2:544]).

so for instance sight and taste (through the *dulcedo*[222] of the divine presence, or of love, apprehended as an effect of His invisible presence). (Yet he has previously referred taste to charity and wisdom.[223]) Those that are perfective of *love* attain to God directly and without medium of any effect. They operate in *ecstasy*. Thus especially spiritual *touch*: it reduces the intelligence to silence; it brings into play the *apex affectus*[224] (this {is} important for spiritual sensitivity and contact with God—cf. also called *scintilla animae*, *synderesis*, etc.); in the action of spiritual touch, love and knowledge are one; the experience of God is obscure; it is an *amplexus* without any intelligible species.[225] This last description is of value especially because it coincides with the descriptions given by the Cistercian Fathers, and in particular William of St. Thierry.[226] It also fits in well with the doctrine of Gregory of Nyssa. This theory is evidently the opposite of Poulain's, for Poulain says that the spiritual sense of touch comes into play in ordinary mystical experience of the lower levels, and sight ("intellectual vision") develops only in ecstasy. There is not much point in arguing about it, because it is simply a matter of following different texts of various authors and attempting to *systematize* and categorize. There is no hierarchy of spiritual senses, at least none that is strictly definable. There is some point in distinguishing those which attain to God mediately and those which attain to Him immediately. (How valid is this distinction?) The lesson of this is that the doctrine of the spiritual senses when it is expressed in scholastic or phenomenological terms is confusing and inconclusive. And it is especially unfortunate that the doctrine gets lost in psychology.

---

222. "sweetness" (Olphe-Galliard, "Sens Spirituels,"189).

223. Olphe-Galliard, "Sens Spirituels,"188.

224. "the high point of the spirit" (Olphe-Galliard, "Sens Spirituels,"188).

225. "embrace" (Olphe-Galliard, "Sens Spirituels,"188).

226. See William's *Commentary on the Song of Songs* (*PL* 180, cols. 490C, 490D, 506C, 507C, 512A).

What about another approach? *Don Anselm Stolz (Théologie de la Mystique*, 231 ff.)[227] opposes and corrects Poulain's theory:

1) Poulain's theory is plausible, but as far as the spiritual senses go, the genuine traditional view is that the spiritual senses are *a restoration of man's* (innocent) *sensibility* which has been materialized by original sin (p. 231).[228]

2) With the loss of man's first state of grace our sensibility was limited to sense objects, whereas before it participated, in its own mode, with the Spirit's mystical union with God—hence in the paradisiacal state the whole man, sense and spirit, enjoyed mystical union with God.

3) The Holy Spirit, by ascetic purification, regains control of the whole man. Hence the exercise of the spiritual senses is not a matter of an extraordinary psychological act, nor is it a matter of special spiritual senses in the soul which are *opposed to the bodily senses*, but rather an exercise of the *spiritualized senses* on a mystical level.

This view has the advantage of being perfectly in accord with the mystical theology of the *Oriental Church*. The Greeks take an entirely different approach from that we have discussed in Poulain and {Olphe-Galliard}. They do not try to *account for mystical apprehensions* by pointing to the senses; rather they try to account for the *share of the senses* in mystical experience. Mystical experience is spiritual, and it *reaches the senses in a spiritual way* through and in the spirit. The "spiritual senses" are thus the senses themselves, but spiritualized and under the sway of the spirit, rather than new spiritual faculties. {See} *Gregory Palamas, The Defense of the Holy Hesychasts* (tr. in French by Meyendorff[229]): "That which takes place in the body coming from the soul filled

---

227. ET: 211-12.

228. ET: 211.

229. Grégoire Palamas, *Défense des Saints Hésychastes,* ed. and trans. Jean Meyendorff, 2 vols. (Louvain: Spicilegium Sacrum Lovaniense Administration, 1959); on March 3, 1961 Merton mentions that this is his "Lenten book" for this year (*Turning Toward the World*, 98).

with spiritual joy, is a *spiritual reality* even though it is active in the body" (Meyendorff I:334-5).[230] "The spiritual joy that comes from the spirit into the body *is not at all corrupted by communion with the body,* but transforms the body and makes it spiritual" (*id.*). Such spiritual activities do not carnalize the spirit but "deify the body" (*id.* 342-43).[231] *One should study in detail this passage* (342-343-344-345). In justice to Poulain we might remark that his observation on the interaction of body and spirit in mystical experience is related to this, but the perspective is quite different.

Spiritual Senses in St. Gregory of Nyssa. Origen's teaching on the spiritual senses plays a central part in the doctrine of Gregory of Nyssa. The first thing that is notable about this is that the *restoration of the spiritual senses is a return to man's paradisiacal state* (cf. Stolz[232]). Here we find the basis of the whole Oriental doctrine. However this return is a matter of mortification of the bodily senses. In the *De Virginitate* {we read}: "We must become again what the first man was . . . . A stranger to the pleasures of sight and taste, he found his delight in the Lord alone. Hence renouncing the illusions of sight and taste we must cling to the only true good";[233] and again: "It is not by using the ordinary faculty of hearing that the spirit comes to hear the celestial music, but by rising above the carnal senses and ascending to the heights it perceives the harmony of the heavens."[234] From these texts it is clear that the senses are certainly spiritualized by ascetic purity and by the *life of virginity.*

One might add, the liturgy has a great part to play. The connection between virginity of spirit and the renewal of the spiritual

230. *Triad* II.2.9.

231. *Triad* II.2.12.

232. Stolz, 231; ET: 211; see also Daniélou, *Platonisme et Théologie Mystique*, 222–24.

233. *PG* 46, col. 374C (c. 13), quoted in Daniélou, *Platonisme et Théologie Mystique*, 224.

234. *In Psalmos*, c. 3 (*PG* 44, col. 440D), quoted in Daniélou, *Platonisme et Théologie Mystique*, 227.

senses is therefore essential. Stolz may be right when he says that the spiritual senses are the ordinary senses on a higher and spiritual level, rather than essentially different faculties in the intellect alone. However this is not absolutely clear in Gregory of Nyssa. The point should be studied further.

Daniélou, commenting on Gregory of Nyssa's teaching,[235] points out that:

a) the doctrine of the spiritual senses is not taken up by the Dionysian tradition;

b) the presence of the doctrine of the spiritual senses in Gregory {of} Nyssa together with his apophatic theology means that he unites in himself the Biblical and Platonic traditions, the apophatic tradition of Dionysius and John of the Cross, with the cataphatic tradition of Diadochos and St. Bernard.[236] This confronting of apparently "opposed" traditions, even when they are "united" in an exceptional figure, is not always satisfactory. The oppositions can be accepted with reserve, but whole doctrines must not be built on them (cf. what we shall have to say below about the thesis of "Western mysticism"[237]).

The awakening of the spiritual senses belongs to an advanced stage of the spiritual life. For Origen they awaken gradually one after another and the *teleios*[238] is one in whom they are all awake. Not only active purification is required but also *passive purification* (trial, the "desert"). Daniélou[239] contrasts "sun mystics" like Origen and St. Augustine, in whom the spiritual senses of vision and taste are most obvious, and mystics of night, like St. John of the Cross and Gregory {of} Nyssa, in whom other senses are most important. In St. John of the Cross it is above all the sense of *touch*. In St. Gregory of Nyssa, the spiritual sense of

---

235. Daniélou, *Platonisme et Théologie Mystique*, 222–52.
236. Daniélou, *Platonisme et Théologie Mystique*, 224.
237. Pages 168–70.
238. "the perfected one."
239. Daniélou, *Platonisme et Théologie Mystique*, 231.

smell is important,[240] {exemplifying the} oriental tendency to speak of God perceived as a perfume or spiritual fragrance in darkness (cf. also St. Teresa of Avila, quoted by Poulain[241]). In "divine darkness" God is perceived as fragrance, tasted as sweetness, "touched" in existential contact. But we must always remember that for St. Gregory of Nyssa and St. John of the Cross these experiences are of God *beyond experience*, in "unknowing," and we should never grasp the experience for its own sake. "For him there is no vision of God but only an experience of the presence of God; that is to say, God is grasped as a person in an existential contact, beyond all intelligence and finally in a relation of love."[242] In Gregory the progress is then from light to darkness, as it is also in St. John of the Cross, rather than a progress from darkness to light as in Origen and Evagrius, etc. Daniélou points out that this is more real, and existential knowledge of God beyond knowledge and beyond light *is the very essence of mystical theology*.[243] (The biblical basis for this is found in Deuteronomy 4:12 ff., Exodus 33.)

In resumé, then: Poulain, following the mystics of light, tends to say that sight is at the top of a supposed hierarchy of spiritual senses. But actually the mysticism of light tends to be light *in its exposition*. The reality of the mystical experience is *expressed in terms of light* when there is need to communicate it to others. Hence what is operative here is not always the "spiritual sense of vision" but rather perhaps more often than we realize the *literary choice of metaphors of light*. Those who use the language of night and darkness not only remain more faithful to their experience but also communicate it in a way that is perhaps baffling but nevertheless more accurate. This is not to say that there are not many mystics who actually experience God in a most positive

240. Daniélou, *Platonisme et Théologie Mystique*, 231.

241. *Interior Castle*, Fourth Mansion, 2.6; Sixth Mansion, 2.14, quoted in Poulain, 112–13.

242. Daniélou, *Platonisme et Théologie Mystique*, 232.

243. Daniélou, *Platonisme et Théologie Mystique*, 232.

way as light. The apophatic mystics themselves are definite about the positive light that they perceive negatively in darkness. It is a true light, not seen by the senses of the body, but by the spiritual senses of the soul. Hence it is seen "in darkness," yet the light seen in darkness is at the same time "brighter than any other light" and indeed it blinds "by excess of light." Hence, in the terms of St. John of the Cross, he who *sees a light* (directly and positively) has not seen the true light, but something far below it.

Texts from *St. Gregory of Nyssa*: commenting on the Canticle, obviously the sense of touch is primary: "*Osculetur me osculo oris sui.*"[244] If these are the opening words of the *Canticum Mysticum*, there is certainly a definite significance in the fact. St. Gregory says: "There is a certain touch of the soul by which it touches the Word . . . by a certain incorporeal contact which falls under the understanding. . . . The odor of the divine ointments is not sensed by the nostrils but by the intelligence, and by any immaterial virtue."[245] (He says the divine names leave a faint trace of the fragrance of God as He really is, like the trace of perfume in an empty container.) The soul does not really touch the Word Himself, but traces and illuminations of Him which are accessible to our intelligence. Here the contact with God is *mediate*. In darkness, "the Spouse is surrounded by divine night in which the Bridegroom approaches without showing Himself . . . but in giving the soul a certain sentiment of His presence while avoiding clear knowledge" (*Hom. XI in Cant.*).[246] This appears to be direct and existential apprehension of the *presence* of the Word rather than of the *Word as He is in Himself*. Light and darkness are one—*lampros gnophos*: "shining darkness."[247]

---

244. "Let him kiss me with the kiss of his mouth" (Cant. 1:1).

245. *PG* 44, col. 780D, quoted in Daniélou, *Platonisme et Théologie Mystique*, 225–26.

246. *PG* 44, col. 1001B, quoted in *Histoire de Spiritualité*, vol. 1, 437; ET: 363.

247. *De Vita Moysis*, 2.163 (*PG* 44, col. 377A), quoted in *Histoire de Spiritualité*, vol. 1, 437; ET: 363.

Religious knowledge starts out as light [the burning bush] when it first appears: for then it is opposed to impiety, which is darkness, and this darkness is scattered by joy in the light. But the more the spirit in its forward progress attains by a greater and more perfect application to the understanding of the realities, and comes closer to contemplation, it realizes that the divine nature is invisible. Having left behind all appearances, not only those perceived by the senses but also those which the intelligence believes itself to see, the spirit enters more and more into the interior until it penetrates, by its striving, even unto the Invisible and the Unknowable, and there it sees God. The true knowledge of Him that it seeks and the true vision of Him consists in seeing that He is invisible, because He transcends all knowledge, and is hidden on all sides by His incomprehensibility as by shadows (*De Vita Moysis* II:162).[248]

(Compare St. John of the Cross, *Ascent* II:3, 4; vol. I, p. 70 ff.[249])

V. Evagrius Ponticus—the "Prince of Gnostics"

A. *The Problem of Evagrius.* Evagrius of Pontus is one of the most important, the least known (till recently), the most neglected and the most controversial of Christian mystics. He merits, with Gregory of Nyssa, the title of "Father of Christian Mystical Theology." He was an Origenist and the greatest of the theologians of Egyptian monachism at the end of the fourth century when

248. *PG* 44, cols. 376D–377A, quoted in *Histoire de Spiritualité*, vol. 1, 436–37; ET: 363–64.

249. In these chapters St. John explains "that, for the soul, this excessive light of faith which is given to it is thick darkness, for it overwhelms that which is great and does away with that which is little, even as the light of the sun overwhelms all other lights whatsoever" (70), supporting his statement by scriptural references, including the pillar of cloud in Exodus, which "was full of darkness and gave light by night," just as "faith, which is a black and dark cloud to the soul . . . should with its darkness give light and illumination to the darkness of the soul" (72–73).

Cassian visited Scete. Being a confirmed intellectualist with very complex and abstruse theories, he frightened the simple-minded monks and clerics of his time in the desert.

The Reputation of Evagrius: Evagrius enjoyed great influence in his lifetime. His doctrine persisted after his death and influenced some of the most important theologians in the West as well as in the East. The paradox is that those who used him, whether knowingly or otherwise, ascribed his teachings to someone else whose name was more "acceptable." For the name of Evagrius became mud, or worse. He fell with the Origenists and was execrated by the enemies of Origen.

Against Evagrius: the Greek and Latin Churches as a whole were against Evagrius. Moschus, in the *Pratum Spirituale*,[250] records the legend that Evagrius' cell at Scete was haunted by a devil. The story was told that Evagrius was in hell among the heretics. St. John Climacus,[251] while being strongly influenced by the Evagrian teachings, nevertheless condemns Evagrius by name. St. Maximus has been proved by Viller (*RAM*, April 1930 ff.[252]) to be clearly a disciple of Evagrius. He is not only full of Evagrian doctrines but can be said *to base his* teaching on Evagrius. However the teachings are ascribed to others. Modern scholars, while admiring him, still do not praise him without qualification. Von Balthasar calls him "Buddhist rather than Christian."[253] Though Evagrius speaks often of contemplation of the Trinity, von Balthasar and Hausherr[254] maintain that this is purely verbal

---

250. John Moschos, *The Spiritual Meadow*, trans. John Wortley, CS 139 (Kalamazoo, MI: Cistercian Publications, 1992), 146–47, 18.

251. St. John Climacus, *The Ladder of Divine Ascent*, trans. Archimandrite Lazarus Moore, 14:12 (New York: Harper & Brothers, 1959), 141.

252. See note 46 above.

253. Hans Urs von Balthasar, "Metaphysik und Mystik des Evagrius Ponticus," *Zeitschrift für Aszese und Mystik*, 14 (1939), 39 (see *Histoire de Spiritualité*, vol. 1, 457; ET: 381); this article is now available in English: "The Metaphysics and Mystical Theology of Evagrius," *Monastic Studies*, 3 (1965), 183–95.

254. Irénée Hausherr, *Les Leçons d'un Contemplatif: Le traité de l'Oraison d'Evagre le Pontique* (Paris: Beauchesne, 1960), 98–99.

and that by "Trinity" he just means "God"—that his mysticism is not fully Trinitarian. Bouyer defends Evagrius on this and on other points.[255]

For Evagrius: The Arabian and Syrian Christians, who were less affected by the Origenist conflict and its passions, had no reason to hate Evagrius. Hence they continued to praise him and to admire him. It is through the fact of his survival in Syrian manuscripts that he has come to light again in our time. The Syrian texts have established conclusively that the great works on *Prayer* etc. are really his and not to be ascribed to anyone else. Isaac of Nineveh (Nestorian mystic and bishop) calls Evagrius the "Prince of Gnostics"—"the wise one among the saints" and "the Blessed Mar Evagrios."[256] When works of Isaac, quoting Evagrius favorably, were translated into Greek, the name of Evagrius was suppressed and names of accepted writers like Gregory Nazianzen would be substituted for it. L. Bouyer is the most outspoken advocate of Evagrius at the present moment.

Life of Evagrius: born at Ibora on the Black Sea, {he} went to Constantinople, then fled from the temptations of the city. {He} went to Cappadocia, was a friend of Basil and the two Gregories, was introduced by them to the writings of Origen, and to the monastic life. {He} was ordained deacon either by Basil or Gregory {of} Nyssa. {He} went on to Jerusalem where he was in contact with St. Melania and the Origenist Rufinus. He became a monk at Scete under St. Macarius, lived in the "desert of {the} cells," and died on the feast of the Epiphany {in} 399, just before the outbreak of the great Origenist conflict which ruined his reputation.

Rediscovery of Evagrius: the most widely read work of Evagrius, in which there is nothing heretical (he is not a heretic), is the *De Oratione*, which was so popular and so influential that

---

255. *Histoire de Spiritualité*, vol. 1, 469-70; ET: 392.

256. See Isaac of Nineveh, *Mystic Treatises*, trans. A. J. Wensinck (1923; Wiesbaden: Sändig, 1969): "the sage among the saints, Mar Euagrius" (72); "the blessed Euagrius" (297, 306, 333, 345); "the holy Euagrius" (334); "one of the holy Fathers, Euagrius, one of the initiated" (383).

it could not help but survive. Its authorship was simply ascribed to another—"St. Nilus." For centuries this treatise was read, praised and used, and Evagrius exercised great influence as "Nilus." In 1912 Frankenberg[257] discovered the works of Evagrius that had been preserved in Syriac. {In} 1923, the *Evagrios Studien* of {Bousset}[258] drew attention to Evagrius. The most important and difficult work of Evagrius, the *Kephalaia Gnostica*, preserved in Syriac, has been re-edited in a better version, with a French translation, in 1958.[259] Fr. I. Hausherr, SJ of the Pontifical Oriental Institute proved definitively that the *De Oratione* was by Evagrius, and twice presented studies and translations, commentaries, of this work in the *RAM*, first in 1934 and then in 1959.[260] This has finally appeared in book form {in} 1960.[261] The *Selecta in Psalmos*, hitherto ascribed to Origen, in *PG* 12, were restored to Evagrius by H. von Balthasar.[262] M. Viller, SJ showed the influence of Evagrius on the teaching (perfectly orthodox) of St. Maximus the Confessor (*RAM*, 1930 f.). Some of the works of Evagrius had survived under his name in the *PG* 40, such as the *Praktikos*, the *Mirror of Monks*, the *Letter to Anatolios*.[263]

---

257. W. Frankenberg, *Evagrius Pontikus* (Berlin: Weidmannsche Buchhandlung, 1912).

258. Wilhelm Bousset, *Apophthegmata: Studien zur Geschichte des ältesten Mönchtums* (Tübingen: Mohr, 1923) (Merton misspells the name as Bossuet, as he does in *Cassian and the Fathers*).

259. *Les Six Centuries des 'Kephalaia Gnostica' d'Évagre le Pontique*, ed. Antoine Guillaumont, *Patrologia Orientalis*, 28.1 (Paris: Firmin-Didot, 1958); this edition includes the original Syriac and French translations for both text traditions of this work, in which each of the six centuries actually consists of only ninety chapters; the so-called "Century Supplement" of sixty additional chapters is, according to Guillaumont, actually a separate work, sometimes given the title *Chapters on Knowledge* (5, n. 2).

260. See n. 45 above.

261. *Les Leçons d'un Contemplatif*.

262. Hans Urs von Balthasar, "Die Hiera des Evagrius," *Zeitschrift für Katholische Theologie*, 63 (1939), 86–106, 181–206 (see *Histoire de Spiritualité*, vol. 1, 457; ET: 381).

263. Cols. 1213–86.

The Teaching of Evagrius: the worldview of Evagrius is based on Origen and has come down to us in Cassian. It is exactly the philosophy behind the *Instituta* and the *Collationes* of Cassian. Hence it runs through all medieval monasticism.

1. A primitive spiritual cosmos (paradisiacal) fell with man into a state of sin and limitation (captivity). Matter has an intimate connection with this fallen condition of the cosmos. Man's primitive state was a pure contemplation of the Trinity with an intellect *naked of all forms*. He fell not only into attachment to forms but to *love of sensible objects* for their own sakes.

2. The demons tempt man through matter, and keep him enslaved to sense and passion.

3. Man's life on earth is a struggle against the demons, in which he attempts to evade their subtle temptations, to spiritualize matter, beginning with his own body, and return to union with God in a paradisiacal state, a life of "pure prayer" on a level with the *angels*. Man must return by the way he fell. First he must purify his body, his senses, his passions (*praxis*—active life), detaching himself from objects. Then he must spiritualize his knowledge of created things in "natural contemplation" (*theoria physike*). After that he must learn to contemplate *spiritual beings*. And finally he must recover *the contemplation of the Trinity without forms and without images*, from which he originally fell.

4. Evagrius does not simply *despise* the material world as a Platonist—his view of it is essentially Christian. "The body is a seed in relation to the wheat it will be [after the resurrection] and so too this present world is a seed of the world that is to come after it" (*Kephalaia Gnostica* II. 25).[264] Man's contemplative restoration in Christ is necessary for the recapitulation of the entire cosmos in Christ. The life of man is divided into *active* (*praktike*) and *contemplative* (*gnostike*). The active life begins in *faith and the fear of God*. This puts us on our guard against the temptations of the devil, and we must grow at the same time in the discernment

---

264. Guillaumont, *Six Centuries*, 71.

of spirits and in self-discipline (*egkrateia*) through patience and hope until we attain to freedom from passion, or *apatheia*. This is the summit of the active life and is required before one can enter into the truly spiritual and gnostic life of contemplation.

5. We must realize that for Evagrius the ascent to *gnosis* is not just a matter of seeking one's own spiritual purity. It is a *response to the will of God* for the restoration of the cosmos to its primitive state. God wills that all should come to the knowledge of the truth, that is of Himself. Hence all should seek to ascend to the purity of contemplation and the angelic life. The beginning, faith and the fear of God, shows us what God asks of all.

6. Furthermore, the summit is not just *gnosis* but *agape*, love. We shall see this later. Though there is indeed a strong emphasis on the intellectual side of contemplation in Evagrius, it is not true that he neglects the aspect of *love*.

7. The emphasis is not primarily on our own ascetic effort, in a Pelagian sense. Rather it is a question of submission and co-operation with God's will. Obscure as God's hidden judgements may be, it is basic to Evagrius' system that *all that God wills tends in some way or other to lead us to truth* and to Him, if we correspond with His will. The sufferings He sends us are remedies destined for our purification and for our good. In all that happens He has no other end than to bring us to contemplation and *agape*, so we must accept all that He sends with gratitude and energetic cooperation.

8. *Prayer* is the greatest of means of cooperating with the will of God. Evagrius repeatedly insists that we should not pray for our own will to be done or for our own desires to be fulfilled, but that God's will may be done—always in the perspective indicated above: God wills our union with Him. We should especially pray for our purification (1) from passions first of all (this is essential to the active life); (2) from ignorance (this is essential to the lower degree of the contemplative life); (3) from all temptation, darkness and dereliction (the higher degree of {the} contemplative life).

9. Finally the man of prayer or gnostic should seek not only his own purification but that of all men, especially men of prayer.

In this way he seeks first of all the Kingdom of God and His justice.

The Active Life (praktike) in Evagrius: time does not permit a detailed treatment of the asceticism of Evagrius. Suffice it to say that beginning with faith and the fear of God it struggles against the bodily passions as well as the more subtle spiritual passions, and strives to attain to *apatheia*, which implies complete control of the passions and is the summit of the active life.

The Question of Apatheia: this raises the question of *apatheia*— is this a genuinely Christian notion? If it can be reconciled with Christian teaching and doctrine, is it not still an extreme? Even if we admit its practicability for some rare souls, should we admit it as the logical term of the ascetic life for all? We must begin with a real understanding of the meaning of the term. *St. Jerome* in his *Epistle* 133 so grossly exaggerated the idea of *apatheia* which he attributed to his Origenist adversaries, that he has brought it unjustly under suspicion. It is not as bad as St. Jerome tries to make us believe. (St. Jerome has never been suspected of attaining to *apatheia*.) The letter of Jerome (133) is in fact directed against the Pelagians and against their idea of *apatheia* and impeccability which is certainly more extreme and less Christian than the *apatheia* of Evagrius and Origen, or of Gregory of Nyssa. (*Apatheia* is clearly stated to be the prerequisite for contemplation in Gregory of Nyssa's *Homilies on the Canticle of Canticles*.[265]) However Jerome lumps them all together. And he makes a special attack on Evagrius, with some very unchristian statements about his adversaries St. Melania and Rufinus, who were reading Evagrius. Jerome says Evagrius wrote to "her whose name of blackness [Melania] signifies the darkness of perfidy, and edited a book about *apatheia* . . . [a state] in which the soul is never moved by any vice of perturbation, and that I may state it simply, *such a soul becomes either a stone or a god*. The books of this man are read curiously in the East by the Greeks and in the West through the

265. See Daniélou, *Platonisme et Théologie Mystique*, 92–103.

translations of his disciple Rufinus. . . ."[266] The rest of the letter is about the Pelagians. However, *apatheia* has had a bad press in the West because of its associations with *Pelagianism* and *stoicism*. Also, the *Quietists* misused the term. In general it can be said that the common doctrine tends rather to follow St. Thomas,[267] who says that the passions are to be *used* and not reduced to complete silence. This is certainly the better understanding of man's condition and of his true vocation to go to God body and soul together. However it is possible that this more moderate view is after all not completely incompatible with Evagrius' idea of *apatheia*.

Defense of Evagrius:

1) If we want to get a less extreme and more humane and more practical notion of *apatheia* we can study the first *Conference* of Cassian, where the *puritas cordis* given as the proximate end of the monastic life corresponds exactly with the *apatheia* of Evagrius.[268] Note also Palladius in {the} Prologue to {the} *Historia Lausiaca*[269] contrasts *apatheia* with the activistic asceticism of some monks who placed their confidence in heroic practices and did not see that real ascetic purification must be achieved by peace, tranquillity, interior liberty—all grouped together as *apatheia*. If we translate *apatheia* as "insensibility" we will undoubtedly go wrong and our concept will certainly end by being unchristian. If we keep in mind that it means interior *peace* and tranquillity, born of detachment and freedom from slavery to inordinate

---

266. *PL* 22, col. 1151.

267. *Summa Theologiae*, 1a 2ae, q. 24 a. 2, ad. 3, cited in G. Bardy, "Apatheia," *DS* 1, col 745.

268. See *PL* 49, cols. 485–90, and Merton's discussion in *Cassian and the Fathers*, 205–10.

269. See Bardy, col. 733–34, and Palladius, *The Lausiac History*, trans. Robert T. Meyer, Ancient Christian Writers [ACW], vol. 34 (Westminster, MD: Newman, 1965), Prologue, 8: "For many of the brethren prided themselves on their labors and almsgiving and boasted of their celibacy or their virginity; they had every confidence in attention to divine prophecies and to acts of zeal, and still they never attained a state of quietude" (25).

passions, we will be able to appreciate it better. Certainly it does not have to mean the complete absence of all temptation, though for Evagrius etc. it certainly seems to mean a *habitual* tranquillity and freedom from temptation.

2) G. Bardy, writing in *DS* I:736, defends the idea of *apatheia* as it is found in the Greek Fathers. "It is not a matter of insensibility towards God Whom one must love above all else, nor of insensibility towards men, but of perfect liberty of spirit, perfect abandonment as the fruit of renunciation, perfect detachment from all things, humility, continual mortification and contempt for the body. This is a very lofty doctrine in which *apatheia* is brought back to human proportions, . . . and no longer has any of the rigorousness which the stoics assigned to it."[270]

3) Bouyer, in *Histoire de Spiritualité* (vol. 1, p. 462 f.)[271] sums up the case for Evagrius as follows:

a) *Apatheia* for Evagrius means control of all movements of passion that are opposed to charity.

b) It implies deliverance from the demons who work on us through the passions.

c) It liberates us and enables us to give ourselves completely to the worship of God.

d) Far from being a matter of insensibility, it purifies and elevates normal human sentiments.

e) It implies the ability to pray without distraction by corporeal images or thoughts inspired by passion.

f) It does *not imply impeccability* or the absence of temptation. One can still be tempted and one remains still subject to sin. But the depths of one's being are really fully committed to the love of God and hence one would have to go against his inmost tendencies in order to sin.

g) It brings a deep abiding peace to the depths of the heart united to God's will.

270. Bardy is referring here specifically to the *De Oratione*, 52 of Evagrius.
271. ET: 386–87.

h) *Apatheia* is not perfection. It still demands to be perfected in contemplation and *agape*, which finally complete the total purification.

i) *Apatheia* is ordered to *gnosis* and love. Love is the "excellent state of the reasonable soul in which it is not able to love anything corruptible more than the knowledge of God" (*Kephalaia Gnostica* I.86).[272]

Comments: when the *apatheia* of Evagrius and the Greek Fathers is interpreted in this favorable manner we can see that there is nothing wrong with it at all except perhaps that it still presents a certain danger—it can be misleading and this interpretation is not the most obvious one to the average reader. However it is certainly conformed to Christian ascetic tradition. What we ought to retain from all this *as a matter of pastoral concern* {includes the following}:

1. We ought to remember that there is no deep contemplative life without *a most serious ascetic purification*. We must not underestimate this. We must not be satisfied with the initial sacrifices required to bring one from the world to the monastery and to monastic profession. The purification must continue. It is a lifelong work.

2. We must understand clearly however that ascetic purification does not mean necessarily the use of very special, extraordinary and heroic practices of bodily mortification. The emphasis is on the end to be attained, which is interior peace. Cassian gives the right principle to follow: practices are subordinated to purity of heart. Those that enable us to attain to purity of heart are good. Others, no matter how good or how necessary they may seem, must be set aside if they stand in the way of purity of heart. (See *Conference* 1.[273])

---

272. Guillaumont, *Six Centuries*, 57.

273. *PL* 49, col. 487B (c. 5): "*Quidquid ergo nos ad hunc scopon, id est, puritatem cordis potest dirigere, tota virtute sectandum est; quidquid ab hac retrahit, ut perniciosum ac noxium devitandum*" ("Therefore whatever can direct us toward

3. It is not only legitimate but even desirable to think of the term of ascetic purification as a *state of peace and tranquillity* due to detachment and freedom from passionate drives that disturb prayer. It is legitimate to expect that this kind of purification may make a real life of prayer easy and simple. This concept of *apatheia*, tranquillity, includes and goes beyond the idea of abandonment to God's will. The monastic life should be so ordered that monks not only "obey" and "abandon themselves" whatever comes day by day, but also their daily life should be so ordered that they are gradually freed from distracting concerns and agitations that keep their minds in a whirl. They should live in an *atmosphere of peace and quiet*. This depends not only on their own obedience but also on the general recollection and detachment of the community and its life. Involvement in special activities, even with a seemingly spiritual purpose, can make this tranquillity impossible and frustrate the real end of monastic asceticism.

B. The *De Oratione* of Evagrius ("St. Nilus"). We now turn to Evagrius' classical work on prayer which, in spite of his disgrace, continued throughout the Patristic and Middle Ages to be a most powerful formative influence in Christian mysticism, attributed to "Nilus."

What is prayer? (Numbers in the following sections refer to the chapters on prayer as given by Hausherr.) Prayer is defined as a *"homilia* of the intelligence with God" (3).[274] *Homilia* is equivalent to *conversatio*, habitual intimacy; intelligence (*nous*) {is} therefore not of the affections only, and not of reasoning. This disposes us to accept the idea of prayer that is immediate intuitive contact with God, a habitual commerce with God, not a conversation in words or thoughts. Prayer of petition is given an important place in Evagrius. {He} also {focuses on} the attention with which we

---

this target, that is, purity of heart, should be followed with absolute commitment; but whatever pulls us away from it, should be shunned as dangerous and poisonous").

274. Hausherr, *Leçons*, 16.

approach God and the reverence with which we address Him: this is couched in terms resembling St. Benedict (see Hausherr, p. 17—references will be given as far as possible to the newly published: Hausherr, *Les Leçons d'un Contemplatif* [text of Evagrius *On Prayer*] Paris, 1960.)

N. 60 is important: "IF YOU ARE A THEOLOGIAN YOU WILL TRULY PRAY. IF YOU TRULY PRAY YOU ARE A THEOLOGIAN."[275] "Theologian" for Evagrius means mystic, one who experiences the things of God without intermediary. This state is not reached by study but by purity of heart. It does not consist in scientific knowledge about God, which can be possessed by the impure. "The Kingdom of God is not in words but in power; power, here, means the purity of the soul, and this comes from *charity*" (Evagrius, *Centuries*[276] V.26; Hausherr, p. 86).

N. 61: we begin to come close to "prayer," he says, "when the understanding, in ardent love for God, begins bit by bit to go forth from the flesh, and casts aside all thoughts that come from the senses, the memory, or the *temperament*, while at the same time being filled with respect and joy."[277] {It is} important to note:

a) The efficacy of love.

b) The setting aside of thoughts based on sense impressions and natural experience.

c) Temperament, *krasis*, is explained by Hausherr[278] to mean the psycho-physical organism which, even when one has attained to *apatheia*, can be worked on by the devil to produce visions. {It would be} very interesting to study this further in the light of Jung's theory of archetypes, for instance. In any case, like St. John

---

275. Hausherr, *Leçons*, 85.

276. This is the same work as the *Kephalaia Gnostica*; Hausherr is quoting from the earlier, less authentic version edited by W. Frankenberg in *Evagrius Pontikus*.—n.b. it is not found in S₁, the text of this version in Guillaumont, *Six Centuries*.

277. Hausherr, *Leçons*, 86–87.

278. Hausherr, *Leçons*, 99.

of the Cross, Evagrius teaches we must rise above all forms based on natural or preternatural experience.

d) The emptiness left by the absence of these experiences and impressions is filled by holy *awe and joy*. (N.B. fear of the Lord which is {the} beginning of wisdom, stressed by St. Chrysostom—see above.[279])

Hence he can define prayer in n. 35 as "AN ASCENT OF THE MIND TO GOD."[280] We shall see later in detail what this means.

Psalmody and Prayer: meanwhile we can clarify our notion of Evagrian prayer when we compare it with psalmody. The two are distinct. Psalmody is not necessarily choral or public prayer. It is vocal prayer. Psalmody belongs particularly to the active life. Not only is it an exterior, quantitative exercise, but psalmody helps to appease certain passions. The precise place of psalmody in the ascetic life is to calm the passion of anger, and to appease the *krasis* so that the devil cannot produce hallucinations. See nn. 83, 85:[281] in 85 we see psalmody described as part of what he calls "multiform wisdom,"[282] that is, the wisdom which deals with separate manifestations of God in created things and events, which goes from one object of thought to another, and from creatures to God, which is occupied with the varied *logoi* of created things.

N. 87: both psalmody and prayer are *charisms*,[283] special gifts of God, and we must pray God insistently to receive them. {There is} no illusion that psalmody is something easy and obvious and that prayer alone is difficult. In a quote from *Praktikos* 1:6 (Hausherr, p. 115) we see a further development that gives us a better *perspective of the ascetic life*: reading, watching and meditation help to settle the wandering mind; fasting, labor and solitude quiet the movements of concupiscence; anger is calmed by *psalm-*

---

279. Page 77 (but note that Chrysostom does not quote this verse).
280. Hausherr, *Leçons*, 53.
281. Hausherr, *Leçons*, 115, 119.
282. Hausherr, *Leçons*, 119.
283. Hausherr, *Leçons*, 122.

ody, patience and pity. All these things must be used at the proper times and in the proper measures, otherwise they do not have their proper effect. In n. 82,[284] the two special qualities of psalmody are *understanding* and *harmony* (unison with other monks??). Psalmody, having these qualities, joined to quiet, tranquil meditative prayer, leads to *apatheia*—one becomes a "young eagle"[285] soaring in the heights above the confusion and turmoil of the flesh. This is a very wise traditional description of the exercises of the *"bios praktikos"*[286] and of the spirit in which they are to be carried out.

Prayer, as contrasted with psalmody: prayer and psalmody must go together as we have just seen. Psalmody is oriented to the control of the body, the emotions, the passions. Prayer "leads the intelligence to exercise its proper activity" (83).[287] This proper activity of the intelligence is to see creatures in the light of God (lower level of contemplation, where prayer and psalmody have more or less the same object, multiform *gnosis*) or God Himself in the light of the Trinity. However, prayer alone is truly worthy of the dignity of the intelligence. To have psalmody without prayer would be to lead a life unworthy of the spirit of man. Psalmody demands to be fulfilled in contemplation without images. If it is not so fulfilled it remains frustrated and abortive, according to Evagrius.

The Summit of prayer is prayer without distraction (34a).[288] The summit of the ascent of the mind to God is a state in which the intelligence is *illuminated by the Holy Trinity*. Only the state of illumination by the Holy Trinity, beyond all concepts and images, can be called true prayer, says Evagrius (*Cent. Suppl.* 30, quoted by Hausherr, p. 86). Hence, there can be no distractions in this

---

284. Hausherr, *Leçons*, 114.
285. Hausherr, *Leçons*, 114.
286. "the 'practical' or active life."
287. Hausherr, *Leçons*, 115.
288. Hausherr, *Leçons*, 52 (this verse is omitted in the *PG* text, hence the "a").

state of pure prayer. Obviously this is a mystical grace and not something achieved by human efforts. (Pastoral note on distractions: obviously when in discursive prayer a man tries to exclude one thought and replace it by another, in "multiform *gnosis*"[289] he will often have a terrible struggle. Undistracted prayer is not, in Evagrius' terms, the ability to remain fixed on a thought or feeling of experience of God, even on God's presence. It is the resting in God's own light, not by our own efforts, but by His gift.) The state of undistracted prayer is variously called "the state of understanding" (*katastasis noos*), "the state of prayer" (*katastasis proseuches*) and theology, or *gnosis* of the Trinity.[290] Hence theology for Evagrius is really an illumination without reasoning, concepts, visions, images or anything of the sort.

The trials that come from the devil: there is a very important element of diabolism in this work of Evagrius. The illusions, hallucinations, temptations, and various assaults that take place on the contemplative are ascribed to the devil, God's adversary, to whose interest it is to prevent the spiritualisation of man, the divine image, and the glory of God fully resplendent in man. The devil therefore does all he can to prevent a man from becoming a true contemplative.

a) In the *Kephalaia Gnostica* (I.10),[291] Evagrius points out that some demons try to prevent us from keeping the commandments, others from attaining to natural contemplation, others from attaining to contemplation of God. In *Kephalaia Gnostica* III.76, he says, when we are formed in the womb we live as plants; when we are born we live as animals; when we are grown up we live as angels or as demons.[292]

b) We are never fully safe from temptation, even in *apatheia*. {It is an} illusion to imagine or to hope for a state in which we will

---

289. See below, n. 342.
290. Hausherr, *Leçons*, 53.
291. Guillaumont, *Six Centuries*, 21.
292. Guillaumont, *Six Centuries*, 129.

not be tempted. Even the perfect are tempted to impurity, especially in the imagination in the time of prayer (Hausherr, p. 123 f.). Evagrius adds that the demon of impurity does things to monks that "cannot be related"[293] for fear of scandalizing those who do not know about it. This is an early reference to the problem of *special impure temptations and accidents*, a problem that is never fully treated, only alluded to through the history of mysticism. Note: Evagrius, accepting the usual tripartite division of the soul,[294] says the following: the EPITHUMIA is renovated and restored by chastity; the THUMOS {by} love; the NOUS {by} contemplation.[295]

c) Special physical assaults of the devil, like those recorded in the life of the Curé d'Ars,[296] are described in nn. 91 ff. Not only does the devil work on the mind and thoughts, but even administers physical violence, striving to *produce terror*. Special hints and instructions are given so that the monk may be courageous and inflexible. Evagrius in his *Antirrheticos* ("The Contradictor") presents the monk with a manual, a collection of Scripture texts with which to defy the devil, to shout him down, to drive him out and treat him with contempt. It is practically a manual of exorcisms. (Practical note: direct argument with the devil {is} not to be encouraged!) {It is} important to note what Evagrius has to say about patience, humility, the help of the good angels, trust in God, etc.

d) *Spiritual temptations*: {these are} the ruses of the devil to produce illusions of spiritual perfection. They try above all to incite us to pride and vanity and self-love. They even pretend to allow themselves to be defeated, in order that we may get a swelled head and think ourselves saints (133, 134, 135, 136).[297]

---

293. *Antirrhetikos*, "Fornication," 65, quoted in Hausherr, *Leçons*, 124.

294. See Plato, *Phaedrus*, 246a-256e, the famous image in which the rational faculty (*nous*) is depicted as a charioteer that must control its two horses, the spirited and appetitive faculties (*thumos* and *epithumia*); the same division is also found in Book 4 of the *Republic*, 436–444, and in the *Timaeus*, 69b–70a.

295. *Kephalaia Gnostica*, III.35 (Guillaumont, *Six Centuries*, 111).

296. See Hausherr, *Leçons*, 126.

297. Hausherr, *Leçons*, 166–69.

They also tempt the saints to a sense of *guilt*: see *Kephalaia Gnostica* III.90: they "calumniate the gnostic"[298] in order to attract his mind to themselves. When he strives to justify himself before them a cloud overwhelms his mind and contemplation becomes impossible.

e) *False visions*: the devil especially tries to destroy contemplation by producing false "forms" under which we imagine we see God. When one has attained the height of prayer, then the characteristic temptation is to consent to a vision of God under some conceivable form. "They represent to the soul God under some form agreeable to the senses in order to make it believe that it has attained to the goal of prayer" (n. 72).[299] The temptation is thus to "localize God and take for the divinity a quantitative object. . . . But God is without quantity or figure" (n. 67).[300] These forms are produced by the action of the devil on the *krasis* (n. 68) and again the result is {that} "the soul becomes habituated to resting in concepts and is easily subjugated; this soul that was going forth to immaterial *gnosis* without form, now lets himself be deceived, taking smoke for the light" (68).[301]

These are very important chapters which may be compared to some of the classical passages of St. John of the Cross in *The Ascent of Mount Carmel*, for instance. The basic principle of St. John of the Cross is {that} "no thing created or imagined can serve the understanding as a proper means of union with God" (*Ascent*, II.8).[302] Read *Ascent* II.8, numbers 4 and 5:[303] "It is clear, then, that none of these kinds of knowledge can lead the understanding

---

298. Guillaumont, *Six Centuries*, 135; see also Hausherr, *Leçons*, 68, 159.

299. Hausherr, *Leçons*, 104.

300. Hausherr, *Leçons*, 96.

301. Hausherr, *Leçons*, 99.

302. Peers, *Complete Works of Saint John of the Cross*, 1.94.

303. N. 4 (Peers, *Complete Works of Saint John of the Cross*, 1.95–96) declares that imagination and understanding, dependent on the senses, cannot serve as a proximate means to union with God; n. 5 (Peers, *St. John*, 1.96–97) states that even a supernatural apprehension or understanding cannot be a proximate

direct to God; and that, in order to reach Him, a soul must rather *proceed by not understanding than by desiring to understand; and by blinding itself and setting itself in darkness rather than by opening its eyes in order the more nearly to approach the ray Divine"* (*Ascent*, II.8, n. 5).[304] *Re*: imaginary visions, read *Ascent*, II.16, nn. 3, 6,[305] and especially the end of 9:

> But there is none like My servant Moses, who is the most faithful in all My house, and I speak with him mouth to mouth, and he sees not God by comparisons, similitudes and figures. Herein He says clearly that, in this lofty state of union whereof we are speaking, God is not communicated to the soul by means of any disguise of imaginary vision or similitude or form, neither can He be so communicated; but mouth to mouth—that is, in the naked and pure essence of God, which is the mouth of God in love, with the naked and pure essence of the soul, which is the mouth of the soul in love of God (*Ascent*, II.16, n. 9).[306]

The Assistance of the Good Angels: the devils try to impede our prayer and create forms and images to keep us from God. The good angels are no less active (n. 74 ff.). First they pacify the soul, keep out distractions and diabolical interventions (74).[307] Their function is to prepare the way to the *locus Dei*,[308] the interior sanctuary of contemplation and *gnosis*. They protect us against sleep, boredom, torpor (devils produce these). They stimulate us

---

means in this life to divine union, which is beyond understanding (as the quoted concluding passage to this section points out).

304. Peers, *Complete Works of Saint John of the Cross*, 1.97 (emphasis added).

305. N. 3 (Peers, *Complete Works of Saint John of the Cross*, 1.131-32) states that both God and the devil can present images to the soul without using the outward senses; n. 6 (Peers, *St. John*, 1.132) emphasizes that the understanding should not cling to these visions, whatever their source, and the soul should remain detached from them.

306. Peers, *Complete Works of Saint John of the Cross*, 1.134.

307. Hausherr, *Leçons*, 108.

308. "the place of God" (n. 57; Hausherr, *Leçons*, 80).

to more pure love for God, thus facilitating prayer. N. 81 reads: "Know that the holy angels urge us on to pray and they remain then at our sides, joyful and praying for us. If then we are negligent and welcome alien {thoughts} we sorely grieve them, since, while they are fighting so zealously for us, we do not even wish to pray to God for ourselves, but despise their aid and abandon God their Lord in order to go out to meet the impure demons."[309] (An echo of this {is found} in Cistercian tradition, the recording angels in choir.[310]) Note that the good angels are always contemplating God and beings. They enjoy *theoria physike* uninterruptedly; men have it sometimes, demons *never* (see *Kephalaia Gnostica*, III.4[311]).

The Ascent of Prayer: "Prayer is an ascent of the mind to God."[312] {The} outline of the *bios theoretikos* (see *Kephalaia Gnostica* I.27[313]) {consists in}: {the} Kingdom of Christ (*theoria physike*) {involves} multiple *gnosis*, {of} beings and their *logoi*: (a) providence;

---

309. Hausherr, *Leçons*, 113–14 ("thoughts" was inadvertently x'd out in the typescript but restored in the mimeo).

310. See St. Bernard, *In Cantica*, 7.4–6 (*PL* 183, cols. 808A–809D), in which Bernard identifies the friends of the Bridegroom to whom the Bride addresses her request for "the kisses of his mouth" with "the holy angels who wait on us as we pray, who offer to God the petitions and desires of men, at least of those men whose prayer they recognize to be sincere, free from anger and dissension. . . . Since they are all spirits whose work is service, sent to help those who will be the heirs of salvation, they bear our prayers to God in heaven and return laden with graces for us." Like Evagrius, Bernard also warns his monks that if they are negligent or asleep in choir, "instead of showing reverence for those princely citizens of heaven you appear like corpses. When you are fervent they respond with eagerness and are filled with delight in participating in your solemn offices. What I fear is that one day, repelled by our sloth, they will angrily depart. . . . It is certain indeed that if the good spirits withdraw from us, we shall not easily withstand the obsessions of the evil ones" (Bernard of Clairvaux, *On the Song of Songs* I, trans. Kilian Walsh, ocso, CF 4 [Kalamazoo, MI: Cistercian Publications, 1971], 40–41).

311. Guillaumont, *Six Centuries*, 99.

312. N. 35; Hausherr, *Leçons*, 53.

313. Guillaumont, *Six Centuries*, 29.

(b) divine judgements; (c) natural created beings; (d) angels; {the} Kingdom of the Father (*theologia*) {involves} contemplation of the Trinity in the *locus Dei* "without forms,"[314] "without multiplicity."[315] The Kingdom of Christ {provides} *gnosis* of the economy of salvation and of the revelation of the Logos in creation and in history. This is not the summit of the contemplative life, but an intermediate stage, a further spiritual and intellectual purification completing the work of the active life.

In the realm of *theoria physike* we are *beyond all passionate thoughts*, and begin to go beyond *simple thoughts* to the *logoi*. These remain *multiple*, *objective*, and *formal*—intuitive and not discursive, however. These intuitions are *mystical*, given directly by God, but they also presuppose or allow for our own cooperation in disposing ourselves, not only by ascetic purity of heart but also by assiduity in reading the Scriptures. Evagrius stresses the fact that *love* is necessary for the *gnosis* of created beings (see *Kephalaia Gnostica* III.58[316]). *Theoria physike* is insufficient. This is stated categorically {in} n. 55: "The mere fact that one has attained *apatheia* does not mean that one will truly pray, for one may remain with *simple thoughts* and be distracted in meditating on them, and thus remain far from God."[317] What are simple thoughts? thoughts of objects that are completely innocent and good, and free from all passionate attachment. But they are nevertheless "multiple" and also somewhat superficial, meaningless, *irrelevant*. We are not yet in the realm of *theoria physike* strictly so called, only on the threshhold. We are purified from simple thoughts by a work of *recollection and deepening*—a new *intuitive seriousness* which penetrates to the *logoi of things*. This deepening by *theoria physike*, this grasp of the *logoi*, is the beginning of a

---

314. *Centuries Supplement*, 21 (Hausherr, *Leçons*, 94).

315. See J. Lemaitre, R. Roques, M. Viller, "Contemplation: III. Chez les Grecs et Autres Orientaux Chrétiens: 1. Étude de vocabulaire," *DS* 2, col. 1778: "La Contemplation de la Trinité n'a rien de multiple."

316. Guillaumont, *Six Centuries*, 121.

317. Hausherr, *Leçons*, 80.

mature interior contemplation. But it is not yet the *locus Dei* or
the true interior sanctuary of prayer. N. 56 {states}: "Even if the
intelligence does not delay among simple thoughts, it does not
by that fact attain to the place of prayer: but it may remain in the
contemplation of objects and be occupied with their *logoi* which,
though they may be simple expressions, nevertheless, *since they
are objects, impress a form* upon the intelligence and keep it far
from God."[318] He says elsewhere (quoted by Hausherr, p. 145):
"He who contemplates God through the consideration of His
creatures does not see His nature but the economy of His wisdom,
and if this is the case, how great is the folly of those who pretend
that they know the nature of God."[319] N. 57 speaks of a further
stripping of the intelligence. It must ascend even beyond the
angels, though to reach the angels it must ascend above "nature"
and proceed in "nakedness without forms";[320] nevertheless there
is multiplicity in this angelic contemplation, and no doubt a semblance of objectivity. It is the "*gnosis* of intelligibles,"[321] and these
intelligibles are multiple. This particular point needs to be much
more thoroughly studied and clarified, and we do not dwell upon
it here. {It is} sufficient to say that the *gnosis* of spiritual beings
and of "intelligibles" is not yet enough and one must pass even
beyond this to pure emptiness and nakedness, to the *locus Dei*.

A qualification of this strict doctrine: what is said here must not
be misunderstood and taken in too strict and absolute a sense. It
is not a mere matter of purifying the intellect more and more so
that it is completely empty and without images. This concept of
prayer could in fact be disastrously misleading. God Himself
purifies our intelligence, and He does so not only by means of
gnosis, but also by *love*. Love remains an important force in the

---

318. Hausherr, *Leçons*, 80.

319. *Kephalaia Gnostica*, V.51 (this is the less authentic version, according to Gullaumont; the S$_2$ text is somewhat longer [Guillaumont, *Six Centuries*,
198/199]).

320. See *Kephalaia Gnostica*, III.15 (Guillaumont, *Six Centuries*, 103).

321. *Kephalaia Gnostica*, I.70, 76 (Guillaumont, *Six Centuries*, 51, 53).

mysticism of Evagrius. Also, the mere fact that one has not attained to absolute purity of intellect does not prohibit occasional flashes of pure and perfect contemplation brought about by the action of the Holy Spirit (n. 62).[322] This short-cut is a matter of *love* which cuts short reasoning and preoccupation with forms. This fact should be remembered. It is easily forgotten when we concern ourselves with the strict logic of the Evagrian ascent. Such things do not obey the logic and forms of {a} rigid system, and Evagrius himself knew it.

"*Theology*"—*the locus Dei*:[323] in the first place, the concept of a "*locus Dei*" is itself a deficiency or seems to be one, according to Evagrius' own standards. Is not this itself a quasi-form, a semi-objective entity within ourselves? Is there not {a} danger that this concept of a *locus Dei* may itself distract us? Of course the concept is used in communication of what is in itself ineffable, hence the imperfection. We must remain on guard.

a) The contemplation of the Holy Trinity is not multiple—the "Three" are "not numerical."[324]

b) Evagrius is here accused of being more philosophical than theological and of using the "Trinity" as an expression of God as monad. This needs to be studied more.

c) In any case the *gnosis* of the Trinity is true theology, and it is a gift of light from God, immediate, without forms, perfect in unity. {It is} *without form*: "The mind has all its strength when in time of prayer it imagines nothing in this world" (*Pract.* 1.37).[325] (This applies to *theoria physike* on {the} higher level—intelligibles.)

---

322. Hausherr, *Leçons*, 88.

323. The phrase, taken from Psalm 75:3, is found in section 57 of the *De Oratione*, and also in *On Thoughts*, cc. 39, 40, *Reflections*, cc. 20, 23, 25, *Letter* 39 and *Scholia on the Psalms* 75:3: see Evagrius of Pontus, *The Greek Ascetic Corpus*, trans. Robert E. Sinkewicz (New York: Oxford University Press, 2003), 180, 213, 273, 286.

324. *Kephalaia Gnostica*, Cent. VI.10-13 (Guillaumont, *Six Centuries*, 221, 223), quoted in Hausherr, *Leçons*, 147–48.

325. Hausherr, *Leçons*, 96.

"I call impressionless the intellect which at the time of prayer imagines no bodily thing" ({the} same remark applies here) (*In Ps. 140*). "The thought of God keeps the mind from all impressions, for God is not a body" (*In Ps. 140*, quoted by Hausherr [p. 96]). Is this translation (of Hausherr) satisfactory? {It} implies a concept of God. The emptiness of Evagrius would seem to demand much more.

Two important numbers, for *theology*: n. 66 {states}: "See no diversity in thyself when thou prayest, and let thy intelligence take on the impression of no form; but go immaterially to the immaterial and you will understand."[326] This by itself is not a full explanation of pure prayer. It is not enough to be "immaterial"; one must also be "beyond intelligibles." Hence, Hausherr quotes from *Cent. Suppl.* 21 (see p. 94): "having entered into prayer [the intelligence] penetrates into *light without form*, which is *the place of God*." Note: this concept of the *locus Dei* within oneself is the most serious flaw in the mystical theology of Evagius—not that it is wrong in itself but it *blocks* further (ecstatic) development. It explains union in such a way that it remains necessarily imperfect; God and the spirit remain face to face, so to speak, subject and *object*. Even the *locus Dei* risks being regarded as "something" objective. Also, in *Cent.* II.63 (quoted *ibid.*), it is said: "Among various forms of *gnosis*, some are immaterial, some are known in material objects. The *gnosis* of the Holy Trinity is beyond all of them."[327] That is to say, it is beyond the *material and the immaterial*. This is important because we tend to imagine that it is sufficient to ascend from the material to the intelligible. Also, note that this transcendent quality of divine *gnosis* postulates once again the activity of *mystical love* and not a mere intellectual light alone. N. 114 {states}: "Aspiring to see the face of the Father Who is in heaven, seek for nothing in the world to see a form or figure

326. Hausherr, *Leçons*, 93.

327. The S$_2$ text is completely different at this point (Guillaumont, *Six Centuries*, 84).

at the time of prayer."[328] There is no need of a form to see God; He gives us a light in which He is seen directly. *Cent*. I:35 is theologically ambiguous, and the ambiguity will be resolved in a characteristic way by later Byzantine mystics. However we reproduce it as it stands: "Just as the light that shows us all has no need of another light in order to be seen, so God, Who shows us all things, has no need of a light in which we may see Him: for He is Himself light by essence" (Hausherr, p. 145).[329] It is to resolve this problem that the concept of the *locus Dei* is developed. Rather than say that God is seen directly by His own light, which would imply a participation in the beatific vision, it is said that He is seen in the *naked and light-filled intellect* which mirrors Him as a pure and perfect image. This pure intellect is itself the *locus Dei*. The light of God received into the mirror gives us a direct intuition of God in our own divinized intelligence. He also speaks of the light "carving out in the soul the place of God"[330] by purifying it of every form. Elsewhere he has something about the "sapphire light"[331] of the *locus Dei*. This is dangerous and misleading.

Note the *Beatitudes of Prayer*: they praise the "formlessness" and nakedness that we have discussed, but they also bring in the element of love, and particularly of fraternal charity. The *unity* produced by contemplation is not confined to individual union of the monk with God—on the contrary, he who is purified by *apatheia* and contemplation is perfectly one with all his brothers because he is perfectly humble and pure. N. 118: Blessed is the intelligence which, in a prayer without distraction, acquires ever new increase of love for God.[332] N. 119: Blessed is the intelligence

---

328. Hausherr, *Leçons*, 144.

329. Both text traditions for this chapter are identical (Guillaumont, *Six Centuries*, 32/33).

330. *Praktikos*, 1.70, quoted in Hausherr, *Leçons*, 81.

331. The phrase, taken from Exodus 24:9-11, is found in *On Thoughts*, c. 39, and *Reflections*, c. 2: see Evagrius, *Greek Ascetic Corpus*, 180, 211.

332. Hausherr, *Leçons*, 153.

which in the time of prayer becomes immaterial and naked of all things.[333] N. 120: Blessed is the intelligence which in the time of prayer has obtained perfect imperviousness to the appeals of sense.[334] N. 121: Blessed is the monk who considers himself the offscouring of all.[335] N. 122: Blessed is the monk who regards the salvation and the progress of all as his very own, in all joy.[336] N. 123: Blessed is the monk who considers all men as God, after God.[337] N. 124: He is a true monk who is separated from all [things] and united to all [men].[338] This last is completed by another saying of Evagrius from a letter (quoted by Hausherr, p. 158): "Christ is our charity and HE UNITES OUR UNDERSTANDING TO OUR NEIGHBOR IN *APATHEIA* BY THE TRUE *GNOSIS* OF THE HOLY TRINITY."[339]

Conclusions:

a) Evagrius has been treated with harsh severity by many authors, and yet he has been used by the greatest saints. There are real riches in his doctrine.

b) It is true that he has a distinctly Platonic, or rather neo-Platonist, tone. He is highly intellectual. He is always in danger of a certain angelism, considering man as a potentially pure spirit, isolating the intelligence from everything else, as if the contemplative life were a question of pure *mind*. He does *not* hold that the body is evil. He says categorically that "*nothing* created by God is evil" (*Keph. Gnost.* III.59).[340]

c) He tends to separate off the contemplative life and to isolate it from the wholeness of the Christian's life in the Spirit.

333. Hausherr, *Leçons*, 154.
334. Hausherr, *Leçons*, 155.
335. Hausherr, *Leçons*, 156.
336. Hausherr, *Leçons*, 157.
337. Hausherr, *Leçons*, 157.
338. Hausherr, *Leçons*, 158.
339. *Letter* 40.
340. Guillaumont, *Six Centuries*, 123.

d) This tendency must not be exaggerated. His extreme statements must be balanced by those others in which he insists on *love*, and on unity in the mystical Christ, and the rare places where he speaks of the action of the Holy Spirit.

e) It would seem right and proper to grant Evagrius the benefit of the doubt and to say that the fullness of Christian mystical theology is implicitly there but that he did not have a theological language that was capable of making it perfectly clear, {and} that his attachment to intellectualist terminology spoiled his theology.

f) Evagrius does not go as far as the later *ecstatic* theologians. He takes us out of all that is not the self, but not out of ourselves. He takes us away from external objects to the *locus Dei*, but no further than this.

g) There remains a considerable danger of misunderstanding him. He is an interesting and important source, but in forming young monks and in preaching the contemplative life it would of course be much wiser to find the same things said much better in great saints like Gregory of Nyssa, Maximus, etc.

VI. Contemplation and the Cosmos—*Theoria Physike*

The topic of *theoria physike* has already been mentioned. Let us now treat it in detail because it is very important. We can in fact say that the lack of *theoria physike* is one of the things that accounts for the stunting of spiritual growth among our monks today. On the contrary, where there is a genuine growth from the serenity of at least a relative *apatheia* to the enriched state of *gnosis* by "natural contemplation," then we are fully and integrally prepared for *theologia* without forms, beyond all ideas and symbols. Note how the modern controversy about a distinction between "acquired" contemplation that is "dark and without forms" and infused contemplation really obscures the essential issue. There must in reality be a flowering of contemplation in the realm of types, symbols, and *logoi*, in the *gnosis* of God's mercy, in His providence and in His judgements, before there can be a normally mature development in the direction of pure *theologia*.

What is theoria physike? Evagrius calls it the "land flowing with milk and honey" (*Kephalaia Gnostica* III.67).[341] It is a contemplation according to nature (*physis*). It is also a contemplation of God in and through nature, in and through things He has created, in history. It is the *multiformis sapientia*,[342] the *gnosis* that apprehends the wisdom and glory of God, especially His wisdom as *Creator* and *Redeemer*:

1) in the spirit of Scripture and not in the letter;

2) in the *logoi* of created things, not in their materiality;

3) in our own inmost spirit and true self, rather than in our ego;

4) in the inner meaning of history and not in its externals ({the} history of salvation, {the} victory of Christ);

5) in the inner sense of the divine judgements and mercies (not in superstitious and pseudo-apocalyptic interpretations of events).

It is a contemplation to which we are led and in which we are illuminated by the angels. It is a spiritual contemplation, a gift, proceeding from *love*, accessible only to the pure, and essentially distinct from the science of nature which is only intellectual, and accessible to the impure as well as to the pure. It is not only the crown of the active life and the beginning of the contemplative life, but it also is *necessary to complete the moral purification* effected by the active life. When the *thumos* and *epithumia* have been ordered and purified by love and chastity, the *nous* is purified by *theoria*.[343] In this purification there is also a transformation and deepening. What were merely "simple thoughts" become penetrating intuitions of the *logoi* of things, in preparation for a further step—the intuition of pure intelligibles.

341. Guillaumont, *Six Centuries*, 125.

342. "multiform wisdom" (*Kephalaia Gnostica*, I.43; II.2, 21; III.11; IV.7; V.84 [Guillaumont, *Six Centuries*, 39, 61, 69, 103, 139, 213]).

343. See above, n. 295.

Theoria gives a supernatural understanding of nature, of history, of revelation, of liturgy and of man himself. It attains to this understanding in types, symbols and *logoi* which are opened up to us by the divine illumination, but also depend on our own cooperation. Hence *theoria physike* is *partly mystical and partly natural*. There is a manifest synergy of God and man in its action. Man does not simply receive these illuminations passively. It is always sustained by faith, or rather by a collaboration between nature and faith: the *logoi* of creatures and the types of Scripture are realities which nurture and preserve faith; faith feeds on these "words of God." They are a kind of angelic nourishment, without which the intelligence fails and dies. In effect, the man who is immersed in the letter of Scripture, the materiality of things, his external self, the externals of history, is in fact completely blinded; his intelligence is starved and shrivels up, and even if he is still alive by "faith," his faith is so languid and weak that it is perpetually on the point of death. His intelligence is deprived of vitally important spiritual nourishment. How can such a one aspire to a life of genuine contemplation? His contemplation will, if it exists at all, be a false illumination nourished by passion and sense stimulation, and by the emotions. *Theoria physike* {is thus the} reception of God's revelation of Himself in creatures, in history, in Scripture. "We must not believe that sin caused this unique masterpiece which is this visible world in which God manifests Himself by *a silent revelation*" (St. Maximus, *Ambigua*).[344] Here St. Maximus uses *theoria physike* to protest against the Origenist idea that the world is in itself imperfect, being made up of fallen spiritual realities. *Theoria physike* is necessary to correct the deviations of Origenism, including those found in Evagrius.

St. Maximus, on whom we rely mostly here, is a great theologian of the seventh century, the Father of Byzantine mysticism. He died in 655. He used Evagrius but corrected him and went beyond him. He used Pseudo-Dionysius but also corrected him

---

344. *PG* 91, col. 1328A, quoted in von Balthasar, *Liturgie Cosmique*, 17; ET: 61.

and went beyond him.[345] {He is} one of the greatest of the Greek Fathers. (Read *Liturgie Cosmique* by H. Urs von Balthasar.) St. Maximus is the great doctor of *theoria physike*. He unites Plato and Aristotle, within the Christian framework. He has the broadest and most balanced view of the Christian cosmos of all the Greek Fathers, and therefore of all the Fathers. St. Maximus says again: "There is in everything a general and unique mode of the obscure and intelligible Parousia of the unifying cause" (*Mystagogia,*[346] quoted in *Liturgie Cosmique,* p. 25). He says again: "The love of Christ hides itself mysteriously in the inner *logoi* of created things . . . totally and with all His plenitude . . . in all that is varied lies hidden He who is One and eternally identical; in all composite things, He who is simple and without parts; in those which have a beginning, He who has no beginning; in all the visible, He who is invisible," etc. etc. (*Ambigua,* 1285, 1288[347]).

Theoria physike is then:

a) Reception of the mysterious, silent revelation of God in His cosmos and in the *oikonomia,* as well as in our own lives. Note—this is not a question of *epistemology,* as it was for St. Augustine. For Augustine (see Guardini, *Conversion of Augustine,* p. 13 ff.[348]), it was a matter of explaining how we know the essences of created things. This knowledge of essences is not attained by

346. 7:91 (*PG* 91, col. 685AB); ET: 70.

345. The second section of *Liturgie Cosmique,* "Les Idées," focuses on Maximus' critique of Pseudo-Dionysius (71-80) and Origen (80-87); ET: 115–26, 127–36.

346. 7:91 (*PG* 91, col. 685AB); ET: 70.

347. Von Balthasar, *Liturgie Cosmique,* 222–23 (the references are to column numbers in *PG* 91); ET: 292.

348. In his second chapter, entitled "The Memory," Guardini finds Augustine raising "epistemology's basic problem: How is the essence—or aprioristic character—of a thing to be grasped?" (12), and explains that "For Augustine, as for Plato, all this comes, not by way of the senses, but directly from the eternal ideas, of which the objects of experience and process are but images. . . . [T]he mind constantly refers itself to that realm of ideas which, ultimately, is none other than the living spirit of God. . . . The whole world, insofar as a man encounters it and it has become the content of his life, exists twice: actually and

sense, but by *"memoria,"* for in his Platonic line of thought the *memoria* is enlightened by God and perceives the reality of things not just in themselves but in the Word. Contemplation of the *logoi* of things is like this, but the perspective is different.

b) It is the knowledge of God that is *natural* to man, with God's help (grace). But note, it is not "natural" in the modern sense, clearly distinct from and opposed to "supernatural." It is natural in the sense that it is what God *intended* for man in creating him. It is proper to him as a son of God, was his when in paradise, is proper to him as a brother of the angels. We must be restored first of all to this "natural" contemplation of the cosmos before we can rise to perfect *theologia.*

c) This contemplation is demanded by the cosmos itself and by history. If man cannot know creatures by this spiritual *gnosis* they will be frustrated of their end. If man cannot spiritually penetrate the meaning of the *oikonomia* it runs the risk of being frustrated and souls will be lost.

d) Hence *theoria physike* is a most important part of man's cooperation in the spiritualization and restoration of the cosmos. It is by *theoria* that man helps Christ to redeem the *logoi* of things and restore them in Himself.

e) This *theoria* is inseparable from love and from a truly spiritual conduct of life. Man not only must see the inner meaning of things but he must regulate his entire life and his use of time and of created beings according to the mysterious norms hidden in things by the Creator, or rather uttered by the Creator Himself in the bosom of His creation.

The vision of *theoria physike* is essentially *sophianic.* Man by *theoria* is able to unite the hidden wisdom of God in things with the hidden light of wisdom in himself. The meeting and marriage of these two brings about a *resplendent clarity* within man himself, and this clarity is the presence of Divine Wisdom fully recognized

---

in the memory" (13, 15) (Romano Guardini, *The Conversion of Augustine,* trans. Elinor Briefs [Westminster, MD: Newman Press, 1960]).

and active in him. Thus man becomes a mirror of the divine glory, and is resplendent with divine truth not only in his *mind* but in his *life*. He is filled with the light of wisdom which shines forth in him, and thus God is glorified in him. At the same time he exercises a spiritualizing influence in the world by the work of his hands which is in accord with *the creative wisdom of God* in things and in history. Hence we can see the great importance of a sophianic, contemplative orientation of man's life. No longer are we reduced to a *purely negative* attitude toward the world around us, toward history, toward the judgements of God. The world is no longer seen as merely material, hence as an obstacle that has to be grudgingly put up with. It is spiritual through and through. But grace has to work in and through us to enable us to carry out this real transformation. Things are not fully spiritual in themselves; they have to be spiritualized by our knowledge and love in our use of them. Hence it is impossible for one who is not purified to "transfigure" material things; on the contrary, the *logoi* will remain hidden and he himself will be captivated by the sensible attractions of these things.

The "will of God" is no longer a blind force plunging through our lives like a cosmic steamroller and demanding to be accepted willy-nilly. On the contrary, we are able to *understand* the hidden purposes of the creative wisdom and the divine mercy of God, and can cooperate with Him as sons with a loving Father. Not only that, but God Himself hands over to man, when he is thus purified and enlightened, and united with the divine will, a certain creative initiative of his own, in political life, in art, in spiritual life, in worship: man is then endowed with a *causality* of his own.

The Three Laws: the best approach to the full idea of *theoria physike* is the synthesis of the three laws as described by St. Maximus.[349] The object of *theoria* is for Maximus something more dynamic and profound than simply the spiritual sense of Scripture and the *logoi* of creatures, with providence etc. (though Maximus

---

349. See von Balthasar, *Liturgie Cosmique*, 221-42; ET: 291–314.

is weak on the importance of *history* in *theoria physike*[350]). The object of *theoria* is not only nature (*phusis*) and the Law (*nomos*) but the two together, fused on a higher level of unity in Christ Who is the fulfillment of both nature and the Law. Hence we have Nature (*phusis*)—the Greeks—(Elias)—*body* of wisdom, {and} Law (*nomos*)—the Jews—(Moses)—*soul* of wisdom, {united in} CHRIST the true Law. Body and soul are united in the higher unity of SPIRIT, which is in Christ, the true Law of the cosmos and its fulfillment, the fullness of wisdom and revelation.[351] (Moses and Elias are here brought in in reference to their position in the Transfiguration on either side of Christ. *Theoria* is then contemplation of the splendor of divine wisdom in Christ with nature [Elias] on one side and law [Moses] on the other, both looking to Him as to their fulfillment. In the full development of *theoria they both disappear* and we see Christ alone.) Von Balthasar says: "The meaning of each natural thing and the meaning of every law and commandment is to be an Incarnation of the divine Word; to realize fully its proper nature or its proper law is to co-operate fully *in the total realization* of the Word in the world" (*Liturgie Cosmique*, p. 224[352]). Note that both *phusis* and *nomos*, without Christ, tend unnaturally and against His intention to *separation* and not to unity. {With regard to} nature, the true *logos* of man demands unity with Christ, in love and in will, and unity with other men. Egoism, however, {is} dominated by the action and desire of *sense*, which separates, produces an unnatural state of division against {the} natural tendency to unity in love. {With regard to} Law, justice as such tends to unity, as nature does. But the *letter* of the Law creates {a} multiplicity of cases, distinctions, problems, decisions, and eventual separation between this one and that one, ending with *inequality*. *Without theoria physike*, which penetrates to the inner *logos*, and {its} orientation to unity and simplicity and wholeness, nature and law tend to disintegration,

350. So von Balthasar, *Liturgie Cosmique*, 127; ET: 179.
351. See *Ambigua*, PG 91, cols. 1161AD, 1164AD, 1165A.
352. ET: 294.

separation and conflict. With the understanding of the *logoi*, in love and in the light given by God, they fulfill their true purpose and tend to unity, {to} recapitulation in Christ.

LOGOI *of things*: hence we now have one important conclusion. The LOGOS of things and the SPIRIT of Law are those inmost and essential elements primarily intended by God, placed in them by God, oriented to unity in love, in Himself.

A. The *logos* of a man is therefore something hidden in him, spiritual, simple, profound, unitive, loving, selfless, self-forgetting, oriented to love and to unity with God and other men in Christ. It is not an abstract essence, "rationality plus animality." It is however the *divine image* in him. More deeply it is CHRIST in him, either actually or potentially. To love Christ in our brother we must be able to SEE Him in our brother, and this demands really the gift of *theoria physike*. Christ in us must be liberated, by purification, so that the "image" in us, clothed anew with light of the divine likeness, is able connaturally to recognize the same likeness in another, the same tendency to love, to simplicity, to unity. Without love this is completely impossible.

B. Creatures: the vision given by *theoria physike* shows us that all creatures are good and pure. This is the first thing, the complement of the active detachment in *apatheia*. Evagrius declares, following the desert tradition (especially St. Anthony) that "nothing created by God is evil,"[353] and St. Maximus adds, "nothing created is impure."[354] (He comments on the vision of Peter at Joppa, the creatures let down in the sheet. {The} accommodated sense {here is that} all created things are seen to be good, made by God and reflecting His goodness.[355]) This implies not mere negative indifference but a positive awareness, by love, of the value of creatures, divinely given to them, placed in them by the

353. *Kephalaia Gnostica*, III.59 (Guillaumont, *Six Centuries*, 123).

354. *Questiones ad Thalassium*, 27 (*PG* 90, cols. 357D, 360A), quoted in von Balthasar, *Liturgie Cosmique*, 140; ET: 194.

355. See *Questiones ad Thalassium*, 27 (*PG* 90, cols. 353B, 356A), quoted in von Balthasar, *Liturgie Cosmique*, 234–35; ET: 305.

Creator to reflect Him in them. Once again it becomes clear how and in what sense *theoria* is necessary to complete *apatheia* and gives it positive meaning. *The right use of creatures* is essential to the proper understanding of them. St. Maximus says[356] we must be attuned not only to the *logoi* of creatures but also to *tropoi* or models of action: we get light from the *logoi*; we get order and love from the *tropoi*. They not only move us to praise but they guide us in action. It is very important to realize that *theoria physike* is actually a dynamic unity of contemplation and action, a loving knowledge that comes along with *use* and *work*. Note, the examples given by Maximus are stereotyped and can be improved upon. They do not give the full depth of his conception. For instance: the heavens—it is almost a stoic cliché to say that the *tropos* of the heavens is their stability and their tranquillity in order, etc.; other ones {include} the eagle, who looks directly at the sun; the lion, whose bones, when clashed together, produce sparks ({an example which} teaches {us} to compare texts in Scripture). Here we are in the realm of allegory, and very tame allegory, while in reality the intuitions of *theoria physike* penetrate far deeper than this. To return to the main point made above: *theoria physike* plus *praxis* is proper to a man who has attained full maturity and integrity in the spiritual life, the *holokleros*.[357] This, we repeat, is arrived at through the proper understanding of the *logos* of things and the natural appreciation of and practical "imitation" of their *tropoi*. Hence the completeness conferred by *theoria physike* is not simply a *gnosis* superimposed upon the virtuousness acquired during the practice of virtues in the active life. It is a twofold, speculative and practical, contemplative gift, a double illumination in the order of action and of contemplation, given by God through the gnostic evaluation of things and events, particularly of Scripture.

---

356. *Questiones ad Thalassium*, 51 (*PG* 90, col. 481B), cited in J. Lemaitre, "Contemplation: III. Contemplation chez les Grecs et Autres Orientaux Chrétiens: II. La Theoria Phusike," *DS* 2, col. 1817.

357. "the whole or complete person" (see I Thes. 5:23; James 1:4).

Logos and Mystery: it must be quite clear that the spiritual sense of Scripture, for instance, is something much more than mere allegory. As we said above in connection with Gregory of Nyssa,[358] it is a direct contact with the Word hidden in the words of Scripture. How do the *logoi* of created things find their expression in relation to the mystery of our salvation? Certain created material things enter explicitly into the framework of ritual mysteries, the celebration of the mystery of our salvation. In so doing they "represent" all creatures, for all creatures not only "groan with us expecting the redemption of the Sons of God"[359] but enter directly or indirectly with us into the great mystery of Christ. To see the *logoi* of creatures we are going to have to recognize in them this "groaning" and this "eschatological expectation" which depends on us—on our knowledge of them, on our use of them, with a directly sophianic and soteriological reference. To begin to realize the *logoi* of creatures we must then always be conscious of their mute *appeal* to us to find and rescue the glory of God that has been hidden in them and veiled by sin. {There is} a special problem of modern time, with its technology: technology, with its impersonal, pragmatic, quantitative *exploitation and manipulation* of things, is deliberately indifferent to their *logoi*. Consideration of the symbolic *logos* of a thing would be an obstacle to science and technology, so many seem to think. Hence the *logos* must be excluded. No interest {is shown} in "what" a thing really is. {This is} a deliberate conversion to the *alogon*, the *me on*.[360] *Meonic* preoccupation {is} a kind of liberation of the *me on* in order that there may take place a demonic cult of change, and "exchange"—consumption, production, destruction, for their own sakes. {Note the} centrality of *destruction* in this process. Technology leads to demonic pseudo-contemplation, {a} mystique of technics and production. The chief effort of Teilhard de Chardin

358. See above, page 74.
359. Romans 8:21-23 (condensed).
360. "the irrational, non-being": Lemaitre, "Contemplation," col. 1822, quoting Eusebius of Caesarea, *Preparatio Evangelica*, 15.17 (*PG* 21, col. 1345B).

in our time has been a noble striving to recover a view of the scientific world, the cosmos of the physicist, the geologist, the engineer, with interest centered on the *logos* of creation, and on *value*, *spirit*, an effort to reconvert the scientific view of the cosmos into a *wisdom*, without sacrificing anything of scientific objectivity or technological utility. The *logoi* and the spirit of Scripture are not discovered merely by study. They are not communicated by the doctors. They are the Kiss of the Word Himself, not the Kiss of His mouth. The Word, {the} *Logos*, teaches us how the *logoi* are oriented to Him, how they are both *in* Him, and *for* Him. The *logoi* of things are in the *Logos*: they are created in the *Logos*. The *logoi* of things are then the *Logos* in things. "In every being there is a *logos sophos kai technicos* beyond our vision" (St. Gregory of Nyssa, *In Hexaemeron*, PG 44.73A).[361] This is the *theoteles logos*:[362] that in the thing which comes from God and goes to God. *Theoria physike* then demands that we enter into the movement of all things from God back to God; and it implies *realization of the obstacle in the way of this movement placed in the world by philautia*[363] *and sin*, which makes things created by God serve our own immediate interests.

Theoria physike implies a sense of *community with things in the work of salvation*. {The} *logos* of bread and wine {is} not merely to nourish man physically but to serve the unity of mankind in Christ sacramentally. Wine is something which points beyond itself to the "new wine" in the Kingdom. The new wine is not something that is purely spiritual and therefore "not material wine." On the contrary, in the Eucharist, material wine is transformed not only

---

361. "a wise and skillful ordering principle" (quoted in Lemaitre, "Contemplation," cols. 1821–22).

362. "the logos tending toward God" (*Questiones ad Thalassium*, 32 [*PG* 90, col. 372B]), quoted in Lemaitre, "Contemplation," col. 1819.

363. "self-love": see von Balthasar, *Liturgie Cosmique*, 132, 142–43; ET: 184, 195; see also ET: 298; see also Irénée Hausherr, sj, *Philautie: De la Tendresse pour Soi á la Charité selon Saint Maxime le Confesseur* (Rome: Pontificale Institutum Orientalium Studiorum, 1952).

into spiritual wine, but into the "mystical wine" which is the Blood of Christ. The *logos* of a table {is} realized in the mystical table which is the altar around which the brethren gather for the fraternal meal at which the Risen Christ will be mystically present and will break bread. Christ Himself is the table of the altar. Hence, St. Maximus sums it up: "The whole world is a GAME OF GOD. As one amuses children with flowers and bright colored clothes and then gets them later used to more serious games, literary studies, so God raises us up first of all by the great game of nature, then by the Scriptures [with their poetic symbols]. Beyond the symbols of Scripture is the Word. . . ."[364] The spiritual knowledge of God in things is given to men in the desert of this world as manna was given to feed the Hebrews in the desert of Sinai (*Quest. 39 ad Thalas.*).[365] Maximus makes clear that the *spiritual senses* function in *theoria physike* as in their proper realm (cf. Gregory of Nyssa[366]). By the *logoi* of things the Divine Creator draws men who are attuned to *logoi*, the logical men, *logikoi*, to communion with the *Logos*. When a man has been purified and humbled, when his eye is single, and he is his own real self, then the *logoi* of things jump out at him spontaneously. He is then a *logikos*.

Art: logos and epiphany: here we can see the importance of *theoria physike* for sacred art. The sacred artist of all people should be a *logikos*. Hence it is not true that he does not need to be purified. He must in some sense be one who has attained to the summit of *apatheia*—not of course in the conventional way in which the average pious Catholic might conceive it. He does not necessarily have to be fully respectable in a conventional sense. A kind of unconventionality may be in him a form of humility and folly for Christ, and part of his *apatheia*. We must not forbid the artist a necessary element of paradox in his life. Conformism will perhaps blind him and enslave his talent. But he must at all costs

---

364. Von Balthasar, *Liturgie Cosmique*, 239, paraphrasing *Ambigua* (PG 91, col. 1413CD); ET: 310–11.

365. *PG* 90, col. 392B.

366. See above, pages 92–96.

have attained to an inner purity and honesty, a sincerity and integrity of spirit. He must be a *holokleros*, who understands the *logoi* of things and is attuned to their *tropoi*. He must be in *communication* with things, in their deepest center, in their most real value. He must be attuned to their voice. He must sense something of their "logic," their vocation. He must also sense in what way they are being prevented by man, and by society, by misuse, from attaining to their true spiritual end. The artist at the present time *is bound* in one way or other to protest against the systematic obscuring and desecration of the *logoi* of things and of their sacred meaning. For that reason an artist who would serve a completely secular society and put his art at the disposal of propaganda for materialistic illusions, would be destroying himself as an artist, especially if he served up conventional forms of "beauty." He would be conniving at the desecration and destruction of art. In so doing he would be betraying created things, and betraying his vocation as artist. This by no means condones any illusion of the artist as a "special kind of man," but his technical gifts as maker demand to be sustained by a spiritual gift as "seer." Note that once again this does not imply allegory or explicit symbolism or some special "message," nor does it imply peculiar forms of "fine art." The perception of the *logos* of a thing by an artist is manifested by the *form* which he gives to things. Examples of work sensitive to *logoi* {include}:

1) Shaker handicrafts and furniture, {which are} deeply impregnated by the communal mystique of the Shaker community. The simplicity and austerity demanded by their way of life enabled an unconscious spiritual purity to manifest itself in full clarity. Shaker handicrafts are then a real *epiphany of logoi*, characterized by *spiritual light*. See also their buildings, barns especially—{they have a} highly mystical quality: capaciousness, dignity, solidity, permanence. {What would be the} *logos* of a barn? "But my wheat, gather ye into my barn."[367] Note: it is never

---

367. Matthew 13:30.

{a} question of a "barn" in the abstract and in no definite place: the Shaker farm building always fits right into its location, manifests the "*logos*" of the place where it is built, grasps and expresses the hidden *logos* of the valley, or hillside, etc. which forms its site. {This} *logos of the site* {is likewise} important in Cistercian monasteries of {the} twelfth century. Note {the} *absence of this in certain religious* settings—pseudo-Gothic, which ignores true *logoi* {and} substitutes an arbitrary and false *logos*, in the head. Modern architecture with its pretended functionalism also is quite arbitrary (cf. Mumford on UN buildings[368]).

2) A primitive painter, Le Douanier Rousseau[369]—some of his paintings might be discussed as unconscious *theoria physike* on an obscure and not explicitly Christian level—but anyway on a kind of "spiritual" level. The "spiritual" content of Douanier Rousseau {is found in his} archetypal symbols. {For example,} *The Sleeping Gypsy* {manifests the} *logos* of passion {as well as} *apatheia*. Whether or not Douanier Rousseau ever attained to "*apatheia*" (in the strict sense) {is} highly doubtful! ({cf.} his loves and angers). But *The Sleeping Gypsy* represents for him the attain-

---

368. Lewis Mumford wrote a number of quite critical articles on the siting, planning and building of the United Nations headquarters in New York City, originally published in *The New Yorker* between 1947 and 1953 and included in his collection *From the Ground Up: Observations on Contemporary Architecture, Housing, Highway Building, and Civic Design* (New York: Harcourt, Brace & World, 1956), 20–70.

369. The reference is to Henri Rousseau (1844–1910), known as "Le Douanier" ("the Customs Officer") from an early job; on September 9, 1958, Merton writes in his journal of borrowing books on Rousseau from the University of Kentucky library (Thomas Merton, *A Search for Solitude: Pursuing the Monk's True Life. Journals, vol. 3: 1952–1960*, ed. Lawrence S. Cunningham [San Francisco: HarperCollins, 1996], 217), evidently in connection with work on his book *Art and Worship*, which remains unpublished (see *Search for Solitude*, 202 [5/9/58], 218 [9/26/58]). The painting of *The Sleeping Gypsy* (1897), now in The Museum of Modern Art in New York, depicts a dark figure stretched out on the bare ground, wearing a multi-colored robe and holding a staff in his right hand, with a lute and a jug placed next to him, and a lion immediately behind him, with mountains and a moonlit sky in the background.

ment of balance and a solution of a long inner conflict of which he was perhaps not even aware. We may see here at least an *analogy* of that *theoria* to which primitives are well disposed.

The Dangers and Limitations of Theoria Physike:
a) *Theoria physike* is between the human and the divine. It involves *sense and spirit* together. It demands man's *activity and divine grace.* It is not yet pure contemplation; it is only the beginning of the contemplative life, the threshold.

b) It involves alternations, and the possibility of delusion. A light that is truly spiritual may be seized upon by the senses and diverted to less pure ends. One may mistake sensible indulgence for spiritual inspiration. When the senses are refined and spiritualized, and yet not completely purified, there remains a danger that a more exquisite form of sense pleasure on a higher and more refined level may be accepted completely as spiritual and mystical.

c) This problem is explicitly treated by St. Maximus in *Quest. 58 to Thalassios.*[370] When sense still predominates, natural contemplation is falsified, because it *seems* natural to us to cling to the beauty of things with sense and spirit at the same time, and consequently sense is not subordinated to spirit. The subordination of sense to spirit *seems to us* unnatural. Hence the complaints and protests of those who, in demanding that nature be respected, are really asserting illusory "rights" for what is *not a natural state*, that is a state in which sense predominates over spirit.

d) The right order {is this}: when sense attains to the material object, the spirit attains to the spiritual *logos* of that object and the sense pleasure is forgotten. There may indeed be a coincidence of *contemplation in the spirit and suffering in sense.*[371] Let us be careful not to be misled by legitimate protests against "dolorism" into

---

370. *PG* 90, cols. 596D–597B; see von Balthasar, *Liturgie Cosmique*, 146; ET: 201.

371. See *Questiones ad Thalassium*, 58 (*PG* 90, cols. 597D, 600A), quoted in von Balthasar, *Liturgie Cosmique*, 212; ET: 280.

asserting that the senses have {a} right to more than is naturally due to them—that is to say, to emphasize sense satisfaction as a natural flowering of the spirit, when such satisfaction has to be disciplined and brought into subordination by suffering and sacrifice. Hence St. Maximus says[372] that just as Ezechias blocked up the wells around Jerusalem in time of danger, so we should abandon *theoria physike* in time of temptation and return to compunction and simple prayer.

VII. The Dionysian Tradition

We now come to the very important mystical tradition of Pseudo-Denys the Areopagite who, by virtue of his tremendous authority as the supposed Bishop of Athens converted by Paul, was the real propagator of Christian mystical theology. He is the one who begins to use the term *Theologia Mystica*. He is the first to write a separate, distinct treatise on this subject. His widespread influence in the West, which grew and grew in the late Middle Ages (n.b. he was thought also to have been Bishop of Paris) had profound effects: it led to the definitive break between mysticism and scholastic theology, among some of his medieval followers. In any case, it is Denys who seems more than any other theologian to represent the birth of mystical theology in its own right. At least later generations ascribed this to him, always believing that he went back to apostolic times. {There is a} curious contrast between the history of Denys and that of Evagrius. Evagrius (actually one of the masters of Denys) was rejected as an Origenist heretic. Denys was accepted as a bishop and martyr of apostolic times, a convert of St. Paul. Through Denys some of the most purely neo-Platonist elements enter into Christianity, and they are accepted without question, to become part of our tradition. It is possible that the writer of the Dionysian texts was a heretic (Monophysite).

---

372. *Questiones ad Thalassium*, 49 (*PG* 90, col. 452AB), commenting on 2 Chron. 32:2-3, quoted in Lemaitre, "Contemplation," col. 1809.

Note however two important qualifications:

a) In spite of the fact of his false identity, the theology of Pseudo-Denys is highly original and very important. In no case must he be dismissed or minimized as a kind of literary forger. The invention of identities was not unusual in those times.

b) The originality of his theology is also contingent upon its *unity*. The *Mystical Theology* must not be separated from all the rest of his works. It is quite likely that the writers of the late Middle Ages who, following Denys, broke away from scholastic theology to become professional "mystical theologians" made this mistake to a great extent.

The *Mystical Theology* of Denys is a very short treatise of only five columns in Migne.[373] It is *beyond* all his other theology. It presupposes all the other Dionysian writings. It presupposes the theology of light and darkness in the *Hierarchies* and the *Divine Names*. It presupposes a strong emphasis on *symbolic and sacramental* theology, which corresponds to *theoria physike* in him. Note that both in the West and in the East there developed a tendency to go directly from the ascetic life to contemplation without forms, without passing through *theoria physike*, in the Middle Ages. This is certainly as meaningful a fact as the separation between spirituality and scientific theology, probably much more meaningful. It is here really that the separation has its most disastrous effect.

We shall study, quite briefly: (1) the Dionysian writings; (2) the Dionysian tradition in the West. Brevity is necessary and very desirable at this point. Our time is running out, and the theme of contemplation in darkness, without forms, is already quite familiar. It is important to advance and to consider the question of "Western mysticism," and the crucial development of mysticism in the late Middle Ages and Renaissance. In this development we will find the key to many modern problems.

---

373. In the Latin translation of John Scotus Erigena: *PL* 122, cols. 1171B–1176C; the Greek, with a Latin translation and extensive commentary, is found in *PG* 3, cols. 997–1064.

1. The Dionysian Writings: *Who was their author?* Three real (?) persons are confused in the legendary figure of Dionysius: (a) the convert made by Paul (Acts {17:34}); (b) a bishop of Athens in the second century; (c) {the} apostle of Paris, bishop and martyr. This legend was widely disseminated in the West by the *Passio Sanctissimi Dionysii* of Hilduin, the Abbot of St. Denis.[374] This is a fabulous piece of writing with all kinds of inventions or at least tall tales. Its purpose was more or less directly to enhance the prestige of the great abbey of St. Denis. {It} was universally accepted until the Renaissance. L. Valla, followed by Erasmus, first questioned it.[375]

Present state of the discussion: nobody knows who the author may have been. {There are} innumerable hypotheses. At present the following are accepted as certain,[376] following the work of Koch[377] and Stiglmayr:[378]

a) the author was a fifth-century churchman at least (later than Evagrius);

b) he depends on Proclus, a late neo-Platonist;

c) he is evidently familiar with the theology of the Council of Chalcedon.

---

374. *PL* 106, cols. 23–50.

375. René Roques, "Denys l'Aréopagite (Le Pseudo-)," *DS* 3, col. 250.

376. See *Histoire de Spiritualité*, vol. 1, 474; ET: 396.

377. Hugo Koch, "Proklus als Quelle des Pseudo-Dionysius Areopagita in der Lehre vom Bösen," *Philologus*, 54 (1895), 438-54; *Pseudo-Dionysius Areopagita in seinen Beziehungen zum Neuplatonismus und Mysterienwesen: Eine Litterarhistorische Untersuchung, Forschungen zur Christlichen Litteratur- und Dogmengeschichte*, 1 (fasc. 2-3) (Mainz: F. Kircheim, 1900).

378. J. Stiglmayr, "Der Neuplatoniker Proclus als Vorlage des Sogen Dionysius Areopagita in der Lehre vom Uebel," *Historisches Jahrbuch*, 16 (1895), 253–73, 721–48; "Das Aufkommen der Pseudo-Dionysischen Schriften und ihr Eindringen in die Christliche Literatur bis zum Laterankonzil 649," *IV Jaresbericht des Öffentlichen Privatgymnasiums an der Stella Matutina zu Feldkirch* (Feldkirch, 1895), 3–96; Dionysius the Areopagite, *Ausgewählte Schriften*, ed. J. Stiglmayr (Kempten und Muenchen: J. Kösel, 1911).

He is most probably a Syrian of the fifth century, with monophy-site tendencies. {He} is in any case strongly influenced by neo-Platonism.

The Writings: the following are the main texts that have survived:

The Divine Names: {this work is} concerned with our knowl-edge of the divine attributes. Cataphatic and apophatic theology {is} explained. God {is seen} as the highest good, {Who} can be known beyond theology in a *passive and ecstatic union* of love in which one "undergoes the divine action," *pati divina*.[379] This phrase became consecrated by traditional use. From then on, mysticism {is} recognized as *passive* and loving knowledge of God in divine union. A key text {reads}: "The great Paul, pos-sessed by divine love, and *seized by its ecstatic power*, pronounced those words: I live now not I, etc. . . . For he who is truly seized by love and made by love to go out of himself does not live by his own life but by the well-beloved life of the One he loves" (*Div. Nom.* IV.13).[380] However, the cosmos as seen by Dionysius is not simply a fallen world in which individuals are called out by love to salvation and ecstasy. The whole cosmos, or at least the *world of intelligences*, is called to one vast ecstasy. God goes out of Himself ecstatically in creation, and His creatures in turn go out of themselves to return to Him and to bring others back to Him. Hence it is a vision of a whole universe of loving intelli-gences, none of which is concerned with itself, all of which draw one another to the One. "Ecstatic love forbids each one to belong to himself."[381]

The Hierarchies: the ecstasy of God reaches down through ordered hierarchies of angels and sacred ministers to attain to those orders that are farthest from Him. Those orders of angels

---

379. *Divine Names*, 2.9 (*PG* 3, col. 674).

380. *PG* 3, col. 712A, quoted by René Roques, "Contemplation: III. Con-templation chez les Grecs et Autres Orientaux Chrétiens: E. Contemplation, Extase et Ténèbre chez le Pseudo-Denys," *DS* 3, col. 1901.

381. *Divine Names*, 4.13 (*PG* 3, col. 712A).

only are in direct contact with Him which form the highest triad: cherubim, seraphim, thrones. The highest in the ecclesiastical hierarchy (bishops) are in contact with the lowest of the angels. *Celestial Hierarchy*: this is the least Christian and the most neo-Platonic of Denys' conceptions. The nine choirs of angels were, however, adopted without question by theology, especially by the "Angelic" Doctor[382] and the whole medieval tradition (see Dante[383]). But it does not go back to the Bible—rather, to Proclus.[384] See also Jewish mysticism: this is an important element that has been neglected in the treatment of Denys.[385]

The Ecclesiastical Hierarchy: {there are} two triads: I. The initiators: bishops, priests, other ministers (down to porter); II. The initiated: monks, the people of God, the ones being purified (catechumens, possessed, penitents). The ecclesiastical hierarchy is in an intermediate state between the celestial hierarchy and the hierarchy of the Old Law. Hence it deals at the same time with the contemplation of intelligibles and with the contemplation of the *oikonomia* through *symbols and sacraments*. However this latter contemplation (*theoria physike*) still has something of the Old Law and is therefore imperfect and provisional only. It must pass away. The bishops perfect all the other orders directly or indirectly: they ordain priests and consecrate monks; priests *illumi-*

---

382. See *Summa Theologiae*, 1a 1ae, q. 108 (Gilby, vol. 14, 120/121-156/157), cited by Joseph Turbessi, "Denys L'Aréopagite: V. Influence du Pseudo-Denys en Occident: A. Au 13e Siècle," *DS* 3, col. 355.

383. In the *Paradiso*, the first nine heavens (from the Heaven of the Moon through the Primum Mobile) are aligned with the nine choirs of angels (from the angels through the seraphim); the tenth heaven, the Empyrean, is beyond the angelic orders.

384. See René Roques, "Denys L'Aréopagite: II. Doctrine du Pseudo-Denys," *DS* 3, col. 270: "The temptation was great, then, to distribute the various angelic groups according to a triadic scheme, and to model their functions on those of the intelligible essences of Iamblichus and of Proclus. Denys has not resisted this temptation."

385. See now Naomi Janowitz, "Theories of Divine Names in Origen and Pseudo-Dionysius," *History of Religions*, 30.4 (May 1991), 359–72.

nate the people of God; other ministers *purify* penitents and catechumens. Hence we see the relation of the various orders as fellows:

(Angels)
BISHOPS
(perfect and perfecting)

Priests	Ministers	Monks
(illuminate)	(purify)	(perfect but not perfecting)
People of God	catechumens, penitents	

In the book on *The Church Hierarchy* he also treats of the sacraments as follows: baptism; sacrament of union (Eucharist); the holy oils; priestly consecration; monastic consecration; funeral rites. {It is} interesting that he regards monastic profession as a sacrament. Note what he says of monks: they are the "perfect" but have no mission to perfect others. They are "pure"; they are "one" and "alone"; they are *the true philosophers*.[386] (What is said in *The Church Hierarchy* needs to be completed by the lost book on *Symbolic Theology*, often alluded to in his other works.)

The cosmos of Denys is then a vast ecstatic communion of intelligences striving to respond to the call of divine Love summoning them to unity in Christ, each according to his rank and degree of purity. In this cosmos, the love of God flows out in a *thearchy*, a divinely ruled order in which the love of the creature, produced in it by God, leads the creature back to Him. The love of God as *agape* awakens *eros* in the creature.[387] *Eros* is divine *agape* responding to itself in {the} creature. The love of superiors for inferiors in the hierarchy resembles the divine *agape* and serves as {an} instrument of the thearchy. The return of created beings to God by love is not an absorption, a plunging into God and

386. See Roques, "Denys," col. 271.
387. See *Histoire de Spiritualité*, vol. 1, 482-83; ET: 404.

disappearing, but a flowering, a perfection, a *divinization*. Created beings reach their full perfection in their return to God. The generosity of creatures toward one another helps them all to return ecstatically to the One.

Symbolism and Mysticism: the merciful love of God, the thearchy, has placed *symbols* at the disposal of men and angels, to help bring about the return of all to God. Angels teach men by means of symbols; {they} do not need symbols themselves. Symbols are appropriate to men as creatures of body and spirit. However there is always a certain risk due to the material element in symbols. To avoid attachment to the sensible element (which would lead to idolatry and illusion) we must be *purified* by asceticism. {This is the} same thing we saw above: *theoria physike* demands purification from passionate thoughts. The real function of symbolic contemplation is to discover the "deiform" content of the symbol. Sacramental symbolism {is} not {a} mere matter of rites or allegorical explanation of ceremonies. Direct contact with the divine life {is} conferred by the sacraments. This demands two things: a spiritual initiation {and} being in one's right place in the "hierarchy." (To attempt by one's own power to accede to a higher level, without the help of the higher ones, is to exclude oneself from the hierarchy.) Beyond symbols: we rise beyond symbols by the apophatic negation of the material elements, but the trans-symbolic contemplation in darkness is not negative; it is positive, transcendent.

Mystical Theology is not just {the} *via negationis*, apophatic theology, dialectical. It is beyond both forms of discursive theology, cataphatic and apophatic.[388] It is the FULFILLMENT OF BOTH AND THEIR JUSTIFICATION FOR EXISTING. It is a transcendent and experienced theology beyond symbols and discourse. It is not relative (apophatic theology is in relation to the cataphatic which it completes and corrects). Mystical theology stands in relation to no other theology. {It} is a pure immaterial vision beyond intel-

---

388. See *Histoire de Spiritualité*, vol. 1, 495; ET: 415.

ligence, beyond reflection and self-correction. It is beyond the division of intelligence and will: hence it is not to be called primarily a matter of intelligence or primarily a matter of love: the followers of Dionysius in the West emphasize it as an act of will and thus tend to diminish it. {It is} passive, beyond activity, {at} the summit of the spirit, invaded and possessed by ecstatic love directly given by God, a pure grace, pure love, {which} contacts God in ecstasy. *Ecstasy* {is} a complete break with sense, with intelligence and WITH THE SELF. Here Dionysius goes beyond Gregory and Evagrius: {it is} outside the intelligence, the will, all created beings and the self. This is the important contribution of Dionysius—the full meaning of ecstasy, not just a going out from all things other than the self, but out of the self also.

Outline of De Mystica Theologia: {it is} addressed to one "Timothy," {and} begins with a prayer to the *Trinitas supersubstantialis et superdea*.[389] Timothy in the prologue is urged to rise above all operations of sense and intellect, beyond all beings and non-beings, and enter into the darkness like Moses. Dionysius refers to his other works (*Divine Names*; *Symbolic Theology*; *Hierarchies*): *descending from God* to creatures he has expanded and explained; *ascending from creatures* to God he will return rather to silence. Hence the *Mystical Theology* which is supposed to crown his other theological writings, is very brief and concise. (Note: it must always be seen in the context of his other work.) God is not sensible but the cause of sensible things. He is not intelligible but the cause of intelligible things. In ascending beyond sensibles and intelligibles to Him we give Him the greatest praise.

Points to emphasize:
a) {It is} not {focused on} darkness as opposed to light, but {on} a point beyond darkness and light in which both are

---

389. "Trinity beyond all substance and all divinity"; Merton is using the Latin translation of John Sarrazin: see *Dionysiaca: Recueil Donnant l'Ensemble des Traductions Latines des Ouvrages Attribués au Denys de l'Aréopage*, ed. P. Chevallier, 2 vols. (Paris: Desclée de Brouwer, 1937, 1950), 565.

transcendently pure: *superignota et supersplendentia*[390] {. . .} *secundum supersplendentem occulte docti silentii caliginem.*[391]

b) {It entails} ecstasy even from the self: EXCESSU TUI IPSIUS . . . MUNDE . . . AD {. . .} DIVINARUM TENEBRARUM RADIUM *cuncta auferens et a cunctis absolutus sursum ageris . . .*[392]

c) {It} is a true transcendent knowledge: {cf.} Moses in the darkness: *eo quod nihil cognoscit super mentem cognoscens.*[393]

d) This seems like pure folly to the non-mystic: *et nunc et caliginem quae est supra mentem introeuntes, non sermonum brevitatem sed irrationabilitatem perfectam et imprudentiam inveniemus.*[394]

These are the classical phrases which were to be echoed everywhere in the West in the late Middle Ages.

2. THE DIONYSIAN TRADITION IN THE WEST: (Note: do not confuse the term Dionysian, referring to Pseudo-Dionysius, with Nietzsche's word,[395] which refers to Dionysus [Bacchus].) What is said now must be remembered when we come to discuss the problem of Western mysticism. One of the chief points on which

390. "beyond all unknowing and beyond all illumination": *Mystica Theologia*, 1.1, which reads ". . . *superignotum et supersplendentem* . . ." in Sarrazin (*Dionysiaca*, 565).

391. "according to the dazzling darkness of the secretly instructed silence": *Mystica Theologia*, 1.1 (*Dionysiaca*, 565).

392. "leaving behind all things and having been released from all things by completely transcending yourself, you will be brought on high to a ray of divine darkness [beyond all being]": *Mystica Theologia*, 1.2, which reads ". . . *ad supersubstantialem divinarum* . . ." in Sarrazin (*Dionysiaca*, 568–69).

393. "for he knows nothing, having knowledge beyond the intellect": *Mystica Theologia*, 1.6 (*Dionysiaca*, 578).

394. "And now, entering the darkness which is above the mind, we will find not briefness of speech but complete mindlessness and thoughtlessness": *Mystica Theologia*, 3.2, which reads ". . . *super mentem* . . ." in Sarrazin (*Dionysiaca*, 589–90).

395. In *The Birth of Tragedy*, his first book (1872), Nietzsche contrasted the orderly, rational Apollonian and the irrational, ecstatic Dionysian dimensions of classical Greek drama, and of the springs of human creativity generally: see Friedrich Nietzsche, *The Birth of Tragedy and The Genealogy of Morals*, trans. Francis Golffing (Garden City, NY: Doubleday Anchor, 1956), 1–146.

the thesis of Dom Butler rests is that "genuine" Western mysticism is "pre-Dionysian" and untainted by the influence of Dionysius.[396] This is an oversimplification. We are going now to treat of Western medieval writers who appeal to Denys as to the *supreme authority* in mysticism. These are Butler's "Dionysians," presumably. Yet though they do this they remain primarily Augustinians for the most part, with rare exceptions, like the author of *The Cloud of Unknowing*. Perhaps the Rhenish mystics, whom we treat separately, are *some* of them (Eckhart) more Dionysian than Augustinian.

a) In 649 A.D. St. Maximus was in Rome, visiting the papal palace, and saw in the library of Gregory the Great *a copy of Pseudo-Dionysius*.[397] But St. Gregory is one of the "purely Western mystics" according to Butler.

b) {Note} the translation of Denys by Hilduin, abbot of St. Denys (832).[398] It is a very poor work. Scotus Erigena did a better one a few years later in the same century. In the ninth century translations of Denys are being made in France. Denys becomes known but is not yet widely read or above all *understood*. One of the first uses of Denys in the West by a mystic was that of Adam the (English) Carthusian in his *De Quadripartito Exercitio Cellae*.[399] John of Salisbury encouraged a new translation of Denys by J. Sarrazin.[400]

c) {In the} twelfth century, *the Victorines*, canons of the School of St. Victor {in} Paris, {were} friends of Bernard, theologians and mystics—they popularize Denys. The School of St. Victor was

396. Butler, *Western Mysticism*, 123.

397. See Philippe Chevallier, "Pseudo-Denys: V. Influence du Pseudo-Denys en Occident: A. Du 6e au 12e Siècle: 1. Origine de l'Influence Dionysienne," *DS* 3, cols. 318–19.

398. Chevallier, "Pseudo-Denys," col. 319.

399. *The Four-Part Exercise of the Cell* (*PL* 153, cols. 787-884; see Eric Colledge, ed., *The Medieval Mystics of England* [New York: Charles Scribner's Sons, 1961], 45–47).

400. See Colledge, *Medieval Mystics*, 48.

founded by William of Champeaux in 1108. William retired to {the} hermitage of St. Victor after his quarrel with Abelard. Disciples gathered round him. The school represented a *spiritual* reaction against the twelfth-century logicians. *Hugh of St. Victor* and the Victorines emphasized: the Bible and the Fathers; the sacraments; the Christian mysteries; contemplation as the culmination and fulfillment of philosophy and theology; interest in psychology and analysis of experience, especially of LOVE; mania for systematic divisions, characteristic of the time; *degrees of love and contemplation. De Contemplatione et eius Speciebus:*[401] *love* {is} more important than knowledge {and} goes further. {The} summit of contemplation {involves} *silence* of the mouth, spirit and reason, *quiescence* of {the} soul, memory and will, {and} *bridal union* with the Word. (*Read* {the} quote from *De Arca Noe* in *Late Medieval Mysticism*, p. 92.[402]) Hugh of St. Victor improved the translation

401. *On Contemplation and its Different Kinds*: this is a treatise attributed to Hugh of St. Victor that may have been put together by his students from class notes; see Bernard McGinn, *The Growth of Mysticism: Gregory the Great through the Twelfth Century. The Presence of God: A History of Western Christian Mysticism*, vol. 2 (New York: Crossroad, 1994), 384 and 586, n. 106. It has been edited by Roger Baron *as Hugues de Saint-Victor: La Contemplation et ses Espèces* (Paris: Desclée, 1958).

402. "The first man was so created that if he had not sinned he would always have beheld in present contemplation his Creator's face, and by always seeing him would have loved him always, and by loving would always have clung close to him, and by clinging to him who was eternal would have possessed life without end. Evidently the one true good of man was perfect knowledge of his Creator. But he was driven from the face of the Lord, since for his sin he was struck with the blindness of ignorance, and passed from that intimate light of contemplation; and he inclined his mind to earthly desires, as he began to forget the sweetness of the divine. Thus he was made a wanderer and fugitive over the earth. A wanderer indeed, because of disordered concupiscence; and a fugitive, through guilty conscience, which feels every man's hand against it. For every temptation will overcome the man who has lost God's aid. So man's heart which had been kept secure by divine love, and one by loving One, afterward began to flow here and there through earthly desires. For the mind which knows not to love its true good is never stable and never rests. Hence restlessness, and ceaseless labor, and disquiet, until the man turns and adheres to Him.

of Erigena and wrote a commentary on the *Celestial Hierarchy*. {He} removes pantheist elements injected into Denys by Erigena, {and} makes accessible *the real meaning of Denys*. The Victorines, who were *above all Augustinians* (very definitely), begin to popularize Denys. It can be said however that the Victorines as a whole belong to the tradition of *speculation and devotion* which can be considered the main line from Augustine to the Franciscans. They are therefore real Augustinians first of all, and Dionysians secondarily. {Also important is} *Richard of St. Victor*—his *De Trinitate*[403] is fundamental. This marks him as a disciple of Augustine. *Benjamin Major*[404] {and} *Benjamin Minor*[405] {are his} two tracts on contemplation. {Their} emphasis {is} on the love that *wounds*, on the *languor amoris*[406] (cf. St. Bernard and *courtly love*[407]), {on} thirst for God {and} the "mystical death" of love in ecstasy. (Read *Benjamin Minor*, ch. 73, 82.[408]) Note these concepts are inseparable

---

The sick heart wavers and quivers; the cause of its disease is love of the world; the remedy, the love of God. . . . In two ways God dwells in the human heart, to wit, through knowledge and through love; yet the dwelling is one, since every one who knows him loves, and no one can love without knowing. Knowledge through cognition of the faith erects the structure; love through virtue paints the edifice with color" (Prologue, Bk. 1, c. 2 [*PL* 176, cols. 619–21D], in Ray C. Petry, ed., *Late Medieval Mysticism*, Library of Christian Classics [LCC] [Philadelphia: Westminster Press, 1957], 92–93).

403. *PL* 196, cols. 887–992.

404. *PL* 196, cols. 63–202.

405. *PL* 196, cols. 1–64.

406. "the languor of love" (Richard of St. Victor, *De Gradibus Charitatis*, 2; *PL* 196, cols. 1198D–1199A).

407. See Gilson, Appendix IV: "St. Bernard and Courtly Love" (170–97).

408. Chapter 73 (*PL* 196, col. 52BD), entitled "*Quam sit arduum, vel difficile gratiam contemplationis obtinere*" ("How arduous and difficult it is to acquire the grace of contemplation"), speaks of the impatient longing experienced by Rachel (symbol of reason) as she awaits the birth of Benjamin (contemplation), which she is powerless to bring about by her own efforts because contemplation is a divine gift; Rachel dies when Benjamin is born because reason is transcended by contemplative awareness. Chapter 82 (cols. 58A-59B), entitled "*Quam sint incomprehensibilia, quae mens per excessum videt ex revelatione divina*" ("How there are incomprehensible things that the mind sees through ecstasy from a divine

from secular trends idealizing *erotic love* in poetry and literature. This influence is very important in {the} development of medieval and modern spirituality. Of Richard of St. Victor, St. Bonaventure said: *Anselmus sequitur Augustinum . . . in ratiocinatione; Bernardus sequitur Gregorium . . . in predicatione; Richardus sequitur Dionysium . . . IN CONTEMPLATIONE.*[409] This is interesting as the view of a mystical doctor concerning the mysticism of the West in the Middle Ages. Even Bonaventure associates the idea of contemplation with Dionysius rather than Augustine or Bernard, and contemplation means mysticism. Note however that when Dante seeks a guide to the highest parts of Paradise he goes to Bernard.[410] Nevertheless Bernard is regarded as a preacher rather than as a contemplative. All three could be regarded as mystics and indeed were. Though Bonaventure places Dionysius *above* Augustine he is really more an Augustinian than a Dionysian.

d) *The Cistercians*: Dom André Fracheboud, ocso, has proved in *DS* (article on influence of Denys—vol. III[411]) that statements of Gilson[412] and Butler[413] that Bernard and {the} Cistercians were not affected by Dionysius are not quite correct. Though it is true that *Bernard* is hardly a Dionysian, the effect of Dionysius' style is seen in Bernard and the *via eminentiae* is there. André Fracheboud disagrees completely that Bernard can be classed as a "Western mystic" unaffected by the negativity of Denys. READ:

---

revelation"), relates the experience of the disciples on the mount of transfiguration to the death of Rachel and the birth of contemplation: the disciples' fall to the ground at the voice of the Father represents the powerlessness of sense, memory and reason to comprehend the divine presence, experienced in both unity of essence and distinction of persons.

409. "Anselm follows Augustine in reasoning, Bernard follows Gregory in preaching, Richard follows Dionysius in contemplation" (*De Reductione Artium ad Theologiam*, c. 6; *Opera Omnia*, 5:321).

410. Dante, *Paradiso*, cantos 31–33 (Singleton, *Paradiso*, 346–81).

411. André Fracheboud, ocso, "Pseudo-Denys: V. Influence du Pseudo-Denys en Occident: A. Du 6e au 12e Siècle: 3. Les Cisterciens," *DS* 3, cols. 329–40.

412. See Gilson, 25.

413. See Butler, *Western Mysticism*, 124.

In Cantica.[414] {As for} *William of St. Thierry*, the direct influence of Denys is clear in the *Speculum Fidei et Aenigma Fidei.*[415] Traces of Denys {are} also clear in *Isaac of Stella* and *Gilbert of Hoyland.*[416] Even *Gertrude the Great* was spoken to by Christ, in vision, in the language of Pseudo-Denys!![417]

e) *The Thirteenth Century*: Denys influenced the Franciscan tradition through *Grosseteste* (through whom he reached Thomas Gallus—see below). *St. Albert the Great* based his mystical theology on Denys. Without knowing Greek he commented on the *Hierarchies*. Note: there is no separation between theology and mysticism in Albert, any more than in Bonaventure. But like the authors of the great *Summae*, including St. Thomas, Albert finds it necessary to state that although in contemplation the spirit *patiendo divina discit*,[418] yet study is no obstacle to this but rather disposes for it. In other words there is already a consciousness of the possible division between them. What produced this consciousness? Undoubtedly the way was paved for it by the struggles of St. Bernard

414. The reference is to *In Cantica* 4:4 (*PL* 183, col. 798AC, quoted in Fracheboud, "Pseudo-Denys," col. 330, who traces the idea of God as the *esse omnium* to *Celestial Hierarchy*, 4.1): "*Omnia omnibus est qui omnia administrat, nec quidquam est omnium proprie. . . . esse omnium est, sine quo omnia nihil. . . . Sane esse omnium dixerim Deum, non quia illa sunt quod est ille; sed quia ex ipso, et per ipsum, et in ipso sunt omnia. Esse est ergo omnium quae facta sunt . . . animantibus autem quod et vivunt; porro ratione utentibus lux, recte vero utentibus virtus, vincentibus gloria*" ("He who controls everything is all to all things, but He is not in Himself what those things are at all. . . . He is the being of all things, without whom all things would be nothing. . . . Of course, I would say that God is the being of all things not because they are what He is, but because all things exist from Him and through Him and in Him. Therefore He is the being of all things that have been made, and to all living creatures He is the source of their life; to all creatures with the use of reason He is light; to all creatures using reason properly He is virtue; to those who are victorious He is glory").

415. See Fracheboud, "Pseudo-Denys," col. 335.

416. See Fracheboud, "Pseudo-Denys," cols. 336–38.

417. See Fracheboud's note to Turbessi, col. 357.

418. "learns divine realities through being acted upon" (*Summa Theologiae*, Prologue, cited in Turbessi, col. 348 [which reads "*patiendo divina didicit*"]).

with the pre-scholastics like Abelard in the twelfth century. The place of William of St. Thierry's tracts on faith, against Abelard's treatment of faith, may be important here. *St. Thomas Aquinas* learned of Denys from Albert the Great, his master; {he} commented on the *Divine Names* (1260-1261). {He} builds his whole *Summa* on the idea of the *exitus* and *reditus* of Dionysius[419]—things going forth from God and returning to Him. {He is} especially indebted to Denys for his ANGELOLOGY[420] but *does not* follow Denys in mystical theology. In the question on *raptus*[421] he holds possible an intuitive vision of God even in this life.

St. Bonaventure, a purely "Western mystic," the pure type of the Western mystic (see below), nevertheless appeals to Dionysius as "higher" than Augustine. Yet he is a pure Augustinian for all that. At the end of the *De Triplici Via* he says there are two ways of contemplation: (a) *per positionem*—the way of Augustine; (b) *per ablationem*—the way of Dionysius.[422] The latter is the *via eminentiae*.[423] Note how the angelic hierarchies are fitted into the complex system of "degrees" in the *De Triplici Via*.[424]

Thomas Gallus (d. 1246): Gallus, a Victorine, is important as one of the first to consciously and explicitly use Denys *against* scholastic theology. Here he simply follows the Victorine tradition. In conscious reaction against Aristotle and the *scholastica levitas*,[425] Gallus stresses the *via negativa* and the suspension of all intellectual activity in favor of an ascent by love to God in darkness. Note that this is

---

419. M.-D. Chenu, *Introduction à l'Étude de Saint Thomas d'Aquin* (Montreal: Institut des Études Médiévale, 1950), 261, cited in Turbessi, col. 354.

420. Turbessi, col. 354.

421. 2a 2ae, q. 180, cited in Turbessi, col. 355.

422. "by attributing . . . by removing": *De Triplici Via*, III.7.11 (*Opera Omnia*, 8.16), quoted in Paul Philippe, "Contemplation VI: Contemplation au XIIIe Siècle," *DS* 3, col. 1980.

423. *De Triplici Via*, III.7.13 (*Opera Omnia*, 8.17), which actually calls the second way *"eminentior"* ("higher") rather than the more technical term *via eminentiae*, associated with Pseudo-Dionysius.

424. *De Triplici Via*, III.7.14 (*Opera Omnia*, 8.18).

425. "scholarly frivolousness".

not exactly the Dionysian ascent at all. It is a view which results from a separation of the *Mystica Theologia* from Denys' other works. {The} true teaching of Denys {incorporates both} (a) {the} intellectual way: two complementary theological approaches, {the} cataphatic, {the} way of light, {and the} apophatic, {the} way of darkness; (b) {the} mystical way: passive, ecstatic, above and beyond the two above ways of intellect; {it} completes and fulfills them.

{According to the} interpretation by the Dionysians of the Middle Ages:

a) {the} intellectual way is to be regarded as secondary;
b) the way of ascent to God is by *love* in darkness.

Thus we arrive at an opposition between *love* and *knowledge*. This is an oversimplification of the classical (including {the} Augustinian) division between *wisdom* and *science*. Here read St. Bonaventure, *Itinerarium Mentis in Deum* (VII.6):

> But if you wish to know how such things come about, consult grace, not doctrine; desire, not understanding; prayerful groaning, not studious reading; the Spouse, not the teacher; God, not man; darkness, not clarity. Consult, not light, but the fire that completely inflames the mind and carries it over to God in transports of fervor and blazes of love. This fire is God, *and His furnace is in Jerusalem.* Christ starts the flame with the fiery heat of His intense suffering, which that man alone truly embraces who can say: "*My soul rather chooseth hanging; and my bones death.*" Whoever loves this death may see God, for this is beyond doubt true: "*No man sees God and still lives.*" Let us die, then, and pass over into the darkness; let us silence every care, every craving, every dream; with Christ crucified, let us *pass out of this world to the Father.* Thus, having seen the Father, we may say with Philip: "*It is enough for us*" . . . (trans. by José de Vinck in *The Works of Bonaventure, Mystical Opuscula*).[426]

---

426. *The Works of Bonaventure*, trans. José de Vinck, 5 vols. (Paterson, NJ: St. Anthony Guild Press, 1960–1970), vol. 1: *Mystical Opuscula*, 58 (which reads, *"No man sees Me . . ."*).

Here love and prayer are contrasted with study, which is incapable of bringing us to union. Note however that St. Bonaventure certainly stresses the *unity* of the intellectual and spiritual lives as much as anyone ever did. However his followers *extracted* this kind of statement from the context and developed the idea independently in *opposition* to speculative theology. This trend was stimulated by the fact that scholastic theology was becoming more and more a speculative science and less and less a wisdom, even though the great theologians kept stressing the sapiential aspect of it.

Followers of Gallus {include} *Hugh of Balma*, a Carthusian (thirteenth century), {who} writes a *Mystica Theologia* which had great influence, as it was for a long time attributed to St. Bonaventure.[427] {It} emphasizes the contrast between *mystical wisdom*, a gift of God, and *human science*, the fruit of study and (scholastic) reasoning. {He} deplores the fact that theologians are seeking the latter more than the former. It is true that with the great love for scholastic thought there was developed a kind of contempt for patristic and strictly religious wisdom, and for contemplation as such. Balma is a good mystical theologian. He sees that *amor mysticus* is not simply opposed to understanding, but above the usual levels of both love and understanding. He respects the transcendent quality of the mystical knowledge of God. *Amor mysticus* leads to union *sine omni investigatione vel meditatione praevia*.[428] This does not mean that meditation and study are useless, but that they do not of themselves directly bring about union, only dispose for it. However, it would be easy to infer from this that they are of no use and should be deliberately suppressed. He uses the classical Dionysian terminology, "ray of darkness,"[429] etc. Both Balma and Gallus situate union in the *apex affectus*,[430] or *apex spiri-*

427. See Philippe, cols. 1976–77.
428. "Mystical love . . . without any previous investigation or meditation" (quoted in Philippe, col. 1977).
429. Philippe, col. 1977.
430. Thomas Gallus, *Extractio in Divinis Nominibus*, c. 7, cited in Philippe, col. 1975.

tus[431] (like St. Bonaventure[432]). This will become the *scintilla* (*vünkelin*) of Eckhart and the Rhenish mystics.

The Dionysian tradition continues strongly through the *fourteenth century*. We will treat of the great fourteenth-century mystics elsewhere. Suffice it to say that the *Rhenish mystics* (Eckhart, Tauler, etc.) brought up under the influence of the school of Cologne etc. where Albert the Great taught, were strongly Dominican and Dionysian, with an *intellectual* stress, even a speculative character, that prevented their Dionysian trend from becoming exclusively affective and anti-intellectual. Normally, we find that the mystics of darkness of the Rhenish and English schools are strongly Thomistic. Note: the chief English work in the Dionysian tradition is the anonymous *Cloud of Unknowing* (fourteenth century), whose author was familiar with the Rhenish mystics and also translated the *Mystica Theologia* of Dionysius into English (*Denys Hid Divinitie*).

The anti-intellectual current: through the fourteenth and fifteenth centuries the Dionysian stream passes also among the more anti-intellectual and affective writers of the *devotional* type, including Franciscans. Gerson, strongly opposed to the Rhenish mystics, is nevertheless a Dionysian, stressing *love and affectivity*.[433] *Henry Herp* (Harphius) (d. 1477), a Franciscan, now little known and studied, is a very important figure[434] among what we are calling the "affective Dionysians." Having received the influence of Denys through Ruysbroeck, he actually goes against many of the fundamental doctrines of Ruysbroeck while considering him still

---

431. Hugh of Balma, cited in Philippe, col. 1977.

432. *Itinerarium*, 7.4 (*apex affectus*) (*Opera Omnia*, 5.312) (cited in Turbessi, col. 349); see also *Sermo V in Epiphania* (*Opera Omnia*, 9:162): "*Apex mentis, quod est summum ipsius animae et quasi centrum, in quo recolliguntur omnes aliae vires*" ("the apex of the mind, which is the high point and center, as it were, of the soul itself, in which are gathered all other powers").

433. See André Combs, "Contemplation: . . . in Occident: 4. Gerson," *DS* 3, 365–75.

434. See Combs, "Contemplation: . . . in Occident: 6. Harphius," *DS* 3, 378–83.

his master. {The} *Theologia Mystica* of Herp {is} actually a compilation of texts from Herp made by Carthusians of Cologne; in it we have a mixture of St. Bernard, Gerson, Ruysbroeck and Hugh de Balma. The *cosmic love* of Denys comes back into prominence. There is a union of the positive and negative aspects of Dionysius. The influence of Herp and the Rhenish mystics traveled to Spain and blossomed out in Osuna and De Laredo[435] who in their turn prepared the way for the great Carmelite mystics of the sixteenth century.

VIII. Western Mysticism

We have already seen that the mystical tradition of Pseudo-Denys is very important in the West and gains importance in the Middle Ages. It must also be recalled here that {a major figure is} *Cassian*, who, although opposed to Augustine in the semipelagian controversy, remained one of the great spiritual masters of the West, particularly of the monastic West. Through Cassian the primitive tradition of Christian mysticism, as represented in St. Gregory of Nyssa and Evagrius, and stemming from Origen, passes on down through the West. Of the Western Fathers, the closest to Cassian is probably *St. Gregory the Great*. In speaking of Western mysticism we have then to take into account the Benedictine tradition, through Cassian and Gregory, which provides a kind of solid substratum to mystical spirituality throughout the Middle Ages. But the solidity of this substratum is due in large measure to the Desert Fathers and to the Evagrian-Cappadocian-Origenist tradition. It can be said that the Benedictine monastic tradition in the West keeps alive all that is most solid, fundamental and traditional in Christian asceticism and mysticism of the fourth century, and this tradition comes to life with the various *monastic revivals*. Hence there is very much of it to be found in the mysticism of the twelfth-century Cistercians. In

---

435. See Jean Krynon, "Contemplation: D. Au 16e Siècle: 1. En Espagne avant Saint Jean de la Croix: 2°. Les Maitres: Osuna et Laredo," *DS* 3, 387–94.

these there is found not only Cassian but the evident influence of St. Gregory of Nyssa, St. Maximus and even of Origen.

In addition to this primitive current we must now account for the dominant personal influence of the great Western Doctor of grace and of conversion: St. AUGUSTINE. The Augustinian theology, inseparable from the drama of Augustine's own conversion and of his whole life, comes to give all the spirituality of the West a special character of its own. Although it is misleading to speak of two separate and clearly contrasting traditions in the West, one Augustinian and the other Dionysian, there is without doubt this overwhelming influence of Augustine. Sometimes this influence is combined with Dionysius, sometimes with the primitive Origenist-Cassianist tradition of the monks, sometimes with both. But always the Augustinian spirit colors all mysticism and all mystical theology except in rare cases, usually after the thirteenth century. We find the Augustinian dominance everywhere: in the Victorines, though they also popularize Denys; in the Cistercians, though they keep alive the deep Cassianist-Origenist tradition; in the Franciscans, especially through St. Bonaventure. (Note: St. Augustine also dominates all Franciscan theology and philosophy in the schools.) The Dominicans begin to break away from the dominance of Augustine and it is in the Rhenish mystics, largely under Dominican influence or actually Dominicans themselves, that we see Dionysius preponderant over Augustine. Yet the influence of Augustine remains clear.

Speaking of the Rhenish mystics, we might mention here a technical distinction that has been made between "bridal mysticism" (BRAUTMYSTIK) and "being mysticism" (WESENMYSTIK):[436]

a) Bridal mysticism {is} affective, cataphatic, erotic, a mysticism of desire and espousal, {with a} stress on the faculties of the soul, especially the will; {it is} generally Augustinian {and} tends to be anti-intellectual.

---

436. See J.-B. P[orion], *Hadewijch d'Anvers: Poèmes des Béguines* (Paris: Éditions du Seuil, 1954), 17–19.

b) *Wesenmystik* {is} speculative, ontological, {emphasizing} union in the substance of the soul, more immediate, {highlighting} the *apex mentis*; {it is} apophatic but not necessarily anti-intellectual; {it} transcends {the} division of intellect and will, {and is} generally Dionysian.

Since in treating Western mysticism we are on more familiar ground we can work faster {and} not {be} concerned with too many details. What follows is a *broad outline*.

The Background of Western Mysticism:

A. *The Pelagian* controversy about grace created problems and emphases which were less noticeable in the East. {There was a} difficulty of adjustment of notions of *grace and asceticism*. {The} root problem {was} the part that must be played by our own effort in the spiritual life. {There are} oscillations between excessive confidence in our own efforts and a carelessness due to misplaced confidence in grace—without fidelity to grace. In the West the question: "What should I do? How much effort should I make? What is the proper balance between God's action and my action?" tends to become a burning one. Note that this problem largely remains dormant until it bursts into full flame with the Augustinian Friar, Martin Luther.

B. *Pessimism of Montanists and Manichaeans*: Tertullian, who retained a great influence in the West in spite of his heresy, rejected the created world as evil. He insisted on an *absolute opposition* between the Gospel and the world. {He had a} juridical spirit {and stressed the} idea of *merit*. The spirit of Tertullian combines extreme rigorism with *brutality in controversy*, the ready assumption that the adversary is a heretic or a crook, that he is a fool, or in bad faith. Note {that} this adversary is not a pagan or a Jew but *a fellow Christian*. {For} the Manichaeans, the power of God is shared with an eternal evil principle. {They preach a} rejection of sacramental life, clergy, etc. This smoulders until {the} twelfth century and then bursts out, {to be} violently repressed by arms and {the} Inquisition.

Note {also the example of} Jerome: his extremely active life {is} marked by incessant conflicts and disputes. {He is} the father of a tradition of monastic mandarins, a *complete stranger to mysticism*, {even} hostile to it. In rejecting Origen he was also rejecting all mysticism except what could be contemplated in the prophets: mysticism was for them, not for us.

In a word, the background of Western spirituality we find {marked by} this uneasy division and anxiety on the question of grace and effort, along with tendencies to activism, to violent controversy (not lacking in the East either), to pessimism, to a juridical and authoritarian outlook, and a pronounced *anti-mystical* current. The West is then to a certain extent predisposed to:

a) water down mysticism, and accept it in a diluted, more *devotional* form, or else reduce mysticism to *speculation* and study;

b) insist on social forms, rules, observances, practices, rites (this is by no means lacking in the East either).

These trends will be assimilated or opposed by Augustine in various degrees, and he himself will add other new elements that will give Western mysticism its own character.

A. St. Augustine—*Life and background*: {Augustine was} born {in} 354 of a pagan father and {a} Christian mother. {He was enrolled as a} catechumen as a child, but due to {a} pagan education fell into {an} immoral life. At 19 {he} reads {the} *Hortensius* of Cicero and starts seeking wisdom. {He} makes a first attempt with the Bible but is bored with it. {He} is in practical despair of ever being pure. {He} becomes a Manichaean for nine years. (Note {the} connection with his personal problem.) {In} 383, at 29, he goes to Rome. Having dropped Manichaeism, {he} cannot accept Christianity, and is close to despair. At Milan, {he is} impressed by St. Ambrose, especially his preaching on *the typology of Scripture*. {He} turns to Christianity intellectually and at *the same time discovers Plotinus*. {The} Epistles of Paul complete his *moral* conversion; {the} *Vita Antonii* strengthens and confirms his high Christian ideal. {In} 387, on the Easter Vigil, {the} night of

April 24-25, {he is} baptized at Milan. {He} forms {a} monastic community at Tagaste ({where he} lives {a} contemplative life {for} four years). {In} 391 {he is ordained} priest. {He} comments on {the} Psalms ({the} summit of his mysticism). {He was ordained a} Bishop {in} 395, {and} died 28 August 430.

The personality of Augustine and his Mysticism: the drama and conflict of Augustine not only profoundly and definitively shaped his own spirituality, but through him reached down to most of the medieval mystics of the Christian West.

a) His mysticism is highly *reflexive and subjective*. All that is said about subjective piety in the West, all the attempts to lay the blame on this or that later mystic, remind us to look to Augustine as to the real source. And yet Augustine was one of the great Fathers of the age when liturgical life flourished in its purity. His "subjectivism" is obviously quite compatible with a deep sacramental and liturgical piety and above all with a *profound sense of the Church*. To this extent there is a "synthesis" in Augustine born of the fervor of his love. It may even be said that perhaps it was the psychological intuitions and sensitivity of Augustine that enabled him to be so keenly aware of the nature of the Church as the Mystical Body, One in the charity of Christ. Perhaps the fact remains that his is a liturgical piety rather than a liturgical mysticism.

b) His mysticism is therefore closely bound up with *psychological observation*, especially reflection on the workings of mystical experience, its roots, etc.

c) This psychology reaches into his anthropology itself, with the Trinitarian structure of the image of God in man. This is found everywhere in the West after Augustine. It even reaches into Augustine's theology of the Trinity and consequently into the Western theology of the Trinity as a whole (the Word as the "thought" of the Father, the Holy Spirit as the love of the Father and the Son, hence proceeding from both the Father and the Son).

d) *The drama of the struggle with evil and the ascent to happiness in love and ecstasy* in Augustine's own life affects his mysticism and that of all the West after him:

1. The starting point {is} a longing for happiness in God, with a despair of ever attaining that happiness because of imprisonment in sin, specifically sin of the *flesh*. Conflict between fleshly and spiritual love becomes the basic conflict of all man's life and the root problem of the moral, spiritual and mystical lives.

2. The solution is not asceticism alone, because Augustine is too conscious of his own helplessness. {He has} a sense of the utter uselessness of man's efforts without the special help of grace. {He stresses} dependence on God, crying out to Him in prayer. This *dependence on grace* will be one of the salient characteristics of Augustinian asceticism, and of Western asceticism as a whole.

3. Hence, {there is an} ever-present consciousness of sin and of the power of grace, {a} sense of the evil of concupiscence, and {a} consequent *pessimism* about nature and natural good. {He has a} realization that we can never fully be without faults: "It is the mark of perfection to recognize our imperfection" (*Sermon* 170, n. 8).[437] The crisis of the Augustinian soul {is the} conflict between the consciousness of sin and the awareness (*MEMORIA*) of the fact that we are made *for God*, in His image. But we have lost our likeness to Him, and long to recover it. This is impossible unless God Himself intervenes to renew the lost likeness.

4. The solution is LOVE, and this love, produced in us by God, gives us also *joy and rest* in God. Hence {there is a} tendency to emphasize {the} *experience* of love, of salvation, that can be verified on reflection. This experience {is} to be nurtured by meditation on {the} positive truths of theology, on the light of revelation. It is by love, the fruit of grace, that the divine likeness is restored to the soul. The anguish of desire fed by the *MEMORIA* of our true nature as creatures in the image of God is appeased by the action of the *will* seeking to see Him above the *intelligence* and all created things.

5. Hence the *ascent to God* {progresses}: *INFRA se*—from inferior and exterior creatures (sensible, vestiges of God); *INTRA se*—to

---

437. *PL* 38, col. 931.

oneself, the soul as image of God; *SUPRA se*—to God Himself, above the soul.[438]

6. *Interior unity*: the three faculties of the soul, intellect, memory and will, correspond to the three divine Persons. In contemplation they are brought into perfect unity, and the *Holy Trinity is mirrored within the soul by its perfect unity.* HENCE THE MYSTICISM OF AUGUSTINE IS CENTERED WITHIN THE SELF, THE TRUE SPIRITUAL SELF NO DOUBT, BUT THE SELF AS MIRROR OF GOD.

7. This interior unity is reached by *gratuitous and pure love*—loving God because He is God, He is our all, seeking no other reward than Him, therefore praising Him with pure praise: *gratis amo quod laudo.*[439]

8. Yet nevertheless this produces the only true rest of our soul. *FECISTI NOS AD TE, ET INQUIETUM EST COR NOSTRUM, DONEC REQUIESCAT IN TE.*[440]

9. The purity of our love for God implies equally love of ourselves in and for God, and of our brother in and for God. {It means} humility and fraternal union without envy, in pure love of {one's} brother, the doctrine that I share all my brother's good by charity, and he mine. Love is everything: *Dilige et quod vis fac.*[441]

10. The summit of love is contemplation, in which the joys of the senses and of fleshly love are exchanged for the joys of spiritual experience and love. God is perceived by the "spiritual senses" as a light, as a voice, as perfume, as food, as an embrace. {There is an} emphasis on these positive experiences.

11. But note an apophatic element: what is experienced is in some sense beyond experience. We do not have the Dionysian

---

438. "beneath oneself . . . within oneself . . . above oneself": Augustine does not use this precise formula, but it represents his basic pattern of spiritual development.

439. "I gratefully love what I praise" (*Enarratio in Ps. 53*, n. 10 [*PL* 36, col. 626]).

440. "You have made us for yourself and our heart is restless until it rests in you" (*Confessions*, 1.1 [*PL* 32, col. 661]).

441. "Love and do what you will" (*Homilies on 1 John*, 7:8 [*PL* 35, col. 2033]).

vocabulary of darkness, but there is nevertheless an essential element of nescience or *unknowing*. NESCIO QUAM DULCEDINEM.[442] . . . NESCIO QUAM OCCULTAM VOLUPTATEM. . . .[443] However this is always corrected with reference to a *higher light*: DELECTATIO CORDIS HUMANI DE LUMINE VERITATIS.[444]

e) *The summit of spiritual experience* is vivid and transient, "like lightning."[445] It is an *immediate* experience, often a touch arousing awe, a *presence* causing a passively received delight. Note {that} Augustine never experienced a direct intuition of the divine essence, but believed such an intuition possible even in this life. This is important because in the West, as a result of this, there is always the strong hope, based on {the} conviction of its possibility, of *very positive experiences of God* or the divine light, presence and sweetness, in love. Later this will be transferred to a special conviction of the possibility of intimate experience of fruitive love for the person of Jesus Christ. In a word, it becomes characteristic of Western mysticism to emphasize a real embrace of love really experienced with God really present in a concrete form as light or some other positive attribute. The experience of God above forms, in darkness, beyond knowledge, tends to be set aside. BUT THIS POSITIVE EXPERIENCE IS ALWAYS IN THE MIRROR OF THE SOUL, hence what it tends to reduce itself to is a created effect in the soul of the contemplative and that effect is a *divinely given love* produced directly by grace. Hence Augustinian contemplation tends to be a direct experience of love as a miracle of grace in the soul and as the manifestation of God's loving presence, as a means of contact with Him. In what sense is this

442. "I know not what sweetness" (*Confessions* 10:40 [*PL* 32, col. 807]).

443. "I know not what hidden pleasure . . ." (*Enarratio in Ps. 41*, n. 9, which reads: "*nescio et . . .*" [*PL* 36, col. 470]).

444. "The delight of the human heart from the light of truth" (*Sermo* 179.6, which reads: "*Delectatio enim . . .*" [*PL* 38, col. 969]).

445. See *Confessions*, VII, c. xvii (23) (*PL* 32, col. 745): "*Et pervenit ad id quod est, in ictu trepidantis aspectus*" ("And it reached that which is, in the flash of a trembling glance").

immediate??? *Ecstasis*—at the summit of all is an ecstasy *beyond all images* (this expression is not Dionysian but came to Augustine from the neo-Platonists). *ALIENATIO A SENSIBUS CORPORIS UT SPIRITUS HOMINIS DIVINO SPIRITU ASSUMPTUS CAPIENDIS ATQUE INTUENDIS IMAGINI-BUS VACET.*[446]

Note {a} comparison of Augustine with {the} Greek Fathers:

> If to any man the tumult of the flesh be silent, if fantasies of earth and air and sea be silent also, if the poles of heaven be silent and the very soul of man be silent to itself, and by not thinking pass beyond itself, if all dreams be silent and all such things as be revealed by the imagination, if every tongue and every sign and every thing that hath its existence by passing-on be silent wholly unto any man . . . if then He only speak, not by them but by Himself, that we may hear His word not by tongue of flesh nor voice of angel nor by the sound of a cloud that is broken by thunder nor by the dark riddle of a similitude, and we may hear Him, Whom in these things we love, Himself, apart from them . . . and this alone might so transport and swallow up and wrap him who beheld it in these intrinsical joys, so that his life might be for all eternity such as was this moment of understanding . . . would not this be that whereof is written: "Enter thou into the joy of thy Lord"? (from Augustine's *Confessions*,[447] quoted in Colledge, *The Medieval Mystics of England*, p. 90).

This text contains familiar neo-Platonic ideas common to {the} Greek and Latin Fathers. It is quite general. Anyone could have written it; {there is} little to distinguish Augustine particularly. We must consider the whole question of approach. *Compare*:

---

446. "Separation from the bodily senses so that the human spirit, taken over by the Divine Spirit, might be empty of all images to be received and seen" (*De Diversis Quaestionibus*, 2.1 [*PL* 40, col. 129]).

447. *Confessions* Bk. 9, c. 10, n. 25 (*PL* 32, cols. 774–75).

St. Augustine	St. Gregory of Nyssa
a) ascent—*extra se* / *intra se* / *supra se*	a) light / cloud / darkness
b) subjective, reflexive, dialectical, psychological	b) less personal and subjective, more ontological
c) cataphatic—culminating in (possible) intuition of {the} divine essence	c) beyond *apophasis*
d) personal crisis and drama of Augustine gives orientation to his mysticism	d) experience not of crisis but of {a} return to Paradise; *normal* state {is} optimism about nature

Hence at the summit of Augustinian contemplation there is an *immediate union with God* in ecstasy, immediate in the sense that it is without any *sensible* form or image but in the direct embrace of love (how intellectual?). Contact with God {comes} by love, beyond sense and vision, out of oneself; *raptus supra se*[448] is then what is meant by immediate union with God in the Augustinian context. At the same time we might still consider that love itself were a medium, a created effect. {The} solution {is that} reflection on the experience of love is of course mediate. Ecstatic love is an immediate contact with God Who IS LOVE (though grace always remains in some sense a created medium). This is apparently *beyond reflection*, until after it has gone.

f) *The Mysticism of the Church in Augustine*: what has been said so far does not show the greatness of Augustine. In these matters he compares perhaps unfavorably with some of the great Eastern mystics. What is important is the *reality of his vision of the Church*, of his mysticism of humility and charity leading to the experience of Christ, the *humility of* God in the *humility of the Church*, as a visible social entity functioning in history for the salvation of mankind.

448. "rapt above itself" (the exact phrase is not found in Augustine).

1) Humility {is} the great characteristic of the Incarnation, and *pride* in man is the great tragedy, {the} refusal of God's humble love. This refusal is a refusal of the humility of the Church.

2) Mutual need, mutual love, mutual prayer is the strength of the Church. *Quia ergo in Christo vos amamus, in Christo nos redamate, et amor noster pro invicem gemat ad Deum (In Joan.* VI.1).[449] {This means} going to Christ together, supporting one another. The humility and love in the relation of the bishop to his priests and flock is an epiphany of Christ.

The role of the Church in contemplation for Augustine is clearly described in the commentary on Psalm 41 (*Quemadmodum desiderat*).[450] This enarration on the Psalm is one {of} the primary sources for Augustine's mystical doctrine, comparable to the vision at Ostia.[451] In this commentary Augustine speaks of seeking God in creation, outside himself, of seeking God within himself, and of ascending to the brief glimpse of the contemplation of heaven in which God is enjoyed (*fruitio*). The key concept of the commentary is that the transition to the glimpse of heaven is made through an intuition of God's beauty in the Church, *in the virtues of the faithful*. Hence what is characteristic of Augustine is the *communal* orientation of his desire for mystical union, his stress on *love*, on *thirst for God*, a thirst that is shared, and increased by being shared, helping all on toward an enjoyment which is all the greater for being shared. It is to be observed, however, that on this level, the intuition of the Church, we have simply a variant of *theoria physike*. The highest experience, ecstasy, is transcendent for Augustine as for all the mystics, and is beyond distinction between persons, beyond the self as distinct from other selves.

---

449. "Therefore, because we love you in Christ, love us in Christ in return, and our love for one another may breathe forth to God" (*PL* 35, col. 1425).

450. *PL* 36, cols. 464–76.

451. See *Confessions*, Bk. 9, c. 10, nn. 23–26 (*PL* 32, cols. 773–75); this is the famous account of the mystical experience shared by Augustine and his mother Monica shortly before her death.

{Here are} some characteristic passages from {the} *Enarratio in Ps. 41* (see {the} translation in Butler, *Western Mysticism*, p. 21 ff.): Introductory (n. 2): "Come my brethren, catch my eagerness; share with me this my longing, let us both love [*simul amemus*], let us be influenced with this thirst, let us hasten to the well of understanding."[452] Characteristic of Augustine is this longing for divine light, longing for love, longing for experience, thirst, desire. "Long for this light, for a certain fountain, a certain light, such as thy bodily eyes know not [note a certain apophatic quality]; a light, to see which the inward eye must be prepared; a fountain, to drink of which the inward thirst must be kindled. Run to the fountain; long for the fountain . . . etc."[453] He then says we must run "like the hart,"[454] which, according to myth, kills serpents. That is to say, we must kill our vices. {Here is the} traditional theme of *purification from passion* necessary for contemplation. (Butler omits a very important part of the sermon [n. 4], the thought that when harts [stags] are crossing a river together, they rest their heads upon the backs of those in front of them and swim across helping one another, and the one at the head of the line, if he gets tired, goes to the end and rests his head on the last one. "To such stags the apostle speaks, saying: bear ye one another's burdens."[455]) After purity of heart has been attained, the contemplative must "pour out his soul above himself"[456] and come to the "house of God."[457] He only comes to the "high and secret place"[458] of God's house by passing through His tabernacle on earth, which is the Church. "It is here that He is to be sought for; it is here that

452. Butler, *Western Mysticism*, 21, which reads: ". . . share with me in this . . . let us both be influenced . . . let us both hasten . . ."
453. Butler, *Western Mysticism*, 21, which reads: "Long thou for . . . thirst is to be kindled . . ."
454. Butler, *Western Mysticism*, 21.
455. *PL* 36, col. 466.
456. Butler, *Western Mysticism*, 22, which reads: "poured out my soul above myself" (n. 8).
457. Butler, *Western Mysticism*, 22, which reads: "house of my God" (n. 8).
458. Butler, *Western Mysticism*, 22, which reads: "high in secret place" (n. 9).

is found the way by which we arrive at His house."[459] *Admiration* of the tabernacle prepares us for ecstasy. "It was thus, that whilst admiring the members of the tabernacle, he was led on to the house of God: BY FOLLOWING THE LEADINGS OF A CERTAIN DELIGHT, AN INWARD MYSTERIOUS AND HIDDEN PLEASURE, AS IF FROM THE HOUSE OF GOD THERE SOUNDED SWEETLY SOME INSTRUMENT; and . . . following the guidance of the sound, withdrawing himself from all noise of flesh and blood, made his way on even to the house of God."[460] The sounds of the perpetual festivity in the house of God are heard by those who withdraw from the noise of the world and walk apart in His tabernacle. It awakens their longing and they seek after it with thirst and desire. To attain to the House of God one must, however, transcend the tabernacle.

This "Churchly" dimension of the Augustinian experience is what saves it from subjectivity. This must be remembered. *In the context of the Church* the love received from God through the Church can be accepted without hesitation and without question. It is the real and genuine expression of Christ living in us, the same who is in ourselves, in our brethren, and in the whole Church—and in heaven. *Hence in this love we transcend ourselves.* Without the context of love in the Mystical Body, reflection on our inner experience of love would be merely subjective fixation on our own psychological experiences.

Rising above change and flesh, the soul attains to a fleeting perception of the Unchangeable. Compare {this} with the vision at Ostia:

> We were discoursing together alone, very sweetly, and we were enquiring between ourselves in the presence of the Truth, which Thou art, of what sort the eternal life of the saints was to be. With the lips of our souls we panted for the heavenly streams of Thy fountain, the fountain of life which

---

459. Butler, *Western Mysticism*, 23, which reads: ". . . sought, for it is in the tabernacle that . . . at the house" (n. 9).

460. Butler, *Western Mysticism*, 23 (n. 9).

is with Thee, that, sprinkled with that water to the measure of our capacity, we might attain some poor conception
of that glorious theme. And as our converse drew to this
conclusion, that the sweetest conceivable delight of sense
in the brightest conceivable earthly sunshine was not to be
compared, no, nor even named, with the happiness of that
life, we soared with ardent longing towards the "Self-same"
[i.e. the unchanging God], we passed from stage to stage
through all material things, through heaven itself, whence
sun and moon and stars shed their radiance upon earth.
And now we began a more inward ascent, by thinking and
speaking and marvelling at Thy works. And so we came to
our own minds, and we passed beyond them, that we might
come unto the region of unfailing plenty, where Thou feed-
est Israel for ever with the food of truth. There Life is the
wisdom by which all things come to be, both those that have
been and those that are to be; and the Life itself never comes
to be, but is as it was and shall be ever more, because in it
is neither past nor future but present only, for it is eternal.
And as we talked and yearned after it, we touched it—and
hardly touched it—with the full beat (toto ictu) of our heart.
And we sighed and left there impawned the firstfruits of
the spirit, and we relapsed into articulate speech, where the
word has beginning and ending (*Confessions* IX.23, 24,[461]
quoted in Butler, *Western Mysticism*, p. 32).

Here instead of the "tabernacle" and the virtues of all the faithful,
it is Monica herself who serves as the medium to prepare for the
contemplative experience: more accurately it is their common
love, which serves them as a stepping stone to a kind of ecstatic
glimpse of the "Self-same." It is to be noted however that this is
not a pure description of mystical ecstasy, but it still savors much
more of *theoria physike* if not of Platonist dialectic. It would be
difficult to call Augustine the "Prince of Mystics" (Butler)[462] on
the basis of these passages.

461. *PL* 32, col. 774 (c. 10).
462. Butler, *Western Mysticism*, 20.

B. Western Mysticism: BUTLER'S THESIS. Let us examine here briefly the arguments advanced by Cuthbert Butler. The whole purpose of his book, doubtless a good one, is to reestablish the rights of traditional Benedictine mysticism and contemplation. He is defending the monastic contemplation of the Middle Ages, based on Gregory, Augustine and Bernard, {contrasting it} with modern mysticism which is either a mysticism of night like that of St. John of the Cross or a mysticism of visions, like that of so many modern saints and mystics with a capital M. Butler's thesis, without being aggressively dedicated to the task of proving Western mysticism absolutely better, certainly presupposes that the mysticism of Augustine etc. is more germane to us in the West, more natural to us, more proper to us, and that we should be formed according to this tradition first of all. Let us examine his arguments and evaluate their worth. According to Butler,[463] "Western mysticism" has the following characteristics:

1. IT IS PRE-DIONYSIAN: that is to say, it is a "pure" Western form of mysticism that antedates the influence of Pseudo-Denys in the West (medieval).

a) Dionysian mysticism is a mysticism of darkness, says Butler. Western mysticism is a mysticism of light: "Contemplation is a revelation of light and knowledge and fullness."[464] Criticism: Pseudo-Denys combines a cataphatic theology and an apophatic theology, and the summit is a synthesis of both, going beyond both, to a *"supersplens lumen."*[465] Hence Butler's division is not accurate.

b) The Dionysian influence in the West is treated as a kind of irruption of neo-Platonism into the West. Criticism: Augustine was just as much a neo-Platonist as Denys. The contention that the mysticism of Augustine, Gregory and Bernard is pre-Dionysian needs to be qualified. There are certain traces of Denys

463. Butler, *Western Mysticism*, 123–28.
464. Butler, *Western Mysticism*, 123.
465. "light beyond light"; the terminology is Dionysian, though the exact phrasing is not his.

in Bernard and even Gregory. *The real problem* is not the division between Augustinian (Western) and Dionysian (Eastern) mysticism: but to bring out the primitive tradition of the East and West united in one like Cassian, and *complicated by* Augustine and later by Dionysian writers of the Middle Ages *who were themselves more Augustinian than Dionysian in any case.*

2. It is pre-scholastic: this is correct. The Victorines begin already to treat mysticism systematically. The scholastics tend to institute a *science of contemplation.* Augustine, Gregory and Bernard are interested in contemplation itself, not in writing about the science of contemplation. However let us remember that the followers of the Victorines and other mystical writers who were themselves Augustinian, preserved the interest in contemplation, but tended more and more *to oppose it to theology and science.* It was certainly due to the influence of Augustinianism more than to that of Denys that scientific theology and mystical theology parted company in the Middle Ages. Both however were responsible. Most responsible of all were the scholastics themselves and the Aristotelians.

3. It is without visions and revelations: this is true. The visions and extraordinary graces attributed to Bernard are of course to be taken into account, but they are quite separate from his own writing and may be apocryphal (???). Note however that the visionaries of the thirteenth century on tend to be very much influenced by the Augustinian-Gregorian-Bernardine tradition and to be formed in it, for instance Blessed Juliana,[466] {an}

---

466. The reference is to Blessed Juliana of Mont Cornillon, or of Liège, who is credited with initiating the feast of Corpus Christi; she is said to have learned more than twenty of St. Bernard's sermons on the Canticle by heart, and her most famous vision was of the moon crossed with a black stripe, which she eventually came to understand as a symbol of the liturgical year without the feast of Corpus Christi. See the *Vita B. Julianiae*, Book I, c. 1, and Book II, c. 2, in *Acta Sanctorum*, ed. Ioannis Carnandet, *Aprilis (Tomus I)* (Paris & Rome: Victor Palmé, 1866), 444D, 457D; an English translation is now available: *The Life of Juliana of Mont Cornillon*, trans. Barbara Newman (Toronto: Peregrina, 1991).

Augustinian nun, who knew many sermons of St. Bernard by heart, and was a visionary.

4. No ecstasies affecting the body {are found}: this is correct, but again it is in the tradition of Augustine/Bernard/Gregory that the ecstatic trend is most clearly developed in the Middle Ages.

5. {There is} no diabolism: this is not fully correct. There is no pathological diabolism. But see the *Dialogues* of St. Gregory, even in the *Life of St. Benedict*. There are at least as many appearances of or frays with the devil as there are mystical experiences recorded, perhaps more; I have not counted them. As for the later monks, just see {the} *Exordium Magnum*[467] and Caesar of Heisterbach!![468]

6. {There are} no quasi-hypnotic symptoms: this appears to be a gratuitous dig at the Byzantine hesychasts and is not worth bothering with. The hesychasts were not hypnotizing themselves.

C. Western Mysticism: Further Notes on Latin Mysticism—The Franciscan Movement

Enough has been said, in speaking of the Victorines, etc., to get a general idea of the Latin mysticism of the Middle Ages. Space does not permit details here. A few notes must suffice. Our approach is now going to be *historical* more than anything else. {It is} vitally important to understand the unparalleled awakening of popular mysticism, both orthodox and heretical, and to try to apprehend something of its tremendous significance. The

---

467. Conrad of Eberbach, *Exordium Magnum Cisterciense*, ed. Bruno Griesser, *Corpus Christianorum Continuatio Medievalis* [CCCM], vol. 138 (Turnholt: Brepols, 1994); ET: *The Great Beginnings of Cîteaux: The Exordium Magnum of Conrad of Eberbach,* trans. Benedicta Ward and Paul Savage, CF 72 (Kalamazoo: Cistercian Publications, 2006).

468. *Caesarii Heisterbacensis Monachi Ordinis Cisterciensis Dialogus Miraculorum*, ed. Joseph Strange (Coloniae: J. M. Heberle, 1851); ET: Caesarius of Heisterbach, *The Dialogue on Miracles*, trans. H. Scott and C. C. Swinton, 2 vols. (London: Routledge, 1929); see also the *De Daemonibus* (*Sui Demòni*, ed. with Italian trans. by Sonia Maura Barillari [Alessandria: Edizioni dell'Orso, 1999]).

way was prepared by the monastic mysticism of the Cistercians and Benedictines and the ferment of monastic reform in the eleventh and twelfth centuries; above all the personal impact of *St. Bernard*, the "friend of God,"[469] on the populations of all parts of Western Europe, prepared the way. Note: {there were} many visionaries contemporary with St. Bernard, v.g., St. Hildegard. {There was} a reawakening of the sense of *charismatic mission* and of *prophecy* as opposed to the clerical and hierarchical structure of Christendom. Everyone was by now disillusioned with clergy and religious who were to become more and more lax in spite of great waves of reform.

The Cistercians (of whom we will treat extensively elsewhere[470]) represent the fine flower of medieval monastic spirituality and mysticism. {Theirs was} a Biblical mysticism, centered on the mystery of Christ, a traditional mysticism, centered on the ancient way handed down by Cassian, St. Gregory the Great and the Benedictines, with a generous admixture of all that is best in Augustine and some notable traces of Dionysius. {It was} a school of experience, in which personal experience is not so much analyzed and dissected, as *expressed* fully and poetically in the traditional images and terms of Scripture. Hence the character of Cistercian mysticism is to *relive* the Scriptural mysteries in one's own personal life, without undue subjectivism. {It was} a school of love, centered on the idea of the recovery of the lost likeness to God, the restoration of the image which is in us by nature. {There is need to} stress the wholeness and originality and sanity of the Cistercian school. {The} originality of particular authors, especially *William of St. Thierry* and *Isaac of Stella*, {is} worthy of a very

---

469. See A. Chiquot, "Amis de Dieu," *DS* 1, col. 493.

470. Merton's course entitled "Cistercian Fathers and Monastic Theology," given to the novices in 1963, is found in volume 20 of the Gethsemani "Collected Essays" collection; Merton also gave conferences to the novices, evidently begun in the latter part of 1961 (see *Turning Toward the World*, 125 [June 10, 1961]), on "The Cistercian Order from the Death of St. Bernard to the Reform of Benedict XII," also found in volume 20 of "Collected Essays."

detailed study; *St. Bernard* of course needs no introduction here. The Cistercian heritage goes down not only in the Franciscan tradition but also among the Flemish, German and English mystics.

Joachim of Flora: one great Cistercian who is usually neglected, and whose memory has been systematically suppressed because of the condemnation of his writings, {is} Joachim of Flora, the prophet. He is *one of the most important figures in the Middle Ages*. His mysticism is somewhat heterodox and apocalyptic, and certainly he is not a model to be followed in the contemplative life. He may well have been a false mystic, though there is no question of his sincerity or subjective probity. We will not discuss his mysticism here—what matters is *the immense influence it exercised*. Born in Calabria in 1132, Joachim was more subject to Byzantine influences than to those from northern Europe, France, etc. However he was regarded as a successor to St. Bernard as {a} preacher and mystical reformer of the Church. {In} 1178, when Abbot of Corrazzo, {he} received papal permission to withdraw to a hermitage and write his prophetic books. These are a powerful criticism of the clergy and its corruption, and point, as divine remedy, to a providential cleansing and a destruction of institutional Christianity, to be replaced by the "Eternal Gospel" of the Holy Ghost. Joachim foretold a new age of "love and freedom" as opposed to authority and despotism. The Church was, in the new age of the Holy Spirit, to be ruled by contemplatives, and by the Holy Spirit through them. Especially {he} foretold two new orders: this was taken to be a prophetic prediction of the coming of the Mendicants. Joachim dies in the odor of sanctity in 1202. His doctrines were developed by disciples. Dante places Joachim in the twelfth circle of heaven,[471] that of the "Prudent"—with St. Bonaventure, St. Thomas, St. Anselm, Hugh of St. Victor, etc.

The *Franciscan* movement is especially tied up with the Joachimite prophecies, and when the crisis of the order ensued,

---

471. Joachim is actually in the fourth circle, the Heaven of the Sun, but it is in Canto XII of the *Paradiso* (ll. 140-42) that he is mentioned (by St. Bonaventure) (Singleton, *Paradiso*, 139).

the *Spiritual Franciscans* looked back to Joachim for their inspiration and carried on a bitter struggle, convinced that they had a mission to carry out what he had predicted. This in turn spread and continued on down through the fourteenth and fifteenth centuries and undoubtedly contributed to the breakaway of the Protestants from the Church. Whatever may be the Church's judgement on Joachim (his ideas were condemned but his holiness was approved, and nothing has ever been said to impugn his honesty or rectitude), it is certainly true that he had a historic and mighty influence which cannot be ignored and should not be too contemptuously dismissed, even though he may have been in great part deluded. His "mission" may not have been directly the work of the Holy Ghost through a true prophet, but there was an element of natural prophetism that responded to the unconscious aspirations and drives of Western history—at least this.

Pourrat[472] attributes the appearance of *flagellantes* to the influence of Joachim. Certainly many obscure and heterodox popular movements responded to his influence. On the other hand he was *not alone* by any means. There were many more heterodox and really heretical movements in the twelfth century, marked by rejection of some of the most important doctrines of the Church, the throwing off of all authority, and frank rebellion. Mention need only be made of *Arnold of Brescia*, the Waldensians, the Albigensians. The fact that in a time when these movements were hated and violently repressed by the Church, Joachim was accepted, trusted and blessed by the popes is surely of significance. He must not be loosely equated with the heretics. He was universally respected and approved by the Church, and his work was posthumously condemned only after his disciples had caused it to be interpreted in dangerous ways, and hotheads had in fact appealed to him to justify rebellion.

---

472. Pierre Pourrat, *Christian Spirituality, vol. 2: In the Middle Ages*, trans. S. P. Jacques (1927; Westminster, MD: Newman, 1953), 80.

The most important aspect of the new piety was the development of the *consciousness of the laity* as a vital and important force in Catholic life. This went hand in hand with the development of the communes, with a growing disrespect for traditional forms of authority, and for the clergy, with a new sense of the evangelical aspect of Christian life. It was combined with growing individualism. Individualism is today a "bad word." However this growth was necessary and inevitable at that time. The Middle Ages witnessed the spontaneous and universal growth of "modern forms of piety" outside the liturgy: devotion to the Eucharist, the Holy Name, to Our Lady (on a larger, more universal scale), to saints and angels, etc.

St. Francis: in the midst of all the turbulent and confusing movements that expressed the new awakening of the laity and the yearning for a more evangelical life, St. Francis represented at once the perfect expression of Christian poverty and humility united with complete obedience and devotion to the Church. Note the crucial importance of the ideal and mystique of *poverty*. It is the very heart of late medieval mysticism from the Franciscans on down through the Rhenish and English mystics to the sixteenth-century Carmelites, in varying forms: from the stripping of all possessions and mendicancy to interior stripping, "annihilation," descent into one's own nothingness, littleness, etc. From the thirteenth to the sixteenth centuries and even beyond, we are in the *mysticism of poverty* (significant as the counterbalance to the great development of *riches and power* in {the} secular sphere). Francis was a providential sign, raised up by the Holy Spirit, to manifest in himself the true Christian life in all its fullness—a perfect reproduction of the loving obedience of Christ crucified, His self-emptying and His glorification. Francis, bearing in his body the marks of the Passion, with his passionate love for the Gospel, the Cross and the Church, was also a perfect witness of the Resurrection by his paradisiacal life, his power over man and beast, his *complete and universal love*, transcending suffering. Francis manifested the fullness of the reign of perfect love in a man, a small group of men, totally dedicated to Christ, in the *new way* of mendicant poverty and itinerant preaching, alternating with periods of eremitical solitude. The great mark of Francis is the *perfect synthesis* of all trends and movements in the likeness to Christ, {the} synthesis of action and contemplation, solitude and society, obedience and freedom, homelessness and being at home everywhere, poverty and mastery over all creation, study and mysticism, etc., etc. In a word, ST. FRANCIS STARTED A CHARISMATIC MOVEMENT OF SPIRITUAL REFORM WHICH BROUGHT MYSTICISM OUT OF THE CLOISTER AND ONTO THE HIGHWAYS AND BYWAYS OF THE WORLD. He met and fulfilled completely all the needs that had been awakened by Bernard, Joachim of Flora, etc., etc.

The Franciscan Crisis: while Francis was abroad, driven by his love for souls and his charismatic zeal for the salvation of Islam (which was certainly not understood by his contemporaries), his *Vicar General Fr. Elias* began the undermining of his work at home, with all the solid motives of a more human wisdom. This crisis is tremendously important and significant to students of spirituality, not only for the effect that it had in the history of the Franciscans and of the Church, but for its symbolic quality. The incident reminds us of the struggles of the Old Testament prophets against human inertia and raises the great question of spiritual ideals: can they ever be fulfilled? Are they even meant to be fulfilled? {Is it a matter of} the mystery and scandal of the Franciscan ideal and the defection (?) of the first followers of Francis? Or were they providential instruments without which the order could not have been preserved? It was a reaction of institutionalism, taking over where Francis had deliberately refrained from creating an institutional structure. {There was} a twofold reaction against St. Francis' own ideal:

a) Introduction of and insistence upon *studies*. St. Francis' opposition to study was *not devotional*. He believed that the friars could, with sufficient fervor, maintain the higher synthesis that would keep them above the dichotomy {of} intellect vs. will, study vs. love and devotion. His followers returned to the dichotomy and resorted to a human synthesis which was a compromise in the eyes of the Founder. {There was a} return to the use of *money*. The *building of churches* and convents, including splendid ones, {began}.

b) Emphasis {was placed} on *conventual discipline* (replacing the hard but free and unpredictable life of the roads and the hermitages). More *numerous fasts* (i.e. systematic penances) {were instituted} to replace the blind spontaneous abandonment to Providence, taking whatever was set before them.

In 1220, St. Francis reacted in characteristic fashion: following the Gospels, he *resigned* in favor of Fr. Elias who was destroying his work and continued to destroy it. This was certainly not the way of human wisdom. {In} 1224 (17 September), St. Francis received the stigmata. {In} 1226 {he} wrote the *Testament* and the *Laudes Creaturarum*: pure joy and perfection must be seen against the background of suffering and defeat. But for Francis there could no longer be any such thing as defeat. {He} died Oct. 3, 1226, listening to the reading of St. John, chapter 13. {He was} canonized {in} 1228.

Reactions against the adaptations of Fr. Elias: Brother Leo and the *Observants* continue to emphasize life in the hermitages as against the Conventuals; {the} Capuchins develop out of the Observants. The *Spiritual Franciscans* were carried away by their singleminded obsession with poverty to the extent of putting it above obedience to the Holy See, and even above charity (says Vandenbroucke[473]). Basing themselves on Joachimist ideas, they resisted the Holy See. They are first recognized officially in 1294, then finally condemned after they refused to admit that the ideal of poverty must be interpreted by the superiors of the order.

St. Bonaventure was outstanding for his spirit of moderation and understanding. He reached a middle position and with his prudence showed the way out of the crisis. Total poverty was not fully compatible with a large communal organization. Where there was an institution the emphasis naturally fell back on in-

---

473. See *Histoire de Spiritualité*, vol. 2, 362; ET: 298.

terior poverty and obedience. Let us briefly outline some of the main themes in Bonaventure's mysticism (cf. E. Longpré in *DS*).[474] *St. Bonaventure*, the "Seraphic Doctor," {created} the great Franciscan synthesis, {which was} essentially mystical. The Word teaches man three kinds of theology, says Bonaventure: (1) *speculative* (*propria*)—rendering truths of faith intelligible; (2) *symbolic theology*, by exemplarism, leads to union with God by universal analogy; (3) *mystical*—{which} leads to {the} ecstasy of love. {There is an overarching} UNITY. (Note: all science leads to mystical contemplation, {according to the} *De Reductione Artium ad Theologiam*.) "*Ut per propriam recte utamur intelligibilibus, symbolicam {recte utamur} sensibilibus, mysticam rapiamur ad supermentales excessus*" (*Itinerarium Mentis in Deum*, I).[475] Tota mystica theologia consistit in dilectione excessiva *secundum triplicem Viam: purgativam, illuminativam et perfectam* (*In Luc.*).[476] Grace re-creates {the} *soul* in {the} image of {the} Holy Trinity; virtues rectify the *powers of the soul*; sacraments heal wounds and strengthen {the} soul; gifts and beatitudes lead to perfection according to {the} directives of God's will. The soul recovers {the} faculty of contemplation lost by original sin. St. Francis is the model of Christian perfection and contemplation, after Christ Himself. {The} purgative {and} illuminative ways {are} characterized by {the} action and initiative of {the} soul, {the} *unitive* way {by} *passivity* of {the} soul under {the} action of grace, {marked by the} primacy of love

---

474. E. Longpré, OFM, "Bonaventure," *DS* 1, cols. 1708–1843.

475. "that through theology proper we might rightly use intelligible things, through symbolic theology we might properly use sensible things, through mystical theology we might be lifted up to raptures beyond the mind" (*Itin.* 1.7 [*Opera Omnia*, 5.298], quoted in Longpré, col. 1772—though Merton reverses the order of the first two divisions).

476. "All mystical theology consists in ecstatic love according to a triple [hierarchical] way: purgative, illuminative and perfective" (*Commentary on Luke*, 13.21 [which reads "*triplicem Viam hierarchicam*"] [*Opera Omnia*, 7.349], quoted in Longpré, col. 1773).

and of *susceptio sponsi*.[477] "St Bonaventure est de tous les écrivains spirituels celui qui a le plus inculqué aux âmes le désir des ascensions mystiques et en a affirmé avec plus de force l'inéluctable necessité" (Longpré, *DS*).[478]

De Reductione Artium ad Theologiam {emphasizes the} unity of all science converging in mystical contemplation (see above). Contemplations {involve} (a) {the} gift of understanding, {which is} *intellectual*, speculative (*per viam* splendoris)—taught by Augustine; (b) {the} gift of wisdom, {which is} *sapiential*, mystical (*per viam* amoris)—taught by Denis.[479]

1. *Intellectual Contemplation—Itinerarium Mentis in Deum* (see *Late Medieval Mysticism*—the best sections are translated in this anthology).

#1. The Supreme Good is above us; {therefore} no one can be happy unless he rises above himself and {this} cannot {be done} by one's own power—hence {the} necessity of prayer.[480]

#2. The ascent to God {takes place}:

a) *extra nos*: *vestigia* (sense; imagination)—symbolic theology;

b) *intra nos*: *imago* (reason; intellect)—theology *ut sic*;

c) *supra nos*: God Himself (intelligence; *apex mentis*)—mystical theology.[481]

---

477. "union with the Spouse" (*De Triplici Via*, 3.1 [*Opera Omnia*, 8.12], quoted in Longpré, col. 1810).

478. "St. Bonaventure is, of all spiritual writers, the one who has most inspired in souls the desire for mystical ascents, and has affirmed with the most force the absolute necessity for them" (Longpré, col. 1815).

479. "through the way of brightness"; "through the way of love" (*Commentary on Luke*, 9.49 [*Opera Omnia*, 7.232], quoted in Longpré, col. 1819; for a similar passage from the *De Reductione*, see above, page 148).

480. *Itinerarium* 1.1 (*Late Medieval Mysticism*, 132).

481. "outside ourselves: traces . . . within ourselves: the image . . . above ourselves . . . the high point of the mind" (*Itinerarium*, 1.2 [*Opera Omnia*, 5.297]; the phrase *"apex mentis"* is not used here but is found in 1.6 [*Opera Omnia*, 5.297]).

These six powers {are}: in us by nature; deformed by sin; re-formed by grace; purified by justice; exercised by knowledge; made perfect by wisdom; all this {is} done by Christ (read #7, *Late Medieval Mysticism*, p. 134[482]).

Contemplation (ch. VII)—{the} summit of contemplation {incorporates} (a) the Passion (#2); (b) reproducing the ecstasy of Francis (#3); (c) {a} passive {stance} (#4):

> If this transition, however, is to be genuine and perfect, then must all labor on the part of the soul's reasoning faculty cease and the soul's deep affection be centered in God and transformed, as it were, into him. So mysterious and sublime is this experience that none save he to whom it has been given knows anything of it, that nobody receives except he who desires it, and this desire comes to him only whose being is inflamed by the fire of the Holy Spirit—sent by Christ upon the earth. Hence it is that the "hidden things" of God were revealed, as the apostle says, by the Holy Ghost (*Late Medieval Mysticism*, p. 140);

482. "In his primitive constitution man was created by God capable of untroubled contemplation, and for that reason was placed by God in a 'Garden of delights.' But, turning his back on the true light in order to pursue the mutable good, he found himself, through his own fault, diminished and removed from his pristine stature. With him the whole human race, through original sin, was afflicted in a twofold manner: the human mind by ignorance and the human body by concupiscence. As a result man, blinded and bent down, sits in darkness and sees not the light of heaven, unless he be strengthened against concupiscence by grace with justice, and against ignorance by knowledge with wisdom. All this is done by Jesus Christ, 'who of God is made unto us wisdom and justice and sanctification and redemption.' He, being the Power and Wisdom of God, the incarnate Word full of grace and truth, is the Author of both grace and truth. He it is who infuses the grace of charity which, when it comes 'from a pure heart, and a good conscience, and an unfeigned faith,' is capable of ordering the whole soul according to the threefold aspect above mentioned. He also taught the knowledge of truth according to the triple mode of theology: by symbolic theology in which he teaches us how we might rightly use sensible things, by theology properly so-called wherein we learn the use of things intelligible, and by mystical theology through contact with which we may be raised aloft to things unspeakable" (*Late Medieval Mysticism*, 134–35 [*Opera Omnia*, 5.298]).

#5 quotes Dionysius (read[483]); #6 {is} *very important*: grace not study, {as well as the} *active choice* of silence rather than thought, etc.

2. *Sapiential Contemplation* {involves the} perfect union of love, {a} knowledge *"per gustum et experientiam."*[484] {It} culminates in *ecstasy of will*—giving an immediate experience of God: *"in vertice est unitio amoris."*[485] {In} *ecstasy*, the soul is united to God outside its (ordinary) self, *in apice mentis*, not *per modum visus et intuitus*, but *per modum tactus et amplexus*.[486] Note the role of the spiritual senses and {the} distinction between them. *"Vis illius unionis est immediate unitiva Deo super omnia ut quodam modo dormiat et vigilet."*[487] {There is} a "death of love": *Iste amor est sequestrativus, soporativus, sursumactivus. Sequestrat enim ab omni affectu alio propter Sponsi affectum unicum. Soporat et quietat omnes potentias et silentium imponit.* Sursumagit *quia ducit in Deum*.[488] In the

483. "O supereminent and transcendent Holy Trinity, inspiration of all Christian philosophy, direct our steps to the unknown, sublime, and resplendent heights of mystic utterances. On these heights are to be found the new, the absolutely unquestionable and unchanging, mysteries of theology, hidden away, as it were, in the obscurity of excessively lightsome darkness and illuminating silence. Here on these heights, so resplendent in their excessive light, men are enlightened and spiritual souls are filled with the splendors of the true good" (*Mystical Theology*, 1.1 [*Late Medieval Mysticism*, 140]).

484. *"ad gustum et experimentalem cognitionem"* ("by taste and experiential realization") (*Commentary on the Sentences*, III, d. 35, a. 1, q. 3, ad. 1, 2 [*Opera Omnia*, 3.778], quoted in Longpré, col. 1825).

485. "at the height is the union of love" (*Collations on the Six Days*, 2.29 [*Opera Omnia*, 5.344], quoted in Longpré, col. 1828).

486. "at the high point of the spirit . . . by means of vision and intuition . . . by means of touch and embrace" (*Commentary on the Sentences*, III, d. 14, dub. 1 [*Opera Omnia*, 3.292], quoted in Longpré, col. 1829).

487. "The power of that union brings about oneness with God immediately, above all things, so that in a certain sense one sleeps and remains awake" (*Commentary on the Sentences*, III, d. 27, a. 2, q. 1, ad. 6 [*Opera Omnia*, 3.604], quoted in Longpré, col. 1830).

488. "This love has the power to separate, to put to sleep, to raise up. For it separates from any other affection because of the unique love for the Spouse. It puts to sleep and quiets all powers and imposes silence. It raises up because

sleep of the powers—{in} darkness—"*Sola affectiva vigilat et silentium omnibus aliis potentiis imponit.*"[489] "*Oportet quod relinquantur omnes intellectuales operationes.*"[490] ({There is a} controversy as to how to interpret this: Longpré thinks[491] it means just leaving behind those intellectual operations *which depend on sense. The total emptiness of intellect is in rapture. Rapture* {entails} immediate contact with God without any thought at all . . . [??] {It is} an extraordinary state like unto prophecy, {involving} direct revelation: "*Ultima pars vitae spiritualis in via.*"[492])

IX. Fourteenth-Century Mysticism

A. *Lay Spiritual Movements:*[493] the thirteenth century continues trends begun by {the} Albigensians, etc. in the twelfth; for instance: *I Fedeli dell'Amore,* {devotees of a} sophianic popular mysticism related to erotic love trends in secular literature; {the} *Brethren of {the} Free Spirit,* {practitioners of} Flemish popular mysticism {in a} secret society; *Brothers of the Apostles,* {who were} violently opposed to the Church of Rome ({their} founders {were} burned); *Lay Penitents,* {who were dedicated} to repair outrages of Albigensians on {the} Blessed Sacrament, etc.; *Humiliati,* {who were} pacifists—some remain in the Church, some break away. N.B. *new orders:* active orders like {the} Crosiers {and} Trinitarians, {were formed} to meet new needs among {the} laity, {the} sick,

---

it leads into God" (*Collations on the Six Days,* 2.31 [*Opera Omnia,* 5.341], quoted in Longpré, col. 1834).

489. "Only the affections remain awake, and impose silence on all other powers" (*Collations on the Six Days,* 2.31 [*Opera Omnia,* 5.341], quoted in Longpré, col. 1834).

490. "One must leave behind all operations of the intellect" (*Itinerarium,* 7.4 [*Opera Omnia,* 5.312], quoted in Longpré, col. 1835).

491. Longpré, col. 1838.

492. "The ultimate part of the spiritual life here on earth" (*Collations on the Six Days,* 23.10 [*Opera Omnia,* 5.455-56], quoted in Longpré, col. 1840).

493. See *Histoire de Spiritualité,* vol. 2, 420–23; ET: 349–51.

captives etc.; *confraternities* {developed, which were} leading a marginal life outside parish and liturgy, but {were} important.

B. *The "FRAUENBEWEGUNG"*:[494] {note} the importance of an ideology centered on "the lady": idealization of the lady in chivalrous literature, {reflecting the} dignity of woman; {the} cult of the Blessed Virgin; the growth of a new society {which was more} commercial, in which woman is less an object of conquest and possession by the strong warrior, {and} exists in her own right. *Vernacular* literature and piety give scope for expression of feminine experience: women ({who} ordinarily didn't know Latin) could now express themselves. {There is an} influence of this on the development towards bridal mysticism. Love, mercy, suffering take on greater importance, as opposed to ascetic aggressivity; the *passive* virtues {are} emphasized. Yet some of the women saints were tremendously strong and active, v.g. Catherine of Siena.

> It was a moment in history in which woman, mother of renewals and of dawns, drew forth from the sacred depths of her being a fresh inspiration for the civilizations of the letter and of iron. In the spiritual order, at such a time, in their simplicity, protected by a precious ignorance, more patient and also more prompt in sacrifice, they give the religious life a new impetus. Hence we see the Béguines create a new language to translate their passionate experiences, seek God in a more immediate and total union, and proclaim as it were an interior gospel of a new demand on the part of eternal love (Dom J. B. Porion, in his introduction to *Hadewijch d'Anvers*).[495]

The Béguines and Beghards[496] began at {the} end of {the} twelfth century {and} prepare {the} way for fourteenth-century mysticism. Originally {they were} grouped around a chapel or church

494. "the women's movement."
495. Porion, 11.
496. See *Histoire de Spiritualité*, vol. 2, 425-30; ET: 353–57.

served by mendicant {religious in} response to {the} Franciscan call to popular devotion and mysticism. {They lived} without vows, {but with a} promise of chastity during residence. {They led a} simple community life, with manual labor—spinning, weaving, {and practiced} simple, personal, individualistic devotions to Jesus and Mary. Reclusion {was} encouraged; ecstatic piety {was characteristic}; {the movements were} very rich in spirituality. But one of the drawbacks of the Béguinages and their popular mysticism was the fact that these uninstructed people, left to themselves, often deviated into queer bypaths of pseudo-mysticism, or at least expressed themselves in terms which invited condemnation. The errors of the Béguines and Beghards (men) condemned by {the Council of} Vienne in 1311–1312 (Denzinger, 471 ff.[497]) are mostly *pre-quietist*, due obviously to misunderstandings by simple minds and exaggerations: that the perfect could become impeccable, and that they did not need to exercise themselves in virtue, obey the precepts of the Church or superiors, pay external reverence to the Blessed Sacrament, or even guard themselves against certain impure acts. With all this, one could attain to perfect beatitude by contemplation in the present life. Note, however, in the majority of cases, with wise direction, these errors were avoided. These errors will be met with again and again and will continue to develop throughout the late Middle Ages and into modern times. We shall see them culminate in *Molinos*. At the same time, note the Béguines were sometimes judged with extreme harshness. Marguerite Porete was burnt at the stake in 1310 principally for some propositions which were later taught by saints and have now become quite ordinarily accepted. One of these {is} that the perfect soul does not care for the consolations of God but occupies herself with Him directly. A book, evidently hers, and containing the censored prepositions, is in print today and accepted without question—*The Mirror of*

---

497. Henricus Denzinger and Carolus Rahner, eds., *Enchiridion Symbolorum Definitionum et Declarationum de Rebus Fidei et Morum*, 31st ed. (Rome: Herder, 1957), 220–21 (nn. 471–78).

Simple Souls. Note: there are also pontifical documents *in favor* of the Béguines.[498] There was a certain *overemphasis on the marvelous and miraculous*, v.g. in the life of St. Christine.[499] Undoubtedly the levitation ascribed to the Béguines contributed to the great craze about witches in the fourteenth-fifteenth centuries. Note the *fear* which was aroused on all sides by these thousands of women living strange mystical lives.

Summary: we must not exaggerate the defects of the Béguines and Beghards. Certainly there were grave dangers and abuses, but the fact is that there were even greater benefits for those thousands of devout souls who were not able to live in convents and who thus had a life of prayer and simplicity opened to them, and attained sanctity. {Note the} *importance* for us: the Flemish Béguinages were important centers of early lay mysticism; the movement that sprang up in them, and the need for directors, led to the whole flowering of mysticism in the Rhineland and Netherlands in the fourteenth century. {We must recognize the} great significance of the dialogue between theologians and mystics in the Béguinages and convents of {the} Low Countries and Germany!

The Cistercian Nuns:[500] the mystics of the Cistercian nunneries of the thirteenth century are very closely related to the Béguines, and help them in preparing the way for fourteenth-century mysticism. *St. Lutgarde* is an example, {along with} the three Idas, Blessed Alice, etc. Most especially *Blessed Beatrice of Nazareth* is important for her mystical autobiography, written in the vernacular, one of the first of its kind (see *Vie Spirituelle*, Supplément,

498. See Porion, 14, referring to J. de Guibert, *Documenta Ecclesiastica Christianae Perfectionis: Studium Spectantia* (Rome: Gregorian University, 1931), nn. 279, 281, 282.

499. There were actually two Christines, of Belgium and of Stommeln (near Cologne), both known as "*Mirabilis*" for their miraculous powers (see Porion, 14 and 15, n. 14).

500. See *Histoire de Spiritualité*, vol. 2, 432–33; ET: 359–60.

{1929}[501]). Beatrice had been formed by Béguines before becoming a Cistercian, as {were} also Ida of Louvain, Blessed Mechtilde of Magdeburg, etc. (Mechtilde was a Béguine).

Hadewijch of Antwerp:[502] little is known of her, but she is generally agreed to be a thirteenth-century Béguine—or rather there are two authors of the series of poems attributed to Hadewijch, including a "deutero-Hadewijch" responsible for the more Eckhartian poems (*Wesenmystik*), while the other was more a "bridal mystic" (*Brautmystik*). They were evidently influenced by the Cistercians, especially Bernard and William of St. Thierry, and also of course by St. Augustine. On the other hand, she (they) is prior to Eckhart. The poems of the Second Hadewijch seem so much like Eckhart that some have thought they follow his teaching. On the contrary, quite probably they *anticipate* it.[503] Ruysbroeck was inspired by the poems of {the} Second Hadewijch.[504]

Special Traits of Popular Mysticism of the Béguines, as exemplified in Hadewijch:

1. {There is an} ardent quest for union with God *without medium* of signs, words and reasoning, and even "beyond virtues."[505] A German poet of the thirteenth century sums up in verse the

---

501. *La Vie Spirituelle*, Supplément, 19 (1929), 320–32; French translation by J. Kerssemakers. This is actually not her autobiography but a short treatise, "The Seven Degrees of Love," which corresponds to a chapter in the *Vita* of Beatrice attributed to William of Afflighem, based on notes written by Beatrice (see *Histoire de Spiritualité*, vol. 2, 432; ET: 359, which erroneously gives the date as 1939, followed by Merton).

502. See *Histoire de Spiritualité*, vol. 2, 434–38; ET: 361–64, and Porion, *passim*.

503. See Porion, 47–51.

504. See Porion, 46–47.

505. See the words of the twelfth Béguine in Ruysbroeck's *Book of the Twelve Béguines*: "To practice virtue in all loyalty—and beyond the virtues, to contemplate God—there truly is what I value" (quoted in Porion, 172, n. 1). See also Porion's comments on the condemned proposition from Marguerite Porete about "taking leave of the virtues," properly understood as "practicing the virtues without being concerned with them" (12, n. 5), and the similar perspective in Jacopone da Todi's *Lauda* 60 (50, n. 65).

spirituality of the Béguines: Sein selbst und aller Dinge frei /
Ohn Mittel sehen, was Gott sei![506]

2. Personal distinction tends to vanish in union. (This was
{a} dangerous doctrine and brought trouble to Eckhart.) This is
properly understood when we see it in the context of total self-
sacrifice out of love, sharing in the poverty and self-emptying of
the Word Incarnate. Also it is inseparable from {a} profound *eucharistic devotion* in Hadewijch and in many saintly Béguines. It
is communion that leads to "union without difference."[507] {There
are} *two levels of mystical rapture*: (a) to be *ravished in spirit*; (b) to
be *ravished out of the spirit*.[508]

3. {There is} emphasis on interior passivity and freedom—
without neglect of duties of {one's} state. (But some expressions
of this tended to suggest contempt for ordinary virtues—hence
needed qualification.) Hadewijch {was} always clear—{she was}
for virtue.

4. {There is} absolute intellectual simplicity, without reflection, "without why"—the theme goes back to the Cistercian mystic Beatrice of Nazareth and ultimately to St. Bernard.[509]

5. {There is a} purity of love {that is} forgetful of personal
advantage, {a} *total self-sacrifice*; *Mary* is the model of pure love.

6. In Hadewijch there is also an *ardent apostolic love for souls*
and great burning concern for the salvation of sinners; but purity
of love demands that the soul refrain from works, since pure love
is itself the highest of all works. Read here the classic statement
of *St. John of the Cross*:

> Here it is to be noted that, for so long as the soul has not
> reached this estate of union of love, it must needs *practise*

---

506. "Free of themselves and of all things, / To see without medium what
God is" (Lamprecht von Regensburg, *Die Tochter Sione*, quoted in Porion, 49, n.
61).

507. Hadewijch, *Vision* 7, quoted in Porion, 32.

508. Porion, 33, following Joseph Maréchal, SJ, *Études sur la Psychologie des
Mystiques*, 2 vols. (Paris: Desclée de Brouwer, 1937), 2.286.

509. See Porion, 49–50, 147, n. 6.

love, both in the active life and in the contemplative; but when it reaches that estate it befits it not to be occupied in other outward acts and exercises which might keep it back, however little, from that *abiding in love with God*, although they may greatly conduce to the service of God; for a *very little of this pure love* is more precious, in the sight of God and the soul, and of greater profit to the Church, even though the soul appear to be doing nothing, than are all these works together. For this reason Mary Magdalene, although she wrought great good with her preaching, and would have continued to do so, because of the great desire that she had to please her Spouse and to profit the Church, hid herself in the desert for thirty years in order to surrender herself truly to this love, since it seemed to her that in every way she would gain much more by so doing, because of the great profit and importance that there is to the Church in a very little of this love.

Therefore if any soul should have aught of this degree of solitary love, great wrong would be done to it, and to the Church, if, even but for a brief space, one should endeavor to busy it in active or outward affairs, of however great moment; for, since God adjures the creatures not to awaken the soul from this love, who shall dare to do so and shall not be rebuked? *After all, it was for the goal of this love that we were created.* Let those, then, that are great actives, that think to girdle the world with their outward works and their preachings, take note here that they would bring far more profit to the Church and be far more pleasing to God (apart from the good example which they would give of themselves) if they spent even half this time in abiding with God in prayer, even had they not reached such a height as this. Of a surety they would accomplish more with one piece of work than they now do with a thousand, and that with less labour, since their prayer would be of such great deserving and they would have won such spiritual strength by it. For to act otherwise is to hammer vigorously and to accomplish little more than nothing, at times nothing at all; at times, indeed, it may even be to {do harm. May God forbid that your salt should begin to} lose its

savour; and yet although in such a case it may seem superficially that it has some effect, it will have no substantial
effect, for it is certain that *good works cannot be done save in
the strength of God* (both quotations from *Spiritual Canticle*,
Peers translation, p. 346-7).[510]

These were difficult truths to explain in acceptable terms,
and those who misunderstood them went very far into error. The
Rhenish speculative mystics and Ruysbroeck were in large measure attempting to justify and clarify the immense, hidden, inar-
ticulate movement of the spirit that had taken place among the
Béguines with so many good and bad effects. The problem was
to channel this spiritual power, not let it run riot.

From the poems of Hadewijch (written in the popular style of
troubadour love-poetry):

I must leave my inheritance, and on the highroads
Walk alone, wherever free love bids me go (II).[511]

He who takes the road of love
Let him give himself faithfully
To every good work.
For Love's honor alone
Let him serve and all his life
Prize his sublime choice.
From Love Himself he shall receive
All the strength that is lacking to him
And the fruit of his desires.
For love can never refuse Himself
To whoever loves Him

---

510. Annotation (2-3) for Stanza XXIX (line dropped by eyeskip in mimeograph) (Peers, vol. 2).
511. Porion, 64 (ll. 17–18) (the poem numbers are taken from Porion's selection, which do not correspond to the critical edition).

He gives more than we expect
And more than He made us hope (IV).[512]

This is the theme of risking all for love, abandonment and going forth one knows not where or how, trusting in His fidelity. (Note: she does not discard good works.) {For the themes of} prayer and insistent desire for love, compare St. Thérèse of Lisieux.[513]

Ah! I have no longer any way of living
Love, you know it well!
I have kept nothing that is my own
Give me what is thine!
But alas, even if you give me much
I will still hunger, for I want all (IV).[514]

Another Carmelite theme:

At the high-point of the spirit,
Of this I am certain
Love must pay love with love (VII).[515]

512. Porion, 70–71 (ll. 13–24).

513. See St. Thérèse of Lisieux, *Story of a Soul*, c. 8: "And now I have no other desire except *to love* Jesus into folly. . . . Neither do I desire any longer suffering or death, and still I love them both; it is *love* alone that attracts me, however. . . . Now, abandonment alone guides me"; c. 9: "The science of Love, ah, yes, this word resounds sweetly in the ear of my soul, and I desire only this science. . . . I understand so well that it is only love which makes us acceptable to God that this love is the only good I ambition"; c. 11: "A scholar has said: '*Give me a lever and a fulcrum and I will lift the world.*' What Archimedes was not able to obtain, for his request was not directed by God and was only made from a material viewpoint, the saints have obtained in all its fullness. The Almighty has given them as *fulcrum*: HIMSELF ALONE; *as lever*: PRAYER which burns with a fire of love. And it is in this way that they have *lifted the world*" (*Story of a Soul: The Autobiography of St. Thérèse of Lisieux*, trans. John Clarke, ocd [Washington, DC: Institute of Carmelite Studies, 1976], 178, 187–88, 258).

514. Porion, 72 (ll. 67–72).

515. Porion, 83 (ll. 68–70).

{There are} frequent complaints at the dolors of love, longing for death, etc., complaints at having been deceived by Love. This is a Cistercian theme (cf. *vicissitudo* [516] and *languor animae amantis*[517]).

> Know well, there are more sorrows in love
> Than there are lights in the starry heavens (VIII).[518]

> Before the all is united to the All
> Many a bitter draught must be tasted (VIII).[519]

> How the All is seized by the all
> This will never be known by strangers (VIII).[520]

(Love is a hell.)

> If a man will face this truth let him beware
> For in the presence of love nothing will serve
> Except to receive at every moment blows or caresses
> Striking even to the center of the faithful heart (XIX).[521]

The "Second" Hadewijch:[522] here we have not complaints at the sufferings and aridities of love abandoned by the Beloved, but praise of naked and essential knowledge in the abyss of luminous darkness, "without modes."[523]

---

516. "alternation": see St. Bernard, *In Cantica*, 31.1 (*PL* 183, col. 940C), 32.2 (*PL* 183, col. 946C); the expression is also found in Guerric of Igny, *In Festo Benedicti, Sermo* 4.5 (*PL* 185, col. 115B) and in Gilbert of Hoyland, *In Cantica* 25.5, 27.7, 30.1, 31.2 (*PL* 184, cols. 133A, 144D, 155B, 161B); see Gilson, 241, n. 215, for a discussion of this term in Bernard.

517. "the languor of the loving soul" (William of St. Thierry, *Expositio in Epistolam ad Romanos*, 5.9, which reads: "*Languor est . . .*" [*PL* 180, col. 645A]); cf. Song of Songs 2:5: "*quia amore langueo*" ("Because I languish for love").

518. Porion, 85 (ll. 17–18).

519. Porion, 87 (ll. 77–78).

520. Porion, 87 (ll. 81–82).

521. Porion, 128 (ll. 206–209).

522. For distinctions in style and focus, see Porion, 45–56.

523. A term perhaps most familiar from the conclusion of Ruysbroeck's *Adornment of the Spiritual Marriage* (". . . a nakedness where all the divine names, aspects, living reasons which are reflected in the mirror of the divine

She is alone in an eternity without shores
Herself limitless, saved by the Unity that swallows her up,
The intelligence, with desires at rest
Vowed to total loss in the totality of the Immense One:
There a simple truth is revealed to her
A truth that cannot but be simple: the pure and naked
    Nothing (I).[524]

In the intimacy of the One these souls are pure and naked
    interiorly
Without images, without figures
So though liberated from time, uncreated
    [cf. condemned proposition of Eckhart[525]]
Freed from all limits in the silent vastness (I).[526]

The noble light shows itself in whatever way it pleases
It is of no avail to seek, or to intend, or to reason:
These must be banished. One must remain within
In a naked silence, pure and without will:
In this way one receives
The nobility which no human tongue can express
And the knowledge that springs forth ever new from its
    untouched source (II).[527]

. . . penetrate into the bareness of the One
Above understanding

---

truth, fall in a simplicity beyond name, beyond reasons, beyond modes" [Porion, 161, n. 1]), but which is found throughout the work of the thirteenth- and fourteenth-century Flemish and Rhenish mystics (see also Porion, 17, 21, 34, 45, 136 [n.1], 146 [n. 3], 147 [n. 5], 156 [n. 1]).

524. Porion, 134 (ll. 13–18).

525. Denzinger and Rahner, 229 (n. 527): "*Aliquid est in anima, quod est increatum et increabile; si tota anima esset talis, esset increata et increabilis, et hoc est intellectus*" ("There is something in the soul that is uncreated and uncreatable; if the entire soul were such, it would be uncreated and uncreatable, and this is the intellect").

526. Porion, 134–35 (ll. 33–36).

527. Porion, 140 (ll. 15–20).

Where all help of light fails us
Where desires meet with nothing but darkness
A noble something, which I know not,
Which is neither "this" nor "that"
Guides us and leads us and absorbs us in our Origin (II).[528]

"Without why":

The multitude of reasons beyond number
Which make me prefer you, Lord, to all things
Escapes me when I turn in nakedness to you alone
Loving you without why, loving yourself for yourself (II).[529]

{She is} evidently influenced by the great theme of St. Bernard: *Amo, quia amo*.[530] Note the place of Christ crucified in this "unknowing" Love:

It is in the wounds of Christ that one acquires nobility
And loses all knowledge (II).[531]

Note also, there is great emphasis on the practice of every virtue, especially meekness, patience, humility, mercy, gentleness, *charity*. Here we see the mysticism of a saintly Béguine at its best.

In the popular mysticism of the Béguines, etc. we must remember the tendency to more and more extraordinary manifestations (though this is contrary to what we see above in Hadewijch). Ecstatic piety is common—visions, revelations, sensible manifestations of spiritual realities—in spite of the insistence of the spirituality against this—levitation, stigmatization, etc. The powerful movement of popular mysticism attracted the attention of the Inquisition, as we have seen above. The Béguines were not only condemned for doctrinal errors but their mysticism tended to be suspect, and it was not unusual for a "mystic" to be condemned to death for some strange manifestations that had attracted notice.

528. Porion, 140–41 (ll. 32–36).
529. Porion, 141 (ll. 51–54).
530. "I love because I love" (*In Cantica*, 83.4 [*PL* 183, col. 1183B]).
531. Porion, 143 (l. 87).

Some people found it hard to draw the line between Béguines, heretical sects, "witches" and so on. There was great confusion: boundary lines were not sharply drawn and many crossed over the boundaries without knowing they had done so.

The Women Saints of the Late Middle Ages: not only did a vastly popular mystical movement exist, but in the late Middle Ages we see the *greatest saints* are not the men and not even women in convents, but *women of the laity*. This is a matter of great significance. The place occupied in the twelfth century by St. Bernard, in the thirteenth by Sts. Francis and Dominic, is occupied in the fourteenth by St. CATHERINE OF SIENA, St. Bridget of Sweden, surrounded by many others of lesser stature. Catherine of Siena, a layperson, {a} Dominican Tertiary, assumes the role of visionary monitor of the popes that had been exercised by St. Bridget of Sweden when the latter died in 1373. The fact that Bridget and Catherine were women only emphasized the surprising power of their supernatural gifts, and helped them to be accepted by the popes as friends and instruments of God. A few notes {are in order} on Catherine of Siena as a woman with a special and prophetic vocation in the medieval Church. There is no question that she was raised up by God for her charismatic role. This brought home to all the fact that heaven was using *special means* to warn men, in a time of crisis when the voice of God had repeatedly been ignored. She had first of all a clear sense of her mission. This was supported by a *perfectly orthodox mysticism* which could not be doubted. She was taught directly by Christ, through the Holy Spirit. She served as His instrument for the good of the Church. At the heart of her mysticism is a burning love for and devotion to the Church and the papacy. Her mission was sealed by a complete mutual giving between herself and Christ. Although a Dominican in spirituality, she nevertheless stands above all schools and movements. She is a spiritual phenomenon in herself. *Her spirituality and mysticism* correspond entirely to the needs of her mission. "I am He who is; thou art she who is not."[532] {Note} her sense of her own nothing-

---

532. See *Histoire de Spiritualité*, vol. 2, 494, 497; ET: 412, 415.

ness and {her} complete abandonment to the action of Christ. Total humility is the guarantee of her efficacy as an instrument in society, and this humility was recognized and respected. It was the "sign" of Christ. {Her} burning love for Christ and for souls {reveals a} perfect likeness to Christ in love for all. *The central idea* in the mysticism of Catherine of Siena is not speculation about various forms of union, not inquisitive examination of how union takes place, or how to ascend to higher degrees of love and fruition: it is rather TOTAL SELF-SACRIFICE FOR THE CHURCH, CONCERN FOR THE PURITY AND PERFECTION OF THE CHURCH rather than her own, {a} LOVE FOR SINNERS AND DESIRE FOR THEIR REDEMPTION. The fact that she was a laywoman is not secondary but absolutely primary: it stresses the *relative unimportance of belonging to this or that order* and the supreme importance of UNION WITH CHRIST CRUCIFIED for the redemption of sinners.

The full import of Catherine's charismatic mission is to be seen only when we realize the background. Catherine dies in 1380. At this time there is a great sense of disillusionment with clergy, hierarchy and with the religious orders. The corruption of the clergy has finally brought the laity to lose confidence in the priests and even in the Church. *Wyclif* at the time of Catherine's greatest activity is preaching that only the holy belong to the Church, which is "purely invisible." He is also denying transubstantiation and the value of the sacrament of orders. At the same time the more or less heterodox mystics, or those on the margin of the Church's life, are tending more and more to *ignore* the Church, her discipline, her worship, her hierarchy, etc. Even the orthodox mystics tend to abstract from the problems and scandals of the visible life of the Church.

{In the} *fifteenth century,* most of the saints are women.[533] *St. Frances of Rome* {is} a mystic who is also a wife and a mother. *St.*

---

533. *Histoire de Spiritualité*, vol. 2, 595–98, 601; ET: 500–502, 505, for all these women except St. Lidwyne (of Schiedam), who is mentioned by Porion (26, n. 27) as coming into conflict with a priest who refused to consider a host, which descended from heaven into the young woman's hands, to be consecrated.

Catherine of Genoa {was} married; her married life {was} a hell. {She is known for her} care of {the} poor and sick, {and her} visions of Purgatory, {which} anticipate {the} Dark Night {of} St. John. *St. Lidwyne* {was a} visionary {marked by} suffering, a Béguine {who had to} struggle with {the} clergy concerning her experiences. *St. Joan of Arc* {had} one of the most extraordinary charismatic missions of all time. {She was} executed May 30, 1431. The "irresistible" prophetic call {came to her} outside of all familiar religious forms, and orders. Her sanctity {consists} in her fidelity to the extraordinary call she received from God. She cannot be regarded strictly as a martyr, and her visions as such do not constitute her sanctity. (Note: in a contemporary document Joan of Arc is called, no doubt loosely, a Béguine.[534])

B{₁}. The German Mystics of the Fourteenth Century

Background – Summary:

1. {Note} the popular widespread movement of mysticism outside the cloister, among Béguines, among unattached groups of lay people, among heterodox groups. This movement tends to be *independent of the clergy*. The use of the *vernacular* is of very special importance.

2. However note that the *mendicant orders*, particularly the Dominicans, encourage and guide the movement. They provide theologians and directors and preachers. The theologians and preachers *learn from* the unlettered mystics they guide, and *disseminate* the doctrine thus learned. They are in many cases mystics themselves, but their mysticism undoubtedly owes a great deal to their penitents.

3. Note the emphasis on poverty—crucial since the twelfth century and {the} mendicant movement. This question is vital; but the emphasis is now on *interior poverty* above all, and the *stripping of self*, "annihilation," so that God can give Himself directly and *immediately*, without impediment.

---

534. The *Chronique de Morosini* (1429), cited in Porion, 26, n. 27.

4. There is a tendency to be *autobiographical*, and to share one's mystical experience with others; see for instance Suso's *Autobiography*.

Forerunners: besides the Béguines and especially Beatrice of Nazareth and Hadewijch, already mentioned, {these include}: *St. Hildegarde of Bingen*, {the} twelfth-century visionary "officially" approved by St. Bernard and Eugene III: she foretold {the} coming of Protestantism (?) {and made} apocalyptic prophecies; *Mechtilde of Magdeburg*, {who was} first a Béguine, directed by {a} Dominican, Henry of Halle, {and} later a Cistercian at Helfta, in her last years; her book of visions, *Flowing Light of the Godhead*, {is} remarkable for her genius as {a} poet. {The} key to her spirituality {is} *immediacy*, hence poverty: "Nothing must subsist between me and Thee—put aside all fear, all shame, and all [undue confidence in] exterior virtues";[535] *St. Albert the Great*, himself a mystic and great *magister* of theology at Cologne, prepared the way for the Dominican mystics who grew up under his influence; he was one of the great Dionysians of the thirteenth century.

Movements:

1. In the center {is} the Rhenish school of mystical (speculative) theologians and preachers: *Eckhart, Tauler, Suso* and members of other mendicant orders besides the Dominicans.

2. The Flemish mystics, centered around *Ruysbroeck*, whom we include here with the Rhenish mystics, due to lack of time.

3. *The Friends of God*: due to {the} Black Death and other tragedies of {the} time {they emphasize} fear of {the} wrath of God, but not stopping at fear they see {that the} only solution lies in being the "Friend of God," loving Him for His own sake alone. {They show the} influence of St. Bernard's distinction {of} slaves, mercenaries, friends.[536] Mechtilde of Magdeburg speaks of the mystic as

---

535. *Histoire de Spiritualité*, vol. 2, 451–52; ET: 376–77.

536. *De Diligendo Deo*, 12–14 ([*PL* 182, cols. 995B–998B]; the progression is also found in *Conference* 11 of Cassian [*PL* 49, col. 853A] and elsewhere in patristic writing).

the "close friend of God."[537] St. Bernard {was} remembered in {the} Rhineland as a holy man and "friend of God."[538] Hence, {for this} popular movement of mysticism, {the goal was} to become a friend of God, in Suso's term, as *one who has completely abandoned his own will.* {See} Suso on "the higher school of Gelassenheit":

> Once after Matins, the Servant sat in his chair, and as he meditated he fell into a trance. It seemed to his inner eye that a noble youth came down toward him, and stood before him saying: "Thou hast been long enough in the lower school and hast exercised thyself long enough in it; thou hast become mature. Come with me now! I will take thee to the highest school that exists in the world. There thou shalt learn diligently the highest knowledge, which will lead thee to divine peace and bring thy holy beginning to a blessed fulfillment." Thereat he was glad and he arose. The youth took him by the hand and led him, as it seemed to him, to a spiritual land. There was an extremely beautiful house there and it looked as if it was the residence of monks. Those who lived there were concerned with the higher knowledge. When he entered he was kindly received and affectionately welcomed by them. They hastened to their master and told him that someone had come who also wished to be his disciple, and to learn their knowledge. He said, "First I will see him with my own eyes, to see if he pleases me." On seeing him, he smiled at him very kindly and said, "Know from me that this guest is quite capable of becoming a worthy master of our high learning, if he will only patiently submit to living in the narrow cage in which he must be confined." The Servant turned to the youth who had brought him there and asked, "Ah, my dear friend, tell me, what is this highest school and what is this learning thou hast spoken of?" The youth replied: "The high school and the knowledge which is taught here is nothing but the complete, entire abandonment of one's

---

537. Chiquot, col. 494; see *Flowing Light of the Godhead*, 1.22, 44, 3.10, 6.1, 7.31.
538. Chiquot, col. 493.

self, that is to say, that a man must persist in self-abnega-
tion, however God acts toward him, by Himself or by His
creatures. He is to strive at all times, in joy and in sorrow,
to remain constant in giving up what is his own, as far as
human frailty permits, considering only God's praise and
honor, just as the dear Christ did to his Heavenly Father"
(Suso: *The Life of the Servant*: "The Higher School of Gelassenheit," quoted in *Late Medieval Mysticism*, pp. 259-60).[539]

The movement was to some extent secret and esoteric, not
exactly anti-clerical but outside the normal sphere of clerical influence. Priests belonged to it and gave direction. It was not anti-
sacramental, but definitely aimed at a *democratic* atmosphere in
which priest and people were not separated by a wide gap. Members included a priest, Henry of Nordlingen, Rulman Merswin,
{the} anonymous author of {the} *Book of the Poor in Spirit*, lords
and nobles as well as many humble people. Tauler and Eckhart
were included as "Friends of God." The *Theologia Germanica*
(*Theologia Deutsch*) is a product of this school. It calls attention to
{the} distinction between true and false friends of God.[540] {It em-
phasizes} a call to deification (Vergottung) by a perfect following
of Christ *above and beyond both action and contemplation* (see
below[541]). The Rhenish mystics seek above all a synthesis in
Christ, born in the soul, liberating the contemplative from all
limited forms, so that he is equally free and united to God in
suffering or joy, action or contemplation, etc., because "happiness
lies not in what is done by the creature but in what is done by
God."[542]

---

539. *Life of the Servant*, chapter 19 ("Gelassenheit": "abandonment").

540. See *Histoire de Spiritualité*, vol. 2, 474; ET: 396.

541. Page 212.

542. *Theologia Germanica*, c. 9 (this and later quotations from the *Theolo-
gia Germanica* do not correspond to either of the available English translations:
Theologia Germanica, trans. Susanna Winkworth [New York: Pantheon, 1949];
Theologia Germanica: The Way to a Sinless Life, trans. Thomas Kepler [Cleveland:
World Publishing, 1952]).

Mysticism of Eckhart and {the} German School: Eckhart (1260-1327) {was} prior and vicar in his order, {the} Dominicans; a highly respected theologian, preacher {and} director, {he} taught as *magister* in Paris, Strasbourg and Cologne. His sermons were transcribed by nuns to whom he preached—Dominicans, Benedictines, Cistercians, etc. Although Eckhart is not the mystic of the German school we most recommend for reading in the monastery (on the contrary he is to be read only with great caution), he is nevertheless the one representative of the school who is *most extensively studied* today, especially by non-Catholics. Dr. Suzuki, the Zen Buddhist, seems to derive most of his knowledge of Christian mysticism from Eckhart, to whom he is greatly sympathetic.[543] Several studies and anthologies of Eckhart (by Protestants) have recently appeared in English.[544] No translation of Tauler is yet available.[545] Only a few texts of Suso and Ruysbroeck are to be had in English. Hence those in the monastery who meet non-Catholics or specialists in these fields need to be at least aware of Eckhart's existence and of what the Church thinks about him. He is perhaps *not* the greatest mystic of the Rhenish school. He is above all a brilliant mind, a genius in speculative theology, but one who was not careful to moderate his language by prudent discretion.

543. See D. T. Suzuki, *Mysticism: Christian and Buddhist* (New York: Harper, 1957).

544. See Raymond Blakney, trans., *Meister Eckhart: A Modern Translation* (New York: Harper, 1941); James M. Clark, *The Great German Mystics: Eckhart, Tauler and Suso* (Oxford: Blackwell, 1949); James M. Clark, *Meister Eckhart: An Introduction to the Study of his Works, with an Anthology of his Sermons* (New York: Nelson, 1957); James M. Clark, trans., *Meister Eckhart: Sselected Treatises and Sermons Translated from Latin and German* (London: Faber and Faber, 1958); a Catholic perspective from this period is provided by Jeanne Ancelet-Hustache, *Master Eckhart and the Rhineland Mystics*, trans. Hilda Graef (New York: Harper Torchbook, 1957).

545. In fact an English translation of Tauler appeared during this very year: see John Tauler, *Spiritual Conferences*, trans. Eric Colledge and Sr. M. Jane (St. Louis: Herder, 1961); Merton mentions this translation in a January 29, 1962 letter to Etta Gullick (*Hidden Ground of Love*, 350).

Doctrines:

1) *Exemplarism*: underlying Eckhart's mystical teaching is the idea of the destiny of all creatures to *return to find themselves in the Word* in Whom alone they have their true being. Return to the exemplar {is a return} to the "eternal luminous image of oneself in the Son of God beyond every sensible image, every sign and every concept."[546] This was propounded by St. Albert the Great following Scotus Erigena and the neo-Platonists.

2) *Immediacy*: God as Creator is immediately present to every being which He maintains in existence. Their being is not *outside* Him in the void, but it is *distinct* from His Being. He alone is; all that He creates is, outside of Him, pure nothingness. But it is in Him, apart from Him. *In man*, this immediacy is also on the level of grace, above nature, for the *Son of God is born in the center of the soul* that is in grace, and thus, intimately united with the one Son of God, we become, with Him, "one Son of God."[547] Hence we are *divinized* in proportion as we are stripped of all that is not the Son of God born in us, in the center of our soul. This is done by the action of the Holy Spirit, taking the *scintilla animae and restoring it to its original source in the Word.* VÜNKELIN—the *scintilla* or spark of the soul—is a light in the center of the soul, above all the faculties, "always opposed to what is not God,"[548] but buried, so to speak, under the ashes of our selfish preoccupation and self-will. GRUND—what is the relation of the "spark" to the "ground" of the soul? The *ground* is the naked, nameless, solitary essence of the soul *flowing directly from God* without medium. It is also treated as the *uncreated grace* of God, i.e. God Himself present to the soul, born in the soul as Son. {This is} a very deep and difficult concept. Most of Eckhart's troubles {are} due to the confusions in explanation of what constituted the immediate

---

546. Raphael-Louis Oechslin, "Eckhart," *DS* 4, cols. 99–100.

547. *Sermon* 6 and *Book of Divine Consolation*, quoted in Raphael-Louis Oechslin, "Divinisation: IV. Moyen Age: C. École Rhénane et Flamande: 1. Selon Eckhart," *DS* 3, cols. 1433, 1435.

548. *Sermon* 22a, quoted in Oechslin, "Eckhart," col. 101.

union of the soul with God in the "ground" or essence. *"Deus illabitur ipsi nudae essentiae animae quae ipsa nomen proprium non habet et altior est quam intellectus et voluntas"* (Eckhart).[549]

3) *The Return to God*: the Word being born in the ground of the soul, it is necessary to return to Him by stripping off everything that is exterior to the inmost depth in the soul. Here we come to propositions that got Eckhart into difficulty regarding asceticism:

a) Active level: there is no problem about the active part of the return to God, by ordinary works, virtues, sacramental life, etc.

b) "Noble" level: but Eckhart insists that perfect union with God is attained only on the level of the "noble" man, the interior man who is one with God "above all works and virtues."[550] Here we find the matter of several condemned propositions which seem to say that all practice of virtue is useless, that sin is not to be regretted and that one can be completely stripped of all that is not divine. These propositions as condemned are not seen in their context but purely and simply as they stand. Eckhart says that we must be stripped even of images of the humanity of Christ. "Strip yourself of all images and unite yourself with the essence without image and without form."[551] "When the soul leaves all forms it goes direct to the formless nature of God."[552] "When thou art completely stripped of thyself and of all that is

---

549. "God will flow into the naked essence of the soul which does not have its own name, and which is higher than the intellect and the will" (quoted in Oechslin, "Eckhart," col. 102).

550. In his brief treatise "The Aristocrat" (or "The Nobleman") Eckhart writes: "St. Augustine says that when the human soul is fully devoted to eternity, turned to God alone, the divine image appears in it shining. When, however, the soul turns away, even if it be to outward deeds of virtue, the divine image is covered up" (Blakney, 77).

551. Raphael-Louis Oechslin, "Dépouillement: III. Au Moyen Âge," *DS* 3, col. 471.

552. Oechslin, "Dépouillement," col. 471 (condensed).

proper to thee, and hast delivered and abandoned thyself to God with full confidence and all love, then all that is born or appears in thee, whether exterior or interior, agreeable or disagreeable, bitter or sweet, no longer belongs to thee but exclusively to thy God to whom thou hast abandoned thyself. . . ."[553] This is his doctrine of "equality" (Glichheit) and abandonment. It is not a doctrine of stoic indifference. When we are completely abandoned to God then all our works, all our sufferings, the small and the great, are all equally great because they all belong to God. It is He who makes them valuable and precious. The secret of all for Eckhart is then total abandonment and complete obedience to God by the "inner work"[554] which is the work of love, the *reception of God's work in us*, and the renunciation and forgetfulness of all else, every other concern. When one is thus perfectly obedient to God "one becomes the Only Son" ({a} condemned proposition[555]). This he sums up in the expression: AMARE DEUM SINE MODO ET QUALIBET PROPRIETATE INCLUDENTE MODUM[556] (note {the} reminiscence of St. Bernard: "*sine modo diligere*"[557]). The key to it all is perfect interior poverty: *Quanto nudius, tanto capacius.*[558] *Quanto humilior, tanto capacior.*[559] On perfect interior poverty, he says: "He is poor who wants nothing, knows nothing and has nothing."[560] One must not even "have a will with which to do the will of

---

553. Oechslin, "Dépouillement," col. 472.

554. Oechslin, "Divinisation," col. 1436.

555. Denzinger and Rahner, 228 (n. 520): "*Quod bonus homo est unigenitus Filius Dei*" ("That the good man is the only-begotten Son of God") (nn. 521 and 522 are similar statements).

556. "to love God without measure and without any property whatsoever including measure" (Oechslin, "Eckhart," col. 105).

557. "to love without measure" (*De Diligendo Deo*, cc. 1, 6 [*PL* 182, cols. 974D, 983D])

558. "the more naked, the more spacious" (*Sermo* 11, quoted in Oechslin, "Eckhart," col. 106).

559. "the more humble, the more spacious" (*Sermo* 35, quoted in Oechslin, "Eckhart," col. 107).

560. Oechslin, "Dépouillement," col. 471.

God."[561] Note {the} hyperbole! In speaking of this poverty Eckhart multiplies paradoxes and speaks in a way that could not help giving offense.

The Errors of Eckhart: the orthodoxy of Eckhart is much discussed today, and even the best Catholic students (see *DS* IV: article on Eckhart[562]) seem to agree that he did not intend formal heresy, but that he made many statements that invited condemnation because of the bold and careless way he expressed them. He used the vernacular to express very difficult truths. His vernacular sermons were often given quite spontaneously and were taken down hastily by nuns and laypeople without much education. He had an extremely original mind and expressed himself very freely and paradoxically, especially when he felt that his audience was hungry for the kind of thing he was teaching. Hence he did not watch himself, and relaxed his control. This lack of caution was extremely dangerous at such a time. His statements had a great effect, in an age when there was much turbulence and independence and many popular movements, some of them heretical and rebellious. The Inquisition was on the watch to prevent the spread of dangerous doctrines and trouble, especially among laypersons and nuns. Eckhart had his enemies. There were serious rivalries between religious orders and theological schools. There were people who were looking for opportunities to make trouble for him, and he carelessly provided them with the opportunity. Note that not all he said was in the vernacular, by any means. His Latin tracts contained dangerous statements too, but here he was on safer ground nevertheless. In 1326 the Inquisition at Cologne condemned some of his statements and he appealed to the Holy See. In 1329, after his death, the Holy See (at Avignon) declared

---

561. See Blakney, 228: "As long as a person keeps his own will, and thinks it his will to fulfill the all-loving will of God, he has not that poverty of which we are talking, for this person has a will with which he wants to satisfy the will of God, and that is not right" (*Sermo* 52 [#28 in Blakney's numbering]).

562. Oechslin, "Eckhart," col. 96.

{that} seventeen propositions from Eckhart were heretical, and eleven were "suspect" of heresy. Considering the times, the situation, and the boldness of some of his statements, what is surprising is not that Eckhart was condemned, but that he got off so lightly compared to many other unfortunates. If he had not been a distinguished churchman, it would have fared very badly with him. Yet many of the things he said have been said, in slightly different words, with greater discretion and theological accuracy, by many of the saints.

Specific Errors (see Denzinger 501 ff.[563]): some concern the creation of the world by God. Eckhart is accused of pantheism; this is a misunderstanding. Some concern sin—statements about how sin can give glory to God, {and is} not to be regretted. His teaching seems to belittle prayer of petition, and says it is imperfect. N. 508 condemns his doctrine of poverty of spirit, that those who have renounced everything, *even the explicit intention to do the will of God*, give God the most glory. {N.} 510 condemns the statement that we are united to God "without distinction." Errors {are found} concerning the necessity of exterior acts of virtue (516, 517, 519), {along with} errors regarding the "divine filiation" in us, in which he too closely identifies the soul and the Son of God (512, 513, 521). NN. 501-515 are heretical, and these are the ones that affect his doctrine of poverty of spirit, and the "not willing not to have sinned,"[564] {and} total union with God "without distinction."[565] Also condemned as heretical is the statement that there is something "uncreated"[566] in the soul (namely the *vünkelin*); but he himself protested against this interpretation of his words: that which is uncreated in the soul is NOT any part of the soul, but God present in the soul. Though Pourrat makes the proper qualifications in regard to Eckhart's doctrine, his whole treatment of Eckhart is based on the condemned propositions

563. Denzinger and Rahner, 227–29 (nn. 501–29).
564. N. 514.
565. N. 510.
566. N. 527.

and not on Eckhart's own work, with which he seems to have no acquaintance.[567] Such a treatment is inadequate and unfair. Oechslin, in *DS IV*,[568] concludes however that "with proper commentary on the obscure and condemned passages, reestablishing the implied context," Eckhart's works can be read today with profit. We add, however, that in the monastery Eckhart should not be read by those who have not finished theology, and even not by all of these, because not all are able to make for themselves or provide for others the "proper commentary" required. Eckhart is for specialists and experts, not for the average contemplative. He *should* be studied by Catholic scholars and not left to non-Catholics to twist as they please. Note however that the extreme statements of Eckhart are mitigated and given an orthodox sense in the writings of Tauler and Ruysbroeck.

Through the influential Rhenish school, which reached the Spanish mystics via Osuna and others in the Netherlands, much of the mysticism of Eckhart, purified of its most extreme statements, survives throughout the later mysticism of Spain and France. The teachers of *holy abandonment*, both orthodox and unorthodox, doubtless owe much to the teaching on poverty of spirit given by the Rhenish mystics. What is valuable and to be saved from Eckhart is present not only in Tauler and Ruysbroeck but also in teachers like St. Francis de Sales and even St. Thérèse of Lisieux, whose *little way* has many elements in common with the "true poverty of spirit" of the Rhenish mystics and doubtless is indebted to their heritage to some extent, since their influence penetrated everywhere. Note: the English Mystics, for instance Walter Hilton, preserve something of the same spirit. Hilton laid down as a basic principle for the interior life the consciousness that "I am nothing and I have nothing and I seek nothing but

---

567. Merton may be referring here to Pourrat's discussion of Eckhart in his *Christian Spirituality* (2.214-17), but he may also be referring to his article on "Abandon" in the *Dictionnaire de Spiritualité*, in which his discussion of Eckhart in the section "Histoire de Faux Abandon" consists almost exclusively of passages quoted and translated from Denzinger (vol. 1, cols. 38–40).

568. Oechslin, "Eckhart," col. 113.

Jesus."[569] Note however that this is completely different from Eckhart who pushed it so far that he said we must not even seek God, or preserve the image of His Incarnate Word.

C. THE MYSTICISM OF JOHN TAULER: there is no question of the orthodoxy of Tauler and Suso. They are accepted by all and Pourrat praises them.[570] The great value of Tauler {is} his perfecting of Augustinian psychology and mysticism, *his synthesis between Augustine and Denys.*

I. *John Tauler* (1300-1361) {was} not a technical theologian but a preacher and director of souls. His sermons also are preserved in notes taken by his hearers (mostly nuns). His doctrine, {of the} same school as Eckhart, based on {the} neo-Platonic and Dionysian background of {his} studies at Cologne, gives {the} essence of what is taught by Eckhart but in a more correct form. His psychology {places} emphasis on the "ground" of the soul, and the *deep will* (*gemüt*) but {there is} no error about an "uncreated element" in the soul. When the *gemüt* is divinized it does *not* become indistinguishable from God.[571]

Psychology of Tauler (the Interior Man): his psychology is based on the traditional (Greek) concept of the threefold division in man: (1) *animalis*—exterior man; (2) *rationalis*—interior man; (3) *spiritualis*—superior man: the "noble" man. It is the superior

---

569. Walter Hilton, *The Scale of Perfection*, II.21 (compressed), in Colledge, *Medieval Mystics*, 247: "Say 'I am nothing, I have nothing, and I want nothing except one thing'; and even though you do not always need to be repeating these words in your thoughts, keep their meaning constantly in your intention and in the habit of your soul. Humility says 'I am nothing, I have nothing.' Love says 'I want nothing except one thing, and that is Jesus.'"

570. Pourrat, *Christian Spirituality*, 2.217-22.

571. See Merton's journal entry for May 23, 1960: "Tauler—*Gemüt* and the *Grund*—turning the whole desire and strength of the soul to the emptiness, the mirror in which God appears—which is the very mirror being of our being!" (Thomas Merton, *Search for Solitude*, 394).

or noble man that is the *gemüt*, or rather the *grund* to which the *gemüt* directs itself to find God.[572]

a) The *grund* is called the *mens* and {the} *summit of {the} soul*. It is the place where the image of God is found. It has no name. It is "closely related"[573] to God (*not* "identified with Him"). It is in and by the *grund* that God is united to us in an ineffable manner. "It is there [the *grund*] that is found profound silence. No creature and no image have ever penetrated there. Here the soul does not act and has no knowledge, here she knows nothing of herself, of any image, or of any creature."[574] It is a *passive receptivity* upon which God alone acts, when He is left free to do so.

b) The *gemüt*—or deep will—is again above the faculties, above their ordinary action. When left free it plunges down into the *grund*, to seek God in His image. It is therefore a *dynamic power of conversion* to God, a gravitational force of love, and the inner source of all our activities. It is that *by which we give ourselves* in the deepest sense of the word. It is the gravitation to God as our origin. Free will can forcibly direct its power to another object, but it still longs for God.

c) {In the} summit of union, the *gemüt* is divinized in divine union. "*The gemüt recognizes itself as God in God, while nevertheless remaining created.*"[575] Here Tauler restates Eckhart's paradox, with sufficient qualification to avoid being condemned. Like Eckhart he describes mysticism as the birth of God in the ground of the soul. Note: behind all this is the Augustinian maxim: *Amor meus pondus meum.*[576] {In} his asceticism and mysticism, like Eckhart

---

572. John Tauler, *Sermon* 64.4, quoted in A. L. Corin, "Introduction Théologique," in *Sermons de Tauler*, trans. E. Hugueny, OP, G. Théry, OP, and A. L. Corin, 3 vols. (Paris: Desclée, 1927), 1.74.

573. *Sermon* 56.5, quoted in Corin, 1.75.

574. *Sermon for the First Sunday after Christmas* (not included in the critical edition of Tauler), quoted in Corin, 1.75–76.

575. *Sermon* 64.7, quoted in Corin, 1.80.

576. "My love is my weight" (Augustine, *Confessions*, 13.9 [*PL* 32, col. 849]); see *Cassian and the Fathers*, 235, n. 618, for a discussion of Merton's use of

he insists on self-stripping and poverty, but he does not go to the extremes of Eckhart in his language. "All that a man rests in with joy, all that he retains as a good belonging to himself is all worm-eaten, except for absolute and simple vanishing in the pure, unknowable, ineffable and mysterious good which is God by renunciation of ourselves and of all that can appear in Him."[577] Tauler reminds {us} of the part played by Mary in the contemplative life. He emphasizes the sacraments, especially the Eucharist. He gives a great place to the *Gifts of the Holy Ghost* in his mysticism[578] (cf. St. Thomas[579]). It is the gifts of wisdom and understanding that lead to the "abyss without name."[580] Tauler clearly emphasizes *passive purification* by the Holy Spirit. Passive purification restores the likeness of the divine image in man. Besides all the other ordinary forms of self-love and attachment from which we must be purified, there is above all that *self-will in the things of God, "wanting our own will to be carried out in all the things of God and even in God Himself."*[581] This purification takes a long time. Tauler believes one is not ripe for deep contemplation before he is forty years old. This is not to be taken as absolute, but there is a certain wisdom in it. Time is important. Tauler thinks the years between forty and fifty are very important—the ideal time for passive purification. "When a man is young he must not travel fully in the land of vision; he can only make sallies into it and withdraw once again, as long as he has not fully grown."[582] Tauler insists on the importance of *meditation* for those who are young in the spiritual life. For those who are progressing, the great thing

---

this quotation in his dialogue with D. T. Suzuki (Thomas Merton, *Zen and the Birds of Appetite* [New York: New Directions, 1968], 127).

577. *Sermon* 46, quoted in G. Théry, OP, "Introduction Historique," in *Sermons de Tauler*, 1.16.

578. *Sermon* 26; see *Histoire de Spiritualité*, vol. 2, 467; ET: 390.

579. For Thomas's discussion of the gifts of the Holy Spirit, see 1a 2ae, q. 68, in *Summa Theologiae*, ed. Gilby, 24:2/3–40/41.

580. *Sermon* 56.5, quoted in Corin, 1.75.

581. *Sermon* 19, quoted in Corin, 1.96.

582. *Sermon* 2.5, quoted in Corin, 1.97–98.

is patience and trust in tribulation, especially in passive purification—not seeking relief from creatures but waiting patiently for the "new birth" of God within them.

Two Texts from Tauler on humility and patience in trial, as the sign of the true spiritual man:

> a) If your boat is solidly anchored, all will go well. Remain in yourself. Do not go running about outside; be patient until the end; seek no other thing. Certain men, when they find themselves in this interior poverty, run around seeking always some new means of escape from anguish, and this does them great harm. Either they go and complain and question the teachers of the spiritual life, and they come back more troubled than they went. Remain without misgivings in this trial. After the darkness will come the brightness of the sun. Keep yourself from seeking anything else, just as you would guard yourself against death. *Be satisfied to wait.* Believe me, there never arises any anguish in man that God does not desire to prepare a new birth in that man. Know that whatever comes to deliver you from oppression or appease it, will be born in you. That is what will be born in you, either God or the creature. Now think about it. If it is a creature that takes away your anguish, whatever may be its name, that creature steals from you the birth of God (*Serm.* 41, #3).[583]
>
> b) When man has tasted this altogether interior piety it makes him plunge down and sink in his own nothingness and littleness, for the more brightly the greatness of God shines for him, the more easily he recognizes his littleness and nothingness. . . . It is by this that one recognizes that there has really been an illumination from God if the light, instead of touching the images and faculties of the soul, has gone straight to the depths. These beloved men are thirsty for suffering and humiliation, to imitate their well-beloved Lord Jesus Christ. They fall neither into false

583. Quoted in Corin, 1.99-100.

activity nor into false liberty and do not divert themselves, flying about like butterflies with their reason. For in their own eyes they are little and nothing and that is why they are great and precious before God.[584]

Tauler and Eckhart and other points:

a) He openly defends Eckhart: "You have not understood this beloved Master because he was speaking from the point of view of eternity and you have judged him from the point of view of time" (*Serm.* 15).[585]

b) He takes up the most characteristic doctrines of Eckhart and corrects them, giving them an orthodox expression.

c) Some think Tauler was, of the two, the truer mystic, that his correction of Eckhart was also based on a more real and more profound experience. (Note—Suso in his *Orologium Sapientiae* also defends Eckhart; for this he was deposed as prior.[586])

d) Tauler, like Ruysbroeck, combated {the} errors of Beghards and {the} Brethren of {the} Free Spirit.

e) Tauler clearly manifested his devotion to and obedience to the Holy See.

f) Luther was a devoted student of Tauler. John Eck attacked Tauler in attacking Luther. Louis de Blois replied in defense of Tauler, stating that his orthodoxy is beyond question. This led to an edition of Tauler by St. Peter Canisius in 1543.[587] Nevertheless the Jesuits forbade the reading of Tauler in 1578—{the} Capuchins also.[588] But he was rehabilitated in the seventeenth century.[589]

g) Tauler, in a warning printed as a preface to his *Sermons,*[590] points out *four errors* to be avoided in following the way of mystical emptiness and freedom. In general the mystical life does seem

---

584. *Sermon* 44.5, quoted in Corin, 1.102-103.

585. Quoted in Théry, 1.26.

586. See Félix Vernet, "Allemande (Spiritualité)," *DS* 1, col. 328.

587. See Théry, 1.44-47.

588. See Théry, 1.52-53.

589. See Théry, 1.54.

590. Tauler, *Sermons*, 1.157-62.

and *is* dangerous to those who cannot abandon themselves, renouncing the inclinations of flesh and blood, and letting go of their thoughts and reasonings, to be guided by the Holy Spirit and by the Friends of God. The *four errors* are:

1) exterior living, by the natural wisdom of the senses; on the contrary one must cultivate the *interior life*, which means for Tauler *living in the present* with a *pure desire to please God alone* and submitting to His will at every moment in privation as well as in plenty of material and spiritual things.

2) revelations and visions—attachment to these is to be avoided, though such things may sometimes come from God; those who seek and cherish them suffer great harm.

3) relying on reason {and making} excessive intellectual effort under the stimulations of natural light, and taking too much pleasure in this kind of activity; {he stresses the} danger of useless speculations.

4) blank passivity, mere inactivity, sleeping in self-absorption, blank and empty stupidity—the inexperienced attach themselves stubbornly to this kind of false emptiness, imagining it is the true emptiness of contemplation.

Remedies {include} genuine zeal for good, without attachment to practices, and with *alert, peaceful attention to the inspirations of grace*, proper use of meditation as long as it is necessary, avoidance of false passivity, especially during youth, *acceptance of suffering and privation, active charity, prayer, patience* and *long experience*. On these we can rest the structure of contemplative unknowing.

Henry Suso {was} a "minnesinger"[591] of mystical love. In reaction to the Eckhart crisis, while defending Eckhart, {he} tries to make mysticism more acceptable. {He} emphasizes his own personal experience {in} autobiographical {writings}. {Among the} qualifications {he makes, in} speaking of the transformation of man in Christ, and deification, {he} no longer declares that there *is* no distinction, but that the mystic *feels* no distinction, between the soul and God.

591. Vernet, col. 327.

The Theologia Germanica (Theologia Deutsch) {is} by an anonymous author, of Frankfurt, {at the} end of {the} fourteenth century, a "friend of God." This is in bad repute because Luther liked it and published an edition of it, appealing to it to support his opposition between faith and works. It was this fact, that Luther relied on the mystics, who minimized personal action, that helped to bring them into disrepute. The orthodoxy of {the} *Theologia Germanica* is hotly debated. It is supposed to have pantheistic tendencies. However the *Theologia Germanica* points out errors of heretical movements, *false* "Friends of God."[592] We meet in it the familiar themes: the union of man with God by complete stripping of the self and of its activity; interior illumination by the "true light which is a seed of God and produces the fruits of God";[593] interior life which is "beyond expression,"[594] in which the activity of God gradually substitutes for the activity of man, culminating in "deification,"[595] {the} synthesis of action and contemplation. These have by now become standard themes, and we are thoroughly familiar with them.

It remains to be said that the *history of these themes* needs to be understood:

a) Remember that parallel to the orthodox Christian mysticism of the Rhineland was an unorthodox popular tradition largely withdrawn from ecclesiastical control. This unorthodox tradition *exaggerated and distorted the themes* familiar in the mystics. *In doctrine*, they tend to say without qualification that man either becomes God or returns to an original supposed "identity" with God which he never had really lost. *In ascetic practice*, if man is really one with God all the time, then *personal responsibility* tends to vanish: either one can pass beyond good and evil by

---

592. See Chiquot, cols. 496–97, citing the introduction to the *Theologia Germanica*, where the "false friends" are identified with the "free spirits, enemies of divine justice, who are so harmful to the Church."

593. *Theologia Germanica*, c. 40.

594. *Theologia Germanica*, c. 21.

595. *Theologia Germanica*, cc. 32, 33, 35, 37, 41, 43.

simply ceasing to act and by remaining "passive," in which case "God acts," or else one need not resist passions or reject sinful tendencies because they are the work of a fleshly self from which one is dissociated, or else God is responsible. There follows a rejection of sacramental and institutional life—of confession, of the Eucharist, of meditation, of personal devotion to Christ, the saints, etc. In many cases these errors can be summed up as a misapplication of figurative language that has meaning only for the rare case of the mystic united with God in passivity. Figures of speech valid for mystical union are taken and put in the context of *ordinary Christian life*. Hence everyone "becomes a mystic" by ceasing to act, by deliberately remaining passive. Everyone is encouraged to pursue this "easy and direct way." Hence people who are weak, who are beginners, who cannot advance without the help of ordinary means provided by the Church, are deprived of those means. In trying to attain to a more direct and immediate union with God, by deliberate passivity, they actually resign themselves to following irrational forces in themselves, and yield to passion and even to sin, at the same time rejecting responsibility for their acts. This false passivity was condemned by the great mystics themselves, notably by *Ruysbroeck*, Tauler, etc.

b) The *Dictionnaire de Spiritualité* sums up its evaluation of the German mystics as follows:[596] the orthodox mystics of the Rhineland and Flanders were not in any real sense *precursors* of Luther; {they} were not pantheists or quietists, but their language could be misinterpreted and has to be carefully understood. Eckhart is a special case: his language is very imprudent and erroneous and consequently he is apart from the safe Rhenish mystics like Tauler; however he is a writer of unparalleled originality and genius, the greatest of the Rhenish mystics in this respect; some doubt whether he was a "mystic" but their doubt is transparently foolish. Tauler and Suso, as well as Ruysbroeck, are fully orthodox, fully acceptable, and should be read by contemplatives, if

596. Vernet, cols. 329–30.

not by Jesuits. The *Theologia Germanica* is acceptable. Some of the Friends of God are to be taken with caution.

D. The Reaction to German Mysticism

1) Defenders and followers of Eckhart: we have seen that Tauler and Suso defended Eckhart. Nicholas of Cusa, {a} cardinal {and} a very important and interesting figure in the fifteenth century, worked for reunion of East and West at {the} Council of Florence; {he} was envoy to {the} Greek emperor at Constantinople {and} studied {the} *Koran* there. {A} friend of Benedictines and Carthusians, {he wrote} *De Docta Ignorantia*, {a work} in {the} Dionysian tradition {of a} speculative {character}, {as well as} *De Visione Dei*, written for Benedictines. In regard to Eckhart, Nicholas of Cusa defended him against {the} charge of pantheism, but admitted he was not to be read by all; the mere fact of his approving of Eckhart made Nicholas himself suspect, in the general reaction.[597] *Luther* pointed to Tauler and to the *Theologia Germanica* as to models and sources, hence bringing them into disrepute[598] (see above).

2) *Attacks on the Rhenish mystics*: Cardinal Peter d'Ailly attacked {the} orthodoxy of Ruysbroeck. {He} substitutes for {the} speculative mysticism of Rhenish and Flemish mystics a "safe mysticism" based on St. Bonaventure, highly systematic, and with emphasis on the *spiritual senses*: thirteen chapters of his compendium on contemplation deal with the spiritual senses.[599] Jean Gerson {is} an interesting case. {As} chancellor of {the} University of Paris {he} attacked William of St. Thierry and Ruysbroeck together as pantheists, {and was} also opposed to St. Bridget and St. Catherine, their visions, etc. Yet {he was} not antimystical as such. He opposes the two extremes of dark and visionary mysticism {and} returns to the "middle"; Evelyn Underhill

---

597. Vernet, col. 328.
598. Vernet, col. 328.
599. See above, n. 205.

calls him a "second Bonaventure."[600] {He} emphasizes spiritual direction, discernment of spirits, but also the positive side of Dionysius, and St. Augustine of course. The trend represented by Gerson and D'Ailly, suspicious of extremes, emphasizing at best a "safe" mysticism, but tending to shy completely away from speculative mysticism, prepares the way for the Jesuit spirituality of the sixteenth century, which we will consider in a moment. This, with the *Devotio Moderna*, represents the accepted doctrine since the Council of Trent, the "main line" of Catholic spirituality in the West—active, devotional, subjective, non-mystical.

The Devotio Moderna was in great part a reaction against the speculative mysticism of the Rhineland and Flanders, as well as against the false popular mysticism with quietistic trends. *Gerhard Groote* (d. 1384) {was a} contemporary of the mystics, but reacted against mysticism, though {a} friend of Ruysbroeck. {He was a} preacher and missionary, {a} deacon only ({who} refused priesthood out of humility), {and} wrote many letters of direction, {along with works of} autobiographical piety. {He was a} *critic* of the infidelities of monks and clergy, {of} the false mystics that abounded, especially with pantheistic and quietistic tendencies, {and of} the speculative mystics. {His} *spirituality* {was} centered on *morality*, good conduct, fidelity of life, charity, humility. Contemplation {was} devaluated, and methodical meditation on Christ, especially on the Passion, {was} preached instead of contemplative prayer. {There was an} insistence that perfection of charity is what matters. In other words, a *duality* of ways of perfection tends to grow up, one active and ordinary, the other contemplative and extraordinary.

The Brethren of the Common Life {was} established at Deventer, Holland, in 1383, and became a center for dissemination of the *Devotio Moderna*. The foundation at Windesheim especially influenced clerical and religious life everywhere. There was considerable discussion of and opposition to the Brethren of the Common

---

600. Underhill, 810.

Life, especially by the clergy who resented {its} criticism of laxity. The Brethren of {the} Common Life were sometimes accused of being unorthodox but such accusations were irresponsible and unjust. Groote was forbidden to preach in 1383 and when he died in 1384 the event was hailed with jubilation by his (clerical) enemies. *Thomas à Kempis* (fifteenth century), accepted as most probably {the} author of the *Imitation {of Christ}*, {is} typical of the Brethren of {the} Common Life. Like Groote, {he places} emphasis on fidelity to ordinary duties, to Christian morality on the ordinary level, to charity and humility, {on} affective, subjective and individualistic devotion, especially meditation on the humanity of Christ and the Passion, {as well as on} simplicity. The *Imitation* is a compendium of all that is most healthy and less extreme in medieval asceticism. It represents the safe way, the middle of the way, and *invites all to seek sanctity* by ordinary means, which nevertheless demand heroism. The *Devotio Moderna* and the *Imitation* are blamed for being non-liturgical, and for substituting individualistic and subjective devotion to liturgical and communal spirituality. However this is not to be blamed on these holy men alone: it was inevitable that they should place this type of emphasis in their time. The times themselves created the situation. Note also {the following} characteristics of this school:

a) a tendency to anti-intellectualism, to a complete separation between sacred learning on the one hand and piety on the other, as if they were opposed.

b) emphasis on {a} *contrast* between nature and grace, nature now taken in the sense of *fallen* nature: {a} radical opposition between the two {is posited}.

In the sixteenth century, the Inquisition tends to condemn or withdraw from circulation all mystical writings. They are automatically considered suspect, and popular reading of them is discouraged, especially the mystics of Germany and the Low Countries.[601] *In the seventeenth century*, J. P. Camus (1640) attacks

601. Vernet, col. 328.

the "passives,"[602] including Tauler. Bossuet, in his reaction against Fénelon, is to a great extent following Gerson's criticism of Ruysbroeck; Bossuet criticizes the Rhenish mystics, with qualifications, admitting Tauler as one of the "more solid of the mystics."[603]

The Jesuits: in general the spirituality of the Jesuits was antimystical, though the Society produced some great contemplatives and mystics. In 1575 Mercurian, the General of the Society {of} Jesus, forbids {the reading of} Tauler, Suso, St. Gertrude, Mechtilde, Harphius, Ruysbroeck, etc. {They are} not to be read by Jesuits because {they are} "not well adjusted to our institute."[604] Note {that} this does not imply a criticism for heresy; it is understood that writers like Eckhart would not even be considered. {It is} important that here we have a great religious order with a well-defined systematic *policy* in spiritual matters—a policy to which mysticism is considered foreign.

St. Ignatius: we cannot treat him adequately here—just a brief note. His *Spiritual Exercises* are not intentionally either pro- or anti-mystical. They are intended to help a man to open up his mind and heart to divine grace and to make, with the help of grace, *a crucial decision*, on which his whole life and vocation depend. One does not normally decide to "become a mystic" or even a contemplative in the intimate sense of the word. But the *Exercises* might conceivably, in an individual case, dispose a contemplative person to receive a special grace that would open up a new way to him. However *systematic means* should be considered normally unfavorable in an advanced mystical life marked by definite passivity. (Note: a precursor of St. Ignatius in *methodical meditation* is the Benedictine *Garcia Cisneros* [sixteenth century]; in the history of methodical meditation, St. Ailred's *De*

---

602. Vernet, col. 329.
603. Vernet, col. 329.
604. Vernet, cols. 328–29.

Institutione Inclusarum[605] is important, also the meditations of Stephen of Salley[606]—both Cistercians of the twelfth century.)

The Jesuits and mysticism in the sixteenth century: it would be false to imagine that the Jesuits conducted a systematic anti-mystical campaign. On the contrary, St. Teresa owed much to her Jesuit confessors and to their support. However, they were very unfriendly to "passivity." *Balthasar Alvarez* (confessor of St. Teresa and novice master of the Society {of} Jesus) {was} considered an exemplary Jesuit, and always retained the confidence of his superiors. But he began teaching {about} "retiring from the noise of creatures, withdrawing to the depths of the heart to adore God in spirit"[607] {and} "remaining in the presence of God with sentiments of love, either dwelling on images if profitable, or not dwelling on them"[608] (when it is no longer profitable). In other words, he was teaching what St. Teresa called the prayer of *simple recollection* and what modern devotional writers have also called the *prayer of simplicity* or *simple regard*. He was censored by the Society and forbidden to teach this. His doctrine was classified as "intolerable"[609] and "contrary to the *Spiritual Exercises*."[610] Is

---

605. Aelred of Rievaulx, *De Institutione Inclusarum*, in *Aelredi Rievallensis Opera Omnia*, vol. 1: *Opera Ascetica*, ed. C. H. Talbot, *CCCL* 1 (Turnholt: Brepols, 1971), 635–82; ET: Aelred of Rievaulx, *Treatises and Pastoral Prayer: On Jesus at the Age of Twelve; Rule for a Recluse; The Pastoral Prayer*, CF 2 (Kalamazoo: Cistercian Publications, 1971). In his *Aelred of Rievaulx: A Study*, CS 50 (Kalamazoo: Cistercian Publications, 1981), Aelred Squire writes, "Aelred's meditative technique had a great future before it in later medieval methods of prayer" (69).

606. Stephen of Sawley, *Treatises*, trans. Jeremiah F. O'Sullivan, CF 36 (Kalamazoo: Cistercian, 1984); Stephen is actually a thirteenth-century writer, probably dying in 1252 (sometimes given as 1245); Dom André Wilmart, in "Le *Triple Exercice* d'Étienne de Sallai," *Revue d'Ascétique et de Mystique*, 11 (1930), sees this work as one of the earliest examples of methodical prayer (356).

607. M. Olphe-Galliard, "Contemplation: A. Enquête Historique: IX. Au XVe Siècle: 6. Contemplation Ignatienne," *DS* 2, col. 2027.

608. Olphe-Galliard, "Contemplation," col. 2027.

609. Olphe-Galliard, "Contemplation," col. 2027.

610. Olphe-Galliard, "Contemplation," col. 2026 (paraphrased).

this strictly true? *Suarez*, who was always respected by the Carmelites and who defended St. John of the Cross, tried to emphasize a certain contemplative orientation in the *Spiritual Exercises*. *Claudio Acquaviva*, {the Jesuit} General, wrote in 1590 an official *Letter on Mental Prayer* in which it was stated that true and perfect contemplation was an aid to virtue and a source of apostolic zeal. *Alvarez de Paz* entered {the} Society {of} Jesus in 1578 and was sent to Peru in 1584. He spent the rest of his life in Peru, taught theology and Scripture at Lima, became provincial, {and} died in {the} odor of sanctity {in} 1620. His doctrine is largely *patristic*, especially influenced by St. Bernard. Since he is also influenced by Hugh of Balma ("Bonaventure") he is in the medieval mystical tradition, and his emphasis on "infused love without previous knowledge"[611] is by no means typical of the Society. Alvarez de Paz first uses the term *affective prayer*.[612] In regard to the desire for contemplation, {his teaching is}: in the sense of extraordinary manifestations, ecstasies, etc.—no; in the sense of "wisdom" which is a great means to perfection—yes. He influenced Surin, and the later generation of Jesuit mystics. Note: here we see contemplation almost ordered as a means to a further end, the apostolate. It is certainly valued in relation to this end.

E. *Summary and Outline*: the separation of mysticism and theology in the West {began in the} late Middle Ages ({for} background {see} Joachim, the prophet {and his} "Age of the Holy Ghost" {in the} twelfth century):

1. {In the} thirteenth century, Thomas Gallus, a Dionysian, uses apophatic theology against scholastic theology, opposes contemplation and science (Franciscan spirituals *idem*).

2. {In the} thirteenth century, the Béguines, Beghards {and} other popular movements not only oppose piety to official theology, but also tend to withdraw from the clergy, and to stress mystical love. In many quarters there is a new stress on the mar-

---

611. E. Hernandez, "Alvarez de Paz," *DS* 1, col. 408.

612. Hernandez, col. 408, citing A. Poulain, "Alvarez de Paz," *Dictionnaire de Théologie Catholique*, 15 vols. (Paris: Letouzey et Ané, 1908–1950), vol. 1, col. 929.

velous and the miraculous. {There is a} "prophetic" sense that God is acting directly among special groups of mystics, and that the mediation of the visible Church is now negligible.

3. {In the} fourteenth century, the speculative mysticism of the Rhineland is an attempt of the Church, through the mendicants and especially the Dominicans, inspired by St. Albert the Great, *to reintegrate mysticism and theology.* There was a successful synthesis, in which theology and mysticism are once again intimately united. Yet scholastic methods and technical theology are to some extent played down.

4. Official theology reacts through the *Inquisition.*

5. The Schoolmen react with *Nominalism,* in which technical theology moves further away from the spiritual life into arid speculation.

6. {The} *Devotio Moderna* is another reaction against speculative mysticism: an affective and moral reaction, individualistic and subjective, pietistic.

7. By the fifteenth century, the break between mysticism and theology is definite and irrevocable. Mysticism is suspect, observed by {the} Inquisition. The popular mystics, who tend more and more to despise authority, go further and further into the extraordinary, the weird, {including} the great growth of superstitions, confusion of strange ideas and devotions, the "end of the world" complex, the "dance of death."

8. *The Humanistic reaction*: from this confusion of decadent theology and degraded mysticism mingled with superstition and magic, healthy minds seek an escape in humanistic culture. This leads to a further dilution and secularization of the spiritual life.

9. By the sixteenth century, Protestants seek a direct return to God in the Gospel, almost entirely discarding theology, retaining only a little of fourteenth-century mystical piety, and in some cases an affinity for the new humanism.

10. Mysticism has now to be revived as a *specialty* for contemplatives by profession. This will be the work above all of the discalced Carmelites. But it is to be noted that in this work, they will strive once more to *reintegrate mysticism and theology.*

X. Spanish Mysticism

1. *The background*: {Note the} importance of the Spanish mystical school. Mysticism was both popular and *deep-rooted*. There are said to have been 3,000 mystical writers in the Golden Age (mostly unpublished). What is especially attractive about the Spanish mystics is their *personality*, their individuality, their "truth": we know these qualities in St. Teresa, but forget they are characteristic of all the Spanish mystics. {Note the} difference between Rhenish and Spanish mysticism: as to background, *Rhenish* mysticism springs up in a time of confusion and decay, amid many anti-authoritarian freely mystical movements, some orthodox, some heretical, {whereas} *Spanish* {mysticism} appears in a time of official reform, unity, centralization, authority, strict control, national expansion and prosperity. The Moors have been driven out, America discovered. {The} national consciousness of Spain {is} wide awake: Catholic consciousness {is} also wide awake. {It is the} Golden Age of literature and painting (painters {more in the} seventeenth century). A general *unity* of life and growth {develops} in {the} arts and in {the} spiritual life, all together. St. Teresa's brother was among the conquistadores in Ecuador. *The authoritarian control grows more and more strict*, but the genuine mystics are not discouraged. They triumph over all obstacles. Note the *suddenness* with which Spanish mysticism begins in the fifteenth {and} sixteenth centuries, with no previous tradition. (Ramon Lull, the only medieval mystic in Spain, is Catalan and has no influence on the Castilians until relatively late; {he is} not even translated until late.) *Some dates*: 1469: Spain {is} united under Ferdinand and Isabella; 1472: the Inquisition becomes permanent under Torquemada; 1492: {the} Fall of Granada and Columbus' first voyage; 1512: {the} Inquisition, previously occupied with Jews and Moslems, now turns to *Alumbrados* and *Erasmians*.

Reformers {include} *Cardinal Francisco Ximenes de Cisneros*, {who} starts {a} movement of reform *before* Trent:

a) {in the} universities: {he} founds {the} University of Alcala {in} 1498; Salamanca {is} reformed—{it} has 8,000 students.

b) {in} printing: Ximenes uses {the} printing press for spiritual reform; {he} compiled {the} *Polyglot Bible*; {in} 1490, {the} *Imitation of Christ* {was} printed; 1500 {saw the} printing of St. Basil, St. Jerome (read by St. Teresa), St. Augustine; Denis the Carthusian {appeared in} three Spanish editions in seven years; {in} 1503 {Ximenes} prints Ludolph the Carthusian, *Vita Christi*, {and in} 1504 {he} prints {a} translation of St. John Climacus (this was also the first book printed in the Americas); also {published were the} life of St. Catherine of Siena, works of St. Mechtilde of Hackbourn, Blessed Angela of Foligno, Hugh of Balma, {the} *Dialogues* of St. Gregory {the} Great, {the} *Vitae Patrum* (some of these were later forbidden by the Inquisition). {Note the} importance of books in the prayer life of St. Teresa and other mystics: they were great *readers*.

Ven. Garcia de Cisneros ({a} relative of the above) {was} the first of the Spanish mystics. Abbot of Monserrate (b. 1455; d. 1510), {he} was sent to reform Monserrate from Valladolid at {the} request of Ferdinand and Isabella. {In} 1500 {he wrote the} *Book of Spiritual Exercises*, intended primarily for monks; {he was} influenced by {the} *Devotio Moderna*. {He also wrote the} *Directory of Canonical Hours* to help the monks recite {the} office devoutly. Neither of these works is mystical. {The} *Exercises* starts with meditations for {the} purgative way, to follow Matins, then {uses the} traditional medieval pattern: *lectio, meditatio, contemplatio.* {He} insists that we should desire contemplation. {His} sources, besides the Western Fathers, especially Augustine and Gregory the Great, {include} Dionysius, Hugh of Balma, St. Bernard; Johann Mombaer's *Rosetum* {is} another source, and Gerson, and Suso. {It is a} paradox {that it was this work of} systematic imaginative meditation which inspired St. Ignatius, with {the} purpose of union with God "without mean."[613]

---

613. Merton's reference is obscure here, since the phrase "without mean" is not found in the *Spiritual Exercises*; he is perhaps referring to the "consolation without previous cause" that Ignatius includes in his Rules for the Discernment

Spiritual trends, deviations, and reactions against them: *eucharistic devotion* was very strong. Francisco de Osuna, recommending daily communion, was withdrawn from circulation by the Inquisition. An extreme practice {arose} of carrying the sacred Host about on one's person, out of devotion. This was of course forbidden. *Erasmianism* {became influential} (Erasmus was translated in 1527). This trend was at once humanistic and evangelical; {it} emphasized *interior* reform, Christ in us, {and had a} tendency to emphasize "freedom of spirit"; {it was} anti-formalistic. {It was a} real renovation, but the authorities were against it and prosecuted it as heretical.

Illuminism (the *Alumbrados*) {was of} two kinds: the *Recogidos*, {with an} overstress on mental prayer, {and} the *Dejados*, {with an} overstress on abandonment. Both {included} strong neo-Platonic and Averroist elements, {and showed the} influence of {the} Rhenish mystics, Beghards, etc. *Errors on prayer* {included} making all perfection consist in interior prayer: by this alone one is saved, {so that} it must be preferred to obedience, to sacraments, etc.; it is *purely* passive. True prayer can be entered simply by becoming passive and excluding all thoughts. *When one is purely inactive then he is, due to that fact, moved by God.* (This is really the crux of the error and is essential to illuminism.) By this inactivity one attains to direct vision of the divine essence. This is essentially the same as the Quietist heresy in regard to mental prayer. It implies a complete misunderstanding and oversimplification of the relations between nature and grace—or even of what they are, {and does} not even {give} a very accurate notion of what constitutes "human activity." In outline, the oversimplification is: *my* activity = natural = bad; God's activity = supernatural = good. Hence, suppress *my* activity and God alone will act. This is a completely mythical conception of man and of God.

---

of Spirits (see *The Spiritual Exercises of St. Ignatius*, trans. Anthony Mottola [Garden City, NY: Doubleday Image, 1964], 133).

The Inquisition was very zealous in stamping out illuminism, but unfortunately went to the opposite extreme, seeing illuminism *everywhere*, even in the *Spiritual Exercises of St. Ignatius*. *Melchior Cano*, op, {was} a "great theologian"[614] and an anti-mystical zealot; he was one of the guiding spirits of the Spanish Inquisition. *Examples of* some of his activities {include}:

a) A Dominican cardinal, a pious man, wrote a *Commentary on the Catechism*. Cano had him condemned and thrown in prison. Even the pope failed to get him out. He was in prison for six years.

b) Ignatius Loyola: Cano attacked Ignatius as a "latter-day seducer"[615] even though Ignatius had been approved by the pope. The *Exercises* were censured for "illuminism." Of him Cano said: "This Company of Jesus has for general a certain Ignatius who fled from Spain when the Inquisition wished to arrest him as a heretic of the sect of the *Alumbrados*"[616] (1548).

---

614. Pourrat calls him "a poor mystic" but "a theologian of the first rank" (Pierre Pourrat, *Christian Spirituality, vol. III: Later Developments: From the Renaissance to Jansenism*, trans. W. H. Mitchell and S. P. Jacques [1927; Westminster, MD: Newman, 1953], 101).

615. Cano applied to the Jesuits the verse from 2 Timothy 3.6 about those who "make their way into houses and captivate silly women who are sin-laden and led away by various lusts" (Confraternity trans.): see Antonio Astrain, *Historia de la Compañía de Jesús en la Asistencia de España*, 7 vols. (Madrid: Sucesores de Rivadeneyra, 1902-25), 1.326: ". . . seduciendo á las mujercillas y llevando en pos de sí á los ignorantes"; Astrain's chapter "Persecución de Melchor Cano" (321–40) provides a thorough discussion of Cano's antipathy.

616. Melchor Cano, *Censura y Parecer contra el Instituto de los Padres Jesuitas*, 4; this work also contains allegations of sexual license (7, 10). For a description, see Terence O'Reilly, "Melchor Cano and the Spirituality of St Ignatius Loyola," in *Ignacio de Loyola y su Tiempo*, ed. Juan Plazaola (Bilbao: Ediciones Mensajero, 1992), 369–80, reprinted (with the same pagination) in Terence O'Reilly, *From Ignatius Loyola to John of the Cross: Spirituality and Literature in Sixteenth-Century Spain* (Brookfield, VT: Variorum, 1995), where it is followed by a complete transcription of the *Censura* from a British Library manuscript. O'Reilly believes that internal evidence dates the document's composition between 1552 and 1556, rather than 1548 (370).

c) Various: Francisco de Osuna {was} put on {the} Index for urging daily communion. Luis de Granada {was} put on {the} Index for teaching lay people to meditate. Blessed Juan de Avila {was} put on {the} Index chiefly because he had Jewish blood. Luis de Leon was five years in prison for translating the Canticle of Canticles into Spanish. In 1551, the Index prohibited the Bible in the vulgar tongue.

d) 1559: the Index of 1559 included books of St. Francis Borgia, Bl. John of Avila, Luis de Granada, Tauler, Herp, Denis the Carthusian (at least in the vernacular).

It will be seen that the chief concern of the Inquisition was not with the Bible or mysticism *as such* but as *preached to the laity*. In so many words, too deep an interest in the interior life was considered dangerous for all but experts. Lay people were to be confined to "*safe*" exterior practices of devotion. It was in the midst of this that St. Teresa and St. John of the Cross not only survived but *flourished*. This should be sufficient indication of the sureness of their mystical doctrine which of course was examined by the Inquisition. (READ: on the state of mind created by this, and the same conclusions reached by Francisco de Osuna, to make up his own mind, see {the} quote of Osuna in Peers, *Studies of {the} Spanish Mystics*, p. 75.[617])

617. In this passage, from Book 5, chapter 2 of *The Third Spiritual Alphabet*, Osuna speaks of a book that had aroused him from spiritual indifference to love for the Lord, which was condemned by one learned man for emphasizing sweetness, and praised by another for being a compendium of teaching expressed more diffusely elsewhere. Osuna concludes, "If in some book thou readest that thou shouldst beware of persons who have raptures, as though they had fits of frenzy, believe it not; and if they tell thee that he that wrote the book was a holy man, say thou that no holy man is bold enough to judge and condemn that which may be good, unless he have first examined it with great circumspection" (E. Allison Peers, *Studies of the Spanish Mystics*, 2 vols., second ed. [London: SPCK, 1951], 1.75; only the first volume of this work, originally published in 1927, was issued in a revised edition; the second, published in 1930, was reprinted unchanged in 1960; a third volume was published posthumously in 1960).

Spiritual Writers {include}: *Blessed Juan de Avila*, {a} secular priest, {wrote the} *treatise Audi filia et vide*,[618] {on} what voices to hear and what to ignore. *Luis de Granada* {was} very popular in Spain and France; {his} chief work {was} the *Sinner's Guide*, {a manual of} asceticism and meditation for lay people, {teaching a} method of meditation, with preparation the night before (see Pourrat III, p. 97). *St. Peter of Alcántara* {was a} friend of St. Teresa {who wrote a} *Treatise on Meditation*. Two Franciscan masters of St. Teresa {were} *Francisco de Osuna*, whom we will treat in detail, {and} *Bernardino de Laredo* (d. 1540), a laybrother {and a} disciple of Osuna, {who wrote} *Ascent of Mount Sion*, {with its} theme {of} ascent above knowledge by love.

2. *Francisco de Osuna*[619] {was} born about 1497 {and} entered the Franciscans quite young; {he} travelled much—{to} Toulouse, Paris, *Antwerp*, {and was} elected commissary general of {the} Order {of} Friars Minor in America, but never went ({due to} ill health); {he} died {in} 1542 (?). A writer held in high esteem in his lifetime, {he had} twenty editions of his works {published} while he was still alive. His *Alphabets* were classed with the writings of St. Teresa. {There were} six *Alphabets*; the *Third* was written first and is the most mystical, dealing with prayer of recollection. {The} other *Alphabets* {include the} *First*, on {the} Passion of Christ; *Second*, for people in active life with little time for prayers; *Fourth*, "The Law of Love," considered by some his masterpiece; *Fifth*, on poverty and riches, to help all love poverty of spirit; *Sixth*, another on the Passion of Christ. {The} *Third Spiritual Alphabet* {was published in} Toledo {in} 1527 "to teach *all* the exercises of recollection."[620] Some of the chief topics he treats {include}:

---

618. *Listen, Daughter, and See.*

619. Merton follows Peers, *Studies*, 1:66-68 here.

620. Osuna says his purpose in this work is "to bring to the general notice of all this exercise of recollection" (*Third Spiritual Alphabet*, Bk. 8, c. 1, quoted in Peers, *Studies*, 1:68-69).

1) {The} vocation to mystical prayer: it is *not for all*—the uninstructed can easily deceive themselves.[621]

2) Yet anyone *may* be called. It is not restricted only to very holy men or for the learned. It is possible for anyone who can love, since it is a matter of friendship with God.[622]

3) {It} requires effort and sacrifice, especially to purify one's heart and thoughts.[623] One must therefore sacrifice worldliness, from which such thoughts arise. An interesting point {is that} created things may at times hinder our prayer, but this is not their fault—it is due to our weakness.[624] When we are more purified they no longer stand in our way.

4) In this regard he treats the question of the *humanity of Christ* which St. Teresa takes up later. It was an axiom of the Alumbrados that the humanity of Christ must be utterly forsaken. For Osuna, it is "more perfect" to rise above it.[625] For St. Teresa one is *never so perfect* that he can go beyond the humanity of Christ.[626] This debate depends largely on misunderstandings, due to the context of mental prayer. A more sacramental spirituality avoids these complications.

5) Prerequisites for interior prayer {include} meekness and humility (see quotes {in} Peers, *Studies of Spanish Mystics*, p. 73[627]); joy—sad souls do not progress in contemplation; love, {which}

---

621. *Third Spiritual Alphabet*, Prólogo and Bk. 8, c. 1, cited in Peers, *Studies*, 1:70.

622. *Third Spiritual Alphabet*, Bk. 1, c. 1, quoted in Peers, *Studies*, 1:70-71.

623. *Third Spiritual Alphabet*, Bk. 1, c. 2, quoted in Peers, *Studies*, 1:71.

624. *Third Spiritual Alphabet*, Bk. 22, c. 5, quoted in Peers, *Studies*, 1:72.

625. *Third Spiritual Alphabet*, Prólogo, quoted in Peers, *Studies*, 1:72.

626. See *Interior Castle*, Sixth Mansions, c. 7 (*The Complete Works of Saint Teresa of Jesus*, trans. and ed. E. Allison Peers, 3 vols. [New York: Sheed & Ward, 1946], 2.302-309).

627. Osuna says in chapter 4 of Book 3 that meekness is the most helpful of the virtues for the spiritual business of which he is speaking, and that a meek soul subjected to God leads to a meek body subjected to the soul; in Book 19 he teaches that humility is the root of meekness and necessary for even the highest spiritual attainment (c. 1).

is of more avail than force; patience and the avoidance of "all superfluous care."[628] "The condition most necessary to every spiritual exercise is to continue therein."[629]

Recogimento—As Peers points out,[630] Osuna has more to say about this than all the rest of the mystical life put together. {It is} characteristic of Spanish mysticism. What it is: it is "mystical theology" as opposed to "speculative theology"; it is wisdom, the "art of love";[631] in Book XXI he quotes his sources: Augustine, Bonaventure (Balma?), Gregory, Dionysius, Richard of St. Victor; the {idea of the} "path of negation" {is} strongly influenced by *Gerson*.[632] {It} is union of wills, in which man becomes *one spirit with God by an exchange of wills* (compare the Cistercian tradition, especially William of St. Thierry[633]). READ {the} quote given by Peers (bottom of p. 76, 77[634])—note the ecclesiological implications, which were certainly not lost on St. Teresa: recollection {is} the gathering together of that which was dispersed. In the quote given by Peers on p. 78 (bottom), note the "deepest recollection" is like a "crystal" filled with the "divine bright-

---

628. *Third Spiritual Alphabet*, Bk. 1, c. 3, quoted in Peers, *Studies*, 1:74.

629. *Third Spiritual Alphabet*, Bk. 14, c. 2, quoted in Peers, *Studies*, 1:74.

630. Peers, *Studies*, 1:76.

631. *Third Spiritual Alphabet*, Bk. 6, c. 2, quoted in Peers, *Studies*, 1:76.

632. See Peers, *Studies*, 1:87, 92, 102.

633. See above, page 65.

634. "Furthermore, it is called Union, for by means of it man draws nigh to God, and becomes one spirit with Him by an exchange of wills, so that the man wills naught but that which God wills, neither does God withdraw Himself from the will of the man, but they are in everything one will, as things that are perfectly united, which lose their own natures, and become transformed in a third: the which comes to pass in this business, for if God and the man before had diverse wills, now they agree in one without dissatisfaction of either. And from this it results that the man is at unity with himself and with his fellows; which if we all were, the multitude of the faithful would be one heart and one soul together in the Holy Spirit . . . Who makes us to be one in love, that He may beget us in grace and bring us all to be made one together with God" (*Third Spiritual Alphabet*, Bk. 6, c. 2).

ness."[635] Note that in the context he speaks of "mansions" of the soul[636]—READ the classical passages of St. Teresa.[637] Peers points out[638] {the} essential ambiguity of Osuna's use of recollection: sometimes it includes all forms of interior prayer, even the most elementary; sometimes it is a higher form, approximating to union. (In any case, as we are not too interested in precise "degrees of prayer," this lack of clarity need not trouble us. St. Teresa and St. John of the Cross will in any case take care of the problem of degrees.) Sometimes it is a general and habitual recollectedness; sometimes it is the actual practice of contemplative prayer,

635. "There remains but the tenth manner of 'recollecting' [i.e. uniting] God and the soul in one . . . which comes to pass when the Divine brightness, as into glass or stone of crystal, is poured into the soul, sending forth like the sun the rays of its love and grace, which penetrate the heart, when they have been received by the highest powers of the spirit. This is followed by the most perfect recollection, which joins and unites (*recoge*) God with the soul and the soul with God" (*Third Spiritual Alphabet*, Bk. 6, c. 4).

636. "The ninth thing recollected is the soul with its powers . . . when the soul is raised above itself, and entirely recollected in the highest mansion (*cenáculo*) of all, . . ." (*Third Spiritual Alphabet*, Bk. 6, c. 4).

637. *Interior Castle*, First Mansions, c. 1: "I began to think of the soul as if it were a castle made of a single diamond or of very clear crystal, in which there are many rooms, just as in Heaven there are many mansions. . . . Let us now imagine that this castle, as I have said, contains many mansions, some above, others below, others at each side; and in the centre and midst of them all is the chiefest mansion where the most secret things pass between God and the soul. . . . Now let us return to our beautiful and delightful castle and see how we can enter it. I seem rather to be talking nonsense; for, if this castle is the soul, there can clearly be no question of our entering it. For we ourselves are the castle: and it would be absurd to tell someone to enter a room when he was in it already! But you must understand that there are many ways of 'being' in a place. Many souls remain in the outer court of the castle, which is the place occupied by the guards; they are not interested in entering it, and have no idea what there is in that wonderful place, or who dwells in it, or even how many rooms it has. You will have read certain books on prayer which advise the soul to enter within itself: and that is exactly what this means. . . . As far as I can understand, the door of entry into this castle is prayer and meditation" (*Complete Works of Saint Teresa*, 2:201-203).

638. Peers, *Studies*, 1:79-81.

which he suggests should occupy two hours in the day (for laymen).[639] {The role of} director {is crucial}: N.B. the eighth Book of the *Third Alphabet* deals with the necessity of a master in this "art."[640] READ {the} quote on p. 84[641]—praise and thanks in the prayer of recollection. {A} second quote on the same page shows {the} distinction between quiet contemplation and sleep: there is a higher and spiritual vigilance (see Peers, p. 84[642] and 96[643]—{the} latter a defense against Quietism). {On} mystical

639. Peers, *Studies*, 1:81-82.

640. Peers, *Studies*, 1:82.

641. "Our Lord is wont to place him, after much prayer, in a state of praise, so that his praises of Him issue from within his soul. So full is that soul of the grace of the Lord, that grace bursts forth, is poured from the lips, and issues in such a giving of thanks that the whole soul would fain melt away, seeing itself in so great happiness, being so near to the Lord, and knowing itself to be so greatly loved by Him, according to the clear witness of a conscience wrapt in the deepest peace" (*Third Spiritual Alphabet*, Bk. 2, c. 2).

642. "As sleep is needful for the body, to sustain bodily life, so to the soul of the perfect man sleep of the spirit is needful also to sustain the life of love, which he receives from God with a quiet (*quietativa*) sweetness which withdraws love from the heart, that the heart may keep vigil and the senses sleep to every creature. And the fumes caused by this heat which rises from the graces close not the channels of the soul, but rather widen them, that the faculties of the soul may work and the natural faculties cease. And the more these latter cease and are at rest, the more truly and delectably do the others work throughout the inner man, which is sovereignly restored and strengthened in such degree that at times he can dispense with bodily sleep, since the spiritual sleep has supplied all his needs; or at the least one that was wont to sleep four hours is content with a single hour, and, when he awakens, returns immediately to prayer" (*Third Spiritual Alphabet*, Bk. 13, c. 4).

643. "Recollected persons in no wise count it perfection to think nothing, for to do this would be to count those who sleep without dreaming, or men in a swoon, as perfect. . . . If the cessation of understanding stopped at this, it would be, not only a lack of perfection, but a loss of time which could be spent in profitable thoughts. . . . Those who follow this path endeavour and study to awaken a love for God. . . . (So) when the understanding has ceased its speculations, the will issues with great power, producing love. . . . See, then, how this nothingness of thought is more than it appears, and how it can in no wise be explained what it is, for God, to Whom it is directed, transcends explanation.

silence, see {the} quote on p. 85 of Peers.[644] The "cloud" and the "tiny spark" {are} evidence of vigilance (Peers, p. 87[645]). {With regard to} dryness and purification, the experience of "dread" (see Peers, p. 92[646]) may be in fact pathological in some cases, and one should consider that perhaps it proceeds from strain and undue insistence on a special "way" to which one is not suited; discretion of the director {is} necessary here. Note: Osuna is con-

---

But I tell thee that this thinking nothing is thinking all things, for we think without words upon Him Who is all things through His marvelous greatness; and the least of the benefits of this nothingness of thought in recollected persons is a subtle and most simple attentiveness to God alone" (*Third Spiritual Alphabet*, Bk. 21, c. 5).

644. "Marvellous indeed, and most worthy of praise with all wonder, is the silence (*callar*) of love wherein most intimately is our understanding hushed to rest, having found, by means of its experience, that which satisfies it greatly. For, as we clearly see, when two that love know each by experience that the other is present, then are both silent, and the love that unites them supplies the lack of words" (*Third Spiritual Alphabet*, Bk. 21, c. 3).

645. "In these manners of recollection the understanding is never so far silenced as to be deprived completely of its powers. For it ever retains a tiny spark, sufficient only for those that are in this state to recognize that they have something that is of God. . . . There come also moments and crises wherein the understanding entirely ceases, as though the soul were without intelligence whatsoever. But then the living spark of simplest knowledge is seen again, which is a thing of wonder, since it is in the total cessation of the understanding that the soul receives the most grace. So soon as it revives again and comes out, as it were, from the cloud, it finds itself with this grace, but knows neither whence nor how it has come; and having it, would fain return to its mortification and the cessation of understanding" (*Third Spiritual Alphabet*, Bk. 21, c. 7).

646. "There is a thing often felt by those that practice recollection, which is a fear most terrible, making it seem as if the soul would leave the body from very terror. This lasts but a short time, though to many it comes with frequency, and so affrights and deters the soul that the soul loses its peace and is filled with dread, not knowing what will become of it. Neither words nor effort nor devotion suffice to calm it. . . . This mighty dread comes often without any thought preceding it, and without any sound—at times, when the soul is recollected and in great devotion. This can be none other than the Devil, who comes to obstruct the soul, and since God allows him to make his presence felt, he causes that new and sudden terror which shakes the whole being" (*Third Spiritual Alphabet*, Bk. 7, c. 3).

cerned with *active* people who practice contemplation, especially laymen. Hence his book is an excellent introduction to the subject. He is as meticulous as a Yogi in his prescriptions on food, sleep, postures, washing, reading, etc.[647] In brief, *he summarizes the tradition of medieval and Rhenish mystics and transmits it to Spain.*

 3. THE CARMELITE SCHOOL: the great Carmelites, St. Teresa and St. John of the Cross in particular, are very well known and there is no need to make a detailed study of their mysticism here. St. Teresa is very widely read and is one of the most attractive of the mystics by reason of her human qualities, her frankness, simplicity, energy, humor and good sense. It will suffice to outline the Carmelite, especially the *Teresian, doctrine* on prayer, and then treat in more detail one or two special practical problems.

 The Teresian School of Prayer (as in the case of the Thomists and St. Thomas, we must distinguish the *followers* of St. Teresa from St. Teresa herself): more than any other school, {this one} *analyzes the experience* of contemplation and of union with God. The approach is essentially *practical*. Stress is placed on "how to get" to union with God, in cooperation with His grace, {as well as on} how to avoid obstacles {and} what the director should do to help one avoid obstacles and progress rapidly. For instance, note the summary on the first page of *The Ascent of Mount Carmel*, which describes the teaching of the book as follows: "Treats of how the soul may *prepare itself to attain in a short time to Divine union.* Gives very profitable counsels and instruction, both to beginners and proficients, that they may know how to *disencumber themselves of all that is temporal and not encumber themselves with the spiritual,* and to *remain in complete detachment and liberty of spirit,* as is necessary for Divine union" (vol. 1, p. 9).[648]

 The Carmelite reform itself aimed at providing austere, recollected convents in which one could rapidly progress in prayer. As to the reception of postulants, St. Teresa says: "Let great care

<hr>

647. See Peers, *Studies*, 1:97-98.
 648. Text reads ". . . itself in order to attain . . . *not to encumber* . . ."; the entire passage is italicized in the text.

be taken that those who are to be received be *persons of prayer* whose aim is complete perfection and contempt of the world" (*Constitutions*, vol. III, p. 224—Read context[649]). The novice mistress is to receive from the novices *a daily account of the progress they are making in prayer* and how they are proceeding in it (*Const.* p. 230—Read context[650]). All the sisters must report to the prioress once a month "what progress they have made in prayer and the way in which Our Lord is leading them" (*id.*). Everything that St. Teresa says about spiritual direction, and indeed about the spiritual life, must be understood in this light. It is written explicitly for nuns whose whole profession is to be persons of prayer, and this means primarily of *mental* prayer. The same is even more true of St. John of the Cross. St. Teresa's whole purpose in founding St. Joseph's Convent, and getting away from the large Convent of the Incarnation where the mitigated observance was in force, was to return to the Primitive Rule of Carmel. The purpose of the Primitive Rule is to permit *constant prayer* in silence and solitude. Chapter 5 of the *Rule of St. Albert* (twelfth century) reads: "Let each one remain alone in his cell or near it, meditating day and night on the Law of the Lord and watching

649, This is the first sentence of the section "Of the Receiving of Novices," which goes on to specify that prospective sisters should be at least seventeen, detached from the world, healthy, intelligent, and possessed of the right temperament and qualities to live the Carmelite life; acceptance must not be predicated on whether the one entering gives alms to the house, or "we shall be paying more attention to the amount of a person's alms than to her goodness and other qualities" (225); the majority of the community must approve of a new novice being received, as well as of each sister making profession.

650. The paragraph on the duties of the novice mistress is part of the section "Of the Obligations of each Nun in her Office" (228–30); it emphasizes that the novice mistress should be "a person of great prudence, prayer and spirituality," who teaches her charges both the outward regulations of the Constitutions and the inward practices of prayer and mortification, attaching more importance to the latter than to the former; she should "treat them compassionately and lovingly, not marveling at their faults, for their progress is bound to be gradual," and should "attach more importance to their not failing in the virtues than to strictness of penance."

in prayer, unless he is legitimately occupied in something else."[651] St. Teresa interprets this in her own way (see *Way of Perfection*, c. 4) {focusing on} silence and solitude in the cell. They *work* alone: "There must be no work-room at St. Joseph's; for, although it is a praiseworthy custom to have one, it is easier to keep silence if one is alone, and getting used to solitude is a great help to prayer. *Since prayer must be the foundation on which this house is built*, it is necessary for us to like whatever gives us the greatest help in it" (vol. II, p. 18{-19}).[652] Elsewhere (*Interior Castle*, V:1, page 247) she says: "All of us who wear the sacred habit of Carmel are called to prayer and contemplation—because that was the first principle of our Order and because we are descended from the line of those holy Fathers of ours from Mount Carmel who sought this treasure, {. . .} in such solitude and with such contempt for the world. . . ."[653] St. Teresa was also very conscious of the apostolic effect of Carmelite prayer: her convents were an integral part of the Counter-reformation. In *The Way of Perfection* (c. 1) she tells her nuns that their vocation is to pray for the salvation of souls, and especially {those} of the Lutherans.[654] In the *Life* (c. 32) she tells how the inspiration to found the first discalced convent followed visions of hell which made her realize her own imperfection and remissness. She was particularly distressed by the fact that she was constantly out of the convent with people of the world, important personages, who could persuade her superiors to send her out to them. It was in a conversation with her cousin Maria de Ocampo that the project of foundation first came up. Then a vision confirmed the project. Her confessor approved it, and her superiors went along with it. But it met with great persecution and opposition and Maria de Ocampo's confessor even

---

651. *Les Plus Vieux Textes du Carmel*, ed. and trans. François de Sainte-Marie, OCD (Paris: Éditions du Seuil, 1944), 88.

652. Text reads ". . . learn to like . . ." (emphasis Merton's).

653. Text reads ". . . this sacred habit . . . treasure, this precious pearl of which we speak, in such great solitude . . ."

654. *Complete Works of Saint Teresa*, 2.3.

refused her absolution. Then the provincial changed his mind. (READ *Life*, pages 219 ff.[655])

Carmelite theologians, typified by Joseph of the Holy Spirit {in his} *Cursus Theologiae Mystico-Scholasticae*,[656] develop the Teresian program. He states: "While all who aspire to perfection should also desire mystical union, the Carmelites are to understand this call particularly directed to them, and not be deterred by the difficulties" (*Isagoge*, I.iv.2).[657] In II, Disp. 11, Q. 4, Joseph of the Holy Spirit considers the question "whether there are some who are *bound* to contemplation."[658] He holds that Carmelites are obligated by their profession *to seek perfection by the way of contemplation*. In order to sustain this opinion he necessarily has to adopt the view that there is such a thing as acquired contemplation, as no one could be bound to attain to perfection by infused contemplation. "*Finis immediatus nostrae sacrae religionis est*

655. Merton has summarized these pages in the preceding sentences; the chapter goes on to relate that a learned Dominican was consulted, and Teresa agreed to abide by his decision; though he initially intended to urge her to give up the project, and was encouraged to do so by others, he finally "became convinced that we should be rendering God a great service and that the scheme must not be abandoned" (1.222-23), and subsequently several saintly persons initially opposed to the idea of the new foundation began to support it.

656. Ioseph a Spiritu Sancto, *Cursus Theologiae Mystico-Scholasticae*, ed. Anastasio a S. Paulo, 6 vols. (Bruges: Beyaert, 1924–1934) (originally published in Seville/Madrid, 1720–1740).

657. This is a paraphrase; the text (#168) reads: "*Omnibus huic sacratissimae unioni inhiandum est et praecipue iis, quorum est in perfectionem ire et die ac nocte in orationibus vigilare. Quamobrem, carissimi, estote fortes in bello et pugnate vigiles cum antiqua serpente . . . suae invidiae ab hac felicitate retrahere sollicitante. Nec vos deterreat asperum certamen, quod aggredimini; sed introspicite fastigium, in quod vocamini*" (1.54). ("This most sacred union should be desired by all, and especially by those who are called to perfection and to remain awake in prayer day and night. Therefore, dearest ones, be courageous in this struggle and fight alertly with the ancient serpent . . . who endeavors to draw you away from this happiness out of envy. Do not let yourselves be frightened away by this bitter struggle which you are waging; but set your sights on the summit to which you are called.")

658. *Cursus*, 2.525–76.

contemplatio."[659] He quotes Thomas of Jesus who states that the Carmelite seeks the perfection of charity above all "by continual meditation and prayer, which is his immediate end, and then by enclosure in the cell, manual labor, most strict abstinence and silence, as means destined to this end."[660] (This sounds like Cassian, *Conference* 1.[661]) Joseph concludes that a Carmelite who would frequently omit "purely mental prayer" ({as} distinct from {the} office) would go against the very purpose of his religious life and hence would sin mortally.[662] How does this compare with the Benedictine concept of *conversatio morum*? It is certainly too formal a statement. The monastic spirit is less juridical, and less centered on *one* means.

The Classical Carmelite Treatment of Prayer and Contemplation: here we give a brief schema of the levels of prayer according to the Carmelite school. This schema is more artificial than the writings of St. Teresa herself.

1. PRE-CONTEMPLATION (this term, suggested by Fr. Gabriel of St. Mary Magdalen,[663] is perhaps arbitrary):

659. *Cursus*, 2.541 (#117): "The immediate end of our sacred religious life is contemplation."

660. *Cursus*, 2.546 (#124), quoting Thomas of Jesus, *Expositio in Regulam Ordinis Carmelitarum*, II, dub. 1 (*Opera Omnia* [1684], I, 451B).

661. In the first *Conference*, Abbot Moses distinguishes between the *scopos*, or immediate purpose of the monastic life, which is purity of heart, and the *telos*, or final goal, which is the Kingdom of God (*PL* 49, cols. 483–85; see *Cassian and the Fathers*, 204–206).

662. Almost the entire rest of *Quaestio IV* (2.543–72; ##145–72) is taken up with defending this proposition and refuting objections to it.

663. This term is not found in Fr. Gabriel's series of lectures: *École Thérésienne et Problèmes Mystiques Contemporains* (Paris: Desclée, de Brouwer, 1935); *Sainte Thérèse: Maîtresse de Vie Spirituelle* (Paris: Desclée, de Brouwer, 1938) (ET: *St. Teresa of Jesus* [Westminster, MD: Newman Press, 1949]); *Saint Jean de la Croix, Docteur de l'Amour Divin* (Paris: Desclée, de Brouwer, 1947) (ET: *St. John of the Cross: Doctor of Divine Love and Contemplation* [Westminster, MD: Newman Press, 1946]); *La Contemplation "Acquise"* (Paris: Lethielleux, 1949) (ET included in *St. John of the Cross*, 99ff.); nor is it found in his contribution to the article "Contemplation" in the *Dictionnaire de Spiritualité*: "Contemplation dans l'École du Carmel

1) Meditation (discursive): a simple method was in favor in the novitiates, {with} emphasis on affectivity rather than reasoning. Meditation in its discursive form is not insisted on with too much rigidity. The Carmelites readily accept the fact that meditation in a formal sense may become impossible. St. Teresa says: "Not all can meditate but all can love."[664] Her corollary is that one should seek above all to *progress in love* rather than in meditation. Note what she says on "loving much rather than thinking much," and not paying too much attention to distractions (*Interior Castle*, IV.l; p. 233).[665]

2) Prayer of recollection:

i) active: {this entails} conscious and willed diminution of discursive acts—deliberate simplification.

ii) passive: discourse is further diminished by {the} intervention of actual grace, but not entirely eliminated.

({Note:} this distinction is rather the work of *modern followers* of St. Teresa than of the saint herself.) {For} examples, {see} *Interior Castle*, IV.3;[666] *Life*, 12:13.[667] (Here St. John of the Cross insists on

---

Thérèsienne" (*DS* 2, cols. 2058–67); in his article on "Carmes: Dechaussés" he speaks of preparation for contemplation but not "pre-contemplation" (*DS* 2, cols. 181–82).

664. See *Foundations,* c. 5: "not everyone has by nature an imagination capable of meditating, whereas all souls are capable of love" (*Complete Works of Saint Teresa*, 3.19).

665. "I only want you to be warned that, if you would progress a long way on this road and ascend to the Mansions of your desire, the important thing is not to think much, but to love much" (*Complete Works of Saint Teresa*, 2.233).

666. *Complete Works of Saint Teresa*, 2.240-46: this chapter is entitled "*Describes what is meant by the Prayer of Recollection, which the Lord generally grants before that already mentioned. Speaks of its effects and of the remaining effects of the former kind of prayer, which had to do with the consolations given by the Lord*"; it emphasizes not straining after spiritual advancement but being receptive to divine action: "The soul must just leave itself in the hands of God, and do what He wills it to do, completely disregarding its own advantage and resigning itself as much as it possibly can to the will of God" (242–43).

667. Chapter 12 has only 7 sections (which in any case are not numbered in the Peers translation); perhaps Merton has mistranscribed from another source

the NIGHT OF SENSE [{to be} discussed later] {with its} preliminary passive purification of the senses.[668]) This pre-contemplative level is not mystical or infused contemplation; at least such seems to be the general opinion. Those who hold the existence of *acquired contemplation* are actually calling by that name the prayer of recollection. This prayer is simple (sometimes called[669] prayer of "simple regard"[670] or "prayer of simplicity"[671]), a plain, undetailed intuition, a global view, generally informed with affectivity: a "gaze of love." Note that many consider that the Night of Sense is already the beginning of mystical action of God in the soul. Such fine distinctions are however not to be taken too seriously, and one must not attempt to "measure" everything in the spiritual life. Nor is it the intention of the Carmelite saints that we should attempt any such thing.

2. CONTEMPLATION:

a) The prayer of quiet (Fourth, Fifth Mansion) {is} like the prayer of passive recollection but deeper and more passive. (Note, for discussion of this rather fine distinction, see remarks that follow the schema.[672]) In the prayer of quiet there is still {the} possibility of distraction. There is still some cooperation on the part of the largely passive faculties. Passivity grows. The intelligence and will have less and less part to play as one approaches the next degree.

---

a reference to chapter 12, sections 1–3, which focus on the soul's own activity in awakening love and nurturing virtues; in the sections of the chapter that follow Teresa warns the reader not to attempt to suspend the working of the understanding by one's own efforts (*Complete Works of Saint Teresa*, 1.70–73).

668. St. John discusses the passive night of sense in *The Dark Night of the Soul*, cc. 8–14 (*Complete Works of Saint John of the Cross*, 1.371-97).

669. The terms are found together in Pourrat, 3.196.

670. See Poulain, c. 2: "Of the Four Degrees of Ordinary Prayer and of the Last Two in Particular" (7–51); the fourth degree is "the prayer of *simple regard* or of *simplicity*" (7), which Poulain considers the highest stage of non-mystical prayer.

671. According to Tanquerey, who describes it at some length (637–48), this term was first used by Bossuet in *Manière Court et Facile pour Faire l'Oraison en Foi, et de Simple Présence de Dieu* (637); see also Poulain, 10.

672. See below, pages 245–46.

b) The prayer of full union (Fifth Mansion: see *Interior Castle*, Fifth Mansion): here passivity is complete. There is no further *ability* to act and direct oneself, or to take any initiative, or to co-operate with grace on one's own. One is passively moved, and "out of oneself."

c) This growing passivity manifests itself in two further ways (Sixth Mansion):

1) positive: ecstasy, rapture and other ways in which the soul is "seized" and "carried away" by the love of God[673] (to be distinguished from the "consolations" described early in {the} Fourth Mansion[674]);

2) negative: exterior and interior trials of all sorts, especially great anguish concerning the validity and divine character of graces that have been received.

(Here distinguish the approach of St. John of the Cross in *The Dark Night of the Soul*, and that of St. Teresa in the Sixth Mansion. St. John of the Cross concentrates on passive and mystical purification by night and desolation, within the depths of the soul. St. Teresa reflects more her own experience: interior and exterior trials combined, the doubt cast upon her spiritual experiences by confessors and good people, and the consequent conflict within her own soul which could not but follow the action of God in spite of all that was said and done to discourage her.)

d) Transforming union, or *mystical marriage*, preceded by *spiritual betrothal* (Seventh Mansion):

A. *Spiritual betrothal* (VII.1):

1) An experience of the Trinity beyond vision—here we rejoin the *theologia* of the Greek Fathers and Evagrius (read p. 331, bottom[675]).

---

673. See Sixth Mansions, cc. 4-5 (*Complete Works of Saint Teresa*, 2.286-97).

674. See Fourth Mansions, cc. 1-2 (*Complete Works of Saint Teresa*, 2.230-39).

675. "It is brought into this Mansion by means of an intellectual vision, in which, by a representation of the truth in a particular way, the Most Holy Trinity reveals itself, in all three Persons. First of all the spirit becomes enkindled and

2) It is not an ecstatic experience {and} does not impede contact with external reality. The presence of the Blessed Trinity is more or less constantly conscious. "The soul is *always aware* that it is experiencing this companionship."[676]

B. *Spiritual marriage*:
1) Takes place in the inmost center of the soul. She mentions in her own case an "imaginary vision" of Christ, but this is accidental.[677] He appears in the center of the soul in an "intellectual vision."[678]

2) The soul and God can no longer be separated. "The soul remains all the time in that center with its God."[679] Yet this does not mean it has attained a state of impeccability, nor are pain, suffering and trial excluded, though they cannot penetrate to this center of the soul. But "they have no aridities or interior trials" (p. 340). "There are *hardly* any of the periods of aridity or interior disturbance which at one time or another have occurred in all [the other mansions], but the soul is *almost* always in tranquillity" (note {the} qualifiers) (p. 341).[680] "They have no lack of crosses, but these do not unsettle them or deprive them of their peace" (343).

3) The effects {include}: (a) self-forgetfulness; (b) {a} great desire to suffer, interior joy, love of enemies, desire for the glory

---

is illumined, as it were, by a cloud of the greatest brightness. It sees these three persons, individually, and yet, by a wonderful kind of knowledge which is given to it, the soul realizes that most certainly and truly all these three Persons are one Substance and one Power and one Knowledge and one God alone; so that what we hold by faith the soul may be said here to grasp by sight, although nothing is seen by the eyes, either of the body or of the soul, for it is no imaginary vision. Here all three Persons communicate Themselves to the soul and speak to the soul and explain to it those words which the Gospel attributes to the Lord—namely, that He and the Father and the Holy Spirit will come to dwell with the soul which loves Him and keeps His commandments" (*Complete Works of Saint Teresa*, 2.331-32).

676. *Complete Works of Saint Teresa*, 2.332 (emphasis added).
677. *Interior Castle*, VII.2 (*Complete Works of Saint Teresa*, 2.334).
678. *Interior Castle*, VII.2 (*Complete Works of Saint Teresa*, 2.334).
679. *Interior Castle*, VII.2 (*Complete Works of Saint Teresa*, 2.335).
680. Text reads ". . . disturbance in it which . . ." (emphasis added).

of God above all; (c) no more raptures and transports, no more fears; (d) deep interior silence.

Some remarks:

A. THE NATURE OF CONTEMPLATION: the Teresian theologians then tend to separate the prayer of passive recollection, which belongs to what they call "pre-contemplation," from the prayer of quiet which is the first stage of real contemplation. In making this distinction they also place the dividing line between so-called *acquired* contemplation and *infused* contemplation at this point, which is not too clearly defined. Is this distinction clear in St. Teresa herself? Certainly not as clear as her followers seem to think. Without taking the academic divisions too seriously, let us consider the texts of St. Teresa herself. {In the} Fourth Mansion (*Interior Castle*, vol. ii; p. 230), she declares that here the "supernatural" prayer begins. Hence she seems to mean that here what is commonly called infused contemplation begins. Does the "supernatural" here apply to the "consolations" which she describes, or to the prayer of recollection which comes in the same book? In IV.3 she makes it clear that "this form of recollection also seems to me to be supernatural" (p. 240).[681] She identifies "consolations" in this context with {the} prayer of quiet (see IV.2; p. 236). *Both* then are "supernatural." Note in IV.1 and 2 there is an added element of confusion: (1) she is comparing "consolations" (prayer of quiet) with "sweetness" (acquired by *meditation*);[682] (2) and she is also implicitly leading up to a comparison between {the} prayer of quiet and prayer of recollection. The danger is that we may confuse these and identify either "consolations" or "sweetness" with {the} prayer of recollection—then we are lost.

Comment: with all these divisions and distinctions, comings and goings and varieties of terms, one tends to become impatient

---

681. Text reads "It is a form of recollection which also seems to me supernatural, . . ."

682. *Complete Works of Saint Teresa*, 2.231.

with the saint. (Walter Hilton, in the *Scale of Perfection* [v.g. II.27[683]], is much simpler and more satisfying.) Read pp. 240 and 241, {her} description of "prayer of recollection."[684] She uses the celebrated

683. This chapter, entitled "How it is very profitable for a soul to be brought by grace into the luminous darkness, and how a man should dispose himself to come to it," discusses the experience of darkness first as a mode of self-knowledge, then as a spiritual seeing of Jesus; the author emphasizes that it is necessary for those without the experience to prepare themselves for it by dying to the world and its recognition, by being poor inwardly and if possible outwardly as well, by not resting in one's own deeds or virtues and by bearing no ill will toward one's fellow-Christians; darkness is equated with dying to the world, as Paul teaches in Gal. 6:15—it is the one and only gateway to contemplation, which is equated with the gain of one-hundred-fold given to those who forsake the world; darkness is compared to coming out of the sunlight into a darkened room and having to refocus one's eyes (see Walter Hilton, *The Scale of Perfection*, trans. Dom Gerard Sitwell, osb [London: Burns Oates, 1953], 215–21); while the reference is to chapter 27, it is possible that Merton is actually thinking of the following chapter, which discusses the work of the Lord in reforming the soul in terms of the four-fold activity of calling, justifying, magnifying and glorifying, which is perhaps more pertinent to the discussion of stages of growth in St. Teresa here.

684. "It is sometimes said that the soul enters within itself and sometimes that it rises above itself; but I cannot explain things in that kind of language, for I have no skill in it. However, I believe you will understand what I am able to tell you, though I may perhaps be intelligible only to myself. Let us suppose that these senses and faculties (the inhabitants, as I have said, of this castle, which is the figure that I have taken to explain my meaning) have gone out of the castle, and, for days and years, have been consorting with strangers, to whom all the good things in the castle are abhorrent. Then, realizing how much they have lost, they come back to it, though they do not actually re-enter it, because the habits they have formed are hard to conquer. But they are no longer traitors and they now walk about in the vicinity of the castle. The great King, Who dwells in the Mansion within this castle, perceives their good will, and in His great mercy desires to bring them back to Him. So, like a good Shepherd, with a call so gentle that even they can hardly recognize it, he teaches them to know His voice and not to go away and get lost but to return to their Mansion; and so powerful is this Shepherd's call that they give up the things outside the castle which had led them astray, and once again enter it. I do not think I have ever explained this before as clearly as here. When we are seeking God within ourselves . . . it is a great help if God grants us this favour. Do not suppose that the understanding

image of the Lord like a hidden shepherd in the center of the soul calling together the faculties like sheep to Himself in recollection, "with a call so gentle that even they can hardly recognize it." This in our opinion puts the prayer of passive recollection in the class of *infused* contemplation. {See also} LIFE, chapter 12: here she seems to rule out a prayer of active recollection that would consist in deliberately suspending the activity of the faculties. But {she} describes how {in} passive recollection, brought about by grace, and aided by *humility and learning* (she keeps insisting that the humble and learned man is at an advantage here), God Himself provides the faculties, passively, with occupation, or else fills the soul with His presence. It is not a mere blank. (READ pp. 71, 72, 73.[685]) Again, {in the} Fourth Mansion (p. 243), this is

---

can attain to Him, merely by trying to think of Him as within the soul, or the imagination, by picturing Him as there. This is a good habit and an excellent kind of meditation, for it is founded upon a truth—namely, that God is within us. But it is not the kind of prayer that I have in mind, for anyone (with the help of the Lord, you understand) can practice it for himself. What I am describing is quite different. These people are sometimes in the castle before they have begun to think about God at all. I cannot say where they entered it or how they heard their Shepherd's call: it was certainly not with their ears, for outwardly such a call is not audible. They become markedly conscious that they are gradually retiring within themselves; anyone who experiences this will discover what I mean: I cannot explain it better."

685. "If anyone tries to pass beyond this stage and lift up his spirit so as to experience consolations which are not being given to him, I think he is losing both in the one respect and in the other. For these consolations are supernatural and, when the understanding ceases to act, the soul remains barren and suffers great aridity. And, as the foundation of the entire edifice is humility, the nearer we come to God, the greater must be the progress which we make in this virtue: otherwise, we lose everything. It seems to be a kind of pride that makes us wish to rise higher, for God is already doing more for us than we deserve by bringing us near to Him. . . . In the mystical theology which I began to describe, the understanding loses its power of working, because God suspends it . . . . What I say we must not do is to presume to think that we can suspend it ourselves; nor must we allow it to cease working: if we do, we shall remain stupid and cold and shall achieve nothing whatsoever. . . . Once more I repeat my advice that it is very important that we should not try to lift up our spirits unless they

further qualified. We should *not suspend all thought*. We should without forcing or turmoil *put an end to discursive reasoning*. One should retain a general sense of the presence of God, a global awareness. But one should not try to understand what is going on or try to understand what this state is because that is a gift bestowed upon the will. This is a very clear and important qualification. It gives us a good and perfectly traditional idea of contemplation, and of the way to dispose oneself to receive the gift of contemplation, the way to cooperate with that gift in its more tenuous and preliminary stage. ABOVE ALL IT MAKES CLEAR THAT WE ARE NOT TO THINK ABOUT OURSELVES AND ABOUT WHAT IS GOING ON IN OURSELVES. This is forgotten by superficial readers of the Carmelite mystics who, on the contrary, become preoccupied with themselves and with their state. If the Carmelites define and describe these states, it is only to remind us at the same time that we must forget all states and all ways. Certain minds can never grasp this approach. For such, the Carmelite mystics are harmful reading. A too rapid reading of Fourth Mansion chapter 3 may lead to confusion rather than clarification as to the difference between prayer of recollection and prayer of quiet. Why? because she takes the prayer of recollection now *after* the prayer of quiet. {See} *Life*, 14 (the second water): {the} prayer of quiet "borders on the supernatural, to which [the soul] could in no way attain by its own exertions" (p. 83). "The faculties are not lost . . . . The will alone is occupied in such a way that, without knowing how, it becomes captive. . . ."[686] The other faculties can help the will but more often hinder it (the "doves") (p. 84). {There are} great consolation and little labor, {and} great fruits of virtue, a "presence" of the Lord, which indicates that He is "about to begin a special work."[687] But the soul that is alone and afraid can become very confused and can turn back. {It is} difficult to understand

---

are lifted up by the Lord: in the latter case we shall become aware of the fact instantly."

686. *Complete Works of Saint Teresa*, 1.83.
687. *Complete Works of Saint Teresa*, 1.85.

the situation, and more difficult to explain it. What has been said is by no means complete, but the fragments of ideas should enable us to piece together a fairly accurate idea of what St. Teresa means by contemplative prayer.

We can come to the following conclusions, without going into further detail:

1) Here we have purely and simply the traditional *contemplatio* of the medieval monastic tradition. It is also familiar mystical prayer as found everywhere in the Rhenish and Flemish mystics.

2) St. Teresa, writing without plan and without system, repeatedly approaches the subject from the point of view of experience and from *different angles*. She brings out ever-new aspects and shades of meaning in simple contemplative experience, and she does tend to distinguish a prayer of recollection, and a deeper form of (almost) the same thing which is the prayer of quiet.

3) The love of order and system among the Carmelite theologians of the Teresian school has led to a systematic schema, a clear-cut division of these various "degrees." But actually this clear-cut division, requiring great ingenuity, is never quite satisfactory, and never quite hits the real point. Whatever may be the merits of the various classifications, since St. Teresa speaks of the prayer of passive recollection as "supernatural"[688] and describes it as a response to the *felt*, experienced *call* direct from God, it certainly seems to be *infused contemplation* and not "pre-contemplation." However the modern Carmelites single this out as a special intermediate form of prayer: (a) they call it "active" or "acquired" contemplation; (b) they claim that it calls for a special kind of direction; (c) it is a question of teaching and helping the soul *to prepare himself* to dispose himself in simplicity for the grace of recollection and unification of the faculties in the love of God.

---

688. See *Interior Castle*, IV.3 (*Complete Works of Saint Teresa*, 2.240): "It is a form of recollection which also seems to me supernatural . . . ."

4) We can never be absolutely and precisely sure what St. Teresa meant, and how she intended to distinguish the prayer of quiet from the prayer of (passive) recollection. The best thing is to read what she has said about both, and accept it all as it stands, making use of the intuitions her descriptions suggest for our own practical purposes.

5) In doing this we will be returning, more or less, to the traditional idea of *contemplatio* which was never reduced to perfect systematization by the monastic fathers, and at the same time we will be profiting by the observations and experience of St. Teresa. In a word, it is very profitable for us to read and understand St. Teresa in the light of the medieval monastic tradition and of the Rhenish mystics. But it is less profitable to introduce into our monastic theology the systematic psychological distinctions favored by more modern writers.

B. The Call to Contemplation: this has been a question which has preoccupied modern writers in mystical theology. What does St. Teresa have to say about it? It is obviously of primary concern to her.

Who is called to (mystical) contemplation?

1. First of all, remember the context: she is writing for members of an order in which everything is directly ordered to a life of recollection, of meditative prayer, of contemplation and contemplative union with God. This, as we have seen, is the express purpose of the Carmelite life. Those then who are called to the Carmelite life are without question called to *tend to contemplation*. They are called to do whatever they can to dispose themselves for it. They are called to the "contemplative life" in the juridical sense, and more than that they are called to the contemplative life in an interior and active sense: that is, to the practice of detachment, silence, solitude, recollection and meditation, which will dispose them to receive the gift of true contemplative prayer.

2. Speaking in this context to her sisters (*Way of Perfection*, c. 19; p. 85), she says that they are all called to the "living waters" of contemplative experience. This text has even been interpreted to mean that *all Christians* are called to mystical prayer in a remote

way. She says: "Remember, the LORD INVITES US ALL [i.e. Carmelites?]; and, since He is Truth Itself, we cannot doubt Him. If His invitation were not a GENERAL ONE, He would not have said: 'I will give you to drink.' He might have said: 'Come all of you, for after all you will lose nothing by coming; and I will give to drink to those whom I think fit for it.' But, as He said we were all to come, without making this condition, I feel sure that none will fail to receive this living water unless they cannot keep to the path."[689]

Comments:

a) As the text seems to refer to John 7:37, it can be taken to apply to all Christians.

b) St. Teresa was a concrete thinker. When she says "we" it is much more likely that she has in mind those who are actually present or those who belong to the group to which she speaks, even if not all are actually present.

c) What does she mean about those "who cannot keep to the path"? At any rate it is a qualification which admits that though all may be called in some way, all may not be able to answer the call and turn out, in effect, to be not called. (It is not at all clear whether they culpably reject the call.)

3. What is this way? In chapter 28 of *The Way of Perfection* (p. 115), she indicates that those who are *able to practice the prayer of recollection* will receive "the water of the fountain" which, in context, is mystical ("supernatural" prayer). She says explicitly that the prayer of recollection is the quickest way to the prayer of quiet. What she means precisely by prayer of recollection here is a prayer which *even though vocal* is centered upon an *awareness of the presence of God within oneself*. "It is called recollection because the soul collects together all the faculties and enters within itself to be with its God. Its Divine Master comes more speedily to teach it, and grant it the Prayer of Quiet, than in any other way."[690]

---

689. Text reads ". . . '. . . I will give drink to those . . .' . . ." (emphasis added).

690. *Complete Works of Saint Teresa*, 2.115.

"Those who are able to shut themselves up in this way in the little Heaven of the soul, wherein dwells the Maker of Heaven and earth, and who have formed the habit of looking at nothing and staying in no place which will distract these outward senses, may be sure that they are walking on an excellent road, and will come without fail to drink of the water. . . ."[691] It is clearly implied that some are *not able* to do this. Hence we can conclude that those who are able to practice the prayer of recollection are certainly (according to her) called to higher prayer, at least to the beginning of mystical contemplation. She does not assert they are the *only* ones so called. It certainly does not seem to be an exaggerated claim to say that all the carefully picked members of a small Carmelite community, picked precisely in view of this kind of aptitude, might be said to be called to mystical contemplation at least in its most elementary form. What does this mean? It does not mean that all Carmelites will automatically reach mystical prayer, by the mere fact of keeping their Rule faithfully. But it does mean that mystical prayer should be considered *ordinary and normal*, not only in Carmel and other similar Orders, but everywhere where a certain amount of silence and recollection are possible, where there is an atmosphere of faith, and where it is not too difficult for the ordinary Christian to be fully aware of the truths of his faith, especially of the presence of God and the love of Christ crucified.

4. NEVERTHELESS, St. Teresa admits in practice:

a) the perfect are not necessarily mystics in the sense of attaining to the grace of the *prayer of union* or even of the prayer of quiet;

b) even in Carmel, though mystical prayer should be ordinary and the nuns all dispose themselves to a life of deep union with God, not every Carmelite will attain to mystical prayer in actual fact;

---

691. Text reads ". . . within this little . . ." (*Complete Works of Saint Teresa*, 2.115).

c) even if one does not attain to mystical prayer, in Carmel or elsewhere, he can be just as holy and perhaps more holy than one who has attained to this prayer.

The cardinal text on this is *Interior Castle*, V, c. 3, which points out that the essence of Christian perfection is union with God by love, that is to say, perfect union with His will, and that an *experience* of union in prayer is not essential to Christian sanctity.

> Despite all I have said, this Mansion seems to me a little obscure. There is a great deal to be gained by entering it, and those from whom the Lord withholds such supernatural gifts will do well to feel that they are not without hope; for true union can quite well be achieved, with the favour of Our Lord, if we endeavour to attain it by not following our own will but submitting it to whatever is the will of God. Oh, how many of us there are who say we do this and think we want nothing else, and would die for the truth, as I believe I have said! For I tell you, and I shall often repeat this, that when you have obtained this favour from the Lord, you need not strive for that other delectable union which has been described, for the most valuable thing about it is that it proceeds from this union which I am now describing; and we cannot attain to the heights I have spoken of if we are not sure that we have the union in which we resign our wills to the will of God. Oh, how much to be desired is this union! Happy the soul that has attained to it, for it will live peacefully both in this life and in the next as well. Nothing that happens on earth will afflict it unless it finds itself in peril of losing God, or sees that He is offended—neither sickness nor poverty nor death, except when someone dies who was needed by the Church of God. For this soul sees clearly that He knows what He does better than it knows itself what it desires (Peers trans., pp. 259–260).[692]

---

692. Text reads " . . . die for this truth, . . ."

Here she is describing the union of wills which is essential to Christian perfection. This is the union of love in which the experience of the prayer of union is rooted and founded. Hence we can say, without the prayer of union, the experience of union, one can still be deeply and perfectly united to God. But without union of wills in love the prayer and mystical experience of union cannot be genuine.

Theologians have developed this in the following terms:

a) Distinction is to be made between *integral* and *substantial* perfection: *substantial* perfection {entails} union of wills with God by love; *integral* perfection {entails} union of wills *plus* an experience of that union in mystical prayer.

b) Integral perfection is or should be the *normal* sanctity of the Christian. It is less according to the Gospels for one to be united perfectly to Christ without having any experience whatever of the fact. (See St. John 14:17 etc., quoted above at the beginning of this series of lectures.[693])

c) It is possible for one to have greater substantial perfection, without experience, than one who has the integral perfection that includes prayer of union. In other words it is possible to be more of a saint and yet less of a mystic or not a mystic at all in the sense of having mystical prayer. (Maritain insists[694] that there is an

---

693. See above, page 39.

694. See Maritain's essay "Action and Contemplation" in Jacques Maritain, *Scholasticism and Politics*, trans. Mortimer J. Adler (New York: Macmillan, 1940): "In the case of other souls it will be primarily the other gifts of inspired freedom; their life will indeed by a mystical and dispropriated life; but it will be such pre-eminently in relation to their activities and works, and they will not have the typical and normal forms of contemplation. They will not be, for all that, deprived of contemplation, of participating and experiencing lovingly the divine states. . . . The contemplation of the 'active' souls will be *masked* and inapparent, but they will have contemplative graces . . . . Mysterious contemplation will not be in their way of praying but in the grace of their behaviour, in their sweet-minded hands, perhaps, or in their way of walking perhaps, or in their way of looking at a poor man or at suffering" (186–87). In a February 10, 1949 letter to Maritain, Merton thanks him for his "kind remarks" on Merton's

"active" mysticism which covers this case, so all saints are in some sense mystics.) In any event, it is held that those who being substantially perfect somehow have to "do without" mystical prayer receive some form of compensation for this.

XI. The Spiritual Direction of Contemplatives

1. *The Nature and History of Spiritual Direction*: it has remained for modern times to take with special seriousness the question of the spiritual direction of contemplatives as well as of those with special apostolic vocations, and others. Spiritual direction has become more and more of an institution. In a course with a more or less pastoral orientation, one cannot ignore the seriousness with which this question is studied today. At the same time one cannot ignore either the change in attitude which is beginning to make itself felt. It is therefore very important to get a well-rounded view of the whole question of spiritual direction. Instead of going into a detailed examination of all the technical ins and outs of the

---

pamphlet *What is Contemplation?* (Holy Cross, IN: Saint Mary's College, 1948), and for his suggestion that those Merton refers to there as "*quasi-contemplatives*" (11) could better be called "masked contemplatives," as in Maritain's own essay: "I especially like the term 'masked contemplatives,' which expresses much better what I mean. As far as I know they are contemplatives but they have no real way of knowing that they are because their gifts of understanding and wisdom are not strong enough to enable them to recognize their experience for what it is. They know God by experience but they can't interpret that experience" (Thomas Merton, *The Courage for Truth: Letters to Writers*, ed. Christine M. Bochen [New York: Farrar, Straus, Giroux, 1993], 24). In the revised edition of *What Is Contemplation?* published in London in 1950 by Burns and Oates, Merton adds two sentences at the end of the paragraph about quasi-contemplatives: "They are much closer to God than they realize. They enjoy a kind of 'masked' contemplation" (this edition is the one that has been reprinted in various formats: see Thomas Merton, *What Is Contemplation?* [Springfield, IL: Templegate, 1981], 32). These same sentences appear in the much more extensive revision of *What Is Contemplation?* that became *The Inner Experience*, though the term "*quasi-contemplatives*" has been replaced there with "*hidden contemplatives*" (Thomas Merton, *The Inner Experience: Notes on Contemplation*, ed. William H. Shannon [San Francisco: HarperCollins, 2003], 64).

direction of mystics, victim souls, etc., etc., we will follow our usual procedure in studying the history of the question, and will then concern ourselves with concrete examples and problems that have arisen in the past, considering the way the problems were solved, or what solutions were attempted. The advantage of this approach will be, once again, to avoid the impression that there is some *magic technique* by which one can became an "expert director" as soon as one has been initiated into the proper theological and pastoral secrets. We must avoid illusions of grandeur both in the matter of direction, as well as in superiorship and in applying psychiatry to members of a religious community. All these offices or techniques are necessary, and must be used humbly, reverently and prudently in union with God's will and the directives of the Church. But great harm can be done by persons who unconsciously exploit souls to magnify their own egos and to substantiate their own illusions about themselves, or about the group with which they have identified themselves (for instance sacrificing the genuine good of individuals and of the community to a program of some movement or to some school of thought).

Questions and Objections: sometimes today, in view of the new developments in the Church, the revival of a more liturgical and objective spirituality, with less emphasis on the individual, the question is asked: HAS THE IMPORTANCE OF SPIRITUAL DIRECTION BEEN EXAGGERATED? And if this is the case, should spiritual direction be de-emphasized? Should it even be discarded altogether? Is SPIRITUAL DIRECTION NECESSARY? Some seem to think that the emphasis on spiritual direction is harmful. In favor of this view, it is argued that:

a) This view is consistent with the whole movement of Catholic thought and spirituality today, which is consistently revaluating all that has taken place since the fourteenth and fifteenth centuries.

b) But, it is argued, a great deal of what has taken place since the fifteenth century has been *degraded and deficient*, and has been evidence of *decadence* in Christian thought and spirituality. In particular, one looks with very special suspicion on all the developments that are characteristic of these periods, and produced by them as manifestations of their own temper.

c) It is further argued that this period has produced an individualistic piety, out of contact with the liturgy, with a distorted view of the sacramental life of the Church, out of contact with the fullness of the Christian mysteries. The developments that seemed like "progress" in this period were in fact deviations from the right path. These developments were doubtless *necessary* but they were also *unhealthy symptoms*.

d) Spiritual direction as a professional concern of certain priests and even congregations arose to fill certain needs created by this individualistic piety, so the argument continues. It therefore took an exaggerated turn, and also *contributed to a further distortion* of the truly Catholic mentality.

e) Therefore (it is concluded) the whole development of spiritual direction as an institution, since the late Middle Ages, will have to be revaluated. The emphasis on direction must stop. We must recognize that it is of far less value than has hitherto been claimed. Souls can very well get along without it. To insist that one needs direction is to perpetuate this false mentality, this unhealthy attitude, etc., etc.

f) Furthermore, direction fixes the attention of the one directed upon himself and leads to morbid introspection or at least to useless concern with one's own perfection.

g) Finally, spiritual direction has been replaced by psychiatry, psychoanalysis, and counselling. These modern techniques are more scientific as well as more adapted to the needs of modern man, and to require spiritual direction *in addition* to them is useless and even harmful.

Such are the arguments advanced. They have some truth in them, but taken as a whole they in their own turn represent a rather unhealthy tendency. What we have to do is evaluate these points rightly, consider what the Church teaches on direction, and make *a sober and wise use of the traditional view of direction.*

Answer: THESE OBJECTIONS, WHILE HAVING SOME TRUTH IN THEM, ARE NOT IN ACCORDANCE WITH CATHOLIC TRADITION, WHICH TEACHES THAT SPIRITUAL DIRECTION IS NOT ONLY USEFUL BUT MAY BE IN SOME CASES NECESSARY, AT LEAST FOR FULL GROWTH IN CHRISTIAN SANCTITY. It is true, however, that the notion of direction has been distorted and exaggerated in the minds of some directors and some schools of spirituality. These exaggerations have harmful tendencies, and must be understood and avoided. In considering the history of the question we shall try to take note of some of the difficulties and problems that have arisen.

The mind of the Church: provisionally we may quote two or three authoritative examples of the Church's teaching on the value of direction, before going into greater detail:

I. In 1260 the Brethren of the Free Spirit were condemned for teaching that one should not ask counsel from learned men *sive de devotione sive de aliis*.[695]

II. Leo XIII, in *TESTEM BENEVOLENTIAE* (22 January 1899, against "Americanism"):

1) reproached some who thought "the guidance of the Holy Spirit was sufficient"[696] for a perfect Christian life;

2) {maintained that} the exterior teaching authority of the Church and the sanctifying action of her ministers is necessary to *complete* the interior action of the Holy Spirit; not that the Holy Spirit is not capable Himself of forming and sanctifying souls, but other impulsions and inspirations not proceeding from Him may be accepted as His; Leo XIII points out that those who seek a higher perfection are more likely to go astray on their own and *have more need than others of a spiritual guide*; *ergo*, all need some direction, but those seeking perfection need it in a special way;

---

695. "whether from devotion or for other reasons" (Gabriel de Sainte-Marie-Madeleine, "Direction Spirituelle: V. Justification théologique," *DS* 3, col. 1175, quoting St. Albert the Great, as Bishop of Ratisbon).

696. Gabriel de Sainte-Marie-Madeleine, "Direction Spirituelle," col. 1176.

3) Christ makes use of intermediaries in dealing with souls, and these are His ministers; to reject this teaching of the Church would be rash and dangerous. Theologians generally agree that since there is a *general call to perfection* and since spiritual direction is needed for this, there is a general need for spiritual direction. It is at least supremely valuable, even when not absolutely essential.

III. In MENTI NOSTRAE, Pope Pius XII (23 September 1950) teaches: in n. 53, without spiritual direction, a "prudent guide," "it is OFTEN VERY DIFFICULT to be duly responsive to the impulses of the Holy Spirit and the grace of God."[697] This teaching is prudent and moderate. In nn. 68, 69 (READ[698]) he praises spiritual directors. In n. 96 he stresses the importance of spiritual direction and formation of seminarians.[699]

IV. THE FRENCH BISHOPS, in 1951, issuing directives for pastoral theology of {the} sacraments, {write}: "No soul must be

697. Gabriel de Sainte-Marie-Madeleine, "Direction Spirituelle," col. 1176.

698. "68. We desire likewise, in this paternal exhortation of Ours, to give special mention to those priests who, in humility and burning charity, labor prudently for the sanctification of their brother-priests as counsellors, confessors, or spiritual directors. The incalculable good they render the Church remains hidden for the greater part, but it will one day be revealed in the glory of God's kingdom. 69. Not many years ago, with great satisfaction, We decreed the honors of the altar to the Turinese priest, Giuseppe Cafasso who, as you know, in a most difficult period, was the wise and holy spiritual guide of not a few priests whom he helped to progress in virtue and whose sacred ministry he rendered particularly fruitful. We are fully confident that, through his powerful patronage, our Divine Redeemer will raise up many priests of like sanctity who will bring themselves and their brethren in the ministry to such a height of perfection in their lives that the faithful, admiring their example, will feel themselves moved spontaneously to imitate it" (*Menti Nostrae: Apostolic Exhortation of Pope Pius XII to the Clergy of the Entire World: On the Development of Holiness in Priestly Life* [Washington, DC: National Catholic Welfare Conference, 1950], 26–27).

699. The section title is "Their Directors Must Instill in Them the Ecclesiastical Virtues" (*Menti Nostrae*, 35).

exposed either to suffer, or to go astray, or to be delayed, due to lack of a guide who may enlighten and aid him."[700]

What is Spiritual Direction? What has been said so far has really clarified nothing. We have not come to grips with the real problem. On the one hand we have enumerated certain questions and objections. On the other hand we have quoted several authoritative statements of the Holy See. But if we imagine that we have even begun from this to understand the problem of "spiritual direction," we are mistaken. And in the first place, to aid this understanding, we must restore the right perspective (if there is any one right perspective—at any rate we can stand back and be critical of wrong perspectives). *It is a mistake to make too much of a problem out of spiritual direction.* Spiritual direction tends to pose more and more of a problem in proportion as we regard it more and more as a *magical technique* of special and irreplaceable efficacy, and as we regard the director as more and more of an official and charismatic instrument or even as one who acts with special jurisdiction from the Church.

Hence we must begin by defining spiritual direction. In a very general way we will expect to find in the spiritual director some sort of *authoritative guidance in the ways of the interior life.* Precisely what is the nature of this guidance and what are its characteristics? This is what we must now consider. Let us, instead of giving a strict definition, limit the field of our investigation by *two possible definitions,* both of which are tenable and which can be said to be at opposite extremes.

A. *The strict, technical and "modern" view:*

1. The director is either a priest or someone with a special office in the Church of God (v.g. a novice mistress in a convent). The position of the director is official or quasi-official. The director is someone who has received more or less of a special technical preparation for his office. Because of his office and because

---

700. *Directoire pour la Pastorale des Sacrements,* n. 49, quoted in Gabriel de Sainte-Marie-Madeleine, "Direction Spirituelle," col. 1178.

he is delegated by the Church, he can count on very special graces of state. His functions are more or less clearly indicated or at least implied in Church Law or the constitutions of religious orders.

2. He has a special function not only to guide souls and resolve certain questions of import, especially at certain crucial moments, as in the choice of a vocation, or in an annual retreat, but especially *to form them* according to some special appropriate way of spirituality which is assumed to be willed for them by God. He exercises constant and vigilant care over the soul. He tests and humiliates the soul. In practice, this concept often means that the director is one who *ex officio* takes on the formation of certain souls confided to him by the very fact that they have entered an institution where he exercises his functions. In such a case his "formation" is carried on according to an *a priori system*. Individual differences are of course respected, but it is the system and the form according to the "spirituality of the institute" that receives major emphasis. The director strictly *guides* the soul and *controls* the development of the penitent.

3. The one directed entrusts himself more or less completely to the director as a representative of the Church and of an institute or school of spirituality. He "puts himself in the hands" of the director, who is conceived to have considerable power in "forming" his charges. Though a vow of obedience may not necessarily be taken, the emphasis is on strict docility to the director, considered as an "expert." Since in practice the direction given is often united with confession, the one directed begins by making a general confession. Otherwise he at least starts out with a complete manifestation of conscience, so that his "case" may be completely clear to his director, who thereafter takes over "professionally," more or less like a doctor or a psychiatrist.

4. The one directed then presents himself regularly at a fixed time for his spiritual direction, in which he manifests his difficulties and problems, or speaks of his prayer and progress in the spiritual life, and the director hands down more or less authoritative answers and detailed directions which are to be followed with fidelity, because the efficacy of the "formation" will depend on this. For the

director is a *mediator* of grace and to fail to follow his instructions is to neglect grace. The director is regarded as an ORACLE.

B. *The broad and pre-technical view*: at the other extreme from this modern professional, technical and institutional concept of direction is a *very broad and informal concept*:

1. The "director" may be anyone at all, man or woman, layperson or religious, at least someone with *spiritual experience*, but not necessarily any official position. In this sense the guidance given by a parent is analogous to spiritual direction. The "director" may simply be a trusted and experienced friend, who in intimate conversations or by letters makes valued suggestions, offers encouragement and inspiration which aid one in spiritual progress. For this to merit the name of direction in any real sense, there must be something of a formal consultation, and not just casual conversation. That is to say, one must really *ask for guidance*, with the awareness that the person is competent to speak with some kind of (very broad and spiritual) authority. {For} example, {see} the part played by Léon Bloy in the conversion of the Maritains and Van der Meer de Walcheren.[701]

---

701. See the two volumes of reminiscences of Raïssa Maritain: *We Have Been Friends Together: Memoirs*, trans. Julie Kernan (New York: Longmans, Green, 1942), especially chapter 5, "Léon Bloy," detailing the Maritains' first encounters with Bloy and his growing influence on their interest in Christianity (104–40), and chapter 6, "The Call of the Saints," bringing the story up through their baptism, with Bloy as their godfather (141–79); and *Adventures in Grace*, trans. Julie Kernan (New York: Longmans, Green, 1945), especially chapter 2, "Some Conquests of the Ungrateful Beggar," which discusses Bloy's influence on the conversion of Pierre and Christine Van der Meer de Walcheren (33–42), and chapter 9, "The Last Years of Léon Bloy" (217–62). See also van der Meer de Walcheren's book *Rencontres: Leon Bloy, Raissa Maritain, Christine et Pieterke* (Paris: Desclée de Brouwer, 1961), which he sent to Merton who was "Moved deeply and to tears" by it (*Turning Toward the World*, 145 [7/26/61]); Merton acknowledges the gift in a letter of July 28, 1961: "It was a joy to receive your book with the very cordial dedication which you inscribed there. I am convinced that you speak the truth, because when I read your pages, a feeling sweeps over me which takes in all of your love for 'our spiritual family.' I feel an extraordinary affinity with that wonderful brilliance of Léon Bloy. . . . The part on Léon Bloy is wonderful. All

2. The relations of the one directed and {the} director are informal, perhaps even in some sense casual. But at least it is clear that one is receiving guidance and help from the other. There is a distinct relationship of "spiritual filiation," in however broad a sense. But there is no question of the one having formal authority over the other.

3. The director discreetly and informally conveys to the one directed the knowledge of a certain spiritual "way," not necessarily systematic at all, not necessarily connected with any spiritual school or institution, but at least conceived as being appropriate for this individual. "This is the way for you to follow."

4. The director is conceived as exercising a divine and spiritual action in the life of the one directed, though perhaps only very vaguely. However this relationship is fluid and so informal that the directives given are not always taken with uniform seriousness. But certain directives are recognized to be of paramount importance to the one directed. They "click." He feels that they are answers to his questions and that he ought to follow them. In this instance there is in a very general way a kind of spiritual direction.

These two descriptions of direction may help us to answer some of the initial questions. *Those who seriously question the value of spiritual direction* and who think it is out of date or undesirable are generally speaking of type A (technical) and usually of this type in its most formal variety. *No one seriously questions that there will always necessarily be* at least some sort of direction of type B, or that such direction is desirable. There is no question that spiritual advice and guidance of an informal kind, at least, is necessary. On the other hand, *when the Holy See stresses the need for direction*, the implication always is that what is meant is direction of type A (see for instance *Menti Nostrae*). However the terms are not rigidly set, and no one has to hold that direction of type A is

---

'my' France comes back to me, with the mystery of my own vocation which my sojourn in France had prepared" (Thomas Merton, *The School of Charity: Letters on Religious Renewal and Spiritual Direction*, ed. Patrick Hart [New York: Farrar, Straus, Giroux, 1990], 139).

the only kind admissible as fulfilling the requirements of the Church. Sometimes direction of type B is heightened by a *definitely or at least seemingly charismatic character*. In this case it retains its informality, its *spontaneity*, but emphasis is on the *supernatural* intervention of grace. The director is regarded as a special instrument of God, and all the more so in so far as jurisdictional and institutional limits are *not* decisive in his exceptional case. We shall see cases of direction of priests by laypersons and even women. Some of them {are} genuine. But here we run into danger of illuminism and superstition. Hence while the Church would not deny the existence of direction of type B, this would receive very little official encouragement. Theologians today would not tend to stress this type of direction, or to take it very seriously.

A practical solution: it seems that the practical solution of our problems lies in a moderate position, including the values of both extremes. This moderate position can be called traditional and monastic.

The monastic view: this view stresses both the *spiritual* authority (as opposed to *juridical* authority) of the director and the spontaneity of the relationship between the one directed and the director. In common with type A, the director, not necessarily a priest or someone with a special office, *is definitely marked out* by his state and holiness of life, his learning and experience, as a guide for others. His authority may be ministerial, charismatic, or both. Hence he is usually one who has received a special preparation for his functions and can be regarded as *representing the Church*, in so far as he speaks with the voice of tradition and in accordance with the Church. He may also have a special office in the Church. But even a layman, in very special circumstances, might conceivably fulfill such a function, preferably in union with the hierarchy and in subordination to them. (The ancient monks were "laymen.") Also in common with type A, the director *definitely guides the soul in the ways of the spirit.* He not only hands down an authoritative instruction on the ways of the ascetic life, but in a very special way he helps his penitent to see and understand God's plan for his own life and to generously put into action his powers in corresponding with God's action day by day. The director, or better, "spiritual father," is to be trusted and followed with docility; he speaks for God, but he does not for all that exercise an absolute authority over the soul. He still suggests and urges, he encourages, he advises, but he does not peremptorily issue orders (except in certain rare cases). He may help the soul in the work of its spiritual formation, but in this case it is clear that *he does not himself form the soul.* Rather he aids the soul to grow and attain the proper stature willed for it by the Holy Ghost. (Note here that jargon about the "soul" is regrettable; it is the whole person who is formed in organic spiritual growth.) The one directed puts himself in the hands of the director, but not under the despotic control of the director. He receives the decisions of the director in faith, and follows the suggestions of the director in *obeying God.* He is not so much in the hands of the director as in the hands of God. But the director is inspired and directed by God and he is empowered to *clarify God's action. The real importance of the director is that without him the action of God cannot really be discovered or properly understood.* (On the other hand it is by no means held that the director has a special power to form the soul according to an approved system and that without him the soul can never receive the proper form.) This view lays less emphasis on the director as *cause, mediator* and *agent* in the physical order. The mediation of the director is exercised above all in *the realm of prayer.* His efficacy is a matter not of professional know-how but of spiritual fatherhood, and this in turn is connected with his humility and charity, rather than with his authoritarian powers and learning. *Openness and manifestation of thoughts* is of primary importance, but still there is less emphasis on direction as a "process" and "system." More important is the *personal relationship* and the *intimate filial rapport* which has its own prime significance, which outweighs anything that is said or done in the direction conversation. (Note the direction is a *familiaris et amica conversatio,*[702] in the terms of Adam of Perseigne.)

702. "familiar and friendly conversation"; the terms, though not the exact phrase, are found in Adam's first letter: "*Nascitur etiam ex amica frequenti et honesta collocutione commendabilis quaedam familiaritas*" ("From frequent friendly and frank conversation is also born a certain praiseworthy intimacy"); "*Religiosa*

In common with type B, besides the informality and casual-
ness of the relationship at times, great emphasis is placed on the
SPONTANEITY AND FREEDOM of the relationship, and particularly
as *regards the initial choice of the director.* IT IS ALIEN TO THE MONAS-
TIC VIEW OF DIRECTION TO INSIST THAT A DIRECTOR BE IMPOSED ON
ANYONE, AND THAT ANYONE SHOULD BE BOUND TO TAKE DIRECTION
AGAINST HIS WILL FROM SOMEONE WHOM HE DOES NOT FULLY TRUST,
OR STILL MORE FROM ONE WHOM HE HAS NOT EVEN CONSULTED IN
SPIRITUAL MATTERS. We must distinguish the sedulously faithful
obedience in *foro externo* which the monk owes in justice to his superiors in all their commands and wishes according to the *Rule*,
from the prudence with which the subject will seek and follow
spiritual advice. He can and should seek such advice from his superiors who may be presumed to know him well. *But obedience
does not require* that one seek this direction from them in all the intimate affairs of the interior life. *One is free to choose* his spiritual
guide. However, ONCE ONE HAS CHOSEN a director, then his direction is to be followed faithfully and with humble charity, even to
a heroic degree. The monastic view seeks to protect the one directed from tyrannical and ruthless interventions and from the
arbitrary imposition of systems, even by superiors.

THE HISTORY OF SPIRITUAL DIRECTION IN THE CHURCH: here
we can profitably consider the development of the idea of direction, in a very general way, with special emphasis on the "professional" and "institutional" concept which belongs to the more
modern period. Material {is taken} from the very long and detailed article in *DS*: "Direction Spirituelle."[703]

---

*magistri conversatio exemplo suae probitatis provocat novitium ad studium aemulan-
dae virtutis. . . . Amica et spiritualis collocatio consulte, ut dictum est, opponitur
acediae morbo"* ("The master's religious conversation encourages the novice by
the example of his own integrity to a desire to imitate his virtue. . . . Friendly
spiritual conversation, as has been said, is deliberately set against the disease of
acedia" (*PL* 211, cols. 586B, 588A).

703. Édouard Des Places, "Direction Spirituelle: I. Dans l'Antiquité Clas-
sique," *DS* 3, cols. 1002–1008; Irénée Hausherr, "Direction Spirituelle: II. Chez
les Chrétiens Orientaux," cols. 1008–60; "Direction Spirituelle: III. En Occident:

A. Classical background: we pass over here the very interesting and important topic of direction in Yoga and in Buddhism, etc., {with} just a word on the master-disciple relationship in classical philosophical schools.

1. The basic idea is that the sage is one who, because of his very unique qualities, his wisdom, his virtue, his gift of insight, makes others better by their very contact with him. Socrates, Pythagoras, etc. (though Socrates disclaims the role of *didaskalos*)[704] *improve and transform* the life of the disciple who comes to them. Hence one seeks out a "master" who will effect this transformation, and make one ready for a higher kind of life.

2. What is the higher life for which the sage prepares? It may be a *political* life (active life) or a contemplative and speculative life of philosophy.

3. An essential element in the relationship of master and disciple, and in {the} disciple with regard to wisdom {is that} it is *gratuitous*. Once the master accepts the disciple, he does not get paid (but he does not have to accept everyone either) and the disciple does not seek wisdom for his own personal profit either. The *didaskalos* moves in a realm of dedication to wisdom.

4. What then are the real conditions, if money has no place in the relationship? First the disciple must open himself completely and confide absolutely in the guidance of the master he has chosen. Then over a more or less long period of time the master *tests* the disciple by special trials, proves his fidelity and his capacity, etc. If after this "novitiate" the relationship is cemented, then direction (philosophical instruction) can begin.

5. Is a master necessary? Varying answers {are given} to this question: normally, yes. However Epicurus distinguishes three kinds of men: those who reach truth alone; those who reach truth

---

C. Période Moderne": André Rayez, "Introduction," cols. 1099–1108; Michel Olphe-Galliard, "Au 16e Siècle," cols. 1108–19; Charles Berthelot du Chesnay, "Du 17e Siècle à Nos Jours," cols. 1119–42.

704. "teacher": *Apology*, 33 (Hausherr, "Direction Spirituelle," col. 1009).

with a guide; those who need a "trainer" (special discipline for more fundamental rough work).

6. {The} concept of the philosophical community in Epicureanism {requires} an enclosed community of friends (the "Garden of Epicurus"; cf. the Stoa, etc.). The formation of this community {is} a reaction against the confusion and degradation of the times, a kind of "refuge of sanity." Its purpose {is} the healing of suffering and anxious souls. Epicurus was a physician of souls, {seeking} to restore them to the ways of peace and happiness. (Note: the Epicureans were atheists.) Epicurus said: "The young man must not put off the study of philosophy, nor must the old man become tired of its study. For it is never too early or too late to occupy oneself with the health of one's soul. And to say that the time for philosophy has not yet come or has passed by is to say that the time to be happy has not yet come, or is no more. Hence it is the duty both of the young man and of the old to study philosophy."[705] Epictetus and Seneca (Stoics) approached the problem in much the same general way, and made use of special techniques for the correction of faults, the development of virtues, and self-discipline. They taught systematic examination of conscience and meditation. Seneca's perspectives {were} centered on the *immortality of the soul*, spiritualization of matter {and} abandonment to the will of the Supreme Ruler.

B. Early Christian monasticism in the Orient: what has been said of the classical period resembles what became traditional in the Christian East. Here again the disciple seeks out a master, either in a community or alone in the desert. He believes that there is one special master *for him* and he must find that one. Having found him, he will believe everything he says and follow all his counsels with complete docility. Here again there is a question of *complete openness*, and of *testing*. The relationship formally begins when these preliminaries have been satisfactorily completed. Then the novice takes up residence with his "senior,"

705. Quoted in Des Places, col. 1005.

"elder" or "presbyter," and simply lives as he does, following his actions and declaring to him his thoughts, so that the elder, with the gift of insight, may explain to him the origin and meaning of each drive and how to deal with it. Ascetic training {is} based on the struggle with the eight principal "spirits" or vices. It is aimed at control of the passions (*apatheia*), in preparation for the contemplative life. Later the master may also initiate the disciple into the mysteries of the *spiritual sense of Scripture* and therefore of *theoria*. Some of the Desert Fathers refused to "teach" anyone the ways of spiritual understanding; others were less hesitant. Some—witness the works of Evagrius—would lead the mature disciple on into the realm of *theologia* and contemplation without concepts.

{There was an} *emphasis on charismatic paternity*. The "senior" is primarily and above all a spiritual father. He is not simply a wiser monk who resolves cases of conscience, teaches a spiritual technique, or initiates into the ways of prayer. He does in some sense carry on the education and the formation of the disciple, but above all he is a "father" who by his prayer, concern, paternal care, guidance and instruction brings forth a higher life in the disciple. *This paternity is supernatural and shares in the action of the divine fatherhood.* It is thus chiefly as spiritual father that the elder represents God. He has usually no juridical or priestly status at all. Clearly his function is not to attach the disciple to himself as his spiritual child but to help him grow as a child of the heavenly Father, so that Christ is formed in him. The fatherly concern of the elder fixes the attention of the disciple on his true Father who is God. He also brings him to know more and more clearly that the Holy Spirit is his true guide and that Christ is his Master. But a long period of trial and instruction is necessary for this. However, when the disciple has been liberated from vices and sins, then he has the unction of the Holy Spirit, and the elder releases him to send him off on his own. After that the monk lives with God, and obeys God directly, until he in his turn becomes a master sought out by others. All this is dependent on the will of God, and directed by Him. No one seeks to set himself up as master;

no one seeks of his own accord to be independent and autonomous, to be "his own master." This is a sign that one is still in need of much discipline. The heart of the direction given by the master is always the *healing of the disciple*, his re-formation in Christ, by the Cross, strengthening him to receive the salutary discipline of God Himself. {He learns} to obey God with loving acceptance of all trials and sufferings, and thus to become free from dependence on worldly happiness and support, able to be guided directly by God. These principles are of great importance for us, and should be learned from the study of monastic sources and especially Cassian and the Desert Fathers.

In medieval monasticism much the same principles prevail: we need not go over them in detail here. See what has been said elsewhere concerning the ideas of Adam of Perseigne on monastic formation, for example.[706]

Direction of virgins and laypeople in the early Church comes under the ordinary life of the parish (see Gregory {the} Great: *Regula Pastoralis*, III[707]). It is a responsibility first of all of the *bishop*. Occasionally the bishop may call in monks or men of special holiness to help in the cure of souls, and generally holy monks themselves often became bishops in Gaul and the West.

---

706. Thomas Merton, "The Feast of Freedom: Monastic Formation according to Adam of Perseigne," in *The Letters of Adam of Perseigne*, vol. 1, trans. Grace Perigo, CF 21 (Kalamazoo, MI: Cistercian Publications, 1976), 3–48; this is a somewhat expanded version of "Christian Freedom and Monastic Formation," *American Benedictine Review*, 13 (September 1962), 289–313, which is itself a longer version of the article "La Formation Monastique selon Adam de Perseigne," *Collectanea Ordinis Cisterciensium Reformatorum*, 19 (January 1957), 1–17.

707. See St. Gregory the Great, *Pastoral Care*, trans. Henry Davis, sj, ACW 11 (Westminster, MD: Newman Press, 1950): Part III of the work (89–233), entitled "How the Ruler Should Teach and Admonish His Subjects by His Holy Life," is made up almost entirely of instructions on adapting pastoral teaching "to the individual in his respective needs" (89); see in particular c. 27, "How to admonish the married and the celibate" (186–92) and c. 28, "How to admonish those who have had experience of sins of the flesh, and those who have not" (192–98).

C. Middle Ages—the mendicants: with the mendicants we see the beginning of the growth of modern spiritual direction. The mendicants come in as shock troops, with special work to do, to revive the Christian spirit and to awaken souls to a new birth in the Christian life which has begun to be dormant. This idea of a reawakening on a large scale, and of special missionaries of the Church to bring it about, had not been so familiar in the early days. The need had not been so acutely felt.

1. Laypeople {receive} direction in the confessional. The "specialist" in religious revival, who is the mendicant friar, instructs the penitent in examination of conscience and in ways of extricating himself from habitual sin, {and} tries to orient {the} penitent to a new life in Christ, often very successfully. Lay penitents embrace deep spiritual life and often become mystics. They enter *confraternities* with regular direction as part of {the} curriculum.

2. Religious—*the formation of religious*: at this time there arises a great concern over the formation of novices as an institutional responsibility. In the medieval monastic orders the formation of novices meant largely their instruction in matters of rule and observance, and chant. Their spiritual instruction they got from the abbot in chapter, from their reading, etc. Undoubtedly there was also spiritual advice given and very wisely. There was direction. But now there arises a new concern over the "method of training novices." A Dominican of the fifteenth century writes a formal TRACTATUS DE INSTITUTIONE NOVITIORUM.[708]

The direction of contemplatives: in many districts, especially in the Rhineland and Flanders, where there was a great wave of fervor sweeping over convents of nuns and communities of Béguines, priests, chiefly of mendicant orders, were in demand. The great mystic movement of the Rhineland, owing its origin to Cistercian influence on Béguines, spreads due to the words, directions and writings of Eckhart and his school. The union of

---

708. *Treatise on the Formation of Novices* (Rayez, col. 1101).

the "*fratres docti*"[709] appointed by the Order {of} Preachers over the seventy convents of contemplative Dominican nuns {was} fruitful in speculative mysticism. In the fifteenth century there follows a *great multiplication of manuals* to instruct confessors and directors. The MANIPULUS CURATORUM[710] of Guy de Montrocher (fifteenth century) distinguishes the *confessio sacramentalis* of the pastor and *confessio directiva*[711] of a "specialist" who may come in from outside the parish on a mission or some other occasion, and may then be kept as one's director. Here we see the modern concept pretty well stabilized. It will develop along these lines.

3. The director and {the} retreat movement: under the influence of men like Savonarola, emphasizing {the} need for reform of Christian life, retreats and missions began to be very popular, and the movement grew all through the fifteenth and sixteenth centuries, especially when SPIRITUAL EXERCISES after the fashion of St. Ignatius became widespread and customary. It was generally on retreat, or making the *Exercises*, that one came in contact with a director, whom one thereafter frequented and obeyed, to keep up the good work begun. Development of seminary education brings the position of director into prominence (especially after {the} Council of Trent). (In the fifteenth and sixteenth centuries, we have come a long way from the Desert Fathers.) THE DIRECTOR BECOMES A SPECIALIST IN TWO THINGS ABOVE ALL: (A) TREATMENT OF SCRUPLES; (B) DECIDING ONE'S VOCATION.

D. The Counter-Reformation: what has been said of the late Middle Ages, becomes a full reality in the Counter-Reformation. {Specialized direction} becomes characteristic of that period, whereas it only existed in embryo in the fifteenth century. After Trent it is widespread and common. An important factor contributing to the development of direction after Trent {is} the *reformation of religious orders*. Habitual spiritual direction becomes

---

709. "learned brothers" (Rayez, col. 1101).

710. *Handbook for Confessors*, published in 1471 but written in 1333 (Rayez, col. 1105).

711. "sacramental confession . . . confession of direction."

a constant and important factor in the reform of religious communities. Direction becomes a special, almost exclusive function reserved to the priest and bishop (except cases of novice mistresses, etc.). Since manuals of direction are numerous, theoretically *any* priest can learn to be a director (but in actual fact special gifts are required). It remains in fact a work for specialists. Direction becomes closely tied up with *emphasis on mental prayer* as an aid to religious reform. Hence the director also normally gives instruction and guidance in mental prayer as a first-aid method in combating religious tepidity. The importance of the director in the realm of mental prayer is also heightened by the necessity to distinguish the "true path" in prayer from illuminism, etc. Hence the director tends, in many cases, to insist on "safe and approved methods" to avoid {the} danger of quietism and other errors. {The} director {functions} as {the} guardian of orthodoxy in the mystic. Savonarola had recommended meditation on the mysteries of Christ, especially the Passion (this in common with the spirit of his time) as a remedy against the evils of spiritual breakdown and tepidity. Luis de Granada also believed in the special importance of mental prayer. Direction stresses methodical meditation on the mysteries.

Certain new *religious congregations* occupied themselves in a special way with direction, retreats, missions, teaching mental prayer and reviving devotion (Barnabites, Theatines). A "great director" was BAPTISTA DE CREMONA who directed two founders of such congregations, St. Anthony Maria Zaccaria, founder of the Barnabites, and St. Cajetan of Thiene.[712] {He also} influenced Scupoli's *SPIRITUAL COMBAT*, characteristic of the spirituality of this period (sixteenth century).

Direction is sometimes intermittent, given only on special occasions like the annual retreat, but more usually *habitual*, at frequent and regular intervals. There are differences in various approaches to direction. Some teach a methodical *way* of perfection,

---

712. See Olphe-Galliard, "Direction Spirituelle: III," cols. 1108–1109.

others interest themselves more in "states of soul" and observing the inner experiences of the subject, in order to guide him (generally *her*) in the ways of union.

The Jesuits: the *Spiritual Exercises* {were} a retreat conducted by a specially trained and qualified director. Rules for the discernment of spirits {were emphasized}. {The} director helps {the} retreatant to go through "crisis" (judgement) and make a decision according to the Holy Spirit. Normally after one has made the *Exercises* one remains under the guidance of a director. In the Society {of} Jesus a spiritual director *other than the superior* {is} required by {the} Constitutions. Confession and direction {are} united usually. St. Peter Canisius made his confession every evening before retiring. Direction of (lay) students in Jesuit schools {was} an essential part of religious training.

Others: {the} French School {includes} St. Francis de Sales, Bérulle, St. Vincent de Paul, Olier, Tronson, etc. {These were} great directors, especially concerned with the direction of *seminarists and priests*, in addition to active and contemplative religious. With St. Francis de Sales we find the director as {a} *liberator* who delivers the contemplative soul from complications and burdens imposed by those less wise.

E.   Lay directors:[713] pious women, female mystics and *beatas* exercised a great influence in sixteenth-century Spain. Many of these were *alumbradas*; many false mystics surrounded themselves with credulous disciples. *St. Teresa* was a great example of a woman who (like Catherine of Siena before her) transformed the lives of most people she came in contact with. She directed several persons outside her own convents, including her brother Lorenzo. In the seventeenth century, particularly {in} France, there were laymen and laywomen who became directors and even gave advice to religious communities: v.g. *Gaston de Renty* (d. 1649), *Jean de Bernières* (d. 1659), who gave direction and conferences to the Ursuline nuns. *Marie Rousseau* (d. 1680), a wife of a wine merchant

713. See Berthelot du Chesnay, cols. 1131–33.

and mother of five children, gave advice to some of the most virtuous souls of Paris; M. Olier highly praised her direction, which he himself followed. *Marie des Vallées* (d. 1656) gave direction to others and was herself directed by St. John Eudes.

The occasional director: since we are concerned with the monastic setting and with "contemplatives," we are considering above all consistent and steady direction by one director, one "spiritual father." However in practice it is important to take account of the fact that for very many people, "direction" in its most elementary form comes when they run into an occasional confessor who, though a stranger to them, can give them some good advice in the particular circumstances in which they find themselves. This applies even in the "Easter duty" situation. An article in *Vie Spirituelle*, Supplément (1955; n. 35) treats this: "Une dimension oubliée du sacrement de pénitence."[714] Starting from the problem of the Christian who may or may not get to the sacraments once a year, it goes on to lay down a principle that is important for all direction. It is stated that in the case of the "Easter duty" penitent it is not enough to remind him of the law of God and get him to fulfill it, but a more constructive and positive approach is desirable—reintegration in the full life of the Church and in God's plan. {A} purpose of amendment {should be} not just to keep the law of God but to really take one's place and one's part in the Church as it actually exists, finding the plan of God for the penitent in the context of the Church. Three principles {are proposed}: to have in mind the *plan* of God rather than the *Law* of God; to be concerned with the active building up of the Church; and not with building up one's *own Church*, i.e. not roping in penitents to one's pet project, necessarily. This remark reminds us of valuable perspectives in direction, and it shows that much good can be done in a case where there is a seemingly chance encounter with an unknown confessor.

---

714. Thomas Suavet, OP, "Note sur une Dimension Oubliée du Sacrement de Pénitence," *La Vie Spirituelle*, Supplément, 35 (1955), 406–11.

Necessity of Spiritual Direction: we have already seen that the Church says more or less officially that spiritual direction is *in some sense necessary*. We can sum up the common teaching on the necessity of direction as follows:

a) In the Sacrament of Penance, the confessor has to give the penitent sufficient direction and help to enable him to make his confession properly, and to receive the sacrament worthily in view of a constructive amendment of life, including advice for the future, at least in a rudimentary form, if the penitent is struggling with habitual sin.

b) There are "good souls" who are leading good Christian lives and receiving the sacraments. No one would hold that for these, spiritual direction is absolutely necessary. They can get along without it, and often have to. Some would argue that they are better off without it, as we have seen. This has to be taken with a grain of salt, and with the aid of careful distinctions. A too formal, systematic and domineering type of direction is useless for them and would do more harm than good. *No* direction at all would be preferable to this.

c) If direction is taken to be THE ART OF LEADING SOULS TO THEIR PROPER PERFECTION ACCORDING TO THEIR PERSONAL VOCATION AND THEIR PLACE IN THE CHURCH, then for everyone desirous of fully corresponding with his vocation, and even of finding his vocation, *some direction is morally necessary and habitual direction is certainly useful*. (*Menti Nostrae* says that without direction it is "very difficult"[715] to correspond with grace as one should. *Testem Benevolentiae* says that those who seek higher perfection have "greater need"[716] than others of a spiritual guide.)

---

715. *Menti Nostrae*, 20 (n. 53).

716. "It must also be kept in mind that those who follow what is more perfect are by the very fact entering upon a way of life which for most men is untried and more exposed to error, and therefore they, more than others, stand in need of a teacher and a guide" (Pope Leo XIII, *True and False Americanism in*

d) This is especially true of "contemplatives." There have been a variety of opinions in the matter, but in general since the sixteenth century at any rate there has been more and more insistence on this. Osuna believed direction to be "absolutely necessary for those who wish to practice recollection."[717] St. Antoninus (fifteenth century) was one of the strongest proponents of regular direction. He claimed: "To arrive at the love of God and devotion, to possess peace . . . it is USEFUL AND NECESSARY to have a spiritual guide to whom you can report at all times your conduct and your failings that he may help and counsel you and allow you to know your own state from hour to hour."[718] (Clearly this is direction of the type A!)

St. Teresa emphasized the importance of contemplative nuns having access to "learned men"[719] in the confessional, for guidance in the ways of prayer. We shall see what she says in greater detail later. She distinguishes: direction is necessary, but a bad confessor can do much harm, therefore no direction at all is better than bad direction. This is a good principle. She says it is more necessary for women than for men. She also places great emphasis on the ascetic value of "obedience" (docility) to a spiritual guide. (She was not in favor of {a} vow of obedience to {one's} director.) The Jesuits placed great emphasis on direction; Alvarez de Paz and Luis de Ponte felt that direction was "necessary for contemplatives."[720] Here direction is usually inseparable from confession. {In the} earlier tradition, Gerson thought direction was necessary "for those called to mystical contemplation."[721]

Religion: Apostolical Letter Testem Benevolentiae, in *The Great Encyclical Letters of Pope Leo XIII* [New York: Benziger, 1903], 447).

717. Quoted in Olphe-Galliard, "Direction Spirituelle: III," col. 1111.

718. Quoted in Rayez, col. 1105.

719. See *Way of Perfection*, c. 5: "*Continues speaking of confessors. Explains why it is important that they be learned men*" (*Complete Works of Saint Teresa*, 2.22-26).

720. See Olphe-Galliard, "Direction Spirituelle: III," col. 1118.

721. See Irénée Noye, "Note pour une Histoire de la Direction Spirituelle," *La Vie Spirituelle*, Supplément, 34 (1955), 262–63.

For St. Francis de Sales, "l'advertissement des advertissements" was to "get a director."[722] In the seventeenth century the belief in the power and value of the director reached its peak. After the seventeenth century, a reaction set in. Caussade felt that a director was more of a hindrance than a help.[723] But he himself was a director and wrote many letters of direction. He meant the kind of director who binds the soul and seeks to control it absolutely—i.e. he reacted against "type A." Dom Marmion was "not in favor of overmuch direction"[724] (again, meaning "type A"). Msgr. Gay, who published four volumes of letters of direction, nevertheless insisted that his penitents should *not depend too much* on direction, but learn to stand on their own feet.[725] All this is healthy. It seems to represent the best Catholic tradition in this matter.

The authority of the director: the question of the authority of the director is studied by those who favor type-A direction. For these the director is normally a priest, or else someone who is placed in a special office by the Church. Direction in the case of priests or those in office is NOT AN EXERCISE OF THE POWER OF JURISDICTION. This is important. Even those who favor type A sedulously distinguish the director from the superior. THE DIRECTOR as such IS NOT A SUPERIOR. (He can of course *also* be a superior.) Therefore as director he has no *potestas dominativa*[726] and cannot demand obedience. Nor has he the power or the right to *dictate* a given way in the spiritual life. He does not formally declare the will of God: he can offer suggestions and counsels. He can never force anyone to follow his guidance. Whether or not he has the right to bind his penitent by a vow of obedience, this vow is certainly not to be recommended. In what sense are the deci-

---

722. "the admonition of admonitions" (*Introduction to the Devout Life*, I.4, quoted in Berthelot du Chesnay, col. 1119).

723. See Berthelot du Chesnay, col. 1133.

724. See Berthelot du Chesnay, col. 1141.

725. See Berthelot du Chesnay, col. 1139.

726. "authoritative power" (Gabriel de Sainte-Marie-Madeleine, "Direction Spirituelle," col. 1183).

sions of a director said to represent the will of God? NOT in the sense that they oblige the penitent to strict obedience under pain of sin (except of course in cases where the director is simply pointing to an obligation that already exists, v.g. a vow, a law of the Church), but in the sense that the path pointed out by the director should be accepted with prudent docility as a sure way to God that can be followed safely. However his authority is *moral and spiritual*. As {a} priest he is a mediator. The power of the priest director flows from his *power of orders*, from his priesthood, and secondarily from his own special spiritual qualities. He is then an AUTHORIZED REPRESENTATIVE OF CHRIST AND THE CHURCH. He can point out the way to correspond with grace and fulfill duties in such a way as to reach perfection. {HE} IS TO BE FOLLOWED WITH FAITH AND DOCILITY. The distinction between the director and the superior may in practice seem academic, since both are to be followed and believed as representatives of God in a spirit of faith. However, the understanding of the docility due to a director is something more subtle and spiritual, because more interior and more mature, than the understanding of obedience due to a superior who exercises power of jurisdiction. To say that one does not formally "obey" a director does not *diminish* his authority or the merit of our docility. The docility to a director requires a more delicate conscience, a more spiritual understanding, a truer fidelity and a more developed love because {it is} more *interior* and *personal*. When there is a good and wise director, and when the one directed is capable of corresponding with this grace with the above dispositions, then direction can contribute to real and rapid progress. (See below what is said about mediatorship and about faith in *Providence* rather than in authority.[727])

The function of the director: we have said that direction is the art of leading souls to their proper perfection according to their personal vocation and their place in the Church, of *leading* or guiding, not pushing or carrying. The director can only point out the

727. See below, page 276.

way and suggest. The one directed has to do the travelling. {The} basic principle behind the whole concept of direction {is that} the penitent is one who *belongs to God,* his Creator and Redeemer. He is *called and sought by Christ.* Christ, through the Church, seeks the *salvation and divinization* of this penitent, partly by leading him *by his own proper way* and partly by giving him *a special place and function in the Church.* These two are inseparable and never really in contradiction, though they may seem to be. The director also recognizes the *spiritual enemy* placing obstacles in the way of the soul. {He} must know how to distinguish between the *true will of Christ* for this soul and the director's own pet plans and projects, not enforcing his own views as those of the Church or of Christ. Hence a certain reserve and hesitation are praiseworthy.

The function of the director has to be seen in the light of the whole Christian life. {In the} *ascetic* {dimension}, he must help the one directed to take up his cross and carry it; he must help him to die with Christ in order to live in Christ; he must help him to purify his life of all that is useless and dead; he must strengthen what is good, and educate it for further growth. {In the} *mystical* {dimension}, he must help the one directed to live in the light of the Resurrection, to recognize that light and appreciate it, to cooperate with that light, to submit entirely to the Holy Spirit. The director is *not* a superior. We shall see what else he is not in a moment. He is a mediator, a master, a father, a physician, a guide. His *mediatorship* is especially clear when he is (as normally he is) a priest. He is a channel of grace. As we have just explained, the juridical channels are not the only channels of grace, nor are they even the most spiritual. In a sense there is a deeper and purer exercise of faith in the mediatorship of the director (i.e. in the fact that he can represent Christ for me) when he is *not* supported by a clear, external, juridical authority. This faith is a belief that Christ can send me *this man* as His representative, and give him special graces with which to guide me in my own peculiar case. This is a faith rather in *Providence* than in *authority.*

As master of the spiritual life the director has the power to educate, to form the soul, in a discreet and broad sense, as an instrument of the Holy Spirit. To be more accurate, he recognizes the Holy Spirit as the true Master of the soul and knows how to bring the one directed into loving and enlightened submission to grace. Hence direction is an *art* rather than a *science*. It implies tact and respect for the individual case in its own uniqueness. The *education* given by the director can take many and varied forms. It is above all a *discipline*: it involves correction, and the prescription of works to be done, or at least counsel of the same. It involves enlightenment, instruction, explanation of the spiritual traditions of the Church, especially as embodied in liturgy and monastic writings or rules. A director in our order gives his direction always in relation to the framework of the *Rule* as a spiritual code and directory. However it is never a question of forcing the soul into a mold, a set pattern. The *Rule* {is} for the soul, not the soul for the *Rule*.

As father {he acts} especially by his *prayers* and *insight*, and a genuine affection, friendship, which must always be detached and spiritual, but can be at the same time deeply human in the right sense. The spiritual father is not just an oracle and a machine for giving out directives. A real spiritual relationship of fatherhood and sonship is established in spiritual direction, with mutual obligations of respect, concern, affection, fidelity and loyalty. It goes without saying that discretion and the respect for secrecy is basic for this kind of confident and trustful relationship. St. Benedict demands that the spiritual father be one who "knows how to cure his own wounds and not make known those of others" (*Rule*, ch. 46 end: READ[728]). NOTE the natural temptation arising in the hearts of those who have no natural family, seeking to acquire spiritual children as consolation and support for themselves.

As physician, he has to *diagnose* spiritual sicknesses, even when they are not apparent and symptoms are almost completely hidden. This involves much experience and grace. The penitent at the

728. Merton has just translated the conclusion of this chapter, "Of Those Who Offend in Any Other Matters" (McCann, 108–109).

same time must take care to cooperate in this work of the spiritual physician by frankly and humbly manifesting his interior state, and not trying to conceal it: openness with a director is of the greatest importance; by being willing to have his condition shown to him frankly, and to take advice. The director has to *prescribe* remedies and *strengthen* the penitent in his good tendencies.

As guide, he must lead the penitent in the "ways of God" by prayer, instruction and example. Here example is most important. Ideally speaking, the director is one who goes ahead (or has long since gone ahead) along the road which the penitent wishes to travel. However as there are many different ways and personal vocations, it is not always possible (indeed it is very rare) to find a director who has gone ahead on the way you yourself are called to travel, if there is question of a rather special vocation. You may have to be guided by someone who himself follows a slightly different way. In the monastery, in so far as all are monks, there is a sufficiently common bond because all follow the *Rule*. But the *Rule* does not prescribe an iron-bound *system* for the regulation of the inner life of each individual monk.

Qualities of a director—in brief he must as far as possible have the following:

Holiness: at least in living up to the obligations of his state and sincerely striving to seek God and follow Christ. No man is without faults, and a temptation of beginners is to judge their director when they find human frailties in him, as if this somehow were a reason for not accepting his guidance with docility.

Learning: it is very important that the director have theological learning and a good comprehension of Christian ascetic and mystical traditions. He should be a *solid moral theologian* with common sense and breadth of view and a sound understanding of human nature. It is also very desirable that he have a thorough grasp of the principles of canon law, especially in the *De Religiosis*[729] (for us).

---

729. See John A. Abbo and Jerome D. Hannan, *The Sacred Canons: A Concise Presentation of the Current Disciplinary Norms of the Church*, second revised ed., 2 vols. (St. Louis: B. Herder, 1960), 1.479-687 (Canons 487–681).

Experience: he should at least have experience of the trials and labors of the ascetic life. Traditionally it is required that a director be one who has attained to a certain perfection in the *bios praktikos*.[730] He should not be the prey of his passions, or at least he should understand the passions and appreciate the vicissitudes of the spiritual combat. It is also very desirable that he be a man of prayer and a contemplative.

Humility: it is especially necessary for the director to be a humble man who puts the interests of the ones directed above his own, and does not simply seek to subjugate them to his own ideas and dominate them by his own "spirituality." He does not want to attract disciples to himself and surround himself with a coterie of dependents. He is interested in truth, in the action of the Holy Spirit, in the will of God for these souls, and not in his own prestige. On the contrary, see the portrait given by St. John of the Cross of jealous and possessive directors:

> And supposing that you have sufficient experience to direct some one soul, which perchance may have no ability to advance beyond your teaching, it is surely impossible for you to have sufficient experience for the direction of all those whom you refuse to allow to go out of your hands; for God leads each soul along different roads and there shall hardly be found a single spirit who can walk even half the way which is suitable for another. Who can be like S. Paul and have the skill to make himself all things to all men, that he may gain them all? You yourself tyrannize over souls, and take away their liberty, and arrogate to yourself the breadth and liberty of evangelical doctrine, so that you not only strive that they may not leave you, but, what is worse, if any one of them should at some time have gone to talk, with another director, of some matter which he could not suitably talk of with you, or if God should lead him in order to teach him something which you have not taught him, you behave to him (I say it not without

730. "the active life."

shame) like a husband who is jealous of his wife; nor is
your jealousy even due to desire for the honour of God,
or for the profit of that soul (for you must not presume to
suppose that in neglecting you in this way he was neglecting God): it is due only to your own pride and presumption, or to some other imperfect motive that concerns you
(*Living Flame* III.59; Peers, III, p. 193).

Together with humility go two other most important qualities:
prudence and *charity*. Of all these qualities the most important are
LEARNING, HUMILITY, PRUDENCE AND CHARITY, as far as spiritual
direction itself is concerned. Holiness and experience are greatly
to be desired, but these alone without learning, prudence and
humble discretion may be useless or even lead to great harm.

2. *Direction and Therapy*
I. *Direction as distinct from counselling, psychotherapy and
psychoanalysis*

COUNSELLING:
a) *What is counselling?* Today many priests and non-Catholic
ministers, as well as professional "counsellors," are called upon to
give "counselling," which is quite distinct from spiritual direction.
Counselling is concerned with moral issues, but it is most directly
concerned with these in *so far as they involve the psychophysical reactions* of the one counselled and *in relation to social adaptation*. Counselling is therefore mostly concerned with ethical problems in so
far as they imply problems of health, especially mental health, and
of social adaptation. Counselling aims at maintaining a normal and
healthy balance in one's personal life by giving general advice on
common problems. Counselling implies a certain insight in the
counsellor and a certain technical training (usually psychological
and sociological), but it deals with general problems and general
norms, though of course applying these to the personal situation
of the one seeking counsel. The counsellor gives advice on common
problems of our time and our society, especially marriage problems,
the sex problems of the adolescent, problems of employment, where

to live, how to get along in the neighborhood where one lives, how to advance in one's field of work, or how to select an employment in the first place, etc. Hence it can be seen that though counselling may often involve spiritual and ethical questions, it touches on these only indirectly, and in the case of spiritual matters it touches on them so superficially that it may be said not to deal with them at all.

b) Secular counselling: counselling is, in effect, a kind of *secular* direction, and very often it prescinds from the whole idea of spirituality or even of morality. In many cases counselling, even by ministers of religion, has become a completely secular substitute for confession and direction. It is, moreover, an American term, and is typical of the American scene. The approach is friendly, spontaneous, simple, practical, not to say quite often pragmatic. It presupposes that the problems of life have simple solutions and that a little good will and "know-how" will help one to find them, or failing this, one will simply learn to "accept the situation" without rebellion and conflict.

{There are} *advantages and disadvantages of counselling*: it can be said *for* counselling that it is often useful for people who do not have deep spiritual or psychological problems. It is a simple aid in the normal difficulties of American life, oriented towards a realistic and matter-of-fact acceptance of ordinary difficulties and of one's own limitations. Generally counselling aims at helping you to help yourself. Against it, one might advance the general impression of superficiality and shallow optimism which it creates, and the fact that it seldom offers any real help in the serious problems of life. At best it brings palliatives or "first-aid" measures of short duration. The knowledge and insight imparted by counselling are little more than the ordinary rule-of-thumb, one might say platitudinous, answers to questions that are generally asked. The *approved* and *generally accepted* answer is what is usually given. Hence counselling tends to perpetuate a kind of passivity and conventionalism. It tends to encourage conformity to group standards. It tends to make organization men. Indeed in many cases counselling is simply the instrument for forming and preserving the mentality of the organization man. If this estimate is biased and unfair, then it may be corrected. *Salvo meliori judicio*[731]—this is the impression given by most (secular) counselling.

c) Catholic counselling: counselling *in a religious milieu* (particularly Catholic) already partakes of something higher. The counselling given by the Catholic priest (*the term is used for advice outside the confessional that is not strictly spiritual direction*) is on the *ethical* plane and very often touches upon the spiritual, or should do so. There is no harm in a certain amount of psychology and sociology entering into this kind of advice, provided that the perspectives of the Gospel and the Church are given first place. Note: a great deal of Catholic counselling deals in practice with points of *Church Law*.

Psychotherapy: whereas counselling is for the "normal" person, the "healthy" person, psychotherapy implies that one is (though not "abnormal") at least suffering from neurosis. Note: it is increasingly common for people who are not really "mentally ill" to consult a psychiatrist. In modern society it is common for those who function well in most respects to have some neurotic symptoms or at least "personality problems" and "emotional problems," or psychosomatic sicknesses which can be helped by psychotherapy. No particular social stigma attaches to this kind of treatment. And the proportion of neurotics in our society is so high that it would be absurd to draw a strict line between them and "healthy people," and make a big issue out of which side of the line one happens to be on. Indeed some who are most convinced that they are not and could not be neurotic are often much more so than others who are aware of neurotic symptoms. In a word, there is nothing wrong in experiencing neurotic symptoms, and realizing their nature, nor is this something to be feared as somehow "ominous" and portending great evil. It can be said

731. "unless a better conclusion can be drawn" (a standard principle in theological reasoning: cf. *PL* 66, col. 290; 78, cols. 448, 583; 153, col. 751; 186, col. 1045).

that the majority of men in our society at one time or other experience these symptoms and difficulties, but learn how to handle them. It is only the person who is completely incapable of handling these difficulties in a valid and mature fashion, who really becomes mentally ill. Neurotic symptoms {include} perfectionism, obsessions, compulsions, scruples, diffuse anxiety, severe uncharitableness.

Psychotherapy differs from *counselling* in that:

a) it presupposes at least a slight degree of neurosis, and *goes deeper* into the *personal problem* of the patient.

b) it not only offers advice, but the therapist "works through" the problem with the patient, aiming at giving him a completely new insight into his situation. The personal relationship between the psychiatrist and his patient is much deeper and more intimate than that of the counsellor who simply proffers advice, exteriorly.

c) the success of therapy depends on the patient *identifying himself* with the therapist so as to see his problem from the therapist's point of view. Also in general it can be said that this identification is important to open up in the patient a *deeper appreciation of "the other" person* as a person in his own right, and not just an extension of one's own thoughts, fears and desires.

Hence in psychotherapy the relationship of the patient and the therapist is both important and significant. It is essential. The aim of therapy is to "heal" (to some extent) *traumatic wounds* in the psyche by bringing them to conscious awareness and showing the patient how to deal with them in a rational and mature fashion, instead of by subconscious and infantile subterfuges, which do not work.

PSYCHOANALYSIS: analysis is a special form of therapy which goes much deeper than ordinary therapy, and generally takes longer. It is much more detailed. It strives to be much more radical, and it aims at a more intimate reshaping of the personality. *Therapy* aims simply at restoring the balance of the psyche by bringing certain unconscious problems to awareness and by dealing with them rationally. *Analysis* aims rather at a reshaping of the self. Freudian analysis generally strives to achieve this by following the problem back to its earliest roots and bringing the patient to "live through" an early stage of his pre-rational life when his development was blocked and "regressed." The emphasis is on the sexual development that takes place unconsciously in infancy and early childhood. Jungian analysis emphasizes more the primitive archetypal religious symbols which belong to the collective unconscious and have been inherited by the entire human race. It seeks to awaken the dormant power of these symbols and bring it into effective play in the psychic life of the patient, whereas in the sick man the *unconscious* power of the symbol tends to be working against him rather than for him. In analysis the relation of the patient to the analyst is even more important than it is in therapy, because the work to be done is more prolonged and is carried out on a deeper level.

DIRECTION differs from all these in ways which should be immediately obvious. The counsellor concerns himself with the externals of social life and with its surface. The director is *concerned with the spiritual depths of the person, and with his relation to God Who calls him* to his supernatural end, sanctity and divine union. The therapist and analyst concern themselves with more or less disordered conditions in the psyche, with the mental and psychological health of the patient. The therapist *is not concerned with sin as sin,* but with the maturity with which the patient is able to face responsibility for sin. Naturally, in so far as the therapist recognizes his own moral responsibility to the patient, he will orient his therapy in an ethical context. Hence the therapist and analyst by no means replace the director. They are concerned with the *pre-spiritual* realm. They are concerned with the mature growth of the psychic and emotional organism, which is necessary for a fully healthy and mature moral and spiritual life.

At the same time, *the director does not replace the therapist in the case of a neurotic or psychotic.* IT IS ERRONEOUS TO SAY THAT THE PSYCHOLOGICAL DIFFICULTIES OF A NEUROTIC CAN SIMPLY BE SETTLED IN THE CONFESSIONAL OR IN SPIRITUAL DIRECTION, BY ASCETIC MEANS. {The} *reason* {is} because ascetic means and to some extent even the sacraments depend for their full efficacy on a healthy psyche. The neurotic is so dominated by unconscious drives that he *is not able to judge* certain spiritual problems in a mature manner. His judgement is falsified, in spite of all his sincere efforts, by passions which dominate him without his knowledge. He is necessarily biased. And he is led to choose the wrong means or to use the right means wrongly. His ascetic efforts, however well meant, *tend inevitably to strengthen his neurosis* instead of liberating his spirit. Hence *whatever he does* tends to aggravate or at least to maintain his condition of psychological immaturity and his lack of spiritual freedom. This may be especially true in his relations with his director. Hence a neurotic and well-meaning person in religion, with a director who knows nothing of this problem, may in his very relations with his director, and in his efforts to attain to sanctity, actually worsen his condition by the means which are meant to solve it and bring him liberty.

In resumé, THE DIRECTOR is concerned not merely with ethical, social, and psychological problems. He deals with these only indirectly. He is concerned with *spiritual problems* above all, and spiritual growth. He is concerned with the soul's *response to grace*, and its fulfillment of its vocation in the Church of God, the Body of Christ. He is concerned with the *growth of the soul in holiness and charity*. He is concerned with the action of the Holy Spirit in the soul. He is concerned with the way the soul makes use of spiritual means of perfection, the sacraments, prayer, virtues, asceticism, etc. His relations with the penitent are spiritual. That is to say they must be seen in the light of faith. The director is the mouthpiece of God and of the Church, the instrument of the Holy Spirit. The Holy Spirit Himself, speaking interiorly, confirms the judgements of the director given exteriorly and moves one to docility and love. Hence the attitude of the one directed is *not merely prudential* as in the case of one receiving counsel, but it is *also supernatural and spiritual*, and God Himself is involved in the direction situation.

II. *Does the director have any use for psychology?* Though not directly concerned with therapy or analysis,

1) the director should have enough understanding of these to know when a penitent is neurotic, and when he needs to be referred to a psychiatrist. N.B. the Holy Office (1961) has recommended a certain amount of caution in referring religious to psychoanalysts (especially Freudian) without a sufficiently serious reason.[732] Permission of the bishop is required, for non-exempt religious.

2) the director may himself find a knowledge of psychology and psychoanalysis helpful, indirectly, in the exercise of his own functions:

A. in *evaluating* the qualities, defects, temperament, character of the penitent. (It is very important to understand at the outset the *capacities* of the penitent and his *ability to receive direction*; hence, what kind of direction to give him, what way to lead him. {It is} useless to spend a lot of time and effort in giving him advice he cannot understand, will not accept, or cannot put into practice at all. In practice much of the effort of direction, in the beginning, is in *preparing the penitent* for direction, gradually. This is especially true in the novitiate. What {the} father master gives is really a *preparation for direction*, at least in the first months. Sometimes one never really gets around to direction in the novitiate, strictly speaking. It is also important to know enough psychology to *evaluate rapidly and accurately* the character one deals with, without having to go into minute investigations and long drawn-out questioning about the past, which is tedious and wearisome to the penitent. One needs to understand him not only by what he tells you but by the way in which he does, and by the other ways in which he reveals himself unconsciously. N.B. in evaluating the strong and weak points of character, often it is the *weak spot* that is surrounded with the most emphatic talk

---

732. "*Acta SS. Congregationum Suprema Sacra Congregatio S. Officii Monitum*" (July 15, 1961), in *Acta Apostolica Sedis*, 53 (1961), 571: "*Sacerdotes et utriusque sexus Religiosi psychoanalystas ne adeant nisi Ordinario suo gravi de causa permittente*" ("Priests and religious of either sex should not consult psychoanalysts except for serious reasons and with the permission of their bishop").

and rationalization. *The penitent may really be weakest and most deficient where he has the most idealism and where he thinks he is strong.* On the other hand, certain weaknesses, which he thinks he has to combat, are often quite illusory, and his efforts tend to overcompensation rather than to realistic grappling with life.)

B. Psychology may help the director *to spare his penitent much useless labor and suffering.*

C. Psychology can help the director understand the way the individual functions in relation to the community, how under pressure of communal action he loses personal initiative and can function only as {a} member of {a} group. {There is a} need to know *group psychology* (especially in monastic-cenobitic life), and to know when an individual will *profit by* collective life as it really is (not as the *ideal* paints it) and where it will do him harm. {A} problem {arises} where an ideal is put forward not because it is really desired but because it is "correct." {This is part of the} ambiguity of community life.

D. In practice, the director needs to know the psychological weaknesses that arise precisely in the area of *culpability*, because the penitent will be talking about *what he considers to be his faults and the obstacles to union with God.* He may have a healthy and realistic view of sin, or he may have a morbid, unhealthy, or un-reliable view. *Types of weakness in the subjective evaluation of sin and guilt* {include}:[733]

1. Neurasthenic: when they feel threatened by {a} fault {or by} guilt, oppressed by constant anxiety and fatigue, the subject feels that almost everything is too much for him, especially where *decisions* are involved. *He has the feeling that he is being rushed into everything* before he is able to decide. *Everything to him is doubtful and uncertain*, and his conscience always bothers him; he is never secure in a feeling of being clearly right or wrong. Hence {he has} doubts, scruples, hesitations, confusion. *Avoid* letting these get

---

733. See Joseph MacAvoy, "Direction Spirituelle: IV. Direction Spirituelle et Psychologie," *DS* 3, cols. 1149–51.

involved in psychology and self-examination. {This would be the} worst possible thing—{it} only increases the agony. If they can get interested in the present reality of the life, and work at it contentedly, without care for past or future, if they can forget themselves to some extent and love others and stop pondering over their "problems," they can make it in a monastery—otherwise not. *Firm, paternal, kind, patient support from {the} director is essential. A typical case {is that of} Fr. Joseph Cassant.*[734]

2. Schizoid: {one who} isolates himself from others by barriers of silence, indifference, *hardness of heart, criticism,* abstract and legalistic thought, intense rationalization, non-participation, coldness, lack of interest. Such ones are usually *attracted to our life and don't belong in it.* False asceticism is common in this type.

3. Cyclothymic: {these exhibit an} alternation of exaltation and depression. When exalted {they are} ebullient, overflowing {with} exaggerated joy, volubility, but also {characterized by a} lack of moral control, {which} can "permit" much dubious activity without qualms of conscience—{there is a} tendency to laxity at such moments. {This is} followed by depression, deep melan-

---

734. Blessed Joseph Cassant (1878–1903) was a French Cistercian of the Monastery of Sainte Marie du Désert near Toulouse, who was beatified by Pope John Paul II on October 3, 2004. Merton wrote a preface for a French biography of Cassant, which was published in 1961: Dom M.-Étienne Chenevière, ocso, *L'Attente dans le Silence: Le Père Marie-Joseph Cassant, o.cist.s.o.,* Préface de Thomas Merton (Paris: Desclée de Brouwer, 1961), 9–13; for the original English version, see Thomas Merton, "Father Joseph Cassant, ocso," *The Merton Seasonal,* 28.4 (Winter 2003), 3–5, in which Merton writes of Cassant's relationship with his novice master and spiritual father, Dom André Malet, as "the one exception that brings relief to his life of frustration, . . . the one great *positive* factor in his monastic life. . . . Through Dom André Malet the Church, the Mother of Souls, sweetly embraced this helpless child and filled his life with the radiance of Christ: and this was what he needed. He needed mercy, he needed the assurance of God's inexhaustible pity and grace. He needed to know that his poverty did not matter because grace is given most abundantly to those who have nothing else. Dom André told him all this many times over, and perhaps after a very long time Père Joseph dared to understand it. If he is a saint, then this is his sanctity" (4–5).

choly and despair, which can be dangerous especially in our life. False mysticism easily occurs in this type. Note that the extremes are really attempts to handle {a} sense of guilt. {The director should} try to lead {these} to a realistic and calm, hopeful state of stability and *humility*.

4. Paranoid: {this state is marked by a} superinflation of the ego, delusions of grandeur and {an} appetite for domination, or else delusions of being a "misunderstood genius," {along with} stubbornness, bitterness, constant fault-finding and agitation to denounce and punish others, {as well as} playing politics and "plotting." These should not remain in the monastery; they cause infinite trouble and upset whole communities. {Such a one} *projects his guilt on others*. In mild forms the sickness can be helped if the person can become humble and charitable.

5. Hysterical: {these} easily become false visionaries; {they are} histrionic, carried away by false raptures in {a} search for attention or applause; {they are} highly suggestible. Is this a form of anguish resulting from a hypersensitivity about their difference from others (in matter of temperament)? ({This is the} solution suggested by MacAvoy, following Hesnard: *Univers Morbide de la Faute*.[735])

In general, all these types will react unfavorably the more stress there is on faults. {The} neurasthenic, crushed by guilt, seeks consolation {and} tends to hang in desperation on {the} director's neck; {he} may get into {the} routine of being pardoned and exempted—"acting out." {The} schizoid {becomes} withdrawn, gloomy, critical, {marked by} abstraction, uncharitableness, negativism. {The} cyclothymic {has a} grand opera {response of} exaltation, {assuming his} fault {is} permitted. {The} paranoid fights back with plots, protean activism, {a} sinister {attitude marked by} legitimizing of hatred. {Both the schizoid and the paranoid} *project* guilt: {they} act out by moving against or away from others.

---

735. Angelo Hesnard, *L'Univers Morbide de la Faute* (Paris: Presses Universitaires de France, 1949), cited in MacAvoy, col. 1149.

III. *Practical use of this psychological knowledge*

Some general "don'ts":
1. {It is} useless just to say "it is all imagination," or "it is all in your head," or to appeal to use of the will, or strong ascetic means. Their problem tends to be all mixed up in the very idea of their religious life itself. Don't try to dismiss it all with a wave of the hand. They do not properly understand themselves or their vocation.
2. Don't be maneuvered into the position of approving whatever their neurosis dictates.
3. *Don't try to bluff.* Don't try to kid them.
4. Don't try to be a psychiatrist if you are not one.

Some basic procedures (for {the} director):
1. *Truth*: again, whatever is clearly true must be emphasized, defended and kept fully in view. They must be guided by truth. But don't insist that something *you want to be true* is necessarily true. Be honest yourself! Break through illusory ideas of religious life and vocation. Oppose all fakery and artificiality.
2. Love: you must take {a} real interest, must really esteem, value and encourage *all the good* that is in them. You have to be on the side of the truly valid forces in their character. In asking {for} *sacrifices*, make them see that what they ought to give up, if possible, is their neurotic way of acting. But you cannot force or cajole them to do this. Favor and encourage *all that is genuinely human.* Avoid a false supernaturalism. *Encourage a productive and fruitful regime*, whether in work or reading or prayer. Encourage humility in the form of a realistic appreciation of truth and love of others.
3. {The} director should help the penitent to take a realistic and sensible view of temptation—*not becoming terrified* of his instincts, not *seeking to escape* from them, and *not building false virtues on repressions* (v.g. not thinking humility is {a} sense of inferiority). Such false virtues are always threatened, and arouse anxiety and strain, because of artificiality.

4. {The} director should oppose tendencies to *obsession* and *compulsion*:

a) *Obsession* poisons {one's} whole life with preoccupation with one's "problems." Everything seems to be a reference to "my problem." Everything arouses the doubt and the question, and the anguish of "the problem." One tries to avoid these stimuli and retreats more and more for "safety." {The} remedy {is} to face normal realities without fear, but not imposing too much burden on the weak.

b) *Compulsion* {involves} pseudo-duty, a mechanical, pseudo-magic rite to exorcise anxiety. {This brings} momentary relief, followed by shame at {an} awareness that one has after all been a little ridiculous (going back again to see that the light is really *out*, etc.).

{The} director must also recognize a certain stubbornness and rigidity in {the} penitent's clinging to a false value; {an} insistence on a demand to do this or that penance can be a fruit of infantile egoism. In all these things what is needed is a *real sense of love and devotion to real values and persons*, not imaginary spirituality and devotion to fictions dictated by fear of anxiety.

5. *The crises of the spiritual and affective life*: {there are} decisive steps in {the} evolution of life, *some of them at normal stages* of growth: childhood, adolescence, middle age. *Others* {come} *under pressure of circumstances*: sickness, vocational crisis, change of superiors and employments, wars, expulsion from {the} monastery, destitution, etc. Very often {there is a} *crisis as a result of unjust treatment* by others, even in {the} monastery—the "raw deal." This is soft-pedaled for obvious reasons, but it may be very real. {The} basic principle {is that} a *crisis* is engendered by the anxiety of *division* and *disproportion* between *one's habitual norms*, personal or social, and by the evolving structure of one's inner life. Psychologically the most important function of the director is to help the penitent fully *to be himself*. This means helping him to reconcile the divisions in himself, especially by encouraging him to *recuperate and salvage* really good and necessary elements in his

life which, for various reasons, he is rejecting. In the contemplative life one of the main duties of the director is to see that the penitent does not compel himself to throw away the best in himself, because he is afraid of it or cannot handle it.

Let us consider the big crises which arrive at moments of division due to growth. Examples {include}:

The adolescent is accustomed to standards of behavior of childhood but his body, his emotions, his self are all becoming different and are exerting the pressure of demands he does not understand and cannot easily cope with. (N.B. this is *not* an "awakening of sex": the infant already knows sensual pleasure connected with sex organs but is not aware of it because {it is} superficial.)

The young man accustomed to his ideas and aspirations for a career in the world finds himself evolving, interiorly, towards a religious vocation. Lack of unity and harmony between his external situation and the demands of his inner self tends to *reject* one or the other—his worldly self or his religious self.

In the vocation crisis, there is very often a *serious problem of interpretation* of the "new" element that is developing. Often the vocation idea is so conventional that it is an *evasion*, not a solution. One tries to "tag" the new development conveniently and accurately, for instance by joining the teaching order by which one was educated, ignoring the fact that the whole problem may be much more subtle and delicate.

{In a} *vocational crisis in {the} monastery*, the structure of rules, norms, ideals ceases to correspond entirely with the evolution of the inner self:

a) Perhaps because of infidelity or imprudence, the young monk has let himself be influenced by desires and aspirations incompatible with monastic life; or he has relaxed his energy and zeal, lost some of his faith in the monastic ideal as it is correctly embodied in his community. There may be a lot of rationalization and false idealism in this: the monastery itself may be unjustly blamed. Sometimes also there is a real lack of adaptation, {of} a real evolution *beyond* the simple norms accepted in the community; {there is} a need for *something more*. *This may be a point where the director can play a crucial part*. The main thing is to lead the penitent *to take the necessary forward step*, kindly and patiently. The Christian principle is that here we have the familiar pattern of "death" and "resurrection" to enter into a new area of life, *a pascha Christi*! {The} problem {is to effect} *a real integration* of the developed inner self and the outer reality, a *new adjustment* that retains what was good and valid before, but casts off what has now become obsolete—perhaps a *sane rejection* of a burden of artificiality and illusion that can no longer be borne. In some cases a *complete sacrifice of a cherished attachment* that has become a fatal menace {is needed}. This may quite usually be the case here. In any case it is a matter of *resolute acceptance* of the simple realities of the case, in a spirit of poverty, humility and trust in Providence (*not* just stultified and inert passivity!). *A crisis that has been gone through successfully and healthily is a victory and a step forward in holiness and spiritual maturity*. A crisis that has been weathered badly, with equivocation and evasion of the issue, leaves a wound, weakens the spiritual energy of the monk, lowers his general tone, decreases his capacity for growth, and in the end, a series of badly handled crises can lead to {a} complete loss of vocation.

b) {A} crisis {may occur} after ordination: due to our priestly formation, oriented toward administration of {the} sacraments and care of souls, at least implicitly, the monk may undergo a *crisis of letdown* when he is left to himself in the common life, after years of study, with "nothing to do." The fault lies with our education of priests and with the weak development of {a} monastic and contemplative spirit in the students. Crises arise from {a} disproportion between secret hopes and {the} actual situation, which frustrates them. Vain hopes must not be aroused.

c) *The crisis of full development*: according to the theories of Jung,[736] man develops full maturity according to the following

736. See MacAvoy, cols. 1154–56.

pattern—without necessarily subscribing to everything said by Jung we can however adopt the essentials of this pattern as revealing for our monastic situation:

1. {The} first stage {involves} the sacrifice of individual elements in order to become a *persona*, socially speaking—to integrate oneself in the monastic community, the exterior world. {There is an} emphasis on regularity, conforming to visible ideals and models. This implies the *rejection* of many capacities and qualities, the sacrifice of important parts of our self, which are not useful for this. But the integration must be made. The sacrifice is *required*.

2. {The} second stage involves the *reintegration* in one's mature life of what was originally set aside or sacrificed, {which is} now reintegrated on a higher level. {There is} a reconciliation of the real and personal depths of the individual with his social and exterior self (not just a rejection of the latter, either!). *Genuine peace depends on this reconciliation.* An imperfect reintegration keeps the senior religious dry and superficial, restless, melancholy, *with very little to give to his younger brethren.* Here above all the director must gently aid in a complete recovery of all that is humanly best and vital in the penitent: warmth, geniality, {an} ability to love and to give. This will help forestall {the} danger of involutional melancholy.

XII. The Spiritual Direction of Contemplatives (continued): Direction in the Crises of the Mystical Life

What has been said in the last series of conferences (XI) is not directly concerned with the guidance of mystics or of "spiritual men." However, very important matters which indirectly affect this question have been taken up. Now, briefly, due to our own lack of knowledge and competence, we can touch on some matters concerning the spiritual direction of contemplatives in times of crisis in the spiritual life. We repeat that the fundamental principles laid down by the Fathers, which we have examined earlier in the series of these conferences, should guide the director in his contacts with the mystical life, the life of the Holy Spirit in Christians reaching their full maturity as members of Christ, and therefore fully participating in His sufferings and His risen life, while still on earth. The direction of "mystics" is therefore to be regarded not as an esoteric specialty, but it is intimately connected with the Christian life as a whole, the Christian life preached by the Gospel, imparted by faith and the sacraments, and lived in liturgical mysteries by the whole Church. We shall here touch on a few classic examples of "crises" of growth in the mystical life and consider the part played in these by directors.

ST. TERESA OF AVILA AND HER DIRECTORS: we shall consider the experience of St. Teresa and note the conclusions she herself drew, in regard to spiritual direction.

I. *The experience of St. Teresa*, with directors, in time of crisis: the fullest exposition of the crises of the mystical life is in the Sixth Mansions (*Interior Castle*). This is the longest section in the *Castle* (about 60 pp.; {the} Fifth Mansion, {on the} prayer of union, is 20 pp. long, {while the} Fourth Mansion, {on the} prayer of recollection and quiet, is 16 pp. long[737]). The Sixth Mansion explains in some detail the exterior and interior trials of the final purification of the mystic, who has reached *union* with God, and is being prepared for the *mystical marriage*. Also it treats of the supernatural experiences, visions, etc. which are likewise part of this preparatory stage, in her case at least. Note: concerning the *Fourth Mansion* St. Teresa says it is the "one which the greatest number of souls enter"[738]—presumably contemplatives. Concerning the Fifth she says, "the majority manage to get inside":[739] this seems excessive until we reflect that she distinguishes between the *prayer of union*, an *experience* not granted to all, and the equivalent union of wills in charity which is substantial perfection (see

---

737. *Complete Works of Saint Teresa*, 2.269–328, 247–68, 230–46, respectively.

738. *Interior Castle*, IV.3 (*Complete Works of Saint Teresa*, 2.246).

739. *Interior Castle*, V.1 (*Complete Works of Saint Teresa*, 2.247).

above[740]). She is saying that most Carmelites reach what is substantially the perfection of union with God by love, though not all experience it in prayer (integral perfection). As to the Sixth Mansion, the way of special purificatory trials and of visions, unusual experiences, she says: NOT ALL SOULS WILL BE LED ALONG THIS PATH.[741] That is to say, not all will have the intense sufferings which are probably the lot of those who are called to the highest mystical life. But it is normal for all contemplatives to have periods of crisis and suffering, and in these crises there will be some elements analogous to those of the higher kind of purification, especially the *exterior* trials.

What we shall be doing then is not regarding the mystical life and its trials in esoteric isolation, as a very special area, but we shall be in reality considering the whole spiritual life from the point of view of the *higher purifications* which *de jure*[742] should be passed through before one attains to perfect holiness and likeness to Christ.

a) Read {the} introductory passage, chapter 1 of {the} Sixth Mansions:

> Oh, my God, how great are these trials, which the soul will suffer, both within and without, before it enters the seventh Mansion! Really, when I think of them, I am sometimes afraid that, if we realized their intensity beforehand, it would be most difficult for us, naturally weak as we are, to muster determination enough to enable us to suffer them or resolution enough for enduring them, however attractively the advantage of so doing might be presented to us, until we reached the seventh Mansion, where there is nothing more to be feared, and the soul will plunge deep into suffering for God's sake. The reason for this is that the soul

740. See the quotation from *Interior Castle*, V.3 (*Complete Works of Saint Teresa*, 2.259-60) above, page 249.

741. See *Interior Castle*, VI.1 (*Complete Works of Saint Teresa*, 2.270), which reads: "Not all souls, perhaps, will be led along this path, . . ."

742. "in principle".

is almost continuously near His Majesty and its nearness brings it fortitude. I think it will be well if I tell you about some of the things which I know are certain to happen here. Not all souls, perhaps, will be led along this path, though I doubt very much if souls which from time to time really taste the things of Heaven can live in freedom from earthly trials, in one way or in another. Although I had not intended to treat of this, it has occurred to me that some soul finding itself in this state might be very much comforted if it knew what happens to those whom God grants such favours, at a time when everything really seems to be lost (from ch. 1, Sixth Mansion; pp. 269-70, Peers translation).

{There are} two kinds of trials: exterior and interior. The exterior are the "least" of them.

1) Here we see the experience of Teresa herself, the "outcry" of good people against her.[743] She scandalizes pious and well-meaning souls. They think she is extreme, that she is deluded (especially in her attempts to reform Carmel, but also her mystical life is somewhat publicized).

2) Especially *pressure is brought on her confessors*. (This of course is altogether irregular and unjustified.)

3) She is abandoned by friends, everyone becomes suspicious of her, and many confessors refuse to have anything to do with her—or at least it seems likely that this may eventually happen.

In the *Life* (c. 28; p. 184 ff.), she recounts how the saintly *Father Balthasar Alvarez* sustained her in her trial when she was first having visions and people were criticizing her on all sides. This is an important and beautiful passage:

a) The confessor suffers himself very much. He does not have the same experience and yet he believes she is to be supported. But he is also humble and does not trust his own opinion.

743. *Interior Castle*, VI.1 (*Complete Works of Saint Teresa*, 2.270).

b) She and the confessor are both attacked; heavy pressure is brought to bear.

c) In spite of all the difficulties, he is faithful to his trust and stands by her.

This is an example of the special difficulties in the life of one called to direct someone with a great and extraordinary mystical vocation with a providential task in the Church. Fr. Balthasar Alvarez met the responsibilities of his task.

However, other confessors were not so helpful. In {the} Sixth Mansion (p. 272), she speaks of the anguish caused by incompetent confessors who do not know how to handle the situation:

a) {A} confessor who is "scrupulous and inexperienced . . . thinks nothing safe." {He} cannot face the responsibility of dealing with "anything out of the ordinary."

b) Above all he does not understand that *imperfection can coexist in the soul of the* contemplative with mystical graces. "He thinks that people to whom God grants these favors must be angels . . ."

c) This being the case, he tends to judge that her experiences are either psychotic delusions or produced by the devil.

d) She goes to him for encouragement and enlightenment, and he condemns her. Naturally she cannot help taking his judgements seriously, especially since she is influenced by the awareness of her own imperfection. Yet at the same time the power of grace is indubitable (at the moment of the experience) so that she is torn between these two forces. Afterwards, however, aridity descends upon her, {so that} she "wonders if she has ever known God or will ever know Him."[744] Then she is troubled by the thought that "she cannot be describing her case properly . . . has been deceiving her confessor."[745] Summary of the situation:

---

744. *Interior Castle*, VI.1 (*Complete Works of Saint Teresa*, 2.273), which reads "the soul feels as if it has never known God and never will know Him."

745. Text reads ". . . has been deceiving him."

READ p. 273.[746] IN THIS SPIRITUAL TEMPEST NO CONSOLATION IS POSSIBLE.

This is a typical case, one which must have reproduced itself thousands of times over in a less marked or extreme way, since that time. What can the ordinary director learn from this? Two things are essential in dealing with extraordinary cases:

a) Recognize one's own limitations. {Do} not judge prematurely. Know where to consult for further information. Know when to refer the person to someone who is better informed or more competent. Get permission to consult someone who has special qualifications, if necessary—permission of the penitent is meant here.

b) Never act in a violent or negative way that simply produces turmoil and confusion. Give whatever comfort and support you can, without committing yourself to the support of what *may* be an illusion. Take your stand on the truth; say what you can say; don't say what you don't know. If you don't know, say you don't know and give what help you can.

c) Positive direction is to {be} given. How? by emphasis on the fundamental and ordinary values of the Christian faith which are always valid for everyone: namely the theological virtues, trust in divine Providence, humble obedience to God in all definite expressions of His will. Often the best direction possible, even of the most difficult mystical problem, is a clear insistence on these fundamentals, in a way that applies to the reality of the case concerned.

Hence it is that if one is called upon to give direction in an extraordinary case, one should first of all realize that one is speak-

---

746. Merton has just quoted from this passage, which concludes, "For there are many things which assault her soul with an interior oppression so keenly felt and so intolerable that I do not know to what it can be compared, save to the torment of those who suffer in hell, for in this spiritual tempest no consolation is possible."

ing as a minister of the Church, that God's grace will sustain our own weakness and supply for our deficiencies, and then in a spirit of humility and truth give principles based on the Gospels and the teachings of the Church, that apply as nearly as possible to the case in hand. The penitent, meanwhile, should not have a fixed idea of what kind of direction is to be expected, before it is given. {He} should approach the director with a completely open mind and in a condition of frankness, humility and readiness to comply in a spirit of faith with any directives given, until it becomes absolutely clear that they are perhaps not the right ones. Even following directives that are not THE right ones can lead to God. One must be humble, detached, and willing to advance in the obscurity of faith.

II. *Further extraordinary cases*: St. Teresa takes up the question of direction in cases of "interior locutions," raptures, visions. She also considers the possibility of psychotic delusions. In {the} Sixth Mansions (pp. 280 ff.), she speaks first of *true locutions*, that are "from God," and of the interior authority by which they make themselves known. Then she takes up those which come from the *imagination* (282, 283), particularly "dreamlike" ones that occur deep in the prayer of quiet. She also says to beware of locutions from the devil, but does not say how they are to be identified in this place. However this leads her to the principle that *whatever may be the nature of the locutions*, even if there are apparent signs that they come from God, one should always consult a director "IF WHAT IS SAID IS OF GREAT IMPORTANCE AND INVOLVES SOME ACTION ON THE PART OF THE HEARER, OR MATTERS AFFECTING A THIRD PERSON."[747] She considers it "very dangerous"[748] for a person to simply follow one of these locutions and trust in his own opinion without consulting a director. The director in turn should have great prudence. Later (p. 317), she insists on the importance of those receiving special favors of this kind "speak-

---

747. *Interior Castle*, VI.3 (*Complete Works of Saint Teresa*, 2.283) (emphasis added).

748. *Interior Castle*, VI.3 (*Complete Works of Saint Teresa*, 2.283).

ing very plainly and candidly"[749] to their director: "UNLESS YOU
DO THIS I CANNOT ASSURE YOU THAT YOU ARE PROCEEDING AS YOU
SHOULD OR THAT IT IS GOD WHO IS TEACHING YOU. God is very
anxious for us to speak candidly and clearly to those who are in
His place, and to desire them to be acquainted with all our
thoughts, and still more our actions, however trivial these may
be. If you do this, you need not be disturbed, or worried, for, even
if these things are not of God, they will do you no harm for you
are humble and have a good conscience."[750] (Read context.[751])

N.B.: since we are on the subject of locutions, it would be
well to refer to the classic treatment of the subject by St. John of
the Cross in *The Ascent of Mt. Carmel*, Book II. {The} general theme
of Book II of the *Ascent* {is that} faith is "night" to the soul,[752] and
faith alone leads to the "highest contemplation."[753] Consequently
all clear apprehensions and forms of knowledge and understanding, even though of a supernatural character, must be set aside
in favor of faith, if we are to attain to perfect union with God.
Chapters 16-20 deal especially with "imaginary visions"; chapter
23 ff. deals with spiritual visions; chapters 28-31 deal with interior
locutions. He repeats his principle: his aim is to "direct the soul,
through all its apprehensions, natural and supernatural, without
deception and hindrance, in purity of faith, to Divine union with

749. The text reads "you should speak to your confessor very plainly and
candidly . . ."

750. *Interior Castle*, V.9 (*Complete Works of Saint Teresa*, 2.318), which reads
". . . with our actions . . . be not of God . . . if you are humble . . ." (emphasis
added).

751. Teresa goes on to warn her sisters not to despise visions but not to
seek after them, and tells of those who desire not to receive consolations so as to
love God with complete detachment (*Complete Works of Saint Teresa*, 2.318-20).

752. See the title of c. 3: "*How faith is dark night to the soul. . . .*" (*Complete
Works of Saint John of the Cross*, 1.70).

753. See the title of c. 4: "*Treats in general of how the soul likewise must be in
darkness, in so far as this rests with itself, to the end that it may be effectively guided by
faith to the highest contemplation*" (*Complete Works of Saint John of the Cross*, 1.73).

God" (vol. I; p. 208).[754] He distinguishes three kinds of locutions: successive (c. 29), formal (c. 30), substantial (c. 31). Successive {are} those which we form for ourselves in meditation and recollection, but which are so helped by grace that it is possible to consider them as "from God." {John indicates} how they can become obstacles, especially if they give rise to vanity and are taken too seriously. (READ p. 211,[755] 213,[756] {showing} how the devil intervenes in these). Formal are directly communicated from "another" without any work on the soul's part, and regardless of whether one is at prayer or not. Dangers are detailed. {The} conclusion (p. 218) {is that} *a learned director must be consulted*. (READ p. 218[757] and refer back to chapters 17-20 of Book II for further

754. Text reads ". . . direction of the soul, . . . deception or hindrance . . ." (Bk. II, c. 28).

755. "For, if humility and charity be not engendered by such experiences, and mortification and holy simplicity and silence, etc., what can be the value of them? I say, then, that these things may hinder the soul greatly in its progress to Divine union because, if it pay heed to them, it is led far astray from the abyss of faith, where the understanding must remain in darkness, and must journey in darkness, by love and in faith, and not by much reasoning" (Bk. II, c. 29.5).

756, "In this type of locution—namely, in successive interior words—the devil intervenes frequently, especially in the case of such as have some inclination or affection for them. At the time when such persons begin to be recollected, the devil is accustomed to offer them ample material for distractions, forming conceptions or words by suggestion in their understanding, and then corrupting and deceiving it most subtly with things that have great appearance of truth" (Bk. II, c. 29.10).

757. "But the words must be repeated to an experienced confessor, or to a discreet and learned person, that he may give instruction and see what it is well to do, and impart his advice; and the soul must behave, with regard to them, in a resigned and passive manner. And, if such an expert person cannot be found, it is better to attach no importance to these words and to repeat them to nobody; for it is easy to find persons who will ruin the soul rather than edify it. . . . And let it be clearly noted that a soul should never act according to its own opinion or accept anything of what these locutions express, without much reflection and without taking advice of another" (Bk. II, c. 30.5-6).

details.[758]) Substantial {are} the most powerful and efficacious of supernatural communication, by "words" in which not so much the word as the reality itself seems present in the spirit. One such word "works greater blessing in the soul than all that the soul has itself done throughout its life."[759] These are subject to special principles. They come from God, but even then {one must} neither desire them nor not desire them; do not attempt to put them into effect: God will put them into effect; {one should} not reject them, but remain in great humility. They help greatly for union with God. In actuality these are closely akin to graces of union and are not words that are "heard" in a physical sense. St. TERESA, in Mansions Six, chapter 3, mentions also these three kinds of locution (see first paragraph).[760] Then she explains that "formal" locutions, which even "seem to be uttered by a human voice,"[761] are heard by persons afflicted by melancholy, by which she means neurotics or psychotics. What to do with these? Take no notice of their locutions. Do not scold these people or upset them by telling them it comes from the devil. Listen patiently and quietly tell them to pay no attention, explaining that "the service of God does not consist in things like these." {Do} not tell them they are crazy "for then there will be no end to it" as they will "simply swear" that they see and hear these things, which, subjectively, they do. "The REAL SOLUTION IS TO SEE THAT THESE PERSONS HAVE LESS TIME FOR PRAYER . . ."[762] and distract them by sane and

758. St. John himself advises the reader (Bk. II, c. 30.7; 1.218) to refer back to these chapters (1.138-62), which point out that even authentic visions may do harm without proper discernment and wise spiritual direction.

759. *Complete Works of Saint John of the Cross*, 2.219 (Bk. II, c. 31.1), which reads "works a greater blessing within . . ."

760. *Interior Castle*, VI.3 (*Complete Works of Saint Teresa*, 2.279).

761. *Interior Castle*, VI.3 (*Complete Works of Saint Teresa*, 2.279); Teresa does not use the term "formal" here, which is that of John of the Cross.

762. *Interior Castle*, VI.3 (*Complete Works of Saint Teresa*, 2.280); "for then" is not found in the text and emphasis is added.

healthy activity, a lighter regime, etc. (See other places in St. Teresa: *vide* index.[763])

ST. JOHN OF THE CROSS: DIRECTION IN THE DARK NIGHT: St. John of the Cross attaches crucial importance to two crises in the spiritual life, one of which is simply a preliminary to the other. They both are called "dark night." The first is the "night of sense" which brings one to the *maturity* of the spiritual life, and the second is the "night of the spirit" which brings one to the *perfection* of the mystical life. These nights are both "active" and "passive." The "stripping" and "annihilation" of sense and spirit are accomplished in part by one's own efforts, in union with grace, but *chiefly by the infused action of God.* It is one of the characteristic doctrines of St. John of the Cross that unless one is *passively purified of all imperfections by the divine action*, one cannot attain perfectly to union with Him; also, that our *cooperation, which is absolutely necessary*, consists more in disposing ourselves to accept God's action, without placing obstacles in His way, rather than in any positive action of our own (on the higher levels—in the lower levels of the spiritual life the initiative belongs to us, and this must not be neglected; if one is not generous in sacrifice in the beginning, one cannot go on to the more difficult and mysterious work of cooperating with the mystical purifications sent by God). It follows then that once there is a definite indication of a call to higher forms of prayer it is *most important that obstacles be removed.* Among the chief obstacles are the *wrong notions entertained by the contemplative* himself, the *ignorance and arbitrariness of his director*, and the intervention of the *devil.* In this connection it is best simply to look at some texts from St. John of the Cross.

---

763. There is an extensive listing under "Locutions" (*Complete Works of Saint Teresa*, 3.389-90).

1. The Prologue to *The Ascent of Mount Carmel*

N. 3: a) he laments the fact that when souls are brought to the dark night by God, and are thus invited to perfect union with Him, they "make no progress."[764]

b) Why? "At times it is because they have no desire to enter it or to allow themselves to be led into it . . . or because they understand not themselves and lack competent guides and directors."[765]

> And so it is sad to see many souls to whom God gives both favour and capacity for making progress (and who, if they would take courage, could attain to this high state), remaining in an elementary stage of communion with God, for want of will, or knowledge, or because there is none who will lead them in the right path or teach them how to get away from these beginnings. And at length, although Our Lord grants them such favour as to make them to go onward without this hindrance or that, they arrive at their goal exceeding late, and with greater labour, yet with less merit, because they have not conformed themselves to God, and allowed themselves to be brought freely into the pure and sure road of union. For, although it is true that God is leading them, and that He can lead them without their own help, they will not allow themselves to be led; and thus they make less progress, because they resist Him Who is leading them, and they have less merit, because they apply not their will, and on this account they suffer more. For there are souls who, instead of committing themselves to God and making use of His help, rather hinder God by the indiscretion of their actions or by their resistance; like children who, when their mothers desire to carry them in their arms, kick and cry, insisting upon being allowed to walk,

764. *Complete Works of Saint John of the Cross*, 1.12.
765. *Complete Works of Saint John of the Cross*, 1.12, which reads ". . . this is because . . . at other times, because they understand not themselves and lack competent and alert directors who will guide them to the summit."

with the result that they can make no progress; and, if they advance at all, it is only at the pace of a child.[766]

Summary: {there are} three lacks which prevent people from entering into the dark night, presuming they are called to it: lack of will, lack of understanding, lack of guidance. (This seems to imply that *all* receive the grace. This is not necessarily to be concluded. He is speaking of cases where *he believes* the grace has been given but the soul was not able to correspond fully for the above reasons.) Where correspondence is only partial or imperfect, there is less merit, there is more suffering, {and} the advance is either very slow or non-existent.

N. 4: hence, he says, he is writing "this book" "to the end that *all, whether beginners or proficient,* may know how to commit themselves to God's guidance, when His Majesty desires to lead them onward . . ."[767] so that they may be able to understand His will or at least allow Him to lead them.

> For some confessors and spiritual fathers, having no light and experience concerning these roads, are wont to hinder and harm such souls rather than to help them along the road; they are like the builders of Babel, who, when told to furnish suitable material, gave and applied other very different material, because they understood not the language, and thus nothing was done. Wherefore, it is a difficult and troublesome thing at such seasons for a soul not to understand itself or to find none who understands it. For it will come to pass that God will lead the soul by a most lofty path of dark contemplation and aridity, wherein it seems to be lost, and, being thus full of darkness and trials, afflictions and temptations, will meet one who will speak to it like Job's comforters, and say that it is suffering from

---

766. *Complete Works of Saint John of the Cross*, 1.12, which reads ". . . high estate), . . ."

767. *Complete Works of Saint John of the Cross*, 1.12-13, which reads ". . . proficients . . ." (emphasis added here and throughout passages quoted from this source).

melancholy or low spirits, or morbidity of temperament, or that it may have some hidden sin, and that it is for this reason that God has forsaken it. Such comforters are wont to infer immediately that that soul must have been very evil, since such things as these are befalling it.[768]

2. Ascent of Mount Carmel, II, chapters 12 to 15: one of the great questions raised and treated by the Carmelite mystics is the question of a crisis in the spiritual life which marks the passage from "ordinary" prayer to "mystical" prayer. The very idea of the passage has become fraught with controversy, and the question of acquired contemplation (whether such a thing exists or not) has been regarded as technically important to this problem. Without entering into the discussion {of} acquired vs. infused contemplation, it may be said that the notion of acquired contemplation may perhaps have been brought into the picture in order to *reduce the intensity of the crisis*. It might seem to be a way of softening the shock of division, the passing over of an abyss, by putting a kind of bridge over it, an intermediate stage, thus creating a sense of confidence and courage in the new contemplative, reassuring him that he is not totally out of his depth. This may or may not be a valid assumption. St. John of the Cross in any case treats the passage from discursive prayer to beginners' contemplation as a "critical" moment in the spiritual life. We shall see that he is especially aware of the fact that the director, by taking a wrong view of what is taking place, *prevents and obstructs* the "passage" into the new level by restraining the penitent and holding him back on the ordinary level, forcing him to produce the familiar and conventional acts which he is now called to leave. It is necessary then to see briefly *in what the crisis consists*, and what are the signs that the soul is truly called to a higher kind of prayer and is consequently in "crisis" and needs the special help that is called for, in the *night of sense*.

---

768. *Complete Works of Saint John of the Cross*, 1.13.

In the *Ascent*, Book II, St. John concentrates on the aspect of the *night of sense in prayer* (this is only *part* of the problem, not the whole story). He also considers it from the active point of view only: *how to cooperate* with God by not placing obstructions, and he especially indicates the signs by which one may know that it is safe and right to proceed from discursive to contemplative prayer.

1) *What causes the crisis?* the passage from discursive and affective prayer to another form of prayer, contemplation, which is silent, apparently inactive, receptive, "passive." In particular the crisis is caused by one entering into a way of prayer in which his faculties are obstructed and cease to act in their ordinary way as means to prayer and fervor. On the contrary, they tend to block the new, deep prayer infused by God. This applies especially to the *imagination*, whether moved naturally or supernaturally (visions), and the *reason*, the *memory*, the *will*. The ordinary spontaneous activity of these faculties is *necessary for beginners* but *harmful to proficients* (i.e. those in whom passive prayer has begun). (Read *Ascent*, vol. I, p. 111, 112; esp. n. 6.[769])

---

769. Bk II, c. 12.4-6: after pointing out that, while images of God according to sense impressions are useful for beginners, God is beyond the grasp of the senses, he continues, "Great, therefore, is the error of many spiritual persons who have practised approaching God by means of images and forms and meditations, as befits beginners. God would now lead them on to further spiritual blessings, which are interior and invisible, by taking from them the pleasure and sweetness of discursive meditation; but they cannot, or dare not, or know not how to detach themselves from those palpable methods to which they have grown accustomed. They continually labour to retain them, desiring to proceed, as before, by the way of consideration and meditation upon forms, for they think that it must be so with them always. They labour greatly to this end and find little sweetness or none; rather the aridity and weariness and disquiet of their souls are increased and grow, in proportion as they labour for that earlier sweetness. They cannot find this in that earlier manner, for the soul no longer enjoys that food of sense, as we have said; it needs not this but another food, which is more delicate, more interior and partaking less of the nature of sense; it consists not in labouring with the imagination, but in setting the soul at rest, and allowing it to remain in its quiet and repose, which is more spiritual."

2) *What constitutes the crisis?* the total unfamiliarity and strangeness of the new state in which one suffers anxiety, anguish, hesitation, doubt whether or not to go forward, irresolution as to how to advance, scruples about whether one is at fault or not, temptations to go back to what is familiar, pressures of the director to go back to what is familiar and conventional though God may be calling and pressing the soul to advance in this new way which is so mysterious.

3) The crisis is manifested above all by *dryness and inability to produce ordinary acts at prayer*, the inability to meditate (when one has previously been proficient at meditation), a sense that one's spiritual life has gone to pieces, an absence of sensible fervor, a deep awareness of one's own weaknesses, limitations, failings; perhaps also many temptations of all kinds, which reinforce the soul in its mistaken conviction that everything is going wrong. The efforts of the soul to recover fervor and light only serve to torment it and increase its anguish, for they are useless. (Read vol. I, p. 113; n. 7.[770])

---

770. Bk. II, c. 12.7: "It is piteous, then, to see many a one who, though his soul would fain tarry in this peace and rest of interior quiet, where it is filled with the peace and refreshment of God, takes from it its tranquillity, and leads it away to the most exterior things, and would make it return and retrace the ground it has already traversed, to no purpose, and abandon the end and goal wherein it is already reposing for the means which led it to that repose, which are meditations. This comes not to pass without great reluctance and repugnance of the soul, which would fain be in that peace that it understands not, as in its proper place; even as one who has arrived, with great labour, and is now resting, suffers pain if they make him return to his labour. And, as such souls know not the mystery of this new experience, the idea comes to them that they are being idle and doing nothing; and thus they allow not themselves to be quiet, but endeavour to meditate and reason. Hence they are filled with aridity and affliction, because they seek to find sweetness where it is no longer to be found; we may even say of them that the more they strive the less they profit, for, the more they persist after this manner, the worse is the state wherein they find themselves, because their soul is drawn farther away from spiritual peace; and this is to leave the greater for the less, and to retrace the road already traversed, and to seek to do that which has been done."

4) *The crisis must not be confused* with similar states of soul caused by tepidity, negligence, sin, laziness, slackness in the spiritual life, real lack of fervor, or perhaps melancholy (neurasthenia).

5) In chapter 13 he explains what are the signs by which one may know that the vocation to simple contemplation is genuine and that the time has come to *lay aside meditation*. This is the active cooperation of the soul, God having already begun to produce passively, by dryness and infused light "which is darkness to the soul"[771] the conditions requisite for contemplation and indeed the beginning of contemplation (whether you choose to call it acquired or infused). He makes it clear that it is of great importance to lay aside the practices of meditation NEITHER SOONER NOR LATER THAN WHEN THE SPIRIT BIDS HIM (n. 1; p. 114); and it is important for him not to abandon meditation "before the proper time *lest he should turn backward.*"[772] This is very important, because unless this distinction is made, anyone who gets the idea that passive prayer is a "good thing" and "better than ordinary prayer" may take it upon himself to abandon meditation and then end up with no prayer at all, since he was not called to do this by God.

One should therefore know the indications that one may safely go forwards in "the night." He gives three signs. *The three signs are*:

a) {an} inability to meditate discursively or affectively, though this was possible, easy and fruitful in the past; lack of pleasure in the meditation that previously brought sweetness.

---

771. See *Ascent*, Bk. II, c. 3: "Hence it follows that, for the soul, this excessive light of faith which is given to it is thick darkness, for it overwhelms that which is great and does away with that which is little, even as the light of the sun overwhelms all other lights whatsoever, so that when it shines and disables our powers of vision they appear not to be lights at all. . . . It is clear, then, that faith is dark night for the soul, and it is in this way that it gives it light; and the more it is darkened, the greater light comes to it" (*Complete Works of Saint John of the Cross*, 1.70, 72). See also *Dark Night*, Bk. II, c. 5 (1.406).

772. *Complete Works of Saint John of the Cross*, 1.114-15 (Bk. II, c. 13.1).

Note {the} crucial importance of the fact that he could meditate before but now can no longer. He had fervor and consolation before, but now finds aridity *precisely where before he found consolation*. This is essential to the "crisis" of the night of sense.

b) no desire to fix the mind or imagination or senses on *any particular object*, "whether exterior or interior."[773] But the imagination still works, and indeed produces distractions. These add to the suffering and aridity of the crisis. It is not an *inability* to fix {the} mind on any particular thing, but a sense of alienation from particular objects as particular, and a movement toward the mysterious reality of God in a general, confused, dark apprehension of love, not under the form of precise and clear ideas.

c) "The soul takes pleasure in being alone, and waiting with loving attentiveness upon God, WITHOUT MAKING ANY PARTICULAR MEDITATION, IN INWARD PEACE AND QUIETNESS AND REST, AND WITHOUT ANY ACTS AND EXERCISES OF THE FACULTIES,"[774] at least without discursive acts, THAT IS, WITHOUT PASSING FROM ONE THING TO THE OTHER. All these elements are very important—this is a positive sign, the other two being negative.

The three signs must all be present together. The first alone, inability to meditate, may proceed from distraction and carelessness. When it does, there is a definite inclination to other particular objects. The second and first, inability to meditate plus distaste for particular objects, indifference, apathy, might proceed from "melancholy," which can produce a "certain absorption"[775] and torpor of the senses, which may even be enjoyable. It is not contemplation. St. Teresa also warns against this.[776] The third sign, positive inclination for loving attentiveness to God in solitude

---

773. *Complete Works of Saint John of the Cross*, 1.116 (Bk. II, c. 13.3), which reads ". . . no desire to fix his meditation or his sense upon other particular objects, exterior or interior."

774. *Complete Works of Saint John of the Cross*, 1.116 (Bk. II, c. 13.4), which reads ". . . and waits . . . without acts . . ."

775. *Complete Works of Saint John of the Cross*, 1.116-17 (Bk. II, c. 13.6).

776. See *Interior Castle*, IV.3 (*Complete Works of Saint Teresa*, 2.245-46).

and quiet, in a general but very definite and positive way, is *decisive*.

These signs should be known by directors. A vague awareness that there exists such a thing as passive and contemplative prayer, that it is a prayer without work of the imagination and faculties, but a failure to understand these precise requirements, leads many to encourage immature and unformed souls to engage in empty daydreaming and torpor or sleepiness. This prevents the real development of the interior life. What is important, then, is that one be ready and disposed to respond to the call of the Holy Spirit whenever and wherever He invites the soul to enter into this quiet, solitary and passive recollection, and that for this end one should be detached, free, unencumbered by particular objects of thought and concern, and by all particular attachments. More important, however, the director must not impede the advance of the soul called by God to this passive prayer.

3. THE LIVING FLAME, BOOK III: *the effects of bad direction*: the soul in aridity and "night," which is necessary for purification, comes to someone who insists that this is the result of sin or some other natural cause—laziness, tepidity, melancholy. Inexperienced and rigid directors tell the soul "that finds no consolation in the things of God"[777] to retrace its steps. They thus retard the soul and "double its miseries"[778] by increasing the load of suffering and self-reproach (cf. what was said above by St. Teresa[779]). "They make these souls go over their lives and cause them to

777. *Complete Works of Saint John of the Cross*, 1.13 (*Ascent*, Prologue 5), which reads: "And there will likewise be those who tell the soul to retrace its steps, since it is finding neither pleasure nor consolation in the things of God as it did aforetime."

778. *Complete Works of Saint John of the Cross*, 1.13 (*Ascent*, Prologue 5), which reads: "And in this way they double the trials of the poor soul; for it may well be that the greatest affliction which it is feeling is that of the knowledge of its own miseries, . . ."

779. See above, page 298.

make many general confessions and crucify them afresh."[780] The great fault of these confessors is that they trust in their own methods and know only one kind of (active) spirituality. They insist on forcing the soul to conform to the "books." They have no respect for the individual needs of the soul. They have no respect for or knowledge of the divine action. And St. John of the Cross insists on the preciseness and efficacy of this mysterious action of God, working secretly in the soul, unperceived, sometimes in great suffering. "THESE BLESSINGS [in contemplative prayer, even though arid] ARE INESTIMABLE; FOR THEY ARE MOST SECRET AND THEREFORE THE MOST DELICATE ANOINTINGS OF THE HOLY SPIRIT, WHICH SECRETLY FILL THE SOUL WITH SPIRITUAL RICHES AND GIFTS AND GRACES; SINCE IT IS GOD WHO DOES ALL THIS, HE DOES IT NOT OTHERWISE THAN AS GOD . . ." (*Living Flame*, III.{40}; p. 182).[781] READ also *Living Flame*, III.41[782] (these anointings {are} understood neither by the soul nor by the director but only by God). (But the slightest active intervention of the soul can spoil the work of God. Naturally this applies only to passive and mystical prayer and the director must know what this is.) READ *idem*, {n.} 42:[783] the great harm done—God's work

780. *Complete Works of Saint John of the Cross*, 1.13 (*Ascent*, Prologue 5), which reads: "such confessors, thinking that these things proceed from sin, make these souls . . ."

781. Copy text reads: "39"; text reads "But the blessings . . . are, as I say, inestimable; . . . the most secret . . ."

782. *Complete Works of Saint John of the Cross*, 3.182: "These anointings, then, and these touches, are the delicate and sublime acts of the Holy Spirit, which, on account of their delicate and subtle purity, can be understood neither by the soul nor by him that has to do with it, but only by Him Who infuses them, in order to make the soul more pleasing to Himself. These blessings, with the greatest facility, by no more than the slightest act which the soul may desire to make on its own account, with its memory, understanding or will, or by the applications of its sense or desire or knowledge or sweetness or pleasure, are disturbed or hindered in the soul, which is a grave evil and a great shame and pity."

783. *Complete Works of Saint John of the Cross*, 3.182-83: "Ah, how serious is this matter, and what cause it gives for wonder, that the evil done should be imperceptible, and the hindrance to those holy anointings which has been in-

defaced. {N.} 43: how great this evil is and how common—the "spiritual blacksmiths" who chide the contemplative for idleness in his prayer because he is not constantly "making acts," "doing something." "These other things are the practices of illuminists and fools."[784] {N.} 44: to make the soul "walk in sense"[785] when God is leading it passively in the ways of the spirit is to make it go backwards. {N.} 46: ESPECIALLY, "LET THEM NOT, THEREFORE, MERELY AIM AT GUIDING THESE SOULS ACCORDING TO THEIR OWN WAY AND THE MANNER SUITABLE TO THEMSELVES, BUT LET THEM SEE IF THEY KNOW THE WAY BY WHICH GOD IS LEADING THE SOUL AND IF THEY KNOW IT NOT, LET THEM LEAVE THE SOUL IN PEACE AND NOT DISTURB IT" (p. 184{-85}).

> These spiritual directors such as we have been describing fail to understand souls that have attained to this solitary and quiet contemplation, because they themselves have not arrived so far, nor learned what it means to leave behind the discursive reasoning of meditations, as I have said, and they think that these souls are idle. And therefore they disturb and impede the peace of this quiet and hushed contemplation which God has been giving their penitents by His own power, and they cause them to follow the road of meditation and imaginative reasoning and

---

terposed should be almost negligible, and yet that this harm that has been done should be a matter for greater sorrow and regret than the perturbation and ruin of many souls of a more ordinary nature which have not attained to a state of such supreme fineness and delicacy. It is as though a portrait of supreme and delicate beauty were touched by a coarse hand, and were daubed with coarse, crude colours. This would be a greater and more striking and pitiful shame than if many more ordinary faces were besmeared in this way. For when the work of so delicate a hand as this of the Holy Spirit has been thus roughly treated, who will be able to repair its beauty?"

784. *Complete Works of Saint John of the Cross*, 3.183, which reads: "there will come some spiritual director who has no knowledge save of hammering souls and pounding them with the faculties like a blacksmith, . . . '. . . Get to work, meditate and make interior acts, for it is right that you should do for yourself that which in you lies, for these other things . . .'"

785. *Complete Works of Saint John of the Cross*, 3.183.

make them perform interior acts, wherein the aforementioned souls find great repugnance, aridity and distraction, since they would fain remain in their holy rest and their quiet and peaceful state of recollection. But, as sense can perceive in this neither pleasure nor help nor activity, their directors persuade them to strive after sweetness and fervour, though they ought rather to advise them the contrary. The penitents, however, are unable to do as they did previously, and can enter into none of these things, for the time for them has now passed and they belong no more to their proper path; but the penitents are doubly disturbed and believe that they are going to perdition; and their directors encourage them in this belief and bring aridity to their spirits, and take from them the precious unctions wherewith God was anointing them in solitude and tranquillity. This, as I have said, is a great evil; their directors are plunging them into mire and mourning; for they are losing one thing and laboring without profit at the other (*Living Flame*, III.53).[786]

How then, we may ask, if you are only a hewer of wood, which signifies that you can make a soul despise the world and mortify its desires; or, if at best you are a carver, which means that you can lead a soul to holy meditations but can do no more: how, in such a case, will this soul attain to the final perfection of a delicate painting, the art of which consists neither in the hewing of the wood, nor in the carving of it, nor even in the outlining of it, but in the work which God Himself must do in it? It is certain, then, that if your instruction is always of one kind, and you cause the soul to be continually bound to you, it will either go backward, or, at the least, will not go forward. For what, I ask you, will the image be like, if you never do any work upon it save hewing and hammering, which in the language of the soul is the exercise of the faculties? When will this image be finished? When or how will it be left for God to paint it? Is it possible that you yourself can perform all these offices,

---

786. *Complete Works of Saint John of the Cross*, 3.189-90.

and consider yourself so consummate a master that this soul shall never need any other? (*ibid.*, 58).[787]

Good Direction {includes}:

1) Recognition of God's action, acceptance of the fact that when He works, no intervention of ours can be of help, but will only hinder. (See {the} Prologue to *Ascent*, p. 14: "Their penitents SHOULD BE LEFT TO THE PURGATION which God gives them, AND BE COMFORTED AND ENCOURAGED TO DESIRE IT until God be pleased to dispose otherwise; for until that time, no matter what the souls themselves may do and their confessors may say, there is *no remedy for them*.") The whole book of the *Ascent* and the *Dark Night* is concerned with instructions on the points mentioned here.

2) The director must be humble and detached from his own methods and acutely attentive to the divine action, objectively, and he must not attempt to impose a program of his own, no matter how much official approval this program may have.

3) The prudent director will try to understand "the way and the spirit by which God is leading" the soul, and in conformity with this way and spirit, to guarantee the following, as far as possible: solitude (interior but also to some extent exterior); tranquillity, liberty of spirit, "a certain freedom SO THAT THE BODILY AND EXTERIOR SENSES MAY NOT BE BOUND TO ANY EXTERIOR THING . . . .";[788] liberation from prescribed forms of prayer, even liturgical, though of course the obligation to participate in public prayer theoretically remains: but it can be fulfilled in solitude, in certain clear cases, which may however remain quite extraordinary. The norm {is} to fulfill all the communal obligations, but in a spirit of liberty and interior freedom, without constraint or pressure. "Let them strive to disencumber the soul and set it in a state of rest, in such a way that it will not be bound by any kind

---

787. *Complete Works of Saint John of the Cross*, 3.192.

788. *Complete Works of Saint John of the Cross*, 3.185 (stanza 3.46), which reads: ". . . so that the spiritual and bodily senses may not be bound to any particular thing, either interior or exterior . . . ."

of knowledge above or below [spiritual or material] or be fettered by any covetousness of any sweetness or pleasure or any other apprehension, but that it will be empty and in pure negation with respect to every creature and will be established in poverty of spirit" (vol. III, p. 185).[789]

Note: {one must} distinguish between *pure* negation and *mere* negation. *Pure* negation is actually in the highest sense positive, a recovery even of all created values in the light of God, darkly. *Mere* negation is simply the exclusion and negation of the creature, which in the first place is impossible, and in the second only encloses the mind in itself, which is disastrous. He says[790] that this is willed for us by Christ (Luke 14:33: "he that doth not renounce himself in all things cannot be my disciple"). This means not only surrender of material things but "the surrender of spiritual things, wherein is included poverty of spirit, in which, says the Son of God, consists blessedness" (p. 185). What is the value of this surrender? It is the cooperation demanded of the soul. If the soul surrenders everything, "IT IS IMPOSSIBLE THAT GOD SHOULD FAIL TO PERFORM HIS OWN PART BY COMMUNICATING HIMSELF TO THE SOUL, AT LEAST SECRETLY AND IN SILENCE."[791] N.B.: this has definite quietistic implications if it is not understood in the real sense in which it is intended by St. John of the Cross. He is referring to one who has clearly been called to infused prayer and has generously disposed himself by previous practice of meditation and active forms of prayer, with self-denial. It is not to be taken to mean that *anyone*, without previous formation, has simply to empty his mind and God will immediately fill it.

789. Text reads: ". . . bound to any particular kind of knowledge, either above or below, . . . by covetousness . . . empty in pure . . ."

790. *Complete Works of Saint John of the Cross*, 3.185.

791. Text reads: "it is impossible, if the soul does as much as in it lies, that God . . ." (Note that the omitted clause speaks to the implications of quietism mentioned in the following sentence.)

Summary: the work of the director is to lead the soul to this *full surrender* and freedom of spirit, according to its own capacities, in the way of evangelical perfection, "which is detachment and emptiness of sense and spirit."[792] This must be brought about by quietness and love, not by force and imprecations. When the soul is thus empty, it does not need to "do anything" further, for God will act in it, says St. John of the Cross (p. 186).[793]

> Oh, souls! Since God is showing you such sovereign mercies as to lead you through this state of solitude and recollection, withdrawing you from your labours of sense, return not to sense again. Lay aside your operations, for, though once they helped you to deny the world and yourselves, when you were beginners, they will now be a great obstacle and hindrance to you, since God is granting you the grace of Himself working within you. If you are careful to set your faculties upon naught soever, withdrawing them from everything and in no way hindering them, which is the proper part for you to play in this state alone, and if you wait upon God with loving and pure attentiveness, as I said above, in the way which I there described (working no violence to the soul, save to detach it from everything and set it free, lest you disturb and spoil its peace and tranquillity) God will feed your soul for you with heavenly food, since you are not hindering Him (65; p. 197).
>
> The soul in this state of quiet must bear in mind that, although it may not be conscious of making any progress or of doing anything, it is making much more progress than if it were walking on its feet; for God is bearing it in His arms, and thus, although it is making progress at the

---

792. *Complete Works of Saint John of the Cross*, 3.186 (stanza 3.47), which reads: ". . . of sense and of spirit."

793. Text reads: "For if it is true that it is doing nothing, then, by this very fact that it is doing nothing, I will now prove to you that it is doing a great deal. For . . . the more it empties itself of particular knowledge and of the acts of understanding, the greater is the progress of the understanding in its journey to the highest spiritual good."

rate willed by God Himself, it is not conscious of movement. And although it is not working with its own faculties, it is nevertheless accomplishing much more than if it were doing so, since God is working within it. And it is not remarkable that the soul should be unable to see this, for sense cannot perceive that which God works in the soul at this time, since it is done in silence; for, as the Wise Man says, the words of wisdom are heard in silence. Let the soul remain in the hands of God and entrust itself neither to its own hands nor to those of these two blind guides; for, if it remains thus and occupies not its faculties in anything, it will make sure progress (67; p. 198).

This is clarified by further statements of principle: the intellect must not be forced to work, because the soul approaches God by faith. (Hence a distinction is necessary, for faith is a work of the intellect as well as the will, but on a level above discourse.) "It is a progress in darkness for faith is darkness to the understanding."[794] Even though the understanding is darkened the *will is not idle*. It may be moved by God without knowledge, "just as a person can be warmed by a fire without seeing the fire" (188).

> In this way the will may oftentimes feel itself to be enkindled or filled with tenderness and love without knowing or understanding anything more distinctly than before, since God is introducing love into it, even as the Bride says in the Songs, in these words: The King made me enter the cellar of wine, and ordained love in me. There is no reason, therefore, to fear that the will may be idle in this case; for, if of itself it leaves performing acts of love concerning particular kinds of knowledge, God performs them within it, inebriating it in infused love, either by means of the knowledge of contemplation, or without such knowledge, as we have just said; and these acts are as much more delectable and meritorious than those made by the soul as the mover and infuser of this love—namely, God—is better than the soul (III.50; p. 188).

---

794. *Complete Works of Saint John of the Cross*, 3.187 (stanza 3.48).

God CAUSES THE ACTS OF THE NATURAL FACULTIES TO FAIL (characteristic of St. John of the Cross) in order to work in them Himself in a way that is not apprehended (p. 190). Finally, OF GREAT IMPORTANCE: the director must *not put obstacles in the way of ascent to a higher and more contemplative form of life* when there are signs that a vocation to higher contemplation exists (see especially p. 194[795]).

4. *THE DARK NIGHT OF THE SOUL:* we will here briefly summarize the main ideas of this classic of the mystical life which is most characteristic of St. John of the Cross. First of all, it must not be regarded as a separate treatise. It forms one single work with *The Ascent of Mount Carmel.* It is in reality the second part of a diptych, the *Ascent* dealing with the active purification (night) of sense and spirit. The *Dark Night* deals with passive or mystical purification. The *Ascent* is the asceticism of purification; the *Dark Night* is the mystical treatment of the same. Note therefore that of all ascetic writers St. John of the Cross really has the least to say and places the least emphasis on exterior works of mortification, and the most to say about interior detachment, giving the greatest place to the work of the theological virtues and the passive activity of the Holy Spirit.

Book I of the *Dark Night* deals with the *night of sense.* Where does the night of sense come in the spiritual life? It is a *transition* by which one passes from the "state of beginners . . . which is the state of those who meditate, to the state of contemplation, which is for the proficient."[796] We have already considered the active aspect of this sufficiently and need not insist further. Chapters 2 to 7 are however important. Here he runs through the

---

795. Stanza 3.62.

796. *Complete Works of Saint John of the Cross,* 1.350 (*Dark Night,* 1.1), which reads: "Into this dark night souls begin to enter when God draws them forth from the state of beginners—which is the state of those that meditate upon the spiritual road—and begins to set them in the state of progressives—which is that of those who are already contemplatives—to the end that, after passing through it, they may arrive at the state of the perfect, which is that of the Divine union of the soul with God."

"spiritual vices,"[797] that is to say, the capital sins, as they are found on a deep spiritual level, not formal sins but principles of semi-deliberate sin and imperfection which keep a man back from true progress. This section can profitably be read by everyone. Every director should know these chapters well. THE PRINCIPLE LAID DOWN IS CHARACTERISTIC: AFTER THE DESCRIPTION OF EACH SPIRITUAL VICE, HE REMINDS THE READER THAT IT CANNOT BE GOT RID OF EXCEPT BY PASSIVE PURIFICATION. This is crucial for the understanding of St. John of the Cross. In reality he does not insist as strongly as some think on active works of mortification (though asceticism and self-denial are absolutely essential). His true stress is on passive purification. Two important corollaries {are}:

a) no amount of active ascetic effort can substitute for passive purification;

b) an unwise insistence on active asceticism can actually interfere with and impede the really important action of inner passive purification operated in the soul by the Holy Spirit.

{For} examples of the spiritual vices, see: p. 351 (n. 3);[798] pride: p. 352, 354, 356;[799] spiritual gluttony *re* communion (p. 366; n. 5[800]).

---

797. See *Dark Night*, Bk. 1, c. 2.2 (*Complete Works of Saint John of the Cross*, 1.352), which reads: "For the devil knows quite well that all these works and virtues which they perform are not only valueless to them, but even become vices in them."

798. This section discusses ascetical practices engaged in by beginners in the spiritual life for the sake of the consolation and pleasure they bring.

799. In this chapter (Bk. 1, c. 2) John speaks of beginners who take pride and satisfaction in their own works of piety and despise others who have what they perceive to be less devotion than themselves (n. 1); who grow despondent about their own imperfections and beg God to take them away, not realizing that thereby their pride would increase (n. 5); who are contrasted with the humble, who acknowledge their own imperfections and are given the grace to cast out evil from themselves by God, "even as He denies it to the proud."

800. "These persons, in communicating, strive with every nerve to obtain some kind of sensible sweetness and pleasure, instead of humbly doing reverence and giving praise within themselves to God. . . . [T]hey have not realized

Chapter 8: here he distinguishes the *night of sense from the night of the spirit*. The night of sense {is} a transition from a sensible and reasonable level to the level where *sense is subject to spirit*. It is, strictly speaking, not the true spiritual life but a preparation for it. {It} is the "adolescence" of the spiritual life. Many enter the night of sense—it is common; {but} few progress in it. Later he will say also (Bk. II, c. 3) that the function of the night of sense is to unite sense and spirit together.[801] The night of spirit then brings *about the real deep purgation of both sense and spirit in one*. This is important for a true understanding of St. John. {In} the night of spirit, the true spiritual life begins: *the spirit is subjected to God*. "It is the portion of very few."[802] The distinction has been ignored or overlooked, says St. John of the Cross: "very little has been said of this."[803]

Chapters 9 to 13 {include} further interesting material on the night of sense, most of which simply elaborates in greater detail and succinctness the points with which we have become familiar above, {so that they} need not be treated here. See chapter 10 for advice on what to do in the night of sense.[804] Chapter 11 stresses the passive elements in the night of sense. Chapter 12 is particularly useful as it lists the *benefits of the night of sense*. If we are fully aware of these benefits and convinced of their importance, we will have less trouble understanding the need to pass through the night of sense with patience and submission to God. We will

---

that the least of the advantages which comes from this Most Holy Sacrament is that which concerns the senses; . . ."

801. *Complete Works of Saint John of the Cross*, 1.402, which reads: "These souls, then, have now become proficients, because of the time which they have spent in feeding the senses with sweet communications, so that their sensual part, being thus attracted and delighted by spiritual pleasure, which came to it from the spirit, may be united with the spirit and made one with it."

802. *Complete Works of Saint John of the Cross*, 1.371 (*Dark Night*, Bk. 1, c. 8.1), which reads: "The night of the spirit is the portion of very few."

803. *Complete Works of Saint John of the Cross*, 1.371 (*Dark Night*, Bk. 1, c. 8.2).

804. The soul is advised to persevere in patience and trust, remaining in peace and quietness beyond all thought and knowledge, even though it appears that it is doing nothing (*Complete Works of Saint John of the Cross*, 1.378-81).

get a better perspective of what it is all about. The night of sense brings one to genuine strength and maturity so that one can truly begin the spiritual life (i.e., mystical life). The benefits are given precisely when they seem to be taken away. Thus in apparent anguish and dryness we receive peace and fervor, on a higher level. The night of sense, while seemingly depriving us of {an} ability to pray, brings us to a state where we are able to pray constantly in *habitual remembrance of God*. Above all it has the advantage of liberating us from all kinds of interior and subtle imperfections. This too is important because it makes us see that we cannot get rid of these imperfections by thinking about them, examining ourselves and "working at" them. On the contrary we must in some sense forget them, and let God take them away in the night of sense. Read pages 392 (nn. 7 to 9)[805] and n. 10,[806]

805. "7. With respect to the imperfections of the other three spiritual sins which we have described above, which are wrath, envy and sloth, the soul is purged hereof likewise in this aridity of the desire and acquires the virtues opposed to them; for, softened and humbled by these aridities and hardships and other temptations and trials wherein God exercises it during this night, it becomes meek with respect to God, and to itself, and likewise with respect to its neighbour. So that it is no longer angry with itself and disturbed because of its own faults, nor with its neighbour because of his faults, neither is it displeased with God, nor does it utter unseemly complaints because He does not quickly make it holy. 8. Then, as to envy, the soul has charity toward others in this respect also; for, if it has any envy, this is no longer a vice as it was before, when it was grieved because others were preferred to it and given greater advantage. Its grief now comes from seeing how great is its own misery, and its envy (if it has any) is a virtue, since it desires to imitate others, which is great virtue. 9. Neither are the sloth and the weariness which it now has concerning spiritual things vicious as they were before; for in the past these sins proceeded from the spiritual pleasures which the soul sometimes experienced and sought after when it found them not. But this new weariness proceeds not from this insufficiency of pleasure, because God has taken from the soul pleasure in all things in this purgation of the desire."

806. "Besides these benefits which have been mentioned, the soul attains innumerable others by means of this arid contemplation. For often, in the midst of these times of aridity and hardship, God communicates to the soul, when it is least expecting it, the purest spiritual sweetness and love, together with a spiri-

{on} how the spiritual vices ({see} above) are purged by aridity, {and the} summary of purification of sense (p. 394, n. 15)[807] {on the} quieting of {the} four passions of joy, hope, fear and grief.

Book I ends with the thought of *transition to the night of spirit* (c. 14). There are references to the special severity of the night of sense in those who are to pass on to the night of spirit. For others, the night of sense remains relatively easy. How long must the night of sense continue? It cannot be said with certainty. This depends on the vocation of each individual. It may be especially long for "the weak" who get it in feeble doses, alleviated by consolations. But also those who are to go on further generally remain a long time in the night of sense. Some remain always "neither in the night nor out of it."[808] These statements might be discussed, but time requires that we pass on.

Book II: the NIGHT OF THE SOUL: the transition continues. After "a long time, even years"[809] in the night of sense, the soul

---

tual knowledge which is sometimes very delicate, each manifestation of which is of greater benefit and worth than those which the soul enjoyed aforetime; although in its beginnings the soul thinks that this is not so, for the spiritual influence now granted to it is very delicate and cannot be perceived by sense."

807. "When, therefore, the four passions of the soul—which are joy, grief, hope and fear—are calmed through continual mortification; when the natural desires have been lulled to sleep, in the sensual nature of the soul, by means of habitual times of aridity; and when the harmony of the senses and the interior faculties causes a suspension of labour and a cessation from the work of meditation, as we have said (which is the dwelling and the household of the lower part of the soul), these enemies cannot obstruct this spiritual liberty, and the house remains at rest and quiet, as says the following line: **My house being now at rest.**"

808. *Complete Works of Saint John of the Cross*, 1.396, which reads: "But those who are very weak are kept for a long time in this night, and these He purges very gently and with slight temptations. Such are neither properly in the night nor properly out of it; . . ."

809. *Complete Works of Saint John of the Cross*, 1.398 (*Dark Night*, Bk. 2, c. 1.1); the text actually says not that the soul spends years in the night of sense, but rather that after leaving "the aridities and trials of the first purgation and the night of sense . . . it is wont to pass a long time, even years, after leaving the state of beginners, in exercising itself in that of proficients." Thus St. John does

is prepared for {the} night of spirit. He does not make clear here, but does elsewhere, that after the night of sense there may be a period of deeply consoled contemplation and prayer of union (betrothal). Note however that even when one has reached this, the purification of the senses is not perfect. The purification of sense is not really complete until one has passed *well into the night of the spirit*. During the consolations of mystical prayer after {the} night of sense, there are also periods of darkness, renewals of {the} night of sense, "sometimes more intense than those of the past,"[810] but they are always transient. {The principal} difference {is that} the darknesses of this period are *not continual*, as those of {the} night of spirit are. In this transition period after {the} night of sense, we run into the "defects of proficients"[811] which, says St. John, require the night of the spirit to be purified. What are these defects? Through weakness, mystical grace causes ecstasies, visions, etc. These are not signs of consummate sanctity, but rather, in his eyes, signs of weakness and deficiency. The body is also affected adversely and suffers illness caused by the force of mystical grace, disrupting the weak organism. Moral imperfections spring from forms of pride and self-complacency; overconfident in one's own perfection and overestimating one's experience, one can become *overfamiliar* with God. One can become deceived as to his true state, imagining himself better than he is, taking himself for a prophet, etc. when he is not. Humility may suffer greatly, and mysticism may turn to presumption. Note {the} genuine problem of the mystic who "goes wrong." {He is} not strictly a "false mystic," but he begins to be led by his own

---

at least suggest here, despite what Merton says in the following sentence, that the night of sense is followed by a period of contemplative illumination.

810. *Complete Works of Saint John of the Cross*, 1.398 (*Dark Night*, Bk. 2, c. 1.1), which reads: "darknesses and perils which are sometimes much more intense than those of the past."

811. St. John speaks of "certain imperfections and perils which belong to these proficients" (*Complete Works of Saint John of the Cross*, 1.400; *Dark Night*, Bk. 2, c. 1.3).

spirit, and that of his group, and does much harm. All this demands the night of the spirit, "so that one may walk in pure faith which is the proper and adequate means whereby the soul is united to God" (c. 2, n. 5).[812]

Now we come to the classical passages on the night of the spirit. Let us look at these chapters in a little more detail. {In} Book II, chapter 4, the dark night is described as "contemplation or detachment or poverty of spirit, which is here almost one and the same thing."[813] The dark night is a "going forth from myself . . . from my poor and limited manner of experiencing God, without being hindered by sensuality and the devil."[814] Remember, he is commenting on his own stanzas: "On a dark night, kindled in love with yearnings—oh, happy chance! / I went forth without being observed, my house being now at rest."[815]

> This was a great happiness and a good chance for me; for, when the faculties had been perfectly annihilated and calmed, together with the passions, desires and affections of my soul, wherewith I had experienced and tasted God after a lowly manner, I went forth *from my own human way and operation to the operation and way of God. That is to say, my understanding went forth from itself, turning from the human and natural to* the Divine; for, when it is united with God by means of this purgation, *its understanding no longer comes through its natural light and vigour,* but through the Divine Wisdom wherewith it has become united. And my will went forth from itself, becoming Divine; for, being united with Divine love, it no longer loves with its natural strength after a lowly manner, but with strength and purity from the Holy Spirit; and thus the will, which

812. *Complete Works of Saint John of the Cross*, 1.402, which reads: "and be made to walk in dark and pure faith, . . ."

813. *Complete Works of Saint John of the Cross*, 1.404, which reads: ". . . which here are almost . . ."

814. *Complete Works of Saint John of the Cross*, 1.404, which reads: ". . . I went forth from myself . . . hindered therein by sensuality or the devil."

815. *Complete Works of Saint John of the Cross*, 1.404.

is now near to God, acts not after a human manner, and similarly the memory has become transformed into eternal apprehensions of glory. And finally, by means of this night and purgation of the old man, *all the energies and affections of the soul are wholly renewed into a Divine temper and Divine delight* (p. 405).

Comment: note the essential elements of the dark night expressed here:

a) a going forth from the human way and operation to the way and operation of God;

b) a total transformation or "divinization" of "all the energies and affections of the soul";

c) implicitly this is the fulfillment of the baptismal vocation, for at baptism grace, and divinization, take possession of the inmost substance of the soul, but the faculties continue nevertheless to be capable of sin and even in good actions to proceed in "a human manner" (i.e. with many imperfections).

Chapter 5, n.1: THIS DARK NIGHT IS AN INFLOWING OF GOD INTO THE SOUL WHICH PURGES IT FROM ITS IGNORANCES AND IMPERFECTIONS, HABITUAL, NATURAL AND SPIRITUAL (p. 405). It is called by contemplatives infused contemplation or mystical theology. It is direct and purely supernatural action of God on the soul, not only purifying but instructing. The purifying power is the Holy Spirit, and divine love. It is "the same loving wisdom that purges the blessed spirits and enlightens them."[816] {He considers} why this night causes torment and suffering:

> But the question arises: Why is the Divine light (which, as we say, illumines and purges the soul from its ignorances) here called by the soul a dark night? To this the answer is that for two reasons this Divine wisdom is not only night and darkness for the soul, *but is likewise affliction and torment.* The first is because of *the height of Divine Wisdom, which tran-*

---

816. *Complete Works of Saint John of the Cross*, 1.406.

scends the talent of the soul, and in this way is darkness to it; the
second, because of its vileness and impurity, in which respect it is
painful and afflictive to it, and is also dark (p. 406).

He then goes on to develop an extensive philosophical argument, based on the principle that "two contraries cannot coexist in one subject,"[817] and the purity of God and the impurity of the soul come into conflict. Also the transcendent greatness of God and the weakness and limitations of the soul cause conflict when they are brought face to face. The mere opposition of divine power and human infirmity causes conflict. Yet this is the merciful love of God which though it causes suffering does so out of tenderness and love.

> Beneath the power of this oppression and weight the soul feels itself so far from being favoured that it thinks, and correctly so, that even that wherein it was wont to find some help has vanished with everything else, and that there is none who has pity upon it. To this effect Job says likewise: Have pity upon me, have pity upon me, at least ye my friends, because the hand of the Lord has touched me. A thing of great wonder and pity is it that the soul's weakness and impurity should now be so great that, though the hand of God is of itself so light and gentle, the soul should now feel it to be so heavy and so contrary, though it neither weighs it down nor rests upon it, but only touches it, and that mercifully, since He does this in order to grant the soul favours and not to chastise it (p. 408).

This is the basic pattern, which he goes on to develop with many illustrations from Scripture and observations from his own experience. We will simply enumerate some of the points he raises:

1) The positive aspect of the dark night is stressed. It is a time of blessings, and although a time of tremendous suffering and darkness it is also a time of deep inner joy. St. Catherine of Genoa

---

817. *Complete Works of Saint John of the Cross*, 1.407 (*Dark Night*, Bk. 2, c. 5.4).

also says this about the souls in Purgatory.[818] The darkness of the dark night is for the sake of light, the misery for the sake of joy; hence joy and light and mercy always have the primacy. Indeed the same light that torments and purifies the soul will also eventually be the source of its greatest delight (see c. 10, n. 3).[819]

2) Aspects of the trial (numbers refer to chapters and sections of Bk. II): it must last several years (7.4); {it is} difficult to believe the director {who is} offering consolation (7.3); intervals of relief come, but followed by worse affliction (7.4-6, 10.7-9; 12.1-6); {there is an} inability to pray or to love (8.1), {an} incapacity for temporal interests and joys (8.1), {an} annihilation of the intellect, memory and will (8.2); the simpler the divine light, the more it purifies (8.2). READ 8.3 (the sunlight in the window)[820] {and} 8.4 (emptiness).[821]

818. See *Treatise on Purgatory*, chapter 12, entitled, "How Suffering in Purgatory is Coupled with Joy": "It is true that love for God which fills the soul to overflowing gives it, so I see it, a happiness beyond what can be told, but this happiness takes not one pang from the pain of the souls in purgatory. . . . So that the souls in purgatory enjoy the greatest happiness and endure the greatest pain; the one does not hinder the other" (*Late Medieval Mysticism*, 408); similar statements are found in chapters 2, 5 and 16 (400–401, 403, 410–11).

819. Here St. John uses the famous similitude of the fire which, in transforming the wood into itself, first prepares it for that purpose: see n. 825.

820. *Complete Works of Saint John of the Cross*, 1.420: "We observe that a ray of sunlight which enters through the window is the less clearly visible according as it is the purer and freer from specks, and the more of such specks and motes there are in the air, the brighter is the light to the eye. The reason is that it is not the light itself that is seen; the light is but the means whereby the other things that it strikes are seen, and then it is also seen itself, through its having struck them; had it not struck them, neither it nor they would have been seen. Thus if the ray of sunlight entered through the window of one room and passed out through another on the other side, traversing the room, and if it met nothing on the way, or if there were no specks in the air for it to strike, the room would have no more light than before, neither would the ray of light be visible. In fact, if we consider it carefully, there is more darkness in the path of the ray of sunlight, because it overwhelms and darkens any other light, and yet it is itself invisible, because, as we have said, there are no visible objects which it can strike."

821. *Complete Works of Saint John of the Cross*, 1.420-21: "Now this is precisely what this Divine ray of contemplation does in the soul. Assailing it with

A reason for the purgation {is that} one *particular* affection that remains is enough to impede the whole general joy of the soul in the "ALL" (9.2). {There is} "substantial darkness"[822] in the substance of the soul (9.3), anguish, "roaring" (9.7),[823] apparent doubt and despair (9.8-9: READ[824]). READ 10.1-2: the fire and the log of wood.[825]

---

its Divine light, it transcends the natural power of the soul, and herein it darkens it and deprives it of all natural affections and apprehensions which it apprehended aforetime by means of natural light; and thus it leaves it not only dark, but likewise empty, according to its faculties and desires, both spiritual and natural. And, by thus leaving it empty and in darkness, it purges and illumines it with Divine spiritual light even when the soul thinks not that it has this light, but believes itself to be in darkness, even as we have said of the ray of light, which, although it be in the midst of the room, yet, if it be pure and meet nothing on its path, is not visible."

822. *Complete Works of Saint John of the Cross*, 1.424.

823. *Complete Works of Saint John of the Cross*, 1.427.

824. *Complete Works of Saint John of the Cross*, 1.427-28: "8. Such is the work wrought in the soul by this night that hides the hopes of the light of day. With regard to this the prophet Job says likewise: In the night my mouth is pierced with sorrows and they that feed upon me sleep not. Now here by the mouth is understood the will, which is pierced with these pains that tear the soul to pieces, neither ceasing nor sleeping, for the doubts and misgivings which pierce the soul in this way never cease. 9. Deep is this warfare and this striving, for the peace which the soul hopes for will be very deep; and the spiritual pain is intimate and delicate, for the love which it will possess will likewise be very intimate and refined. The more intimate and the more perfect the finished work is to be and to remain, the more intimate, perfect and pure must be the labour; the firmer the edifice, the harder the labour. Wherefore, as Job says, the soul is fading within itself, and its vitals are being consumed without any hope. Similarly, because in the state of perfection toward which it journeys by means of this purgative night the soul will attain to the possession and fruition of innumerable blessings, of gifts and virtues, both according to the substance of the soul and likewise according to its faculties, it must needs see and feel itself withdrawn from them all and deprived of them all and be empty and poor without them; and it must needs believe itself to be so far from them that it cannot persuade itself that it will ever reach them, but rather it must be convinced that all its good things are over. The words of Jeremiah have a similar meaning in that passage already quoted, where he says: I have forgotten good things."

825. *Complete Works of Saint John of the Cross*, 1.429-30: "1. For the greater clearness of what has been said, and of what has still to be said, it is well to

After Book II, chapter 11, he goes into a further treatment of the more positive aspects and the union for which the soul is being prepared.

3) Union: the wound of love (c. 11: study and comment). Note especially, he says that this perfection of pure love is the true fulfillment of the first commandment which "sets aside nothing pertaining to man."[826] It is very important to stress this here. *This is the recovery, the reintegration* of all that is good in man, all

---

observe at this point that this purgative and loving knowledge or Divine light whereof we here speak acts upon the soul which is purged and prepared for perfect union with it in the same way as fire acts upon a log of wood in order to transform it into itself; for material fire, acting upon wood, first of all begins to dry it, by driving out its moisture and causing it to shed the water which it contains within itself. Then it begins to make it black, dark and unsightly, and even to give forth a bad odour, and, as it dries it little by little, it brings out and drives away all the dark and unsightly accidents which are contrary to the nature of fire. And, finally, it begins to kindle it externally and give it heat, and at last transforms it into itself and makes it as beautiful as fire. In this respect, the wood has neither passivity nor activity of its own, save for its weight, which is greater, and its substance, which is denser, than that of fire, for it has in itself the properties and activities of fire. Thus it is dry and it dries; it is hot and heats; it is bright and gives brightness; and it is much less heavy than before. All these properties and effects are caused in it by the fire. 2. In this same way we have to philosophize with respect to this Divine fire of contemplative love, which, before it unites and transforms the soul in itself, first purges it of all its contrary accidents. It drives out its unsightliness, and makes it black and dark, so that it seems worse than before and more unsightly and abominable than it was wont to be. For this Divine purgation is removing all the evil and vicious humours which the soul has never perceived because they have been so deeply rooted and grounded in it; it has never realized, in fact, that it has had so much evil within itself. But now that they are to be driven forth and annihilated, these humours reveal themselves, and become visible to the soul because it is so brightly illumined by this dark light of Divine contemplation (although it is no worse than before, either in itself or in relation to God); and, as it sees in itself that which it saw not before, it is clear to it that it is not only unfit for God to see it, but that it deserves His abhorrence and that He does indeed abhor it. By this comparison we can now understand many things concerning what we are saying and purpose to say."

826. *Complete Works of Saint John of the Cross*, 1.434 (Bk. 2, c. 11.4).

his energies and faculties, and the total consecration of them to God, purified and divinized. Nothing human is excluded or lost; all is transfigured. The humanism of St. John of the Cross and of the Church is here seen at its highest level.

> In this way it can be realized in some measure how great and how strong may be this enkindling of love in the spirit, where God keeps in recollection all the energies, faculties and desires of the soul, both of spirit and of sense, so that all this harmony may employ its energies and virtues in this love, and may thus attain to a true fulfilment of the first commandment, which sets aside nothing pertaining to man nor excludes from this love anything that is his, but says: Thou shalt love thy God with all thy heart and with all thy mind, with all thy soul and with all thy strength (p. 434).

This must suffice as our treatment of the great theme of the dark night. These too brief notes may be enough to enable some to enter upon a personal study of this classic.

APPENDIX TO MYSTICAL THEOLOGY

Appendix I: The *SCALA CLAUSTRALIUM*

The Scala Claustralium sive Tractatus de mode orandi[827] (PL 184—note other contents of this volume[828]) {is} a typical medieval treatise on the interior life, by Guigo (?) the Carthusian, important because it is a first-class example of the medieval approach to *lectio, meditatio, oratio, contemplatio,*[829] and contains not only pure doctrine but clear examples of the language of medieval spirituality—largely the language of St. Bernard.

---

827. *The Ladder of Monks, or Treatise on the Way to Pray* (PL 184, cols. 475A-484D).

828. This volume includes works falsely attributed to St. Bernard, including sermons by Gilbert of Hoyland, treatises by William of St. Thierry, including the *Golden Epistle*, the treatise on *Jesus at Twelve Years* of Aelred of Rievaulx, and various other sermons and meditations, most dating from the twelfth century.

829. Col. 475C: "reading, meditation, prayer and contemplation."

{It opens with the} *Epistola ad Gervasium*.[830] Note {its} brevity, succinctness, unction: "*quoniam de servitute Pharaonis, te delicata solitudine laudabili furto surripiens, in ordinata castrorum acie collocasti; ramum de oleastro artificiose excisum prudenter inserens in oliva*."[831] Chapter 1.2: at manual labor, meditating on {the} spiritual life, he thinks of four steps of a ladder "reaching from earth to heaven":[832] *lectio quaerit—cibum ori apponit—inspectio;*[833] *meditatio invenit—masticat et frangit—studium*.[834] (Further development {is found in} chapter 11: by meditation: *ruminando succum eliciamus; {et} transglutiendo* usque ad cordis intima {*transmittamus ut*} *ex his {diligenter} consideramus statum nostrum et studeamus {eorum} opera agere*.[835]) *Oratio postulat—saporem acquirit—devotio*.[836] (Special emphasis {is placed} on prayer because by it we *open our heart* to God, and submit, *consenting to His grace*, and this is essential. *Ad hoc ut fructuosa sit meditatio, oportet ut sequatur* orationis devotio, *cujus quasi effectus est* contemplationis dulcedo.[837]) *Contemplatio*

830. "Letter to [Brother] Gervase" (col. 475BC).

831. Col. 475BC: "because by a praiseworthy theft you have stolen yourself away from the slavery of Pharaoh in delightful solitude and have placed yourself in the ordered ranks of the camp; you have prudently grafted onto the olive tree a branch skillfully cut from the wild olive."

832. Col. 475C.

833. Col. 476C: "reading seeks—puts food in the mouth—examination"; the text reads "*inquirit*" but then, in reference to Mt. 7:7, adds, "*Quaerite legendo*" ("Seek by reading"); the final word here, as in the three subsequent groupings, is adapted from a phrase quoted in full below.

834. Col. 476C: "Meditation finds—chews and breaks up—study."

835. Col. 481D: "by chewing let us draw out the juice; by swallowing let us pass it on all the way to the center of the heart so that through these words we might reflect on our state and be eager diligently to do the same works" (copy text reads: "*eliciamus; transglutiendo . . . transmittimus ex his consideramus . . . studeamus opera . . .*").

836. Col. 476C: "Prayer begs—receives a taste—devotion."

837. Col. 482C (c. 11), which reads: "*Ad hoc ergo . . .*": "And so for meditation to be fruitful, it must be followed by the devotion of prayer, the effect of which is, as it were, the sweetness of contemplation."

degustat—est ipsa dulcedo *quae jucundat et reficit—dulcedo.*[838] (See chapter 12: *Lectio sine meditatione arida; meditatio sine lectione, erronea; oratio sine meditatione tepida; meditatio sine oratione, infructuosa; oratio cum devotione contemplationis acquisitiva; contemplationis adeptio sine oratione, aut rara, aut miraculosa.*[839])

Definitions: *lectio—sedula scripturarum cum animi intentione inspectio;*[840] *meditatio—studiosa mentis actio, occultae veritatis notitiam ductu propriae rationis investigans;*[841] *oratio—*devota cordis intentio *in Deum pro malis amovendis, et bonis adipiscendis;*[842] *contemplatio—mentis in Deum suspensae elevatio, aeternae dulcedinis gaudia degustans.*[843]

End of chapter 2: *lectio—*how it operates: he takes an example of a text from Scripture, *"Beati mundo corde."*[844] {The} reader says, "There is something good here,"[845] very precious, this purity of heart, which gives {the} vision of God. Redibo ad cor meum, *et tentabo si forte intelligere et invenire potero munditiam hanc.*[846] Note

---

838. Col. 476C: "Contemplation enjoys—it is sweetness itself which delights and revives—sweetness."

839. Col. 482CD, which reads: ". . . *arida est; . . . est tepida; . . .*": "Reading without meditation is dry; meditation without reading is erroneous; prayer without meditation is lukewarm; meditation without prayer is unfruitful; prayer with devotion leads to contemplation; attaining contemplation without prayer is either rare or miraculous."

840. Col. 476C (c.1): "reading [is] the careful examination of the scriptures with an attentive mind."

841. Col. 476C (c.1): "meditation [is] the diligent activity of the mind, seeking out knowledge of hidden truth under the guidance of one's own reason."

842. Col. 476C (c.1): "prayer [is] the fervent focus of the heart on God in order to banish what is evil and acquire what is good."

843. Col. 476C (c.1): "contemplation [is] the raising up of the mind beyond itself to God, tasting the joys of eternal sweetness."

844. Col. 476D: "Blessed are the pure of heart, [for they shall see God]" (Mt. 5:8).

845. Col. 477A, which reads: *"Potest aliquid boni esse"* ("There can be something good").

846. Col. 477A: "I shall return to my heart, and see if perhaps I am able to understand and discover this purity."

{the} emphasis on returning to the heart, "finding the heart." *Lectio* awakens this desire.

Chapter 3: *officium meditationis*[847] (continues {the} example {by} meditation on "*Beati mundo corde*")—*Sedula meditatio, non remanet extra, interiora penetrat, singula rimatur.*[848] But note how:

1) by comparison and contrast:

a) what is said and what is excluded (*corde—non corpore*[849]);

b) Scripture is brought in to give light (other passages where *cor mundum* is used[850]);

c) seeing the Face of God—contrast the "vile aspect"[851] of the suffering servant and the beauty of God seen by the pure of heart.

2) by summarizing: all satiety {is} included in {the} vision of God: *satiabor, cum apparuerit gloria tua.*[852] He takes a word of Scripture which ties all up in one bundle, then comments: *Videsne quantum liquoris emanavit ex minima uva; quantus ignis ex hac scintilla ortus est.*[853] And yet the well is deep—much more water can be drawn from it.

Chapter 2, n. 4: *spiritual senses* begin to come into action: *fracto alabastro suavitatem unguenti praesentire incipit, necdum gustu, sed quasi narium odoratu.*[854] This leads to another inference from

---

847. Col. 477A: "The Exercise of Meditation" (title of c. 3).

848. Col. 477B, which includes an additional phrase between "*extra*" and "*interiora*": "earnest meditation does not remain on the surface but penetrates to the center and investigates each particular point."

849. Col. 477B, which reads: "*non dixit,* Beati mundo *corpore; sed* corde" ("It does not say, 'Blessed are the pure of body; but of heart'").

850. Psalm 23[24]:4, Psalm 50[51]:12, but also passages where the precise phrase is not found (Ps. 65[66]:18; Job 31:1).

851. Col. 477C.

852. Col. 477D: "I shall be satisfied when your glory appears" (Ps. 16[17]:15).

853. Col. 477D: "do you see how much juice has come forth from the smallest grape; how much fire has sprung up from this spark?"

854. Col. 477D: "when the jar has been broken it begins to make evident the sweetness of the ointment, not yet by taste, but as though by its fragrance to the nose."

the sweetness of the meditation: what must be the sweetness of the reality experienced. *But* this in turn leads to conflict and crisis, {a} sense that one does not have the capacity to attain to such experience, yet {has a} great desire for it. *Habendi desiderio aestuat, sed non invenit apud se quomodo habere possit: et quanto plus inquirit, plus sitit. Dum apponit meditationem, apponit et dolorem.*[855] For the experience is not to be attained by our own efforts, only through the gift of God. It is a gift of wisdom—*sapidam scilicet scientiam, quae animam, cui inhaesit, inaestimabili sapore jucundat et reficit.*[856] The Lord alone gives this wisdom and this experience for He alone can operate the transformation necessary in the soul that is to experience divine things. *Hic est qui sapientiae saporem dat, et sapidam animam facit. Sermo siquidem datur multis, sed sapientia paucis; quam distribuit Dominus cui vult, et quomodo vult.*[857]

Chapter 4: *officium orationis:*[858] seeing that it cannot attain by its own action to pray—that is a pure gift—*humiliat se et confugit ad orationem*[859] (a very Bernardine phrase[860]). Note the *prayer* that flows from the same Scriptural text under consideration. Study this prayer as {a} typical example of the *oratio* that flows from *lectio* and *meditatio*. The importance lies in its coherent relationship to the other activities, its *use of Scripture* to seek God *non jam*

855. Col. 478A: "It grows warm with the desire to possess, but does not discover within itself how it can do this; and the more it searches, the greater it thirsts. All the while it experiences meditation, it is experiencing suffering also."

856. Col. 478B: "that sweet-tasting knowledge which rejoices and restores the soul to which it is joined with unimaginable sweetness."

857. Col. 478C: "It is he who gives the sweetness of wisdom, and makes the soul wise. Certainly the word is given to many, but wisdom to few; the Lord bestows it on whom he wills, and as he wills."

858. Col. 478C: "The Exercise of Prayer" (title of c. 4).

859. Col. 478C: "he humbles himself and flees to prayer."

860. See *In Psalmo Qui Habitat, Sermo* 6.1 (*PL* 183, col. 197B): "*recurrere ad orationem, refugere ad meditationes sanctas*" ("to run back to prayer, to flee back to holy meditations").

in cortice litterae, sed in sensu experientiae[861] (*ergo, experientiae =
"spiritus"*)—ending with *quia amore ardeo*[862] (theme song of {the}
twelfth-fourteenth centuries—*languor animae amantis*[863]—the
twelfth-century *Eros*).

Caput 5: officium contemplationis:[864] {there is} more on prayer
at {the} beginning of the chapter. Prayer consists in *ignitis elo-
quiis*[865]—arousing and expressing love; {and} *incantationibus*[866]—
calling the Spouse. God, attracted by prayer, brings consolation
to the soul. N.B. this description does not fit passive or infused
contemplation, but is a kind of active contemplation—at least in
the manner in which it begins. {Its} effects {are} described in {the}
usual language: *coelestis rore dulcedinis circumfusus, unguentis op-
timis delibutus: animam fatigatam recreat, esurientem reficit, aridam
impinguat; facit eam* [*animam*] terrenorum oblivisci, memoria sui
[*Dei*] *mirabiliter eam* fortificando, vivificando, inebriando *et sobria
reddendo.*[867] {These are} classical terms (comment: *memoria* [*prae-
sentia*],[868] *sobria ebrietas*[869]). Summary: just as in some carnal acts
a man is overcome by flesh {and} ceases to be *rationalis*, becomes
totus carnalis,[870] so in contemplation, *consumuntur et* {*absorbentur*}
carnales motus ab anima [cf. night of sense {of} John {of the}

---

861. Col. 478D: "not in the rind of the letter, but in direct experience."

862. Col. 478D: "because I burn with love."

863. See above, n. 517.

864. Col. 479A: "The Exercise of Contemplation" (title of c. 5).

865. Col. 479A: "burning words."

866. Col. 479A: "addresses."

867. Col. 479A, which reads: ". . . *et facit . . . eam mirabiliter . . . et inebriando ac sobriam . . .*": "sprinkled with the dew of heavenly sweetness, steeped
in the finest ointments: he renews the weary soul, restores the hungry soul,
nourishes the dry soul; he makes it oblivious of earthly things; he strengthens
and enlivens it wondrously with the memory of God, inebriating it and making
it sober again."

868. "memory"; "presence": the connection is obscure, but Merton perhaps intends to point out that memory has the power to make the past present
and so effective in the soul now.

869. See above, n. 185.

870. "rational . . . totally fleshly."

Cross[871]], *ut in nullo caro spiritui contradicat; et fiat homo* TOTUS SPIRI-TUALIS[872] (cf. St. Bernard on Wisdom: *Sermo 85 in Cantica*[873]).

Chapter 6: signs of the coming of the Spirit (cf. St. Bernard *in Cantica*[874]): the interior baptism of tears ({note the} quotations from {the} psalms). *Si adeo dulce est flere pro te, quam dulce erit gaudere de te?*[875] (again *memoria* {as} *presentia*). {Then follows a} digression: why speak of these things? *Legis in libro experientiae:*[876] a Bernardine expression[877]—letter and spirit, the inner gloss and *commentary of the heart*.

Chapter 7: then the spouse withdraws (*vicissitudo*);[878] the sweetness of contemplation departs. [*Sponsus*] *manet tamen praesens quantum ad gubernationem.*[879]

871. See *Ascent*, Bk. 1, cc. 4-13 (*Complete Works of Saint John of the Cross*, 1.24-63) and *Dark Night*, Bk. 1, cc. 8-14 (1.371-97); see also above, pages 320–24.

872. Col. 479B, which reads ". . . *quasi totus* . . ." (text reads "*absorbuntur*"): "fleshly motives are consumed and drawn out of the soul, so that the flesh does not go contrary to the spirit in any way; and he becomes a completely spiritual person."

873. The third section of this sermon (nn. 7-9; *PL* 183, cols. 1104A–1105D) presents the Word as the source of both wisdom (*sapientia*) and virtue (*virtus*), the latter requiring effort and strength (*vis*), while the former consists in rest and peace in the enjoyment of goodness, a taste (*sapor*) for goodness that has replaced an inclination toward evil.

874. St. Bernard associates the Holy Spirit with the mourning "voice of the turtledove" (Song of Songs, 2:12, referred to Romans 8:26) in section 6 of *Sermo 59 in Cantica*: "*Ipse inducitur gemens, qui gementes facit*" ("He who makes mourners is introduced as mourning Himself") (*PL* 183, col. 1064B).

875. Col. 479D: "If it is so sweet to weep for you, how sweet will it be to rejoice in you?"

876. Col. 479 D, which reads "*legant in libro experientiae*" ("they [you] read in the book of experience").

877. See *In Cantica*, 3.1 (*PL* 183, col. 794A): "*Hodie legimus in libro experientiae*" ("Today we are reading in the book of experience").

878. See above, n. 516.

879. Col. 480B: "[The Spouse] still remains present in so far as he remains in charge of us."

Chapter 8: *occultatio gratiae:*[880] {this is the} traditional teaching on aridity. *Ne existimes te contemni, si paulisper tibi subtrahit sponsus faciem suam. Omnia ista cooperantur tibi in bonum.*[881] Why aridity? *venit ad consolationem, recedit ad cautelam:*[882] as a humiliation; as a way of teaching us to rely on grace, in order to arouse greater desire; to fix our eyes on heaven. *Ne exsilium deputemus pro patria.*[883] Summary: *"et ita quasi alis expansis supra nos volitans, provocat ad volandum."*[884]

Chapter 9: {there is a} danger of growing indifferent in aridity, and turning to "other lovers":[885] {hence the} importance of special care and delicacy of conscience in {a} time of aridity.

Chapter 10 returns to {the} main topic {with a} resumé of the four activities.

Chapters 11-12: the vital interrelationship between reading, meditation, etc. {is emphasized}:

1. {it is} useless simply to read without "chewing"—*ad cordis intima transmittere*[886]—and putting into practice;

2. meditation without reading goes off the beam, gets away from {the} tradition of the Fathers;

3. meditation without prayer {is} useless because we need prayer to ask God's grace *and open our hearts* to it;

4. prayer without meditation is tepid;

5. contemplation without prayer is rare or miraculous (see above[887]).

---

880. Col. 480B: "the Concealment of Grace" (part of title of c. 8).

881. Col. 480B: "Do not think to despise yourself if the Spouse withdraws his face from you for a little while. All these things work together for good for you."

882. Col. 480B: "he comes for consolation, he withdraws for a warning."

883. Col. 480C, which reads *"Ne ergo . . ."*: "Let us not consider our place of exile our homeland."

884. Col. 480D: "and so flying above us as if on outspread wings, he encourages us to fly."

885. Col. 481A, which refers to a single other lover (*"alium amatorem"*).

886. Col. 481D, which reads ". . . *transmittamus*": "to pass on to the inmost part of the heart."

887. This passage was quoted earlier: see note 839.

The "blessed life"[888] (of the monk) is to be free of all other concerns and occupied only in these four things (col. 483). All the traditional language in praise of contemplation is used here: *vacare et videre quam suavis est Dominus.*[889] {There are} references to the *Transfiguration*, to *Jacob and Rachel.*[890] {There is a} warning against turning again to worldly things. Though we cannot always be contemplating, we keep going up and down the "steps" from one to another as circumstances permit. This is very practical and reasonable. Contemplation is enjoyed *only at rare intervals and briefly.*

Chapter 13 discusses reasons for {a} failure to live in this way. Some {are} inevitable and excusable: {a} duty to act, human infirmity; one {is} culpable: "worldly vanity."[891] A prayer and lament {follows} over the folly and infidelity of those who, having tasted contemplation, return to worldly vanities. {This is} beautiful and moving in its spirit of compunction and simplicity. Finally, {there is an} aspiration toward the perfect contemplation of the blessed in heaven.

Appendix II. A NOTE ON BRAINWASHING ("THOUGHT REFORM") (material from R. J. Lifton: *Thought Reform and the Psychology of Totalism* [New York, 1961][892])

1. Note the word has been exploited in political mythology and has become emotionally loaded. Promiscuous use of the term to cover any form of indoctrination one does not approve of has confused the issue. There is left a vague notion of brainwashing as a quasi-magic power of gaining control over the mind. {There has been a} *sensationalist* perversion of the concept in {the} U.S. press.

---

888. See col. 483A, which reads "*Beatus homo cujus animus,* . . ." ("Blessed the man whose life, . . .").

889. Col. 483A: "to be empty and to see how sweet the Lord is."

890. See col. 483B.

891. Col. 483D ("*mundialis vanitas*").

892. Robert Jay Lifton, *Thought Reform and the Psychology of Totalism: A Study of "Brainwashing" in China* (New York: W. W. Norton, 1961).

2. The reality: "thought reform" or "ideological reform"[893] {as} practiced by the Chinese Communists {consists in} systematically and "scientifically" organized use of pressures and appeals, intellectual, emotional and physical, "aimed at social control and individual change."[894] {It is} centered on an *artificially induced crisis, analogous to a spiritual crisis*, a synthetic "conversion," involving (a) confession—rejection of the past, perhaps induced by {a} breakdown; (b) re-education—reorientation for the future, with a total new self-commitment.[895] This is where the study of thought reform is important for us.

3. The most crucially important point about thought reform, totally neglected by Western propagandists, is that it is *sincerely considered and intended by {the} Chinese as a therapy*, which they view as a "morally uplifting {. . .} and scientifically therapeutic experience."[896] *Physical torture plays a small part or no part* in it (propaganda to the contrary). Underlying it is a sincere but misguided attempt to "save."

Mao Tse Tung said re-education depends on two things: (1) "punishing the past to warn the future"; (2) "saving men by curing their ills." But punishing is not the most important. *"The entire purpose is to save the person, not to cure him to death"* (Mao).[897] This is what constitutes the originality and difference of Chinese persecution from that of {the} Nazis or Imperial Rome. In a way it is *easier to resist* mere savagery and cruelty. Here it is the "ministry of love" (Orwell).[898] Prisons are sometimes called "houses of

893. Lifton, 4.
894. Lifton, 5.
895. See Lifton, 5.
896. Lifton, 15.
897. Lifton, 13.
898. In George Orwell's *Nineteen Eighty-Four* (New York: Harcourt Brace & World, 1949), the Ministry of Love "maintains law and order" in Oceania (6); Room 101 in the Ministry of Love is the torture chamber to which Winston Smith, the main character of the novel, is brought (239 ff.); he is told, "There are three steps in your reintegration, . . . There is learning, there is understanding, and there is acceptance" (264), and by the conclusion of the book he has

meditation."[899] Thought reform = a spiritual retreat—a *death and rebirth* (terms actually used[900]). *Chinese Communist prison regulations* read as follows: "In dealing with the criminals, there shall be regularly adopted measures of corrective study classes, individual interviews, study of assigned documents, and organized discussions, to educate them in the admission of guilt and obedience to the law, political and current events, labor production, and culture, so as to expose the nature of the crime committed, thoroughly wipe out criminal thoughts, and establish a new moral code."[901] Sounds like a novitiate!!

The process of thought reform:

A. negative—"purgation":

1. On arrest the prisoner may be put in a cell with other prisoners far advanced in thought reform, themselves "convinced" and "apostolic." They immediately work on him in the "struggle session,"[902] insisting on his wrong-headedness. Note {the} importance of putting {the} prisoner in with others so that he is never alone, so that his intimate acts are subject to their scrutiny (he may be in chains and others may have to help him to urinate, etc.), so that his personal private life is reduced to zero.[903]

2. *Interrogations*, lasting ten or twelve hours {are followed by} returning to further "struggle" in the cell. {The} aim {is} to make one *"confess"*—not just specific imaginary crimes, but anything that can be regarded as {a} crime—real acts, seen as "crimes." They either invent crimes or tell everything they can think of with the implication that it had something wrong with it. No sleep {is} allowed for many days. The prisoner gets to *feel*

---

become successfully "reintegrated": "But it was all right, everything was all right, the struggle was finished. He had won the victory over himself. He loved Big Brother" (300).

899. Lifton, 14.
900. Lifton, 20, 66.
901. Lifton, 17.
902. See Lifton, 21.
903. See Lifton, 22.

he is completely in the power of his judge and says what the judge wants.
He becomes completely compliant, {and} denounces friends {and}
acquaintances, indiscriminately.

B. reconstruction:

1. *Recognition of crimes*: one now is made to see all this "information" from the "people's standpoint,"[904] to use Communist
language. Immediately better treatment is given, {and a} promise
of kindness and leniency is given. The abrupt change produces
hope. Note here the importance of *changes of regime and of policy*
which frequently take place in the prison. With changes in the
party line, more reasonable and humane officers come and go,
alternating with rigid and cruel types. The appearance of kinder
men helps soften up the prisoner and make him more coopera-
tive. Sincere admission in one case that a cruel prison policy had
been unjust ({an} admission by {a} new prison administration)
led to {the} submission of a priest-prisoner.[905]

In this atmosphere he works over his confession material
with great zeal in orthodox Communist language. {He} joins {a}
group study program {which lasts} ten or twelve hours a day,
{with} *active participation required*, {and} with profound self-examination as to {the} sources of one's errors and open lucid criticism
of one's own thinking. {One is} *not allowed to be quiet*, or to "relapse
into subjectivism or individualism."[906] *Progress* is evidenced by
"spontaneous" confidence in the people and in the value of one's
re-education, and skill in criticizing others. (At this point the foreign prisoner signs his confession and reads it publicly, after *several years' work* on it, and is sent out of China.[907])

Analysis of thought reform: "The penetration by the psychological forces of the environment into the inner emotions of the individual person is perhaps the outstanding psychiatric fact of

904. Lifton, 24.
905. See Lifton, 55 (though the cause-effect relationship is less clear-cut
than Merton suggests here).
906. See Lifton, 29.
907. See Lifton, 32.

thought reform" (p. 66).[908] {There is a} death, by physical and emotional assaults and pressures, {and a} rebirth, by leniency and developing confession. {An} *assault upon identity*[909] {is made through}:

a) pressures to break down one's idea of who he is, {and} direct assertions that you are someone quite different than you claim to be;

b) breaking down one's sense of relatedness to others, particularly former associates;

c) {the} *result* {is a} reduction to {a} state of infancy or quasi-animality, completely in the hands of the "trainer,"[910] a regression in which one is deprived of the power of adult existence. {There is a} surrender of personal autonomy. Attempts to assert previous identity are regarded as rebellion and produce more assaults. {There is a} *reduction to {a} hypnagogic state* of susceptibility to destructive influences.

Establishment of guilt:[911]
a) {the} prisoner must not only verbally admit guilt but really experience it, for definite things he before considered right. {There must be a} *sense that punishment is deserved.*

Self-betrayal:[912] denunciations of friends {are required}, not just to get {the} dope on *them* but to destroy *your* integrity and your bond to them, subverting the structure of your own life {and} renouncing the matrix of your former existence. In betraying friends one betrays {the} vital core of his own existence. "The more of one's self he is led to betray, the greater is one's involvement with his captors; thus the captors reach down into the doubts, ambivalences and antagonisms which we all carry beneath the surface of our

908. Text reads "This penetration . . ."
909. See Lifton, 67–68.
910. Lifton, 67.
911. See Lifton, 68.
912. See Lifton, 68–69.

loyalties."[913] Once the captor has gained access to these weaknesses, *the victim has to depend on the bond established between himself and his captor*. Note {the} demonic quality of this use of weakness and passion to subvert and subject the whole person.

Breakdown[914] {is} produced by total isolation in {the} midst of completely hostile and aggressive fellow prisoners, who assert you are wrong and deluded. {There is a} total break of {the} relatedness which is necessary for survival. *Fear of total annihilation* is produced, {with} suicidal depression or psychotic delusions.

The bridge to safety:[915] at the point of breakdown, *leniency* supplies the sudden hope which is a bridge, crossing over to new relatedness with the captors. Here the judge is changed or a new character enters who acts in a human and gentle way, saying, "The government does not want to kill you, just to *cure* you."[916] With this hope, he gets a desperate desire to save himself at all costs. {This leads to} *the compulsion to confess*. Under pressure and suffering the confession tends to be wild; {there is a willingness to} confess *anything*. After the breakthrough the prisoner *takes the same view of himself as the government does*. He now goes over his actual words and deeds, reviewing them over and over in the light of the new viewpoint, seeking to find everything that can be considered "wrong" from the new viewpoint. He then makes a "full confession" of all these *real* actions, but slanted and distorted. {There is} a real inner *compulsion to confess*.[917] This implies *commitment to the new beliefs and receptivity to them.*

---

913. Lifton, 69, which reads: "The more of one's self one is led . . . captors; for by these means they make contact with whatever similar tendencies already exist within the prisoner himself—with the doubts, antagonisms, and ambivalences which each of us carries beneath the surface of his loyalties."

914. See Lifton, 69–72.

915. See Lifton, 72–73.

916. Lifton, 73, which reads: "The government doesn't want to kill you. It wants to reform you."

917. See Lifton, 74–75.

Channeling of guilt:[918] now he learns to *feel real guilt* for relatively indifferent or innocent acts which, in the light of the new faith, are "crimes against the people." How is this done? by taking the inevitable resistances and oppositions within every man, for which all feel guilty, and centering everything on this guilty "resistance." This leads to a feeling of guilt for whatever one *is*, in the face of the group standards. The mechanism is then {that a} harsh group morality makes common cause with {a} harsh superego, and vague free-floating guilt becomes *guilt for specific actions which the society considers criminal*. N.B. {the} cleverness of {this} technique: with a missionary who was a sincerely liberal mind and who already regretted some of the defects of missionaries and of their approach, they pushed him to admit that the missionaries had *betrayed Christianity* and had been essentially unchristian.[919] {Here is a} use of Marxian dialectic: Christianity = thesis; personal deficiencies and doubts = antithesis.[920]

Progress and harmony:[921] as "reform" develops, the prisoner receives recognition and acceptance and becomes integrated in the new milieu; {he} finds satisfaction and comfort in the new way of thinking. It is now possible to talk freely, man to man, with the captors, who are friendly. One feels human again. More self-expression is permitted and one begins to feel that he *really means* what he is saying.

Final confession:[922] it is now time for the "conclusive statement," the final and "correct" version of the confession, *which now the prisoner himself fully accepts and believes*. This is the purpose of the long process. They demand that their accusations become the prisoner's self-accusations. After this the *recovery* of one's normal self is permitted. One is the same person again but *reborn* as a Communist—for instance, a *priest working with* the Communists, convinced they are right.[923]

---

918. See Lifton, 75–76.
919. See Lifton, 55–56, 105.
920. See Lifton, 77–78.
921. See Lifton, 79–80.
922. See Lifton, 80–82.
923. See Lifton, 83, and chapter 11 (207–21).

Thought reform: {one must also take into account} "apparent resisters"[924] {and} their thoughts:

a) analysis and understanding of what is going on:[925] this gives {a} capacity to predict {and} dispels fear of {the} unknown; {it gives the ability} to enter in while maintaining contact with {one's} own spiritual tradition.

b) avoidance of emotional participation:[926] remaining outside {the} system of communication, maintaining {a} private world and {one's} own symbols; a neutralizing attitude towards assaults (humor, stoicism)—*humor creates a bond of sympathy antithetical to the reform.*

c) non-violence,[927] if based on {a} deep supernatural tradition, {is} affirming a moral position higher than {the} claims of thought reform.

d) identity reinforcement:[928] {this is an} essential protection against disintegration: clinging to one's own tradition, {e.g.} seeing things in terms of Catholic theology, {provides} *reminders of who you are.*

Pseudo-strength represents a psychological danger:[929]

a) denial and repression of one's own weakness;

b) denial of one's *attraction* to the thought-reform propaganda (protestations that one has not given in).

(Note a case where this emotional weakness leads to a *war now* attitude[930] and {a} constant struggle against {the} breakthrough of despair.)

---

924. See Lifton, chapter 8 (133–51).

925. See Lifton, 145–46.

926. See Lifton, 146–47.

927. See Lifton, 147, which does not use the term "non-violence" but does refer to "passive resistance in the Gandhian tradition."

928. See Lifton, 147.

929. See Lifton, 148–49.

930. See Lifton, 142, 148–49.

APPENDIX A

TEXTUAL NOTES

Readings Adopted from Mimeograph

1   **AN INTRODUCTION]** *preceded by* (Title Page). *preceded on separate page by* "The essence of mysticism being not a doctrine but a way of life its interests require the existence of groups of persons who put its principles into effect." Evelyn Underhill

3   **FOREWORD]** *preceded by* p 2

15   **Ascetical and Mystical Theology]** *preceded by* Myst Theol.

       1-2. Introd

       3-4. St John's Gospel

       5. Martyrs

       6. Gnostics. Divinisation

       7. Xtological controversies. / Mysticism.

       (8. Greg. Nyss. Spiritual Senses)

       9. Greg. Nyssa. Cappadocians.

       10. Evagrius *followed by added* (13)

       16 Pseudo-Dionysius + Dionysian Trad. in West *preceded by cancelled* 11 *preceded by interlined* (14-15. Theoria Phys *and followed by cancelled* 14. Dionysius + his trad *marked with arrow for placement before* 16

       17 Western Mysticism *preceded by cancelled* 12

       Franciscan Tradition etc. *preceded by cancelled* 13 *and followed on separate line by cancelled* 14 Dionysian tradition in West and outline of separation of Myst + Theol.

       18 *written over* 15 *followed by*—The Rhenish Mystics

       19—Quietism *preceded by cancelled* 18

       20—Jesuits St. Theresa *preceded by cancelled* 19 *and followed by added* + later Carmelites

       21—St John Cross Dark Night *preceded by cancelled* 18-19 *preceded by* 20-21 *added in left margin and cancelled*

20—Later Carmelites] 20 *circled and marked with arrow to precede* 21

22—Byz. Myst. Conclusion *preceded on separate line by cancelled* 21–22. Byzantine Mysticism

18—The Rhenish . . . Byzantine Mysticism *cancelled and replaced in right margin by*

1—Denys.

2—Dionysians in West

3—Western Myst.

4—The 14th–15th Cents.

5—Quietists.

6—Jesuits + St Theresa.

7—St John of +.

5–14 **Table of Contents** . . . thought reform] *omitted in copy text*

35 However] *preceded by* (Remarks—continued)

43 I would . . . p. 108–9).] TEXT READ (copy) St Ignatius, to *the Romans*, n. 2, (Fathers of the Church, Apostolic Fathers, p. 108) *followed by* (insert text from Romans *interlined following cancelled* Text here.

44–45 I am writing . . . p. 97).] COPY here, Romans n. 4 p. 109, the famous passage Let me be thrown to the wild beasts, through them I can reach God. . . I am the wheat of Christ . . ." and n. 5. COPY also, Magnesians, n. 5, p. 97.

46 "Carnal . . . p. 90)] copy Ephesians 8 (last 4 lines, p. 90

91 another approach] followed by (Here insert notes on Dom Anselm Stolz.) p 27a

96 Religious knowledge . . . II:162).] Here quote classical passage from De Vita Moysis COPY (see notes Cassian + the Fathers top of p 31

112–13 It is clear, . . . n. 5).] (copy the last 7 lines of n. 5)

113 But there . . . n. 9).] (copy this last part as marked in our book).

151 *Itinerarium . . . Opuscula*).] from last # of *Itinerarium Mentis in Deum* (VII.6) (late Medieval Mysticism p 141) (COPY) 1st 12 lines—down to "darkness")

162 If to any . . . p. 90).] (Copy text quoted in Medieval mystics of England p 90.)

166–67 We were discoursing . . . p. 32).] read the quote given by Butler on p. 32 (COPY)

179 If this transition, . . . p. 140);] read [COPY]

186–88 Here it is . . . p. 346–7).] (copy—SPIRITUAL CANT. Vol II p.

195 B. THE GERMAN] *preceded by inserted penciled contents page:* Myst Theol.

Mᴀʀᴄʜ *written vertically in left margin to include nn.* 1–6
1—Introduction
2—Introduction
3—St John's Gospel
4—Martyrs + Gnostics—Irenaeus, Clement etc.
    Gnostics] *preceded by vertical line with* 5 *interlined above*
    and cancelled
6—Divinisation. Xtological Controversies. 7 "Mysticism"
    6] *interlined above and preceded by cancelled* 5
    7] *interlined above and preceded by vertical line*
6—St Gregory of Nyssa. Pseudo-Macarius 8 (Sp. Senses—
    Wm of St Thierry)
    8] *interlined above and preceded by vertical line*
Aᴘʀɪʟ *written vertically in left margin to include nn.* 9–14
9—Evagrius Ponticus
    9] *preceded by cancelled* 7
10—Pseudo-Denis
    10] *preceded by cancelled* 8
11—"Western Mysticism" *written over erased words*
10—Dionysian Tradition in the West
    10] *followed by cancelled* 12
    West] *followed by* 12 *[written over* 13*]* Franciscans—
        Rhenish Mystics *added in right margin and*
        marked for insertion and followed by 14 Complete
        Separation of Myst + Theol *added in right*
        margin and cancelled
11—Quietism *written over erased words*
12—Post Trent – Jesuits – St Theresa.
13—St John of the Cross
14—Dark Night.
Mᴀʏ *written vertically in left margin to include nn.* 15-22
15—Later Carmelites—mod. Debates
16—*followed by cancelled* Semi Quietists etc
17—*followed by cancelled* Modern Writers—Saudreau
    Poulain
18—Non-Xtian mysticism?
19—Hallaj—Sufis
20—
21—Byzantine Mysticism
22—St Gregory Palamas
197–98 Suso on . . . pp. 259–60).] (copy) Read here Suso on *Gelassenheit*
    in Late Med. Myst. p. 259.

216   *In the sixteenth century] preceded by* READ:

249   Despite all . . . pp. 259-260).] READ (copy) p. 259 from "Despite
all I have said . . . . . to top p. 260, "what it desires."

279–80   And supposing . . . p. 193).] READ Living Flame III, 59 Peers
III p. 193 (copy marked passage)

296–97   Oh, my God, . . . translation).] (copy pp. 269 begin line 10 "O
my God how great are these trials . . ."–270 ending with
the words "at a time when everything really seems to be
lost") (line 11)

305–306   And so . . . child.] "And so it is sad to see many souls . . .
READ (copy from line 10 to end of n. 3)

306–307   For some . . . befalling it.] then READ (copy) p. 13 "For some
confessions . . . down to end of n. 4)

314–16   These spiritual . . . (*ibid.*, 58).] COPY (Read)—#s 53, pp. 189–190
also #58, p 192.

318–19   Oh, souls, . . . p. 198).] Copy here #65. p. 197. #67. p 198.

319   In this way . . . p. 188).] READ (copy) n. 50, p. 188.

326–27   This was . . . (p. 405).] Copy n. 2 Page 405.

327–28   But the question . . . (p. 406).] Copy n. 2, p. 406.

328   Beneath (p. 408).] COPY n. 7, p. 408.

332   In this . . . (p. 434).] COPY n. 4, page 434.

347   of despair.)] *followed by*
Zahn
Friedensbund Deutscher Katholiken—founded by F.
Stratmann after WW I. Had as many as 40,000 members
before Hitler. Much official encouragement. 13 Bishops
were supposed to be active members. Incl. Faulhaber
+ Bertram (Cardinals). Was wiped out by Nazis as a
traitorous organization—officially dissolved July 1, 1933.
leaders exiled or imprisoned. At most a few members
were active as pacifists during the war. 7 men on record
as refusing service 6 executed 3 *Austrians* 1 indefinitely
imprisoned in mental inst. *In any case no support from
spiritual leaders.* nb. "objector" might be a Gestapo agent
seeking to trap priest.
Destruction of Friedensbund—
1)   Resistance or even lack of enthusiasm could mean
death
2)   Death for unknown or trumped up disgraceful cause
("homosexuality")
3)   Total hopelessness of protest, inability to make protest
known.

4) Fear for dependents.

5) anger at air raids

"The German Catholic who looked to his religious Superiors for spiritual guidance + direction regarding service in Hitler's wars received virtually the same answers he would have received from the Nazi ruler himself" p. 17. Prisoners even were denied sacraments by chaplains, for their attitude—at least until just before execution. Bec. Their resistance was considered violation of Xtian duty.

Hitlers wars—supported by Catholics—40 percent of the population—Soldiers swear *unconditional personal oath* to Hitler.

1) Aggression, with Russia, on Catholic nation— Poland—after faked "incident" to claim Polish "aggression" (on a Radio Station).

2) Why?—opposition wd have brought on extreme anti-Catholic persecution
—opposition might (after war with Russia) have helped Communism
—some elements of justice in the German cause.
—earlier support of Hitler before War—as "pacifier" of Germany, bringing order + preventing revolution + Hitler first promised support of religion

See *quote* from pamphlet by a theologian—p. 57.

The 7 objectors—Executed—3 Austrians Fr. Franz Reinisch—Franz Jägerstätter—Cath Action leader—J. Mayr-Nesser 3 Germans in Xt Kg Soc. Fr Metzger—Br Maurus—Br Michael 1 German layman interned—Josef Fleischer.

Von Galen—Heroism of his protests agst Nazi injustice. Staunch defense of war—as for Germany's rights. agst Western Freemasons + godless Bolshevism (but inconsistency) Von G. a "perfect" bishop acc to all standards since M.A. His very perfection + virtues made him unable to see real issue. made him work for forces of destruction Faulhaber—defended OT + implicitly Judaism (Had received iron cross in WW I—chaplain genl. of Armies of Bavaria) Had been official protector of Friedensbund. but did not come to its defense. Yet in 1932 had called for a "new ethic of war + preparation for

peace." 1932 "Moral theology will speak a new language.
It will remain true to the old principles but in the question
of the permissibility of war new facts will be taken into
account:
1) communications – shd make war more avoidable
2) war technology now too destructive. "no longer
    human not to mention Christian"
3) After war—both would be "losers"—no
    proportionality between objectives + price to be paid.
1930 "I work for peace today because I am convinced that
it is no longer human to wage war with clouds of gas that
smother all personal bravery, with airborne poison bombs
that destroy all life from nursing infant to aged invalid in
a few brief hours . . ."
Gröber against war—addressing national conclave of
peace movement 1931 p. 124. but against pacifism in
1934. sacrificial death of the soldier. p. 126
German bishops. 1) convinced that WW I had been just— +
that it had been unjustly settled hence WW II was just. 2)
Disagreed with Hitler on many things + protested
outspokenly
a) But H. was legitimate authority + must be obeyed
b) And he was against Bolshevism. Hence could be
acclaimed as "providential." But they supported Hitler
also when he was *allied* with Stalin in war agst Poland +
Hitler's attack on Poland, then on Russia—questionable
morality!

Additions and Alterations

3   and probably . . . errors] *interlined with arrow for placement*
           It has not . . . unfinished.] *interlined with arrow for placement*
           These lectures] *interlined above cancelled* They
           broaden] *interlined above cancelled* widen
           and positive] *interlined with a caret*
           non-Catholic] *interlined with a caret*
           by us] *interlined above cancelled* here
4   lived] *followed on separate line by cancelled* Abbey of Gethsemani
15   1. *Aim of the Course*] *interlined*
           obviously] *interlined above cancelled* of course
           assimilated] *followed by x'd out* along the
           monk] *added on line*

to cover] *followed by x'd out* the whole field, as if one were

The main] *preceded by x'd out* To situate

16   there is] *added on line*

combined] *preceded by x'd out* anti-mysticism

affected] *followed by x'd out* the Church

after . . . St. John's Gospel] *added on line*

17   we will see] *preceded by x'd out* with a brief

18   easily] *preceded by x'd out* found in books

However it . . . mysticism.] *opposite page*

school] *followed by cancelled* marked the

19   It is treated . . . sufficient] *added on line after cancelled* Augustine

can be discussed elsewhere. Passing reference is here suf-

ficient. So also for Gregory the Great.

It is] *interlined above cancelled* They are

reading lists] *added in lower margin*

(Homer uses . . . art.")] *interlined*

applied to . . . *training.*] *added on line*

19–20   The whole of . . . 109 end.] *opposite page*

20   d) *oversimplification* . . . maintained] *added below and marked*

with arrow for placement

22   arisen] *followed by cancelled* a distinction between

Mysticism and . . . whole.] *added on line*

infused] *preceded by x'd out* the

be separated,] *preceded by x'd out* properly

23   difficult] *interlined above cancelled* dangerous

24   and must] *interlined below and marked with arrow for insertion*

cf. . . . Stace.] *interlined above and marked with arrow for insertion*

25   Görres' . . . diabolical mysticism.] *added on line*

Before] *preceded by x'd out* We must dis

affected] *preceded by x'd out* more or less taking into

26   hereafter *RAM*] *added on line*

hereafter *VS*] *added on line*

26–27   Also . . . Avon-Fontainebleau.] *opposite page*

27   There is no . . . high.] *added on line followed by x'd out* The early

writers of the 20th Century

attitudes to mystical theology] *added on line after cancelled*

approaches:

in 1896] *interlined with a caret*

28–29   tends to . . . position] *added on line*

29   reappraisal] *preceded by x'd out* theological synthesis, free from

be defended.] *followed by x'd out* The book may

an attempt at] *added in left margin before cancelled* a

30   takes up] *followed by x'd out* the
31   Butler's thesis] *interlined to replace* This *with arrow for placement*
        tends to] *followed by x'd out* emphasize
        exalts] *preceded by x'd out* ignores the main tradition.
32   (in *Revue* . . . *RAM*)] *added on line*
        RAM)] *preceded by cancelled* hereafter
        clarification] *preceded by x'd out* identification of the Pseudo
            Macarius
33   new edition of St. Bernard] *added on line*
        Studies for . . . Bernard] *interlined*
34   very rich] *preceded by x'd out* field which
35   people to church] *followed by cancelled* in America
        in the monastery] *added on line before cancelled* where we are
36   modern world] *interlined above cancelled* monastery
37   especially . . . bread] *interlined*
        but not . . . in us] *interlined*
        faith who] who interlined above cancelled which
38   center] *followed by cancelled* to life
39   *Some Remarks:* . . . beyond liturgy.] *opposite page*
        consent . . . struggle] *added in left margin with arrow for placement*
        external . . . Reality] *added in left margin with arrow for placement*
        leading] *preceded by cancelled* N.B.
        in the Father] in *interlined with a caret*
40   mystical doctrine] mystical *interlined with a caret*
        this has been done] this *interlined above cancelled* it
41   Spirit of Love.] *followed by x'd out* Romans
42   Note—a very . . . this light.] *opposite page*
        A. *Martyrdom*] *interlined*
43   to the Father."] *followed by x'd out* Other deaths may
45–46   la. *The Mystical* . . . living in us.] *opposite page*
45   He who fails . . . incomplete.] *added in left margin*
46   martyrdom brings . . . God] *interlined below cancelled* it
            certainly does this.
        Martyrdom is . . . baptism] Martyrdom *interlined above
            cancelled* it
47   in this text] *interlined with a caret*
        of the three . . . union.] *added on line*
        N.B. Secret . . . beginning."] *added on line*
        relationship] *followed by x'd out* with the
47–48   St. Ephrem . . . (violent) experience.] *opposite page*
48   of the "essence"] *preceded by cancelled* fully

49   superficial.] *followed by x'd out* The

50   as opposed to liberation from the flesh.] *added on line*
           Above all . . . Spirit.] *opposite page*

51   Christ as] *added in left margin and marked for insertion*

52   of its mysteries,] *followed by x'd out* helps
           as contributing to Christian gnosis.] *added on line*
           cast.] *followed by x'd out* In this

53   He defines . . . means."] *opposite page*
           should be] *interlined below cancelled* is
           equals mystical] mystical *interlined below and marked for insertion*
           However, it is still *debatable.*] *added on line*

54   mystery of the divine] *preceded by x'd out* union
           The Scriptures are . . . of Scripture.] *opposite page*

56   man becomes] *interlined above x'd out* to become
           also] *added in left margin and marked for insertion to replace*
              cancelled later
           (including by Clement himself)] *added on line*
           where he is] he *interlined below cancelled* it

57   with present-day theologians] *interlined with a caret*
           part of] *interlined below and marked for insertion*
           Note: Dom . . . p. 283] *added in lower margin*
           nourished by] *interlined above cancelled* flowering in *preceded by*
              cancelled based

58   We will . . . Senses] *added in upper margin*
           A. *Theosis—Deificatio—Divinization.*] *interlined*
           It is a term . . . implications.] *interlined*
           Epimenides and Aratus] *added on line*
           Read . . . wisdom.] *interlined*
           For Plato,] *preceded by cancelled* The actual term divini
           For Paul, . . . of God.] *interlined*

59   For Clement, . . . speculation.] *opposite page*
           Prot.] *followed by cancelled* I.85
           Origen also . . . *DS*, III:1379] *opposite page*
           shalt have] *preceded by x'd out* hast become God

60   Note: already . . . divinization.] *opposite page*

61   made Himself] *preceded by x'd out* was made man in order
           by nature belongs] *preceded by x'd out* is by nature God
           last end.] *followed by x'd out* It is not
           in other words] *followed by x'd out* all
           His body] *preceded by x'd out* this life
           (*De Incarn.* 54; see below)] *added on line*

62   nature] *interlined above x'd out* life,

63   the full] *preceded by x'd out* divinization
       A note:. . . . Resurrection.] *opposite page*
       n.b. Leclercq, p. 271] *added in left margin*
64   Observe . . . p. 228] *opposite page*
65   *Pastoral . . . "self."*] *added in left margin*
66   against the Macedonians, . . . deifies us.] *opposite page followed*
            by cancelled St Gregory Nazianzen agst
       Cappadocian Fathers] *added on line*
       St. Maximus] *added on line*
66–67 Note: Pseudo-Denis . . . God in Christ.] *added in lower margin*
67   B.] *interlined above cancelled* 2.
       Theoria Mystike, Theognosis:] *Mystike interlined with a caret*
       hidden on] on *altered from* in
68   It cannot . . . of Christ.] *opposite page*
69   and *theoria mystike*] *interlined with a caret*
       Joannem *of Origen.*] Joannem *altered from* Jo. *and* of Origen *added*
            on line
       disposes] *preceded by x'd out* makes
70   intervene,] *followed by cancelled* but
       angels] *followed by x'd out* having
       He unites . . . *visionis.*] *interlined*
70–71 Note . . . ancient sense.] *opposite page*
71   closing his] *followed by x'd out* exterior
72   stress] *preceded by x'd out* sufficiently
       dogmatic] *followed by cancelled* theologian
       mystical] *altered from* mystic
       theologian, . . . a mystic.] *added on line*
73–74 In St. Gregory . . . *both* to us.] *opposite page*
73   basic truths] *preceded by cancelled* the
74   three] *interlined above cancelled* two
       secondly through Cassian] *added in left margin and marked for*
            insertion
77   But the living . . . Phil. 4:7.] *opposite page*
       statements] *preceded by cancelled* made
       traditional . . . of wisdom."] *added on line*
78   pastoral . . . true contemplation.] *interlined*
       St. Chrysostom . . . SC p. 166)] *opposite page*
       inexpressible] *preceded by cancelled* invisible *and followed by*
            God *interlined with a caret*
       mortal] *added in right margin and marked for insertion*
       seraphim] *followed by cancelled* comprehend him contemplate
            Him (fully)

(obscurity)] *interlined with a caret*
(*gnosis*)] *interlined with a caret*
79   "Holy of Holies,"] *interlined with a caret*
union] *followed by cancelled* the quest
gnosis but] *preceded by cancelled* for
but *ousia.*] *preceded by cancelled* for
to *ousia* by love.] *added on line*
example of . . . be revealed.] *opposite page*
This divine . . . says Gregory.] *added on line*
ecstasy] *interlined with a caret*
The following . . . important:] *added on line*
which remains . . . knowledge of God.] *added on line*
80   N.B. this . . . exhortation.] *added on line*
81   or apophatic] or *interlined above cancelled* fr
role of] *interlined with a caret*
state] *interlined above cancelled illegible word*
82   fulfilled] ful *interlined with a caret*
a progress] *preceded by cancelled* an infini
C.] *added on line before cancelled* 3
rather] *preceded by x'd out* more
by the bodily senses.] *added on line*
an experience] an *interlined above cancelled* a sense
by the exterior senses.] *interlined*
He is really . . . what it is.] *added on line*
(We bypass . . . Cassian.)] *opposite page*
83   not visions, etc.] *followed by cancelled* That other category
presents other problems, but it does not involve spiritual
senses because the vision is presented to the bodily or
at least to the interior senses. Or at least it is *translated*
completely into bodily terms in order to be expressed.
(vg when St Bernadette "saw the Lady" it may or may not
have involved the "spiritual senses" but the experience
reduced itself for her to a *bodily vision*, literally seeing
Mary present. The problem of the spiritual senses is
the problem of explaining an experience of what is by its
very nature *inaccessible to sense*. A glorified body does not
come in this category. Or does it?)
St. Bonaventure . . . *Dei*"] *opposite page*
mystical action of] *interlined with a caret*
literary] *interlined with a caret*
84   and in disguise. . . . images.] *added on line*
Origen] *followed by illegible cancelled word*

84–85   The doctrine . . . developed.] *opposite page*
85   involve] *interlined below cancelled* mean
         sensible] *preceded by cancelled* a
         on a miraculous] on a *interlined above cancelled* of a
         plane] *preceded by cancelled* nature
         objective] *interlined with a caret*
         the Sacred] *preceded by cancelled* Christ in His
87   Poulain does . . . Two Nights.] *interlined after cancelled*
         They would exclude a form of mystical prayer in which
         precisely there is *no feeling of presence* of God "as object."
         It would completely exclude the mystical prayer of the
         Dark Night. (Perhaps P. would try to fit this in under
         ligature).
88   (God and angels)] *interlined with a caret*
         c)] *added in left margin*
         The sense of *touch* . . . level of mystical prayer.] *opposite page*
            followed by cancelled The sense of spiritual touch
         The sense of spiritual] *preceded by cancelled* the principal and
            most mystical of these senses is that of *touch.*
         (The expression . . . mystical.)] *parentheses added*
88–89   Spiritual touch "can . . . take place.] *interlined followed by*
            cancelled Poulains doctrine of the spiritual senses is
            inadequate and arbitrary.
89   Poulain does well . . . mystic" (!!)] *opposite page*
         while admitting] *preceded by cancelled* Attempts an explanation
            that is more satisfactory
         little] *added on line preceded by cancelled* nothing at all
         It easily . . . verbalism.] *added in lower margin followed by*
            cancelled It gives no practical help to us.
         between the spiritual senses] *followed by x'd out* of
         (though we . . . unsatisfactory).] *added on line*
         Those senses] senses *interlined with a caret*
90   This theory] *preceded by cancelled* St Gregory of Nyssa, and the
            Spiritual Senses.
         and sight] *followed by x'd out* alone
         How valid . . . distinction?] *added on line and followed by*
            cancelled It seems certain that the "senses that perfect the
            intellect" attain to God mediately and those that are
            connected with Love attain to Him immediately. But that
            does not mean that either the one or the other operate
            only on certain levels of prayer, in certain degrees.
         And it is . . . psychology.] *interlined*

doctrine] *followed by cancelled* of Olphe Gaillard
91   opposes and] *interlined with a caret*
original] *preceded by cancelled* sin
pointing to] *interlined with a caret*
share] *preceded by cancelled* part
"spiritual senses"] *preceded by cancelled* senses
92   Here we find . . . doctrine.] *added on line*
One might . . . play.] *added on line*
94   But we must . . . own sake.] *added in lower margin*
The biblical . . . Exodus 33.] *opposite page*
tends to] *followed by x'd out* throw much emphasis on the
96   A. *The Problem of Evagrius.*] *interlined*
Origenist and] *followed by x'd out* one
97   Being a . . . the desert.] *interlined*
97–98 Though Evagrius . . . points.] *opposite page*
97   contemplation of the Trinity,] *preceded by cancelled* Trinitarian
98   L. Bouyer . . . moment.] *interlined above and marked for insertion*
became a monk] *preceded by x'd out* was accep
most widely read] *interlined above cancelled* chief
99   The most . . . in 1958.] *opposite page*
This has . . . 1960.] *added on line*
100 fell . . . (captivity)] *interlined above cancelled* limited with the
    fall.
Man's primitive . . . sakes.] *opposite page*
and keep . . . passion.] *added on line*
Man must . . . cosmos in Christ.] *opposite page*
101 5] *interlined above cancelled* 4
for . . . primitive state.] *interlined above and marked with arrow*
    for insertion
6] *added on line before cancelled* 5
in Evagrius, . . . love.] *added on line*
7] *added on line before cancelled* 6
8] *added on line before cancelled* 7
higher degree . . . life).] *followed by cancelled* 4 and for the
    purification of all [ ] of the [ ] itself
9] *added on line before cancelled* 8
102 notion?] *followed by x'd out* What are we to
idea of *apatheia*] *followed by x'd out* as he atti
(St. Jerome . . . *apatheia*).] *added on line*
The letter] *preceded by x'd out* According to Jerome
Jerome says] *interlined*
103 exactly with] *followed by x'd out* Cassian's

104   Certainly . . . from temptation.] *added in lower margin*
105   i) *Apatheia . . . I.86*).] *opposite page*
      retain] *followed by x'd out* for it
106   habitual intimacy] *added on line*
      or thoughts.] *added on line*
107   without intermediary] *interlined with a caret*
      This state] *added in left margin before cancelled* It
      power, here,] *preceded by cancelled* and
      he says,] *added on line*
108   stressed . . . see above] *added on line*
      stressed] *interlined below cancelled* mentioned
109   In n. 82, . . . flesh.] *opposite page*
110   *that come from*] *interlined above cancelled of*
      a) In the . . . as demons.] *opposite page*
      b] *added on line before cancelled* a
111   Note: . . . contemplation.] *opposite page*
      c] *added on line before cancelled* b
      devil,] *followed by x'd out* as
      d] *added on line before cancelled* c
112   They also . . . impossible.] *opposite page*
      e)] *added on line*
      to the soul] the soul *added on line after cancelled* it
114   alien] *followed by x'd out* thoughts while they are *[n.b. thoughts*
          cancelled erroneously]
      Note that . . . III.4).] *opposite page*
      (see *Keph. Gnost.* I.27)] *added on line*
115   revelation] *preceded by x'd out* cosmic revela
      and begin . . . beyond] *added on line before cancelled* but still in
          the realm of
      to the *logoi*] *interlined above cancelled* logos, and
      objective, and *formal*] *added on line*
      Evagrius stresses . . . III.58] *opposite page*
      only on the threshold] *added on line*
116   He says elsewhere . . . of God."] *opposite page*
118   *In Ps. 140*, quoted . . . p. 96] *added in lower margin and marked*
          for insertion
      Note: this . . . objective.] *opposite page*
      subject] *preceded by cancelled* as [ ]
119   This is . . . misleading.] *added on line*
120   harsh] *interlined above x'd out* great
      real] *interlined below cancelled* great
      question] *interlined below cancelled* matter

He does . . . evil.] *added on line*
He says . . . III.59).] *opposite page*
He tends] *preceded by cancelled* As a result of this
121 f) . . . than this.] *opposite page*
g] *written over* f
We can . . . say] *interlined above cancelled* It can in fact be said *and marked for insertion*
without forms,] *followed by cancelled* and
distinction] *preceded by illegible cancelled word*
122 Evagrius . . . III.67)] *interlined*
especially . . . Redeemer:] *added on line*
It is a spiritual . . . pure intelligibles.] *opposite page*
123 *Theoria* gives] *Theoria added in left margin before cancelled* It
123–24 *St. Maximus, on whom . . . von Balthasar.] opposite page*
124 He unites] *preceded by cancelled* He corrects Evagrius while using him. He corrects Pseudo Denys.
mysteriously] *preceded by x'd out* interiorly
1288)] *followed by x'd out* In St Maximus Quest 51 ad Thalassios
125 But note, . . . creating him.] *opposite page*
this "natural" contemplation] *quotation marks added*
126 political] *preceded by x'd out* events, in art
for Maximus] *preceded by x'd out* not merely
127 In the full . . . alone.] *added in lower margin*
both] *interlined with a caret*
Von Balthasar says:] *preceded by x'd out* Hence St Maximus says: "For love of us Christ hides himself mysteriously in the inner logoi of created things . . . totally and with all his plenitude . . . in all that is varied lies hidden
128 A] *added in left margin*
the complement . . . apatheia.] *added on line*
128–29 This implies . . . meaning.] *opposite page*
The right use] *preceded by x'd out* Created things are seen
130 Certain created] *followed by x'd out* realities
pragmatic,] *followed by x'd out* indifferent
change,] *followed by x'd out* destruction and
131 immediate] *preceded by x'd out* ends
wine] *followed by x'd out* what
132 real self, then] *followed by x'd out* he
133 obscuring] *followed by x'd out* of the
Examples of] *followed by x'd out* artistic
135 *58 to Thalassios*] *to interlined above cancelled* ad
136 Hence St. Maximus . . . prayer.] *added in lower margin*

simple] *interlined below cancelled* vocal

VII] *added on line*

definitive] *preceded by cancelled* break

among . . . followers.] *added on line*

its own right.] *preceded by x'd out* the

was rejected] was *interlined with a caret*

was accepted] was *interlined with a caret*

to become . . . tradition.] *added on line*

137   developed] *interlined above cancelled* was

modern] *added in lower margin with arrow for placement*

138   tall tales.] *followed by x'd out* (cf the II Nocturn of the

later than] *interlined above cancelled* after

139   is in any case] *added in left margin before cancelled* and

140   Doctor and] *followed by x'd out* Dante

between the celestial hierarchy] hierarchy *added in right margin*

consecrate] *preceded by cancelled* receive

141   *Eros* is . . . creature.] *added on line*

divine] *interlined with a caret*

143   This is the . . . self also.] *added in lower margin*

the full] *preceded by cancelled* a full

De] *interlined*

intellect,] *followed by x'd out* to enter

Divine . . . Hierarchies] *added in right margin*

144   (Note: . . . [Bacchus].)] *added on line*

145   We are going . . . Augustinian.] *opposite page*

These are . . . presumably.] *added above with arrow for placement*

primarily] *interlined above cancelled* purely and simply

whom we] *interlined above cancelled* who [*altered to* whom] a

"purely Western mystics"] *quotation marks added*

One of the . . . Sarrazin.] *opposite page*

they popularize Denys.] *added on line*

146   The school represented . . . logicians.] *opposite page*

Hugh . . . p. 92] *opposite page*

Hugh of St. Victor improved] *preceded by x'd out* c)

147   *above all*] *interlined above cancelled* also

tradition of *speculation*] *preceded by x'd out* line of

They are . . . secondarily.] *added on line*

147–48 *Richard . . . spirituality.*] *opposite page*

147   73] *interlined above cancelled* 75?

148   Of Richard] *preceded by x'd out* It is a

rather than . . . Bernard] *interlined with a caret*

means mysticism.] *followed by cancelled* Bonaventure appeals

three could] *followed by x'd out* and were
Though Bonaventure . . . a Dionysian.] *interlined*
Dom] *added in left margin*
vol. III] *added on line*
is there.] *followed by cancelled* Also of course D's angelology
    influences Bernard. *followed by* Read from *Sententiae added*
    on line and cancelled

149   Even *Gertrude* . . . Pseudo-Denys!!] *interlined*
150   *St. Bonaventure,* . . . in the *De Triplici Via.*] *opposite page*
        Here he . . . tradition.] *added on line*
151   other works] *followed by cancelled* and a more or less explicit
        rejection of cataphatic theology, which is not according to
        the mind of Denys.
        regarded as secondary] *interlined above cancelled* rejected as
        external and trivial.
        wisdom and *science.*] *followed by cancelled* In this new approach
        to mysticism, it is stated that one must formally reject the
        activity of the intellect and replace it by the activity of
        love.
151–52 Here read . . . speculative theology.] *opposite page*
152   and prayer] *interlined below and marked for insertion*
        trend was stimulated] *interlined above cancelled* deviation was
        made possible
        study and] *followed by x'd out* effort
153   (like St. Bonaventure)] *added in right margin*
        devotional] *followed by x'd out* and
        including] *preceded by x'd out* mostly
154   The influence . . . century.] *added in lower margin*
        traveled] *interlined above cancelled* goes
        and blossomed out in] *interlined with a caret above cancelled* with
155   inseparable] *preceded by x'd out* based on the dr
        misleading] *added in left margin and marked for insertion to*
        replace cancelled not true
        separate and clearly] *interlined with a caret*
155–56 Speaking of . . . generally Dionysian.] *opposite page*
155   stress on . . . will] *interlined above and marked with arrow for*
        insertion
156   Since in . . . outline.] *added in lower margin*
        excessive confidence in] *followed by x'd out* grace and
157   contemplated in] *preceded by x'd out* found i
        A] *written over* I
158   (lives . . . four years)] *added on line*

sacramental] *followed by x'd out* mysticism
To this extent . . . his love.] *interlined*
and the ascent . . . ecstasy] *interlined with a caret*
159 The crisis . . . lost likeness.] *opposite page*
revelation.] *followed by x'd out* Hence the *ascent to God*
It is by . . . created things.] *opposite page*
160 9] *written over* 8
Love is] *preceded by cancelled* 10
10] *written over* 11
11] *written over* 12
161 e)] *added on line*
In what] *preceded by x'd out* Whether or
162–63 Note . . . nature] *opposite page*
163 more ontological] more *interlined with a caret*
(how intellectual?)] *added on line*
though grace] *followed by x'd out* can
This is . . . gone.] *added on line*
God in the] *followed by cancelled* Church.
166 This "Churchly" . . . experiences.] *opposite page*
168 B] *added on line before cancelled* II.
170 C] *added on line before cancelled* III
THE FRANCISCAN MOVEMENT] *interlined*
permit] *followed by cancelled* further
170–71 Our approach . . . of reform.] *opposite page*
171 to become] *interlined above cancelled* becoming
172 The Cistercian heritage . . . mystics.] *interlined*
one of the most] *preceded by x'd out* a most
Dante places . . . Victor, etc.] *opposite page*
173 contributed] *preceded by x'd out* led to the
breakaway . . . Church.] *added on line after cancelled*
Reformation
His "mission"] *added in left margin and marked for insertion to*
replace cancelled This
and his work] *preceded by x'd out* until his disc
and hotheads . . . rebellion.] *added on line*
174 The most important] *preceded by x'd out* The important
expressed the new] *preceded by x'd out* sought to
Note the . . . sphere).] *opposite page*
great development] *preceded by cancelled* tendency of the
transcending suffering.] *added on line*
175 study and mysticism] *interlined below and marked with arrow for*
insertion

more human] more *interlined below cancelled* purely

resorted] *preceded by x'd out* selected one half of it

a compromise] *preceded by x'd out* perhaps

176   More *numerous*] *preceded by x'd out* Greater

Providence] *followed by cancelled* and

joy and perfection] *followed by x'd out* seen

They are first] They *added in left margin*

He reached] He *added on line after cancelled* who

prudence] *preceded by x'd out* spirit

177   Let us briefly . . . DS).] *added in lower margin*

says Bonaventure] *followed by cancelled* divides theology into

(1) *speculative*] *preceded by cancelled* Word teaches 3 kinds of
        Theol. *in left margin*

(*propria*)] *interlined*

lost by] by *written over* in

initiative of {the} soul] *followed by cancelled* in grace

178   gift of understanding] *interlined below and marked with arrow
        for insertion*

gift of wisdom] *interlined below and marked with arrow for
        insertion*

1. *Intellectual Contemplation*] *preceded by cancelled Intellectual
        Cont – Itinerarium* ascends by 6 degrees 2 in each of them
        a) Through universe. b) Through the Soul itself c) above
        the soul cf. Augustine in Ps 40 extra se intra se supra se
        (culminates in *ecstasy of* admiration

180   Note the role . . . between them.] *interlined*

180–81 In the sleep of the powers] *interlined*

181   on sense] *followed by cancelled* but this would be short of
        traditional standards which demand cessation of even
        purely spiritual thought

in via."] *followed by cancelled* The DS article is unsatisfactory.
        More so—the section devoted to St. B in Spiritualité du
        Moyen age.

IX] *added on line*

Brethren . . . secret society] *added on line*

Humiliati, . . . away] *interlined*

N.B.] *added in left margin*

181–82 among . . . captives etc.] *added on line*

182   B. The *"F*RAUENBEWEGUNG*"*] *interlined*

the importance . . . d'Anvers).] *opposite page*

in their simplicity] *added in left margin to replace cancelled* [ ] in
        their simpleness

seek God] *followed by cancelled* with
183   ecstatic piety] *interlined*
very rich in spirituality] *interlined*
left to] *preceded by cancelled* mostly women, without sound
          formation
or at least . . . condemnation.] *added on line*
and Beghards (men)] *interlined below and marked with arrow for*
          insertion
Note, . . . avoided.] *added on line*
183–84   At the same . . . mystical lives.] *opposite page*
183   care] *preceded by cancelled* bother
184   *Summary:*] *preceded by x'd out* Note: popular attitude to these
          groups reflected in words that have come down in the
          language, derived from Beghard, for instance bigot and
          bugger.
and attained sanctity.] *added on line*
lay] *interlined above x'd out* mysticism
great . . . and Germany!] *interlined*
185   Beatrice had . . . a Béguine).] *added on line*
been formed by] *interlined below cancelled* lived with
authors] *followed by x'd out* to
On the other . . . Second Hadewijch.] *added in lower margin*
signs,] *preceded by cancelled* thoughts,
185–86   A German . . . sei!] *opposite page*
186   This is properly . . . *the spirit.*] *opposite page*
difference."] *preceded by cancelled* distinction
6. In Hadewijch . . . *Cross*] *opposite page*
188   wherever] *interlined above cancelled* as
desires.] *followed by cancelled* IV
190   *The "Second"*] *interlined above cancelled Deutero*
191   loss in] *followed by cancelled* total
in whatever] *preceded by illegible cancelled word*
bareness] *interlined above cancelled* nakedness
192   not only] *preceded by x'd out* Out o
193   The place] *preceded by x'd out* Where the Lo
woman with a] *preceded by x'd out* typical
Christ, through] *preceded by x'd out* the
194   "purely invisible."] *quotation marks added*
Even the orthodox . . . Church.] *added on line*
195   a Béguine] *added on line*
struggle . . . experiences.] *added on line*
Note: in . . . Béguine.] *added in lower margin*

196   see . . . *Autobiography.*] *added on line*
        between me] me *interlined above cancelled* us
199   Although Eckhart . . . discretion.] *opposite page*
200   neo-Platonists.] *followed by cancelled* God as Creator
        light] *followed by cancelled* centered
        flowing] *preceded by cancelled* but above nature, in grace
        confusions] *followed by cancelled* arising from
201   *proprium*] *interlined with a caret*
        ground] *preceded by illegible cancelled word*
        depth] *followed by cancelled* the [ ] element
        got Eckhart] *preceded by illegible cancelled word*
        regarding asceticism] *added on line*
        problem] *added in left margin to replace cancelled* difficulty
        as they stand.] *followed by x'd out* But without qualification
            they probably do
202   note . . . *diligere"*] *added on line*
203   Note . . . hyperbole!] *added on line*
        bold and careless] *interlined below and marked for insertion*
        watch] *preceded by x'd out* take
        heretical] *interlined below x'd out* erroneous and sapientes
            haeresi
203–204 Considering . . . saints.] *opposite page*
204   *Specific*] *added in left margin before cancelled* His
        Eckhart . . . pantheism] *added on line*
        this is a misunderstanding] *interlined*
        statements] *preceded by illegible cancelled word*
        not to be regretted] *added on line with* sin is used by God etc.
            interlined above and cancelled
        N. 508 condemns] condemns *altered from* condemn *preceded by*
            cancelled seems to
        "not . . . sinned,"] *quotation marks added*
        "without distinction."] *quotation marks added*
        (namely . . . present in the soul.] *added on line*
204–205 Though Pourrat . . . unfair.] *opposite page*
205   Oechslin, in] *preceded by x'd out* The question of
        Eckhart's] *interlined above cancelled* his
        be read] *followed by x'd out* The errors as they stand in Denziger
        even] *added in left margin after cancelled* perhaps
        Eckhart is for . . . please.] *added on line*
        survives] *preceded by x'd out* reached the Spanish
        throughout] *followed by cancelled* much of
        of Spain and France.] *added on line*

their influence] *interlined below cancelled* it
laid down] *preceded by x'd out* said
206   C. . . . Tauler] *added in upper margin above cancelled Tauler
and Suso*
Tauler and Suso] *interlined above cancelled* these two mystics
technical] *interlined above cancelled* professional
doctrine,] *followed by cancelled* based on
206–207 Psychology . . . *pondus meum.*] *opposite page*
207   of the word] *followed by cancelled* either to God or to self.
208   simple] *interlined above cancelled* pure
Eucharist] *followed by cancelled* (Daily com by [ ]
can only] *preceded by cancelled* must
withdraw] *preceded by cancelled* return
209   in yourself] yourself *interlined above cancelled* thyself
that creature] *followed by cancelled* is born in you.
210   and other points] *interlined below Tauler and Eckhart*
In general] *added in left margin before cancelled* First of all
211   with *alert,*] with *interlined*
212   a "friend of God."] *added on line*
synthesis . . . contemplation.] *added on line*
doctrine,] *followed by x'd out* where Rhenish Mystics
213   figurative] *preceded by x'd out* language
however he . . . foolish.] *added in lower margin and marked for
insertion*
214   D] *added in left margin*
and followers] *interlined with a caret*
orthodoxy of] *followed by x'd out* Gerson
215   consider] *added on line after cancelled* see
This, with . . . non-mystical.] *added on line followed by cancelled*
16th Century: The Inquisition condemns all disapproves
the reading of all mystics, on general principles, at least
for general consumption. The Rhenish and Flemish
mystics are withdrawn from circulation, good and bad
alike.
as well as . . . trends.] *added on line*
centered on] *preceded by x'd out* A return to
matters] *followed by cancelled* and this is implicitly opposed to
contemplation or divorced from it.
extraordinary] *followed by cancelled* and by [ ] suspicious
There was] *preceded by x'd out* F. Radewijns
considerable] *followed by cancelled* and
discussion] *followed by cancelled* on

216 (fifteenth century)] *interlined with a caret*
demand] *preceded by x'd out* are
also] *interlined*
217 precursor] *preceded by x'd out* predecessor
218–19 Is this strictly true?] *added on line*
219 tried] *followed by cancelled* also
E. *Summary and*] *interlined*
clergy,] *preceded by x'd out* teaching Church teaching of the
    Church
stress] *followed by x'd out* remarkable phenol
220 visible] *preceded by x'd out* Church
methods] *followed by x'd out* are to some ex
Protestants] *preceded by x'd out* those who seek God might hav
10] *added in left margin*
221 What is especially . . . all the Spanish mystics.] *opposite page*
Golden] *preceded by cancelled* Birth of Sp
Note the . . . until late.] *opposite page*
1472: . . . Torquemada] *added in right margin*
students] *followed by cancelled* in 16th cent.
222 compiled . . . *Bible*] *added in right margin and marked with arrow*
    for insertion
1490, . . . seven years] *added in left margin and marked with*
    arrow for insertion
1503 . . . *Vita Christi*] *added after* 1504 . . . Americas) *and*
    marked with arrow for transposition
insists . . . contemplation] *added in right margin and marked*
    with arrow for insertion
St. Bernard] *interlined with a caret*
225 In 1551, . . . tongue.] *added in left margin and marked for*
    insertion
227 or for the learned] *interlined with a caret*
228 in Book . . . *Gerson*] *added in left margin and marked for insertion*
230 director] *added in left margin*
232 St. Teresa is very . . . good sense.] *opposite page*
as in the case . . . herself] *interlined*
For instance, . . . p. 9] *opposite page*
233 be *persons*] *preceded by x'd out* are
(twelfth century)] *interlined with a caret*
234 St. Teresa interprets . . . world. . . ."] *opposite page*
send her] *preceded by x'd out* let
235 Carmelite theologians,] *preceded by x'd out* Fr Pedro Ibanez, a
    Dominican, supports St. Theresa and encourages her to

go ahead

"While all] *preceded by x'd out* Carmelites

236   This sounds . . . 1.] *added on line*

a Carmelite] *interlined with a caret above cancelled* one

"purely . . . office)] *interlined above x'd out* meditation

How does . . . means.] *added on line*

This schema . . . herself.] *added on line*

(this term, . . . arbitrary)] *added on line*

237   emphasis on . . . reasoning.] *interlined*

Meditation in its . . . p. 233)] *opposite page*

this distinction . . . saint herself] *interlined*

Interior . . . 12:13] *added on line*

238   degree.] *preceded by x'd out* form

240   But "they have . . . 343] *opposite page*

241   A. THE NATURE OF] *interlined above cancelled* 2

In making . . . to think.] *opposite page*

Without taking] *preceded by cancelled* This distinction is not at
all clear. Especially since some of them tend to identify
the prayer described in IV Mansion, c. 3 as "passive
recollection." It becomes a very fine distinction and
one which would seem to be useless and misleading
*especially since the dividing line between pre-contemplation
and infused contemplation is placed here.* This is all the more
[followed by x'd out regrettab dubious*]* surprising since
for the Carmelites the passage from one to the other is
regarded as a crucial question.

academic] *interlined*

consider] *preceded by cancelled* rather

begins.] *followed by x'd out* She It is not completely clear whether

Does] *added in left margin*

apply] *altered from* applies

clear that] *followed by x'd out* the

She identifies . . . "supernatural."] *added on line*

241–42 Note in IV.1 . . . satisfying.] *opposite page*

243   This in our . . . contemplation.] *added on line*

244   too rapid] *interlined above cancelled* careful

may] *interlined with a caret*

lead] *altered from* leads

Why? . . . of quiet.] *added on line followed by cancelled* I have
not found the words Prayer of Quiet in this chapter or
in this Mansion. In the Life, C 14, the term is used and the
prayer is formally discussed.

245	never quite hits] *interlined below cancelled* always misses
	point.] *followed by cancelled* In the end it tends to falsify the picture.
	Whatever may be . . . love of God.] *opposite page*
246–47	remote way.] *followed by x'd out* This does not seem to be clear
247	effect, to be] *preceded by x'd out* some
248	4] *preceded by x'd out* 5
	b)] *added in left margin*
249	c)] *added in left margin*
251	1. . . . Direction] *interlined*
	others.] *followed by x'd out* The
	technical] *interlined with a caret*
252	a religious] a *interlined with a caret*
	offices or techniques] *added in left margin before cancelled* things
	reverently] *preceded by cancelled* and
	exploit] *interlined above cancelled* use
	and of the community] *interlined below and marked for insertion*
	to some school] to *interlined below cancelled* of
	and Objections] *added on line*
	Some seem . . . harmful.] *interlined*
	is argued] is *interlined below cancelled* may be
	that] *added on line after x'd out* that the whole mentality of the
	view] *interlined with a caret*
	a great deal] *preceded by x'd out* everything
	the fifteenth century] *interlined above cancelled* then
253	(it is concluded)] *interlined with a caret*
	f) . . . harmful.] *opposite page*
	require] *preceded by cancelled* add
254	I.] *added in left margin*
	II.] *added in left margin*
	complete] *followed by x'd out* and guide
	have more need] *followed by x'd out* of others
	ergo, . . . special way] *added on line*
255	It is at . . . essential.] *added on line*
	III.] *added in left margin*
	a "prudent] *preceded by x'd out* by priests appo
	IV.] *added in left margin*
256	really] *interlined with a caret*
	We have not . . . problem.] *added on line*
	mistake] *interlined above cancelled* wrong and misleading perspective
	In a very . . . now consider.] *opposite page*

view] *followed by interlined and cancelled* This view is not strictly "wrong" but it is misleading and it tends to create more problems than it solves

257   His functions . . . orders.] *interlined*
indicated] *interlined above cancelled* defined by chur
special function] *followed by x'd out* to
He exercises . . . humiliates the soul.] *added in left margin and marked for insertion*
often] *interlined with a caret*
The director strictly . . . penitent.] *interlined*
the development] the *interlined below cancelled* its
"forming"] *quotation marks added*
considered as an "expert."] *added on line*
often] *interlined with a caret*
united] *followed by x'd out* in confess
presents] *preceded by x'd out* subjects himself
at a fixed time] *interlined with a caret*

257–58   For the director . . . ORACLE.] *added on line*

258   *view*] *followed by interlined and cancelled* This view is not completely wrong but it is so broad and so vague that it does not fulfil the requirements of genuine direction
at least] *preceded by cancelled* but
The "director"] *added in left margin before cancelled* It
the name of] *added in left margin and marked for insertion*
example, . . . Walcheren.] *interlined*

259   no question] no *altered from* not *followed by cancelled* necessarily any
formal authority] *interlined below cancelled* jurisdiction

260   *or at least seemingly*] *interlined with a caret*
not decisive . . . case.] *added on line after cancelled* overstepped
laypersons] *preceded by x'd out* laywomen
this would] this *interlined above cancelled* it
or to take . . . seriously.] *added on line*
(as opposed . . . authority)] *interlined with a caret*
In common] *followed by x'd out* view

260–61   He not only . . . be trusted] *opposite page*

261   and followed] *preceded by cancelled* He is to be trusted
that jargon] that *altered from* the
despotic] *added in left margin*
form.] *followed by x'd out* Less tress

262   MATTERS.] *followed by cancelled* BUT ONLY IN FORO EXTERNO.
We must distinguish . . . guide.] *opposite page*

in all the . . . interior life] *interlined below and marked with
 arrow for insertion*
interventions . . . by superiors.] *added in lower margin*
263 just] *interlined below cancelled* but
dedication to wisdom.] *followed by x'd out* Only through his
 mediatorship, for which no payment is adequate, can one
 enter into this realm.
(philosophical instruction)] *interlined with a caret*
264 Christian] *interlined above cancelled* Oriental
in the Orient] *interlined above added and cancelled* (Orient)
265 each drive] each *interlined below cancelled* this
emphasis . . . paternity] *interlined*
shares in the action of] *added in right margin and marked for
 insertion to replace cancelled* has a part in
guide] *interlined above cancelled* teacher
266 always] *followed by x'd out* along
See what . . . example.] *added on line*
267 C. Middle Ages] *preceded by x'd out* Medieval Period
the mendicants] *added on line*
The need . . . felt.] *added on line*
instructs the penitent] penitent *altered from* penitents
orient {the} penitent] penitent *interlined above cancelled* them
enter] *preceded by cancelled* then
writes] *altered from* write *preceded by cancelled* can
formal] *interlined with a caret*
268 over the seventy] over *interlined above cancelled* and
fruitful . . . mysticism.] *added on line*
outside] *preceded by cancelled* the
the parish] *interlined with a caret*
In the fifteenth . . . Fathers] *added on line*
After Trent . . . common.] *added on line*
269 function] *followed by x'd out* of the
Since manuals . . . specialists.] *opposite page*
distinguish] *followed by cancelled* between
from illuminism] from *interlined above cancelled* and
director {functions} . . . the mystic.] *added on line*
Direction . . . mysteries.] *added on line*
Certain new] *interlined with a caret*
(Barnabites, Theatines)] *added on line*
Direction is sometimes] *preceded by cancelled* These directors
 concern themselves especially with the
270 *The Jesuits: . . . less wise.*] *opposite page*

Olier, Tronson] *interlined with a caret*
271   duty" penitent] penitent *interlined above cancelled* character
        purpose] *preceded by x'd out* will
272   A too formal, . . . to this.] *added on line*
273   "for those . . . contemplation."] *quotation marks added*
274   set in] *interlined with a caret*
        (again, . . . A")] *added on line*
        It seems . . . matter.] *added on line*
        as such] *interlined with a caret*
        (He can . . . superior.)] *added on line*
        as director] *added in left margin and marked for insertion*
        does not] *added in left margin and marked to replace cancelled* has
            no power to
274–75 In what . . . safely.] *opposite page*
275   the way to correspond] the *interlined with a caret*
        To say . . . our docility.] *added on line*
        because . . . *personal.*] *added on line*
        See below . . . authority.] *interlined*
275–76 we have said . . . to the Holy Spirit.] *opposite page*
276   basic . . . praiseworthy.] *added below and marked with arrow for
            insertion*
277   implies] *interlined above cancelled* has *followed by x'd out* infinite
        code] *preceded by x'd out* [ ] and
        NOTE . . . themselves.] *added in lower margin after x'd out* As
            Physician
278   The director has to] The director *added in left margin to replace
            cancelled* He
        prescribe] *interlined below cancelled* lay down
        for the regulation . . . monk.] *interlined*
279   labors] *preceded by x'd out* pitfalls
280   2. *Direction and Therapy*] *added in upper margin*
        I] *added in left margin*
        a)] *added in left margin*
        though of course . . . counsel.] *added on line*
281   b) Secular counseling] *interlined*
        or failing . . . conflict.] *added on line*
        asked.] *preceded by x'd out* known and a
282   impression] *followed by x'd out* of the present
        c) Catholic counseling] *interlined*
        Note: . . . *Law.*] *added in lower margin*
        often] *interlined below and marked with arrow for insertion*
283   Neurotic . . . uncharitableness.] *opposite page*

a)] *added in left margin*
b)] *added in left margin*
deeper] *followed by x'd out* than
c)] *added in left margin*
PSYCHOANALYSIS] *preceded by x'd out* Psychotherapy
personality.] *preceded by x'd out* inner
285   full] *added in left margin*
judge] *followed by x'd out* spiritual
wrongly] *followed by x'd out* in order to
aggravate] *preceded by x'd out* reinforce
neurotic] *followed by x'd out* but
and spiritual growth.] *added on line*
286   penitent is] *followed by cancelled* a
287   problem . . . community life.] *interlined*
when . . . guilt] *added in right margin*
clearly] *added in left margin*
Avoid] *followed by cancelled* psychology
288   False . . . type.] *interlined*
289   histrionic] *followed by cancelled* become
In general, . . . from others.] *opposite page*
crushed . . . consolation] *added in left margin*
may get . . . out."] *interlined above and marked with arrow for*
    insertion
290   *Some general* . . . of others.] *opposite page*
4. Don't . . . not one.] *added in right margin*
3] *added in left margin before cancelled* 1
291   4] *written over* 2
penitent's] *interlined with a caret*
5] *written over* 3
wars,] *preceded by cancelled* etc.
291–92 Psychologically . . . to growth.] *opposite page*
292   In the vocation . . . delicate.] *opposite page*
293   The main thing . . . passivity!)] *opposite page*
This may . . . here.] *added on line*
arise from] from *interlined above cancelled* between
294   set aside] *preceded by cancelled* suppressed
help] *followed by cancelled* prevent in dan
295   I] *added in left margin before cancelled* a)
Also it treats . . . least.] *added on line*
296   and of visions, . . . experiences] *interlined with a caret*
Christ] *added in lower margin*
297   1] *added in left margin*

2] *added in left margin*
3] *added in left margin*

298   vocation] *followed by x'd out* in the
299   typical case,] *followed by x'd out* though
300   a fixed] *preceded by x'd out* a priori demands
304   once there . . . of prayer] *interlined with a caret*
      entertained by] *interlined with a caret above cancelled* of
306   presuming . . . to it] *added on line*
307   chapters] *interlined above cancelled* nn.
      problem.] *preceded by x'd out* question.
      from discursive . . . contemplation] *interlined with a caret*
308   Book II] *interlined with a caret*
      1] *followed by x'd out* What does not consti
      In particular . . . n. 6.] *opposite page*
      spontaneous] *interlined with a caret*
      vol. I] I *interlined above cancelled* II
      111] *preceded by cancelled* 110
309   The efforts . . . n. 7.)] *added on line*
310   the vocation . . . and that] *interlined with a caret*
      One should . . . three signs.] *interlined*
      affectively,] *followed by x'd out* as before
311   It is not contemplation. . . . against this.] *added on line*
312   More important, . . . passive prayer.] *added in lower margin*
      3. . . . III] *added in upper margin*
      3] *interlined above cancelled* 2
      Inexperienced . . . directors] *interlined with a caret above*
          cancelled They
313   can spoil] *preceded by x'd out* or the
316   LEFT] *preceded by x'd out* LED TO
      pleased to] *preceded by x'd out* disposed
      mentioned] *followed by cancelled* (continue, Living Flame,
          p. 185) *followed by cancelled* do not type this
      The prudent . . . try] *interlined with a caret above cancelled*
          Trying
      "the way] *followed by x'd out* in
      pressure.] *followed by x'd out* The point is that for spiritual
317   fill it] *followed by x'd out* without
319   person] *preceded by x'd out* soul
320   Finally] *added in left margin*
321   This section . . . well.] *added on line*
      p. 351, . . . n. 5] *added on line*
322   is the "adolescence" . . . life.] *added on line*

Later . . . of St. John.] *opposite page*

323   so that . . . begin] *interlined above cancelled* in
(i.e., mystical life)] *added on line*

324   how the spiritual . . . aridity] *added on line*
quieting . . . grief] *added on line*
(c. 14)] *added on line*

325–26 Note {the} genuine . . . much harm.] *added on line*

326   detail] *followed by x'd out* with the book at our elbow always.

327   PURGES] *preceded by x'd out* IS

328   greatness] *followed by x'd out* and

330   the "ALL"] the *added on line*

332   consecration] *followed by x'd out* to them
These too . . . may] *interlined above cancelled* It will
some] *interlined below cancelled* those who wish
upon] *interlined below and marked for insertion*
a typical] *preceded by cancelled* authorship?
because] *followed by cancelled* of its

333   *solitudine*] *altered from solitudinis*
meditating] *interlined above cancelled* and
Further . . . *agere.*] *opposite page*
Special . . . *dulcedo.*] *opposite page*

334   See . . . *miraculosa.*] *opposite page*
he takes . . . Scripture] *interlined above cancelled* example

335   and contrast] *interlined*

337   *Caput* 5] *preceded on opposite page by* (Do not type this) Our
lady in the world Dark night—God isolates the soul,
burning away bonds + attachments unites it to Himself.
acts in + through the soul united to Him—effects are now
of a different kind. Brainwashing – men play God's part,
isolate the prisoner destroy bonds to old society + old
ways unite him to themselves in order to make him an
instrument. Difference DN alienation from outside +
lower self to full discovery of self in God (above one's
own level) BW alienation from self, loss of self in the
totalitarian mass.
a man] *interlined above cancelled* the bad man

340   II] *interlined before to Spiritual Direction*
Reform and the] *Reform interlined above cancelled* Control

342   insisting] *preceded by cancelled* urging
Note . . . zero.] *opposite page*
in with others] *followed by cancelled* with
"confess"] *followed by cancelled* crimes he never committed

343   Note here . . . priest-prisoner.] *opposite page*
        submission] *followed by cancelled* by
        outstanding] *followed by cancelled* fact
346   personal deficiencies] *preceded by cancelled* Personal failures

APPENDIX B

FOR FURTHER READING

A. Other Writings by Merton on Topics Treated in *An Introduction to Christian Mysticism*

Ignatius of Antioch
"Church and Bishop in St. Ignatius of Antioch." *Seasons of Celebration.* New York: Farrar, Straus and Giroux, 1965: 28–44.

Clement of Alexandria
Clement of Alexandria: Selections from the Protreptikos. New York: New Directions, 1963.
"Clement of Alexandria." *Cassian and the Fathers: Initiation into the Monastic Tradition.* MW1. Kalamazoo, MI: Cistercian Publications, 2005: 20–22.

Gregory of Nyssa
"Vision and Illusion." Chapter 1 of *The Ascent to Truth.* New York: Harcourt, Brace, 1951: 21–29.
"St. Gregory of Nyssa." *Cassian and the Fathers,* 52–60.

Evagrius
"Evagrius Ponticus on Prayer." *Cassian and the Fathers,* 88–96.

Maximus the Confessor
"St. Maximus the Confessor on Non-Violence." *The Nonviolent Alternative,* ed. Gordon Zahn. New York: Farrar, Straus & Giroux, 1980: 172–77; *Passion for Peace: The Social Essays,* ed. William H. Shannon. New York: Crossroad, 1995: 242–47.

Augustine
Introduction to St. Augustine, *The City of God,* trans. Marcus Dods. New York: Modern Library, 1950: ix–xv.
"The Christian in World Crisis: 3. War in Origen and St Augustine." *Seeds of Destruction.* New York: Farrar, Straus and Giroux, 1964: 134–51.

Meister Eckhart

"The Study of Zen." *Zen and the Birds of Appetite*. New York: New Directions, 1968: 1–14.

Spiritual Direction

Spiritual Direction and Meditation. Collegeville, MN: Liturgical Press, 1960: 3–42.

"The Spiritual Father in the Desert Tradition." *Contemplation in a World of Action*. Garden City, NY: Doubleday, 1971: 269–93.

"Spiritual Direction." *The Merton Seasonal*, 32.1 (Spring 2007), 3–17.

John of the Cross

"The Transforming Union in St. Bernard and St. John of the Cross," *Thomas Merton on St. Bernard*. CS 9. Kalamazoo, MI: Cistercian Publications, 1980: 159–240.

The Ascent to Truth. New York: Harcourt, Brace, 1951.

"St. John of the Cross." *Saints for Now*, ed. Clare Booth Luce, 1952; *A Thomas Merton Reader*, ed. Thomas P. McDonnell. New York: Harcourt, Brace, 1962: 306–14; rev. ed. Garden City, NY: Doubleday Image, 1974: 295–304.

Devotions in Honor of Saint John of the Cross. Philadelphia: Jefferies & Manz, 1953.

"Light in Darkness: The Ascetic Doctrine of St. John of the Cross." *Disputed Questions*. New York: Farrar, Straus and Cudahy, 1960: 208–17.

"Thomas Merton's Practical Norms of Sanctity in St. John of the Cross," ed. Robert E. Daggy. *Spiritual Life*, 36.4 (Winter 1990): 195–201.

B. Significant Writings by Other Authors on Topics Treated in *An Introduction to Mystical Theology*

General Studies

Bouyer, Louis, Jean Leclercq, and François Vandenbroucke. *The History of Christian Spirituality*. Vol. 1: *The Spirituality of the New Testament and the Fathers*. Trans. Mary P. Ryan. New York: Seabury, 1963; Vol. 2: *The Spirituality of the Middle Ages*. Trans. Benedictines of Holme Eden Abbey. New York: Seabury, 1968.

Clément, Olivier. *The Roots of Christian Mysticism: Text and Commentary*. Hyde Park, NY: New City Press, 1995.

Jones, Cheslyn, Geoffrey Wainwright, and Edward Yarnold, eds. *The Study of Spirituality*. New York: Oxford University Press, 1986.

Kannengiesser, Charles. *Early Christian Spirituality*. Philadelphia: Fortress, 1986.

Louth, Andrew. *The Origins of the Christian Mystical Tradition from Plato to Denys*. Oxford: Oxford University Press, 1981.

McGinn, Bernard, John Meyendorff, and Jean Leclercq, eds. *Christian Spirituality: Origins to the Twelfth Century.* World Spirituality: An Encyclopedic History of the Religious Quest, vol. 16. New York: Crossroad, 1985.

McGinn, Bernard. *The Presence of God: A History of Western Christian Mysticism.* Vol. 1: *The Foundations of Mysticism: Origins to the Fifth Century.* New York: Crossroad, 1992; Vol. 2: *The Growth of Mysticism: Gregory the Great through the 12th Century.* New York: Crossroad, 1994; Vol. 3: *The Flowering of Mysticism: Men and Women in the New Mysticism—1200–1350.* New York: Crossroad, 1998; Vol. 4: *The Harvest of Mysticism in Medieval Germany —1300–1500.* New York: Crossroad, 2005.

Raitt, Jill, ed. *Christian Spirituality II: High Middle Ages and Reformation.* World Spirituality: An Encyclopedic History of the Religious Quest, vol. 17. New York: Crossroad, 1987.

Spidlík, Tomás. *The Spirituality of the Christian East: A Systematic Handbook.* Trans. Anthony P. Gythiel. CS 79. Kalamazoo: Cistercian Publications, 1986.

Williams, Rowan. *The Wound of Knowledge: Christian Spirituality from the New Testament to St. John of the Cross.* London: Darton, Longman and Todd, 1979.

Ignatius of Antioch

Ignatius of Antioch. Trans. Robert M. Grant. The Apostolic Fathers: A New Translation and Commentary, vol. 4. Camden, NJ: Nelson, 1966.

* * * * *

Corwin, Virginia. *St. Ignatius and Christianity in Antioch.* New Haven: Yale University Press, 1960.

Trevett, Christine. *A Study of Ignatius of Antioch in Syria and Asia.* Lewiston, NY: Mellen, 1992.

Clement of Alexandria

Alexandrian Christianity: Selected Translations of Clement and Origen. Ed. J. E. L. Oulton and Henry Chadwick. Library of Christian Classics, vol. 2. Philadelphia: Westminster Press, 1954.

Christ the Educator. Trans. Simon P. Wood. Fathers of the Church, vol. 23. New York: Fathers of the Church, 1954.

The Exhortation to the Greeks; The Rich Man's Salvation; and the Fragment of an Address Entitled, To the Newly Baptized. Trans. G. W. Butterworth. Loeb Classical Library. Cambridge, MA: Harvard University Press, 1968.

* * * * *

Ferguson, John. *Clement of Alexandria.* New York: Twayne, 1974.

Hägg, Henny Fiska. *Clement of Alexandria and the Beginnings of Christian Apophaticism*. New York: Oxford University Press, 2006.

Lilla, Salvatore. *Clement of Alexandria: A Study in Christian Platonism and Gnosticism*. Cambridge: Cambridge University Press, 1971.

Osborn, Eric. *Clement of Alexandria*. Cambridge: Cambridge University Press, 2005.

Gregory of Nyssa

Ascetical Works. Trans. Virginia Woods Callahan. Fathers of the Church, vol. 58. Washington, DC: Catholic University of America Press, 1967.

Commentary on the Song of Songs. Trans. Casimir McCambley. Brookline, MA: Hellenic College Press, 1987.

From Glory to Glory: Texts from Gregory of Nyssa's Mystical Writings. Ed. Jean Daniélou and Herbert Musurillo. New York: Scribners, 1961.

The Letters. Trans. Anna M. Silvas. Leiden: Brill, 2007.

The Life of Moses. Trans. Everett Ferguson and Abraham J. Malherbe. Classics of Western Spirituality. New York: Paulist, 1978.

Life of Saint Macrina. Trans. Kevin Corrigan. Toronto: Peregrina, 1987.

The Lord's Prayer. The Beatitudes. Trans. Hilda C. Graef. Ancient Christian Writers, vol. 18. Westminster, MD: Newman, 1954.

The Soul and the Resurrection. Trans. Catharine P. Roth. Crestwood, NY: St. Vladimir's Seminary Press, 1993.

Treatise on the Inscriptions of the Psalms. Trans. Ronald E. Heine. New York: Oxford University Press, 1995.

* * * * *

Balthasar, Hans Urs von. *Presence and Thought: Essay on the Religious Philosophy of Gregory of Nyssa*. Trans. Mark Sebanc. San Francisco: Ignatius Press, 1995.

Laird, Martin. *Gregory of Nyssa and the Grasp of Faith: Union, Knowledge, and Divine Presence*. New York: Oxford University Press, 2004.

Meredith, Anthony. *Gregory of Nyssa*. New York: Routledge, 1999.

Smith, J. Warren. *Passion and Paradise: Human and Divine Emotion in the Thought of Gregory of Nyssa*. New York: Crossroad, 2004.

Evagrius Ponticus

The Praktikos; Chapters on Prayer. Trans. John Eudes Bamberger. CS 4. Spencer, MA: Cistercian Publications, 1970.

Ad Monachos. Trans. Jeremy Driscoll. Ancient Christian Writers, vol. 59. New York: Paulist Press, 2003.

The Greek Ascetic Corpus. Trans. Robert E. Sinkewicz. New York: Oxford University Press, 2003.

* * * * *

Driscoll, Jeremy. *The "Ad Monachos" of Evagrius Ponticus: Its Structure and a Select Commentary*. Studia Anselmiana, 104. Rome: Pontificio Ateneo S. Anselmo, 1991.

———. *The Mind's Long Journey to the Holy Trinity: The* Ad Monachos *of Evagrius Ponticus*. Collegeville, MN: Liturgical Press, 1993.

———. *Steps to Spiritual Perfection: Studies on Spiritual Progress in Evagrius Ponticus*. New York: Newman Press, 2005.

Dysinger, Luke. *Psalmody and Prayer in the Writings of Evagrius Ponticus*. New York: Oxford University Press, 2005.

Maximus the Confessor

The Ascetic Life; The Four Centuries on Charity. Trans. Polycarp Sherwood. Ancient Christian Writers, vol. 21. Westminster, MD: Newman Press, 1955.

On the Cosmic Mystery of Jesus Christ: Selected Writings from St. Maximus the Confessor. Trans. Paul M. Blowers and Robert Louis Wilken. Popular Patristics Series. Crestwood, NY: St. Vladimir's Seminary Press, 2003.

Selected Writings. Trans. George C. Berthold. Classics of Western Spirituality. New York: Paulist Press, 1985.

* * * * *

Balthasar, Hans Urs von. *Cosmic Liturgy: The Universe according to Maximus the Confessor*. Trans. Brian E. Daley. San Francisco: Ignatius Press, 2003.

Cooper, Adam. *Body in St. Maximus the Confessor: Holy Flesh, Wholly Deified*. New York: Oxford University Press, 2005.

Louth, Andrew. *Maximus the Confessor*. Early Church Fathers Series. New York: Routledge, 1996.

Thunberg, Lars. *Man and the Cosmos: The Vision of St. Maximus the Confessor*. Crestwood, NY: St. Vladimir's Seminary Press, 1985.

———. *Microcosm and Mediator: The Theological Anthropology of Maximus the Confessor*. 2nd ed. Chicago: Open Court, 1995.

Pseudo-Dionysius

The Complete Works. Trans. Colm Luibheid. Classics of Western Spirituality. New York: Paulist Press, 1987.

* * * * *

Gersh, Stephen. *From Iamblichus to Eriugena: An Investigation of the Prehistory and Evolution of the Pseudo-Dionysian Tradition*. Leiden: Brill, 1978.

Hathaway, Ronald F. *Hierarchy and the Definition of Order in the Letters of Pseudo-Dionysius: A Study in the Form and Meaning of the Pseudo-Dionysian Writings*. The Hague, Nijhoff, 1969.

Louth, Andrew. *Denys the Areopagite*. Wilton, CT: Morehouse, 1989.

Rorem, Paul. *Pseudo-Dionysius: A Commentary on the Texts and an Introduction to Their Influence*. New York: Oxford University Press, 1993.

Augustine

The Complete Works of Saint Augustine. Ed. John E. Rotelle, OSA. 34 vols. to date. Hyde Park, NY: New City Press, 1997–.

Confessions. Trans. Henry Chadwick. New York: Oxford University Press, 1991.

Major Writings. Ed. Benedict J. Groeschel. New York: Crossroad, 1995.

Selected Writings. Trans. Mary T. Clark. Classics of Western Spirituality. New York: Paulist Press, 1984.

* * * * *

Brown, Peter. *Augustine of Hippo: A Biography*. Berkeley: University of California Press, 1967.

Burnaby, John. *Amor Dei: A Study of the Religion of St. Augustine*. London: Hodder & Stoughton, 1960.

Chadwick, Henry. *Augustine*. New York: Oxford University Press, 1986.

Clark, Mary T. *Augustine*. Washington, DC: Georgetown University Press, 1994.

O'Donnell, James J. *Augustine*. Boston: Twayne, 1985.

———. *Augustine: A New Biography*. New York: Ecco, 2005.

Scott, T. Kermit. *Augustine: His Thought in Context*. New York: Paulist Press, 1995.

Sullivan, John. *Image of God: The Doctrine of St. Augustine and Its Influence*. Dubuque, IA: Priory Press, 1963.

TeSelle, Eugene. *Augustine*. Nashville: Abingdon Press, 2006.

Joachim of Flora

Apocalyptic Spirituality: Treatises and Letters of Lactantius, Adso of Montier-en-Der, Joachim of Fiore, the Franciscan Spirituals, Savonarola. Trans. Bernard McGinn. Classics of Western Spirituality. New York: Paulist Press, 1979.

* * * * *

McGinn, Bernard. *The Calabrian Abbot: Joachim of Fiore in the History of Western Thought*. New York: Macmillan, 1985.

Reeves, Marjorie. *Influence of Prophecy in the Later Middle Ages: A Study in Joachimism*. Oxford: Clarendon Press, 1969.

———. *Joachim of Fiore and the Prophetic Future*. New York: Harper & Row, 1977.

Tavard, George H. *Contemplative Church: Joachim and His Adversaries*. Milwaukee: Marquette University Press, 2005.

Wessley, Stephen E. *Joachim of Fiore and Monastic Reform.* New York: Peter Lang, 1990.

Francis

Francis and Clare: The Complete Works. Classics of Western Spirituality. Trans. Regis Armstrong, OFMcap, and Ignatius C. Brady, OFM. New York: Paulist Press, 1982.

Francis of Assisi: Early Documents. Ed. Regis Armstrong, William Short and J. A. Wayne Hellmann. 4 vols. Hyde Park, NY: New City Press, 1999–2002.

St. Francis of Assisi: English Omnibus of Sources. Ed. Marion A. Habig. 4th ed. Chicago: Franciscan Herald Press, 1983.

* * * * *

Boff, Leonardo. *Francis of Assisi: A Model for Human Liberation.* Maryknoll, NY: Orbis, 2006.

Cunningham, Lawrence S. *Francis of Assisi: Performing the Gospel Life.* Grand Rapids, MI: W. B. Eerdmans, 2004.

Fortini, Arnaldo. *Francis of Assisi.* New York: Crossroad, 1981.

Bonaventure

Bonaventure: Mystical Writings. Ed. Zachary Hayes (New York: Crossroad, 1999).

The Soul's Journey into God, The Tree of Life, The Life of St. Francis. Trans. Ewert Cousins. Classics of Western Spirituality. New York: Paulist Press, 1978.

The Works of Bonaventure. Trans. José de Vinck. 5 vols. Patterson, NJ: St. Anthony Guild Press, 1960–70.

Works of Saint Bonaventure. 9 vols. to date. St. Bonaventure, NY: Franciscan Institute Press, 1955–.

* * * * *

Bougerol, Jacques Guy. *Introduction to the Works of Bonaventure.* Paterson, NJ: St. Anthony Guild Press, 1964.

Cousins, Ewert H. *Bonaventure and the Coincidence of Opposites: The Theology of Bonaventure.* Chicago: Franciscan Herald Press, 1978.

Delio, Ilia, OSF. *Crucified Love: Bonaventure's Mysticism of the Crucified Christ.* Quincy, IL: Franciscan Press, 1998.

———. *Simply Bonaventure: An Introduction to His Life, Thought, and Writings.* Hyde Park, NY: New City Press, 2000.

Hayes, Zachary. *The Hidden Center: Spirituality and Speculative Christology in St. Bonaventure.* New York: Paulist Press, 1981.

Hadewijch

The Complete Works. Trans. Mother Columba Hart. Classics of Western Spirituality. New York: Paulist Press, 1980.

* * * * *

Dreyer, Elizabeth. *Passionate Spirituality: Hildegard of Bingen and Hadewijch of Brabant*. New York: Paulist Press, 2005.

Mommaers, Paul, with Elizabeth Dutton. *Hadewijch: Writer, Beguine, Love Mystic*. Louvain: Peeters, 2004.

Eckhart

Meister Eckhart: Teacher and Preacher. Ed. Bernard McGinn. Classics of Western Spirituality. New York: Paulist Press, 1986.

The Essential Sermons, Commentaries, Treatises and Defense. Trans. Edmund Colledge and Bernard McGinn. Classics of Western Spirituality. New York: Paulist Press, 1981.

* * * * *

Davies, Oliver. *Meister Eckhart: Mystical Theologian*. London: SPCK, 1991.

Hollywood, Amy. *Soul as Virgin Wife: Mechthild of Magdeburg, Marguerite Porete, and Meister Eckhart*. Notre Dame: University of Notre Dame Press, 1995.

McGinn, Bernard, ed. *Meister Eckhart and the Beguine Mystics: Hadewijch of Brabant, Mechthild of Magdeburg, and Marguerite Porete*. New York: Continuum, 1994.

McGinn, Bernard. *The Mystical Thought of Meister Eckhart: The Man from Whom God Hid Nothing*. New York: Crossroad, 2001.

Smith, Cyprian. *Way of Paradox: Spiritual Life as Taught by Meister Eckhart*. London: Darton Longman & Todd, 1987.

Tobin, Frank. *Meister Eckhart: Thought and Language*. Philadelphia: University of Pennsylvania Press, 1986.

Woods, Richard. *Eckhart's Way*. Wilmington, DE: Michael Glazier, 1986.

Tauler

Sermons. Trans. Maria Shrady. Classics of Western Spirituality. New York: Paulist Press, 1985.

Theologia Germanica

Theologia Germanica of Martin Luther. Trans. Bengt Hoffman. Classics of Western Spirituality. New York: Paulist Press, 1980.

Theologia Germanica: The Way to a Sinless Life. Ed. Thomas S. Kepler. Cleveland: World Publishing Co., 1952.

Osuna

The Third Spiritual Alphabet. Trans. Mary E. Giles. Classics of Western Spirituality. New York: Paulist Press, 1981.

* * * * *

Calvert, Laura. *Francisco de Osuna and the Spirit of the Letter*. Portland, OR: International Scholarly Book Service, 1973.

Ignatius of Loyola

Spiritual Exercises and Selected Works. Ed. George E. Ganss, SJ. Classics of Western Spirituality. New York: Paulist Press, 1991.

* * * * *

Caraman, Philip. *Ignatius Loyola: A Biography of the Founder of the Jesuits*. San Francisco: Harper & Row, 1990.

Egan, Harvey. *Ignatius Loyola the Mystic*. Wilmington, DE: Michael Glazier, 1987.

Lonsdale, David. *Eyes to See, Ears to Hear: An Introduction to Ignatian Spirituality*. New York: Orbis, 2000.

Silf, Margaret. *Companions of Christ: Ignatian Spirituality for Everyday Living*. Grand Rapids, MI: Eerdmans, 2004.

Teresa of Avila

Collected Letters. Vol. 1. Trans. Kieran Kavanaugh, OCD. Washington, DC: Institute of Carmelite Studies, 2001.

Collected Works. 3 vols. Trans. Kieran Kavanaugh, OCD and Otilio Rodriguez, OCD. Washington, DC: Institute of Carmelite Studies, 1976–85.

The Interior Castle. Trans. Kieran Kavanaugh, OCD and Otilio Rodriguez, OCD. Classics of Western Spirituality. New York: Paulist Press, 1979.

Mystical Writings. Ed. Tessa Bielecki. New York: Crossroad, 1999.

* * * * *

Bielecki, Tessa. *Teresa of Avila: An Introduction to Her Life and Writings*. Tunbridge Wells: Burns & Oates, 1994.

Frohlich, Mary. *Intersubjectivity of the Mystic: A Study of Teresa of Avila's Interior Castle*. Atlanta: Scholars Press, 1993.

Luti, J. Mary. *Teresa of Avila's Way*. Collegeville, MN: Liturgical Press, 1991.

Williams, Rowan. *Teresa of Avila*. New York: Continuum, 2003.

John of the Cross

Collected Works. Trans. Kieran Kavanaugh, OCD and Otilio Rodriguez, OCD. Revised ed. Washington, DC: Institute of Carmelite Studies, 1991.

Selected Writings. Trans. Kieran Kavanaugh, OCD. Classics of Western Spirituality. New York: Paulist Press, 1987.

* * * * *

Arraj, James. *From St. John of the Cross to Us*. Chiloquin, OR: Inner Growth Books, 1999.

Collings, Ross. *John of the Cross*. Collegeville, MN: Liturgical Press, 1990.

Dicken, E. W. Truman. *Crucible of Love: A Study of the Mysticism of St. Teresa of Jesus and St. John of the Cross.* New York: Sheed and Ward, 1963.

Dombrowski, Daniel A. *St. John of the Cross: An Appreciation.* Albany: State University of New York Press, 1992.

Doohan, Leonard. *Life and Vision of John of the Cross.* Notre Dame, IN: Ave Maria Press, 1995.

Herrera, R. A. *Silent Music: The Life, Work, and Thought of St. John of the Cross.* Grand Rapids, MI: W. B. Eerdmans, 2004.

Kavanaugh, Kieran. *John of the Cross: Doctor of Light and Love.* New York: Crossroad, 1999.

Welch, John. *When Gods Die: An Introduction to John of the Cross.* New York: Paulist Press, 1990.

Guigo the Carthusian

The Ladder of Monks: A Letter on the Contemplative Life and Twelve Meditations. Trans. Edmund Colledge and James Walsh. CS 48. Kalamazoo, MI: Cistercian Publications, 1981.

ACKNOWLEDGEMENTS

Cistercian Publications gratefully acknowledges permission to cite the following works:

The Correspondence of Thomas Merton: *The Hidden Ground of Love of Love: Letters on Religious Experience and Social Concerns*. New York: Farrar, Straus & Giroux, 1985. Quoted with permission.

The Journals of Thomas Merton: *Turning toward the World: The Pivotal Years. Journals, volume 4: 1960–1963*. San Francisco: HarperCollins Publishers, 1996. Quoted with permission.

The Apostolic Fathers, trans. Francis X. Glimm, Joseph M.-F. Marique, sj, Gerald G. Walsh, sj. Fathers of the Church series. Washington DC: The Catholic University of America Press, 1947. Used with permission.

Dom Cuthbert Butler, Western Mysticism: *The Teaching of SS. Augustine, Gregory and Bernard on Contemplation and the Contemplative Life*, 2nd ed. London: Constable, 1926. Used with permission.

E. Allison Peers, *Studies of the Spanish Mystics*, 2 volumes. second ed. London: SPCK, 1951. Used with permission.

The Complete Works of Saint John of the Cross, ed. and trans. E. Allison Peers, volumes 1 & 3. Westminster, MD: Newman Press, 1946. Used with permission.

The Complete Works of Saint Teresa of Jesus, trans. and ed. E. Allison Peers, volume 2. New York: Sheed & Ward, 1946. Used with permission.

INDEX

Index   405